HENRY VIII

The Decline and Fall of a Tyrant

HENRY VIII

The Decline and Fall of a Tyrant

Robert Hutchinson

WEIDENFELD & NICOLSON

First published in Great Britain in 2019 by Weidenfeld & Nicolson
an imprint of The Orion Publishing Group Ltd
Carmelite House, 50 Victoria Embankment
London EC4Y 0DZ

An Hachette UK Company

1 3 5 7 9 10 8 6 4 2

A CIP catalogue record for this book is
available from the British Library.

ISBN (hardback) 978 1 4746 0579 3
ISBN (audio download) 978 1 4091 8553 6
ISBN (ebook) 978 1 4746 0581 6

Typeset at The Spartan Press Ltd,
Lymington, Hants

Printed and bound by CPI Group (UK) Ltd,
Croydon, CR0 4YY

MIX
Paper from
responsible sources
FSC® C104740

www.orionbooks.co.uk

For Sally and Alicia

Contents

List of Illustrations

INTEGRATED

Introduction

Down the centuries, Henry VIII has aroused powerful passions. Cardinal Reginald Pole, the exile who fought tooth and nail to defend Holy Mother Church, told him: 'Your butcheries and horrible executions have made England the slaughterhouse of innocence.' As Henry had massacred his kith and kin, one can sympathise.

In the eighteenth century, the Anglo-Irish satirist Jonathan Swift scribbled his thoughts about the old ogre in the margin of one of his books: 'I wish he had been flayed, his skin stuffed and hanged upon a gibbet. His bulky guts and flesh left to be devoured by birds and beasts for a warning to his successors for ever. Amen.' Hardly appropriate sentiments for the Dean of St Patrick's Cathedral in Dublin.

More than a century later, Charles Dickens, in his *Child's History of England*, described Henry 'as the most intolerable ruffian ... with blood on his hands, a disgrace to human nature and a blot of blood and grease' on the fair face of his realm.

In our own time, the king has been defined more by his six marriages and by sometimes trite television dramas, rather than by who he truly was. Much of the drama and intrigue of Henry's last years has been lost sight of, as well as his achievements and painful failures. You will discover that historical truth is stranger than any fiction – and just as gripping.

Because of the Tudor dynasty's insecurity, Henry was obsessive about his health. His sweeping reforms of the medical profession outlawed quacks and superstition, removed it from religious oversight and placed it firmly in the realms of science. His regulatory regime laid the foundations of the modern health care system across the world. Remember him when you next visit your family doctor or local hospital.

He established the Royal Navy and his diplomacy placed his

dominions firmly at the centre of European politics, instead of being regarded as a remote group of rain-swept islands at the edge of the known world.

The king's break with Rome created the Church of England. Henry was a rampant egomaniac, so when he prayed, God listened. After all, he was God's own deputy on earth. I once joked with the then Archbishop of Canterbury at the Hay Festival that 'without my man, you would be out of a job!' Henry, however, would not recognise the modern Anglican Church and would be less than enamoured by its active role as the social conscience of British governments.

One of his measures continues in force to this day. The last remnant of his autocratic rule by proclamation – the so-called 'Henry VIII clauses' – is an administrative instrument sometimes used by British governments to implement decisions or policy changes, without the tiresome inconvenience of parliamentary debate.

He may be England's most famous king, but he was also a totalitarian tyrant, reigning over subjects living in mortal fear of his retribution, as well as a court locked in febrile, dark conspiracy by those jockeying for influence or power.

Henry saw everything in stark black and white terms. You were either for him, or against him, with no 'ifs' or 'buts' in between. Those subjects who did not show absolute fidelity must therefore be treated as enemies. Treason was extended to punish those uttering disloyal words, or failing to support the king's predilections in religious liturgy or beliefs, his choice of wives, their status, or that of any royal offspring. Many would die horribly as a result.

It is time to examine what drove the king in his religious, domestic and diplomatic policies. They included what we would recognise as the genocide he brutally exacted upon the inhabitants of Scotland and northern France, the bare-faced fraud of his 'Great Debasement' of England's currency and the reckless borrowing that swept his kingdom down the perilous path to bankruptcy – all pursued in a relentless quest for military glory. There were also the assassins he hired to murder the reviled traitors who had fled abroad, like the elegant but utterly ruthless Italian gangster Ludovico da l'Armi.

Henry also allegedly plotted to kidnap a king together with various troublesome papal emissaries and funded the assassination of Scotland's Cardinal David Beaton, although he was careful to ensure that his own role in the conspiracy was well-hidden. Such business, he declared with breathless hypocrisy, was 'not meet for kings'.

Since I published *The Last Days of Henry VIII* in 2005, there has been remarkable progress in understanding afresh the ageing despot. With the benefit of new research, both historical and medical, I hope this book will demonstrate for the first time that his complex psychology and his litany of physical ailments and disorders were major contributory factors in shaping his decisions and actions. Much of its content comes from contemporary documents, with the words spoken or written by the protagonists, revealing the astonishing workings of a meticulous Tudor bureaucracy.

This is an account of the epic tragedy of Henry's last seven turbulent years, as the vultures of disease roosted around him and he fought and lost his final frustrating battle against geriatric decay, becoming ever more irrational, mercurial and unpredictable.

The athletic Renaissance prince had long since withered away, leaving a paranoid and psychotic monarch with a dangerous hair-trigger temper, suspicious of everyone, including those close to him. You could smell the putrid stench of his suppurating legs from three rooms away.

The book begins in 1539 for two compelling reasons. Europe was ganging up on the blustering Henry, with the Vatican plotting a three-pronged attack on England, from Scotland, France and Spain, to finally destroy this 'schismatic and heretical' king. Foreign invasion became a more dangerous threat to his throne than the northern rebellions of 1536–7.

Out of this crisis was born a grand strategy. First, fight a war with France and recover the tribute owed him, with the chance to fulfil the ancient claim of English monarchs to the French crown. Second, neutralise Scotland, by making his son king consort to the infant Mary Queen of Scots. After declaring himself king of Ireland, Henry came close to creating the United Kingdom, more than 250 years before the Act of Union was passed.

By 1539, the effects of Henry's insidious disease were also becoming more telling. Here is a new, unfamiliar Henry VIII; a vulnerable, frightened and lonely old man, for whom time was rapidly running out, with none of his childhood dreams of battlefield victory and personal glory achieved.

Obsessed by the need to continue the Tudor dynasty, he was determined to pass on a secure realm to his precious sole male heir, the precocious nine-year-old Prince Edward, no matter at what cost to those who might stand in his way.

Despite his reputation, foul deeds and cruel sense of humour, after reading this book, you might even feel a scintilla of sympathy in your heart for Henry VIII, England's most feared and ruthless king.

1

Royal Obsessions

William Shakespeare's epigrammatic line 'Uneasy lies the head that wears a crown'[1] vividly describes the precarious reigns of the Tudor monarchy, constantly plagued by fears of losing the English throne. Henry VIII lived in the uneasy knowledge that his imperious rule rested on a tenuous, if not legally fragile, claim. This depended on the descent of his grandmother Margaret Beaufort from Edward III's third surviving son John of Gaunt and Katherine Swynford, his mistress of twenty-five years and later third wife. Their four bastard children were legitimised by Richard II and Pope Boniface IX in 1396 but were barred from inheriting the crown by Henry IV a decade later.

His father, Henry VII, tacitly acknowledged the innate weaknesses of the Tudor entitlement to the crown when he addressed his first Parliament in early November 1485. His right to be sovereign came not only through lawful inheritance, but also by the dreadful judgement of God.[2] This had been bloodily delivered on the battlefield three months earlier when Richard III had been butchered, the last of fourteen Plantagenet kings who had ruled England since 1154. The victor of Bosworth's confident words hid dark foreboding about the survival both of his fledgling kingship and the glorious Tudor dynasty he intended to establish.

His uneasiness stemmed from the threat of overthrow by those waiting in the wings, armed with robust claims to the monarchy. A string of insurrections or invasions followed in support of Yorkist pretenders to the throne, every one ruthlessly suppressed. Six-year-old Prince Henry and his mother sampled the sour stench of revolt in June 1497, when they were forced to shelter inside the Tower of London after 15,000 Cornish rebels encamped south of the River Thames, spreading panic through the City of London.

Henry VIII never forgot that hard lesson in kingship, nor the necessity to employ merciless cruelty to destroy any opposition to the House
of Tudor. During his own reign, those suspected of ambitions to occupy
the throne continued to be brutally eliminated, culminating in 1538,
with the slaughter or imprisonment of the noble Montagu, Courtenay
and Neville families.

The other troubling facet of Tudor insecurity was their chronic lack
of male heirs. A plentiful supply of lusty sons was vital to guarantee
their grip on the monarchy and unfortunately, during the last half of
the 118-year-long dynasty, the Tudors were denied male heirs of the
Blood Royal, let alone the comfortable insurance of 'spare heirs'.

Henry was the second of three sons with four sisters,[3] of which three
siblings died in infancy.[4] His eldest brother, fifteen-year-old Arthur, died
in April 1502 after marrying a Spanish princess, Katherine of Aragon.
Edmund was born in February 1499, but died eighteen months later. In
just over a thousand days, Death had snatched two of the three Tudor
princes and the dynasty's continuance rested solely on Henry's survival.

As duke of York, he was never intended for the trials of kingship.
His formative years were spent in a cosy feminine world at his mother's
knee, thoroughly spoilt and tenderly protected from the knocks and
bruises of childhood. Did this cosseted early life, far from male influence, forge a deep psychological flaw within him that later spawned
some of his marriage problems? Some psychiatrists believe he possessed an unconscious craving for an incestuous union, perhaps even
an Oedipus complex, about his gentle, blonde-haired mother, Elizabeth
of York.[5]

After Arthur's death, Henry was forced to live within the cocoon of
his father's stifling protection from all possible dangers to his life and
limb. The prince spent much time alone in 1508, forbidden to leave
the palace precincts at Richmond or Greenwich, except for exercise,
and was closely guarded by carefully chosen companions. No one else,
'on his life, dared approach him', according to the Spanish ambassador
of the time.[6] He was also forbidden from jousting, being restricted to
tilting with his lance at a metal ring, suspended from a swivel beam
on a post.[7] This might be excellent training for horse and rider but,
compared to the excitement of the tournament, hardly enthralling.

The prince suffered a stormy relationship with his father. Long
afterwards, Henry Pole, Lord Montagu, claimed that the king 'had no

affection nor fancy' for his surviving heir. There were even unsubstanti-
ated diplomatic reports that Henry VII had tried to kill his son during
a violent quarrel.[8]

Following his accession to the throne in 1509, the frustrations of this
cloistered upbringing ensured that the king rarely accepted denial of
his wishes and frequently displayed wanton wilfulness, backed by an
infamous temper. Not a monarch to argue with or test. The Imperial
ambassador Eustace Chapuys believed the king had 'no respect or fear
of anyone in the world'.[9] His French counterpart, Louis de Perreau,
observed: 'I have to deal with the most dangerous and cruel man in the
world, for [when] he is in a fury, he has neither reason nor understanding left.'[10]

In his youth, the king was vain and jealous of his looks, stature
and fitness. In 1515, Henry asked the Venetian Lorenzo Pasqualigo to
compare his physique with that of King Francis I of France: '"Is [he]
as tall as I am?" I told him there was little difference. "Is he as stout?"
I told him he was not. "What sort of leg has he?" I replied: "Spare".
Whereupon, he opened the front of his doublet and placing his hand
on his thigh, said: "Look here. I have a good calf to my leg."'[11]

Henry's self-obsessive behaviour comfortably fits into the classic
profile of an individual suffering from 'narcissistic behaviour disorder', a condition that normally develops in early adulthood. This is
characterised by exaggerated feelings of self-importance, an excessive
need for admiration and a chronic lack of empathy towards others. The
king could never be wrong and when boxed into a corner, would lash
out violently.[12] You may well recognise that some of today's political
leaders could be suffering from this disorder. In the king's case, the sure
conviction that he ruled, not by the will of man, but with God's divine
approval, intensified the symptoms immeasurably.

He had other dominant character traits. Like many of his subjects,
Henry possessed an utter dislike and distrust of foreigners – particularly the Scots or French. This galloping xenophobia was exemplified by
his draconian policies. In 1530, legislation was passed to deport 'certain
outlandish people called Egyptians'[13] or Romanies. Seven years later,
the authorities in the Welsh Marches were ordered to banish gypsies
from the nearest port, the ship to sail 'on the first wind'.[14] Others were
forcibly sent packing to Norway and Calais in 1544.

Then there were the Jews, expelled from England by Edward I in

1290. In late 1541, the king ordered the imprisonment of the 'New Christians' who had arrived from Portugal. These were Jews who, despite their conversion to Christianity, had been thrown out of Spain. Henry considered them 'crypto-Jews' and, casting rapacious eyes on their wealth, confiscated their money and possessions as the price of freedom.[15] In January 1542, Chapuys cynically reported that 'however well they may sing, they will not escape their cages without leaving their feathers behind'.[16]

Playing the xenophobic card brought political benefits for Henry. Fears about immigration into England are nothing new. In 1540, an Act 'concerning strangers' was passed, assuaging popular concerns about 'the infinite number of strangers and aliens... which daily increase and multiply in excessive numbers to the great detriment, hindrance, loss and impoverishment of the subjects... of this realm'.[17] The legislation banned aliens from trading, assembling together or the employment of more than four foreigners at any one time.

These were superstitious times and the king shared the prevalent fears about black magic and the power of demons. When the fires of love and lust for his second wife Anne Boleyn were extinguished, Henry claimed that he had been 'seduced and forced' into the marriage by her '[sorcery] and charms' and regarded their union nullified.[18] The Witchcraft Act of March 1542 was the first legislation to make practising magic a felony, punishable by death and forefeiture of the accused's property. It prohibited the invocation or conjuring of 'spirits, enchantments or sorceries with the intent to find money or treasure, or to waste, consume or destroy any person in his body members, or to provoke any person to unlawful love'.[19]

Henry VIII's preoccupation about the Tudor succession would have a cataclysmic impact on English society and political life during the sixteenth century.

Henry's first wife was Katherine of Aragon and the torment of their lack of a living son ran like a thin line of poison through nearly three decades of his reign. She suffered a tragic natal record of six pregnancies during 1510–18, resulting in the miscarriages of two girls, one stillborn boy and three live births – Prince Henry on 1 January 1511 (who lived for just fifty-three days), another boy in September 1513, who died hours later[20] and Princess Mary, born in February 1516, who survived.

The king discarded Katherine because he believed their lack of sons was God's judgement on him for marrying Arthur's widow. More despondency followed when his second wife Anne Boleyn gave birth to Elizabeth in September 1533. Anne suffered one probable phantom pregnancy the following year and miscarried a fifteen-week-old male foetus in 1536.[21]

Recently, there has been speculation about the king's ability to sire children, but this is something of a red herring. Such conjecture ignores the fact that Henry impregnated four women, producing at least ten pregnancies. Aside from the two princesses, he sired the bastard Henry Fitzroy by his first mistress, the eighteen-year-old blonde Elizabeth ('Bessie') Blount, in 1519. He finally obtained the longed-for heir Prince Edward on 12 October 1537 by his third wife Jane Seymour, who died twelve days after the birth by Caesarean section[22] probably from puerperal sepsis, or a pulmonary embolism, or perhaps food poisoning.

It is also plausible that he fathered Catherine (born about 1524) and Henry (born two years later), the children of Anne Boleyn's elder sister (and another royal mistress) Mary, after her marriage to William Carey, an Esquire of the Body in his Privy Chamber, in February 1520.[23] Salacious gossip about Henry's affair with the elder Boleyn girl was probably common in the 1530s: John Hale, elderly vicar of Isleworth, Middlesex, recalled having 'young Master Carey' pointed out to him as 'the king's son by ... the queen's sister, whom the queen may not suffer to be at court'.[24]

The popular view is that Henry contracted syphilis, causing Katherine's terrible obstetric history, and we will investigate this hoary fallacy later in this book. Others believe that Henry possessed a translocation of his chromosomes which meant that his sperm cells had extra or missing genetic material that caused miscarriages. About one person in 500 has a chromosome translocation but this does not necessarily cause a miscarriage, or mean that healthy children cannot be produced.[25]

Another theory claimed he was afflicted with Kell blood antigenicity, causing impaired fertility (inherited from his maternal great-grandmother, Jacquetta Woodville), coupled with McLeod's Syndrome.[26] Henry displayed no symptoms of McLeod's Syndrome and Katherine of Aragon's initial miscarriages and perinatal deaths are not typical of Kell antigen sensitivity.

We must consider the stark facts of life in Tudor England. Soap was a luxury used by the few and most laundry was undertaken using an effusion of cow-dung, hemlock and nettles. The rich, possessing several houses, moved when one became so malodorous that it had to be 'sweetened' by sweeping out the accumulation of rotting plant material covering the floors and fresh herbs such as sweet woodruff laid down to counter the stench.[27]

Given the unhealthy nature of Tudor diet and poor hygiene, it is more likely that Katherine of Aragon and Anne Boleyn suffered nutritional imbalances or common infections like listeriosis, which can trigger spontaneous abortion or stillbirth. This also manifests itself as meningitis or pneumonia in new-borns. The two boys that Katherine safely delivered in 1511 and 1513 died soon after birth, their deaths possibly caused by these two medical conditions.

This then was a very dangerous world and even after the happy birth of Prince Edward, there was no spare heir to allow the king to sleep easier at night. Understandably, he was anxious about the threat of disease to his young son.

Henry VIII's own health dictated the stability of the realm, as well as physically symbolising England's majesty and might.

He had good reason to be fearful. The relentless risk of disease, misadventure and other forms of sudden death meant that life expectancy was far lower than in the twenty-first century. Only ten per cent of Tudor citizens lived beyond their fortieth birthday and the average life expectancy of males was just thirty-seven. No wonder Henry became obsessed with his medical care and displayed all the symptoms of a rampant hypochondriac.

The king was terrified of bubonic plague, introducing the first quarantine laws to counter the disease in 1518. The epidemic of 1499–1500 had killed 30,000 people in England (equivalent to half London's population then)[28] and further outbreaks occurred in 1509–10, 1516–17, 1523, 1527–30, 1532, 1540 and 1544–6. The poor were worst afflicted because of their insanitary living conditions: two-thirds of England's urban population in the 1520s lived below or very near the poverty line.[29] The bacterial strain *Yersinia pestis* infiltrated the human lymphatic system, causing painful swellings – called buboes – in the armpits, groin and neck. Early symptoms resembled influenza: high fever, muscle cramps and headaches, but then blood was vomited, together with gangrene on the fingers, nose and toes. Death could follow within twenty-four hours after the first symptoms, especially if the lungs were primarily infected.

Confronted by such a virulent and deadly disease, Henry ordered that when the royal court embarked on summer progresses in the Thames Valley or elsewhere, harbingers should investigate whether the destination, or towns en route, were infected. At Calais in 1532 and at Windsor in 1540,[30] the sick were dragged out of their homes, carted outside each town's precincts and left to die in the fields to reduce the danger to the court. Henry at least paid for the cost of expelling them at Windsor.

In July 1543, a proclamation forbade Londoners 'entering the gates of any house where the king or queen lay' and banned servants from going to the infected city and then returning to court.[31] Another ordered that crosses be daubed on every house inhabited by plague victims. The burning of straw mattresses and refuse was imposed as a rudimentary means of disinfection and those in contact with the disease were forced to carry white rods as warnings to passers-by.[32]

Another silent killer was the 'English Sweating Sickness' or *sudor anglicus*, probably introduced by the 3,000 French mercenaries with Henry VII when his small army splashed ashore near Milford Haven, Pembrokeshire, in 1485. After Bosworth, his troops were ravaged by the disease and his coronation postponed. Two lord mayors of London died from it within a week.[33]

The name was derived from the erroneous belief that it struck only at Englishmen. There were major epidemics in England in 1485, 1507–8, 1517, 1528 and 1551 and the disease was probably a form of viral pneumonia.[34] The physician John Caius noted that the Sweating Sickness 'immediately killed some in opening their windows, some in playing with their children at their street doors. As it found them, it took them, some in sleep, some [awake], some in mirth, some in care, some fasting, some full, some busy and some idle ... In one house, sometimes three, sometimes five, sometimes all [died]. If the half in every town escaped, it was thought a great favour.'[35]

Victims became leaden-limbed and drowsy. Delirium and vomit-
ing were followed by heart palpitations. Death could strike within
twelve to twenty-four hours. The disease claimed a high proportion
of victims among young, wealthy urban males. Around 40,000 people
were infected in London during the 1528 epidemic, of whom fifty died
daily, including Thomas Cromwell's wife Elizabeth and probably their
two daughters, Anne and 'little Grace',[36] together with Mary Boleyn's
accommodating husband, William Carey.[37]

After some pages in his bedchamber died, Henry fled London and
frequently moved residences, sometimes almost every night.

One preventative measure, claiming to be 'a very true medicine',
combined prayer with the superstitious power of the number seven and
the Biblical promise of fulfilment of a divine mandate.[38] Those wishing
to avoid infection should say seven paternosters ('Our Fathers...') and
seven Ave Marias ('Hail Marys'), every time making the Sign of the
Cross with the thumb on seven parts of the body – under the ears,
armpits and thighs and lastly at the heart. If these were said daily, 'with
the grace of God, there is no manner [to] dread [it].' Reassuringly, the
advice concluded: *Quod pro certo probatum est cotidie* – 'It has daily
been proven for sure.'[39]

There were many other Tudor mortal diseases. Pulmonary tuberculosis killed Henry VII, probably Prince Arthur and Henry VIII's
illegitimate son Henry Fitzroy, duke of Richmond.[40] Edward VI also
fell victim in 1553, coupled with measles and administrations of noxious stimulants. Henry VIII contracted a severe dose of smallpox in
December 1513 and survived. Anne of Cleves was also a victim, as was
Elizabeth I in 1562, when she nearly died from the disease.[41] Typhus
or 'gaol fever'[42] 'killed many honest persons... throughout the realm'
in 1540.[43] Dysentery, or 'the bloody flux', sometimes called 'laskes'
or 'lax', was caused by contaminated water or poor hygiene in food
preparation. Malaria, or 'tertiary fever', spread by mosquitoes became
endemic after the 1520s in marshy areas. The first catastrophic epidemic
of influenza occurred in England in 1510.[44] Scurvy afflicted wealthy
households, as the occupants did not eat fresh fruit or vegetables as
sources of vitamin C.

Medicine fascinated the king. In 1546, he questioned William Foxley, potmaker at the mint in the Tower of London, who had slept continuously for fourteen days and fifteen nights, despite rather uncaring attempts to wake him up by 'pricking, cramping or burning' his slumbering body. The cause of his prolonged sleep remained a mystery. Foxley 'was found at his wakening to be as if he had slept but one night'.[45]

Henry experimented with his own cures for a variety of diseases, producing a 'plaster' for his fourth wife Anne of Cleves, before she was discarded.[46] The British Library retains a book[47] which contains 114 recipes, thirty-two devised by the monarch himself, for a range of balms and poultices, including 'The King's Own Grey Plaster' 'to take away inflammation, cease pain and heal ulcers'. Its ingredients included roots, buds, raisins, linseed, vinegar, rosewater, long garden worms, ivory scrapings, powdered pearls, (poisonous) red lead, suet of hens and fat from the thighbone of calves.

He also developed his own cure for bubonic plague, sending it to his secretary Sir Brian Tuke in 1518. History does not record whether it was efficacious, although significantly, divine intervention was essential.

Henry also tried to rationalise medical science and structure the profession by passing seven separate parliamentary Acts during his reign. He established the Royal College of Physicians in 1518 to 'withstand the attempts ... of those wicked men who profess medicine more for ... their avarice than assurance of any good conscience'. These wicked persons included 'common artificers [such] as smiths, weavers and women who boldly take upon themselves great cures ... They use sorcery and apply medicines very noxious to the displeasure of God ... and grievous hurt to the king's people ... who cannot discern the cunning from the uncunning.'[48]

To achieve this, Parliament had to override the bishop of London's traditional right to grant licences to practise medicine in the city. Henry's royal charter was confirmed by parliamentary Act in 1523, which extended the college's jurisdiction to the whole of England.

In 1540, Henry granted a royal charter to the 'United Company of Barber Surgeons' uniting two city companies, the Mystery of Barbers and the Company of Pure Surgeons, which placed physicians firmly at the top of the profession. Surgeons were now prohibited from applying 'outward remedies' especially for sciatica, ulcers or any kind of wound, but could undertake blood-letting and cutting into a patient's body. At the bottom, barbers were limited to shaving and pulling teeth.

Much of the king's gamecock bravado was deflated by a rapid decline in his health at the end of the 1530s.

Major forensic obstacles have to be overcome when investigating Henry VIII's poor health. Medical science was manifestly less advanced than today, so the royal doctors had imperfect diagnostic skills – except for bubonic plague, smallpox, syphilis or Sweating Sickness, which were all too familiar. There are few surviving letters by his physicians because possessing information about the royal medical condition was dangerous. Finally, we only have evidence supplied by his courtiers or gossipy foreign ambassadors who were hardly expert clinicians.

Yet after nearly five hundred years, we can build a reasonably accurate picture of Henry's medical history.

He contracted smallpox in 1513, when his physicians 'were afraid of his life' – but he rose from his bed, 'fierce against France'.[49] He suffered from malaria in 1521, 1528, 1540 and 1541.[50]

In March 1524, Henry sustained his first jousting injury, recklessly riding with his helmet visor raised, against his friend Charles Brandon, first duke of Suffolk, whose blunted lance caught his forehead. He was lucky not to break his neck or fracture his skull, but was badly bruised. With characteristic swagger, Henry ran six more courses but suffered headaches or 'rheums' afterwards.[51] These may have been caused by bouts of catarrh and coughs, as in July 1528, when the king complained of headaches and was not disposed to write, in 'consequence of his head'.[52] He was also prone to sore throats and hoarseness, as in March 1545, all of which suggest a case of sinusitis.

In 1525, he almost drowned while vaulting over a water-filled ditch while hawking near Hitchin, Hertfordshire. The pole he was using suddenly snapped 'so that if Edmond Moody, a footman, had not leapt into the water and lifted up his head which was fast in the clay, he [would] have drowned'; the king was safely pulled out, feet first.[53] Two years on, Henry strained his foot playing tennis at Whitehall. He was forced to wear a loose black velvet slipper to ease the pain while walking, because of a weak ankle tendon. It prompted a new fashion in footwear as his courtiers sycophantically wore the same slipper. Two years later, he wrenched his foot again during another tennis match.[54]

In 1527–8, Henry was confined to bed at Canterbury with a 'sore leg' by a deep vein thrombosis or varicose ulcer on the left leg,[55] caused by the constrictive garter he wore beneath the knee, or possibly an injury sustained during jousting.

The king was hurt again during jousting on 24 January 1536 at Greenwich. His one-ton charger fell on him as both contestants closed in the lists at a combined closing speed of forty miles (64km) per hour. There were reports that the king lay 'for two hours without speech' probably through severe concussion, rather than bruising of his cerebral cortex, as symptoms of this would have lasted much longer.[56]

His most painful affliction was the purulent and weeping ulcers on one or both legs. The first contemporary reference comes in March 1537 and, a few weeks later, it was reported that Henry 'seldom goes [abroad] because his leg is something sore'.[57] In June that year he wrote to the duke of Norfolk: 'To be frank with you, which you must keep to yourself, a humour has fallen into Our legs and Our physicians advise us not to go far in the heat of the year.'[58]

These ulcers were almost certainly recurring chronic osteomyelitis, which can develop in the long bones of the leg following an injury, or afflicts those suffering from conditions that affect blood supply, such as diabetes.[59] Symptoms include bone pain, fevers, fatigue, pus draining from the sinus tract and local swelling. Today, this is treated by antibiotics and 'debridement' – cutting away the diseased bone and draining the pus – but these methods were unavailable in the sixteenth century.

The following May a fistula in one leg closed up: 'For ten or twelve days, the humours which had no outlet were like to stifle him so that he was some time without speaking, black in the face and in great danger.' In today's medical terms, Henry was probably suffering from a thrombosed vein in his leg and dangerously, a clot may have become detached. Being 'black in the face' was possibly caused by a lung infection or a pulmonary embolism. He was very fortunate to survive.[60]

The king suffered from other kinds of discomfort as well. In September 1539, Henry complained of acute constipation, doubtless because of his substantial consumption of red meat and lack of roughage.

There were more severe infections caused by the fistulas – tube-like ulcers – on his legs suddenly closing up, as in February 1541 when his life seemed threatened. He sank initially into a deep melancholy and then flew into a prolonged violent rage.

The king could never be said to be weak or cowardly and he tried hard to maintain the pretence of regal normality. Despite his legs being regularly cauterised by hot irons by his doctors, Henry insisted on creeping (on his knees) to the cross of the Chapel Royal at Easter 1539 as part of the pre-Reformation liturgy. He served at the altar throughout Mass, piously kneeling.[61]

By 1540, the king was walking with a staff. Sir John Wallop, his ambassador to France, reported that the French king was limping after being 'pricked in the leg [by a] sword, lacking a scabbard'. He added: 'I wished to myself that I had one of your highness' staves to have presented to him in your name. If it shall please your majesty to send him one... he would take it very gratefully.'[62]

The agonising ulcers on his legs were to curse Henry until the end of his days but another, more insidious, medical problem began to consume him by the end of the 1530s; a condition that radically changed his personality and endangered all those around him, as a dark veil of paranoia and suspicion shrouded the monarch and he grew ever more irascible and unpredictable.

2

Safeguarding the Realm

During early 1539, Henry VIII faced an international crisis that endangered his crown, religious supremacy and dominions. More than two years before, he had survived uprisings in northern England against the dissolution of the monasteries only by bluffing and lying to the insurgents' representatives. Afterwards, 216 abbots, priors, monks and rebels were executed, as the king demanded ever more bloody vengeance on his disaffected subjects. 'You shall cause dreadful execution ... upon the inhabitants of every town, village and hamlet that have offended in this rebellion,' he ordered Norfolk, 'by hanging them up on trees and setting their heads and quarters [up] in every town ... [to] be a fearful spectacle to all.'[1]

The king's subsequent voracious destruction of saints' shrines – particularly Archbishop Thomas Becket's at Canterbury in 1538 – and his dialogues with the German Lutheran Protestants to create an alliance against the Vatican, were the last straw for Pope Paul III. He sought assistance from the Catholic monarchs in Europe to destroy this 'most cruel and abominable tyrant' and return England to the spiritual leadership of Rome. Cardinal Alexander Farnese reported in January 1539: 'The new and great impieties and heinous offences of the king of England have disgusted the Christian princes ... so that his Holiness hopes that God will work ... for the reduction of that realm.'[2]

Paul prepared to promulgate the three-year-old Papal Bull excommunicating Henry as a schismatic heretic and releasing his subjects from any allegiance to him or to his evil laws. The king's chief minister Thomas Cromwell, that 'limb of Satan', was to be cast out into utter damnation and Hell's all-consuming fires.[3]

The pope also created the Scottish abbot David Beaton a cardinal and commissioned him to cajole James V of Scotland into attacking

England from the north. Charles V, king of Spain and Holy Roman Emperor, and his neighbour Francis I of France had agreed a ten-year truce in June 1538 under papal sponsorship. Their signing of the Treaty of Toledo the following January (which ruled out any diplomatic agreements with the English king) sparked rumours of impending war, fanned by whispers that the Imperial and French ambassadors would be recalled from Henry's court as a curtain-raiser to hostilities.

Meanwhile, Paul III secretly dispatched Henry's bête noire, the exiled Cardinal Reginald Pole, to Spain and France to rally them to the papal colours, but ill-health prevented him travelling to the Imperial court at Toledo and he only arrived in February 1539.

Pole's mission demonstrated his fortitude and determination in advancing his unfaltering faith. Three years before, he had enraged Henry by writing *Pro unitate ecclesiæ* ('For Church Unity'),[4] an eloquent and violent attack on the king's supremacy over the English Church. Like a cardinal's red rag to an angry Tudor bull, he had been sent to France in 1537 to stir up support for the 'Pilgrimage of Grace' rebels in England, armed with letters of papal credit to raise cash for their revolt and instructions to encourage further uprisings.

Henry had required Pole's extradition as a traitor, but Francis I, who found himself in the painful position of alienating either his brother king or the pope, took the easy way out and merely banished Pole. The cardinal sought refuge at Liège in the Spanish Low Countries, but Henry demanded revenge on this turbulent priest. He instructed his ambassadors in France to 'secretly appoint some fellows' to kidnap him, adding: 'We would be very glad to have Pole trussed up and conveyed to Calais,'[5] the English stronghold on the European mainland. Cromwell, who contemptuously derided Pole as 'brainsick', also launched a covert operation, sending Sir Thomas Palmer, Knight-Porter of Calais, and four accomplices into Flanders to assassinate him.

The cardinal repeatedly escaped Henry's grasp, despite the generous reward of 100,000 gold crowns (£15.3 million at current prices) for the delivery of Pole 'alive or dead'. He defiantly branded Henry and his Privy Council 'enemies of the whole human race'. His mission might have proved unsuccessful but at least he had survived.

His kith and kin back in England had not. In November 1538, Cromwell arrested Pole's sixty-five-year-old mother, Margaret, count-ess of Salisbury,[6] his eldest brother Henry, Lord Montagu, Henry

Courtenay, marquess of Exeter and Sir Edward Neville. The three men were beheaded on Tower Hill that December for treason and, for that most damning of all crimes, conspiring with Pole. Margaret was attainted by Act of Parliament in 1539 and imprisoned in the Tower of London, as was Montagu's eighteen-year-old heir Henry, who mysteriously disappeared within that forbidding fortress some time after September 1542, and Exeter's twelve-year-old son Edward, who was not freed until 1553.

Henry may jubilantly have destroyed the last survivors of the Yorkist 'White Rose' faction of the bitter civil wars of the previous century, but he now faced a more immediate and tangible threat than any latent Plantagenet claimant to his crown.

In Spain, William Ostrych, leader of the English merchants in Andalusia, had intelligence from Charles V's court in January that confirmed the triple alliance of France, Scotland and Spain against England. Henry and his subjects would be 'proclaimed heretics and schismatics, to be treated as Jews and infidels whenever taken'. The emperor 'will have war with the king next March and the Spanish army in Flanders will go against England'.[7]

Thomas Wriothesley, ambassador to Queen Mary of Hungary, Regent of the Spanish Netherlands, warned London of an invasion planned for the summer of 1539 and added dejectedly: 'England is but a morsel amongst these choppers'.[8] A French spy warned in March of 'great preparations being made secretly... You must fortify your places and harbours'. Lapsing into the vernacular, he cautioned that Francis 'intends to do you a bad turn'. Another French agent reported the concentration of 'great numbers of troops between Orleans and Paris... [who] are going into Normandy to sail for Scotland'.[9]

Panic gripped England. This intensified in April 1539 with reports of 8,000 mercenaries mustering in the Low Countries and then a threatening fleet of sixty-eight ships was spotted off Margate on the Kent coast. Troops were mobilised at Ashford in the same county and at Hayling Island, Hampshire, but both incidents were false alarms. The ships sailed on to Spain to join Charles V's campaign against the Turks and the mercenaries ended up in the Baltic region.[10]

A group of religious reformers in London wrote to their Protestant friends in Germany: 'We are to have war with the French, Italians, Spaniards and Scots [all] at once. When the secret machinations...

were reported to the king, he said he should not sleep at all the worse for it . . . [and would] now promote the Word of God more than he had ever done before . . . We have a king of noble spirit.'[11]

Despite Henry's bullish confidence, an unprecedented emergency faced his Tudor dynasty. A holy crusade against him seemed under way and he could face simultaneous attack on at least two fronts against his largely undefended realm, dividing his forces. After the northern rebellions, he was wary about the loyalty of many subjects who still hankered after the certainties of the old religion. Popular discontent was also fuelled by rumours of new taxes – an issue that had sparked the earlier uprisings.[12]

The king launched an emergency programme to defend his coasts and the Scottish border, trusting that Cromwell's omnipresent network of informers would detect and crush domestic treason. How much time did he have before the first invasion ships appeared on the horizon?

The 'King's Device' was an ambitious plan for a chain of artillery fortifications, greater in both cost and extent than those built against invasion by the French three centuries later.[13] Money and resources, at a time of such national danger, were not considerations although Henry was delighted that proceeds from the monastic suppressions would pay for many forts and some would be built with materials recycled from demolished religious houses.

During March and April 1539, military preparations galvanised England. Stone-built defences would take too long to complete, so turf-faced bulwarks and dry moats were hastily thrown up and excavated, protected by earth and gravel-filled 'gabions' – tall wickerwork baskets that absorbed cannon shot. One of Cromwell's aides-memoires listed twenty vulnerable locations where fortifications were essential – potential landing beaches, anchorages and the approaches to ports, as well as bolstering existing defences of the northern borders.[14]

Undaunted by the enormous scale of the task, the minister organised a legion of labourers not only to construct the earthworks but also dig ditches and erect barricades to delay invaders once landed. Lord Chancellor Thomas Audley reported that at Harwich, Essex, 'The people have been most willing and earnest, making both trenches and bulwarks before we came. You should have seen the women and children work with shovels in the . . . bulwarks there,' he noted approvingly.[15] On the exposed Isle of Wight, the gentry were determined 'to defend their country and daily make themselves more ready, saying they will stake their coasts [with wooden obstacles] and [dig] their ditches ... towards low water mark, that when enemies land it shall be dangerous to them. They also make their bulwarks stronger.'[16]

Beacons were set up along the south and east coasts of England, to warn of enemy approach or invasion. Foreign ships were impounded in London and Southampton (under pain of death if they sailed), for naval service. Weapons and armour were bought from merchants in Antwerp and Hamburg and German mercenaries hired to stiffen the ranks of the untrained and ill-equipped county militias, now augmented by conscripted men aged seventeen and over. Garrisons on the Scottish border were reinforced.

Equally important was the battle for the hearts and minds of Henry's subjects. The Tudors invented propaganda in its modern sense, skil-fully harnessing the power of the printing press with that of the visual impact of drama, pageantry and spectacle to raise morale and convince everyone of the absolute justice of the king's cause.

Cromwell's polemicist Richard Morison published *An Exhortation to styre all Englishe men to the defence of their countreye* that March, combining reassurance that England would defeat her enemies with strident appeals that the population's duty lay in supporting their king against the Catholic powers. 'Is it possible that any [of] his grace's subjects can refuse pain, when his highness rides about from haven to haven, from castle to castle [spending] days and nights devising all the ways that wit can invent for our assurance ... ? What a realm will England be, when his grace has set walls [and] ditches that run round about us! England will be much [more] like a castle than a realm ... [When] his highness diligently watches [so] that we may safely sleep [and] spends his treasure ... were it not [to] our great shame to suffer him to travail [labour] alone?'[17]

Morison evoked memories of famous English victories to fire his readers' patriotism: 'We may forget the battle of Agincourt but they [the French] will remember and are like never to forget with how small an army ... King Henry V vanquished that huge host of Frenchmen ... Let us fight this one field with English hands and English hearts.

Perpetual peace, victory, honour, wealth, all is ours.' God was with those who defended their true faith and also with Henry, 'whom God had advanced to the throne as the scourge of superstition'.[18] Cromwell paid the author £20 (£13,000 at today's prices) in April 1539, probably for penning the *Exhortation*.[19]

On Thursday, 8 May, a morale-boosting parade of citizens in full military array was staged in London, mustering in the fields between Whitechapel and Mile End before six in the morning in three great battalions, each led by four field guns, followed by troops carrying morris pikes,[20] bills[21] and bows and arrows. Among them were a 1,000-strong contingent, whose equipment cost Cromwell the princely sum of £117 16s 3d, more than £75,000 in 2019 money.

The London recruits, led by their drum and fife bands, proved a brave and stirring sight. Dressed in white coats and feathered caps, the sun glinting on a forest of weapons, they marched behind their fluttering banners bearing the blood-red cross of England, the City of London's arms and the Tudor colours of green and white. The chronicler Charles Wriothesley saw them tramp through the streets 'to the number of 16,500 and more, [although] a man would have thought they had been above 30,000, they were so long passing by ... There was never a goodlier sight in London'.[22] Another eyewitness, John Husee, thought they numbered between 20,000 and 25,000 and was convinced that foreigners who saw the spectacle 'did little rejoice' at this valiant show of strength.[23]

The long column wound through the city and on to Westminster, where Henry and his Privy Councillors watched as each battalion fired salutes with their field- and hand-guns, the noise judged 'very terrible'. Then it was once around St James's Park, before again parading past the king, now standing atop the Holbein gateway of Whitehall Palace, before dispersing at five o'clock. Henry 'rejoiced' at the muster, although someone with his military acumen would have noticed a worrying dearth of hand-guns among the troops.[24] However, as we shall see, behind that smile of delight creasing the king's bloated face lay secret knowledge that made the day still more gratifying.

The propaganda war against the Holy See continued. On 17 June, Cromwell staged a rumbustious 'triumph' on the River Thames by Whitehall Palace. This spectacle involved two large barges, armed with guns firing darts, or *flechettes*, made of harmless reeds. One boat's crew wore the colourful robes of the pope and his cardinals, complete with tall mitres; the other represented Henry and his sober-sided council. They were to stage a sham fight to delight the Londoners and Henry himself, viewing from a prominent vantage point above the river entrance to Whitehall, decorated with green boughs and roses. Two other vessels, flying banners and pennons bearing St George's cross, carried an orchestra to provide a suitably stirring musical accompaniment. Beneath the laughter and mirth lay a hard-nosed political message: the power of the king's supremacy.

Three times the barges laboriously rowed up and down the river, exchanging volleys of darts. The outcome was, of course, carefully choreographed. At the fourth pass, the papal party were ignominiously thrown into the river. No one drowned, as those taking part were hand-picked beforehand as good swimmers. Cromwell, with a concern for health and safety centuries ahead of his time, had also stationed one of the royal barges nearby to pluck the vanquished 'papacy' out of the water. It was, as a watching Charles Wriothesley pointed out, 'a goodly pastime'.[25]

Quite suddenly, the crisis faded away. Cardinal Pole failed to convince Charles V of Spain to join the holy league against Henry as he had quite enough on his hands fighting the infidel Turks in the Mediterranean and grappling with Lutheran Protestants in Germany. The emperor was already championing the True Religion by tackling these twin evils, at no small cost to his exchequer.[26] Charles promised, however, that when Francis 'who was not so hampered as he, found some plan, they could deliberate more maturely what to do'.

Pole was discouraged by Charles's rebuff but continued to press for French assistance. Henry, he said, was a 'cruel wolf who seeks only to devour the flock of God' ... 'The whole hope of remedying the evils of England and delivering the Church from oppression rests in the king of France who, in this, it is hoped, will imitate his glorious ancestors' in the defence of Catholicism.[27]

Despite the immediacy of his appeals, Pole postponed visiting Francis I and withdrew to Carpentras in south-east France to await papal instructions. He explained to Cardinal Farnese: 'I did not wish in so important a matter to go too far and did not see what more could result, except that I might compromise again my own life and the honour of the Apostolic See, as I did when I went to Flanders.' He had learnt 'from those who know the king of England's practices in France, with how many means he procures my death and chiefly in that kingdom where he has more ways and methods on account of its nearness to [England]'.[28]

Francis initially seemed willing to join the enterprise against England, but then doubts drained his resolve. He was ready to do his duty in supporting the Church, but only when Charles would act in unison. Furthermore, it was inadvisable for Pole to visit him, as this would only arouse suspicion. Then in March, the French king unexpectedly sent Charles de Marillac to London as ambassador, following this up on 18 April, with a private letter to Henry assuring him that his war preparations were aimed at the Spanish in Flanders, not against England at all.

According to Marillac, this letter 'dispelled all remains of distrust from the king and his council' who seemed 'quite delighted'. The king, recovering his old sangfroid, graciously informed Marillac that his defence preparations had been spurred by Charles V's military activities in Flanders and were nothing whatsoever to do with France. He merely 'wished to be on his guard and to see what forces he could muster, if attacked'.[29]

This was the secret knowledge that so cheered Henry as he watched the Londoners marching past in all their martial splendour. There was no threat from France and with luck, no covert French interference in Scotland. The perils of having to fight on two fronts had disappeared like battlefield smoke in a breeze.

By August, Pope Paul had grudgingly abandoned his great crusade and urged Pole to return to Rome and safety.[30] Papal face was saved by Paul's somewhat limp assertion that all he ever intended was to impose French and Spanish trade sanctions that would goad the English into settling their own destiny by fighting a civil war.

The crisis was over, but it had been a testing time. Three years later, Henry confided to Marillac that 'it was true that when the [French] king and the emperor were on terms of agreement ... they had pushed him into a narrow corner but, thank God, he was still alive and not so little a king as had been supposed'.[31]

Henry always proudly maintained that he had far greater expertise in foreign relations than any of his ministers and council – Cardinal Thomas Wolsey and Cromwell included – and had a consistent record of happily ignoring their advice because he knew better. In diplomacy, the king was unpredictable, revelling in his unorthodoxy, a veritable *enfant terrible* of European politics. Francis I once commented miserably on his dealings with Henry: 'Sometimes he treats me like a subject... He is the strangest man in the world and I fear I can do no good with him. But I must put up with him, as it is no time to lose friends.'[32]

The running sore of the break with Rome, the execution of those who opposed his royal supremacy and the dissolution of the monasteries left Henry a pariah in Catholic Europe. John Dymock, his commissary in the Low Countries, was assailed by vehement criticism of the king in Dordrecht in 1546. He was deeply shocked when an official told him 'what the king has done will give him a warm arse one day' and could only lamely reply that he would be judged by God.[33]

Diplomatic embarrassment is one thing; the agony of torture quite another. The unfortunate Thomas Perry, an English merchant in Seville, found himself in the remorseless hands of the Spanish Inquisition in 1539 because of Henry's religious policies. The judge, Pedro Diez, asked Perry repeatedly whether he believed that his king was a good Christian, given his 'putting down of the monasteries, taking away the [church] bells and that he is pope within his realm'. The merchant answered stoutly that he believed 'his grace was a good Christian and the rest I believe well done'. No surprise then that Perry was thrown into the Inquisition's jail in the Castillo de San Jorge in Triana[34] – notorious as the 'Prison of Torments'.

Perry recounted his ordeal: 'Then came the judge and his notary and he set himself down in a chair, [with] a cushion of tapestry work under his feet. Then I knelt down, desiring him to be good to me and do me justice. Diez said: "Confess now the truth and we ask no more".' Then 'the porter and another took me by the arms and ... set me down upon the *burrito* [wooden donkey] and brought one of my arms over the other and cast a rope five times about them and so drew the rope with all their might.

'I thought they would pluck the flesh from the bones and cried to the judge to show me mercy, saying this is a house of justice but it is more like a house of murder... He said he would give me good advice... "Your king... now is the greatest heretic in the world and if we had him here, we would burn him. All the world should not save him." '[35]

Perry was forced to take part in the Inquisition's *auto-de-fé*, an act of public penance. Wearing a yellow habit adorned with red crosses and carrying a candle, he staggered through the crowded Seville streets to the church of St Anna where he heard Mass. Then he was sent to the 'Prison of Perpetuity' where he was told his possessions had been confiscated, half going to the Inquisition and half to Charles V. There he remained 'abiding the mercy of the Lord and [I] might die for [lack] of comfort'.

In July 1540, twenty-five English merchants in Spain, headed by their governor, William Ostrych (whom we met earlier), wrote to Roger Basing, in Henry's household, complaining of their treatment by the Inquisition. 'Other merchants, prisoners with Perry, were present when he was tormented. Four or five Englishmen remain in prison. The Inquisition have searched Seville, Pérez, Sanlúcar and elsewhere for English merchants.'[36]

The following month, Basing was in Seville, ostensibly investigating the fate of these unfortunate victims, but, in reality, tasked with a more mundane mission. He promised to send the emperor's response to complaints about the persecution, but happily, Perry 'with all such Englishmen as were in prison here... for the bishop of Rome's matters, were [freed] on 9 August'.

Then on to the real reason he was in Spain; he had £450 in his bulging purse to purchase bloodstock horses from the Imperial stud for Henry. 'I have bought six horses and four mares of the best and largest I can find which I sent to England from Seville on 26 July,' he reported. He could not leave yet because, ironically, he had been accused of heresy by a Frenchman from Bordeaux. 'He alleges... that I am a Lutheran, because the king has granted me the lease of an abbey... Notwithstanding, I trust to God to ride hence within these ten days.'[37]

His trust in providence was misplaced. Basing was thrown into jail for owing a debt of 1,400 gold ducats. The wheels of Tudor government sometimes revolved slowly and it was not until that November that the Privy Council summoned the Imperial ambassador to complain.

They described 'soberly and modestly' how badly the king's subjects were treated in his country and that he should immediately request Charles V to grant them redress and protection from the Inquisition's attentions.

This appeal proved fruitless, so Sir John Mason, reputedly on good terms with the emperor, was sent to Seville in December 1540. If Basing, the king's servant, could not be liberated without money changing hands, Mason was authorised to spend £40 'or under, rather than leave him in prison'.

Henry was more concerned about his horses which 'are to be at once sent hither'.[38] The 'jennets' and mares eventually arrived in England, but in February 1541 the issue was still taxing the Privy Council. In case Basing 'cannot shortly come home himself' he should report on what had happened to the king's cash 'delivered at his going out and also about the £60 paid out for bringing the horses over'.[39] In the event, the unfortunate Basing seems to have returned to England safely and rehabilitated in Henry's favour, as in December 1542, a man of that name was appointed 'vice-admiral of his majesty's navy'.[40]

The problems of his subjects abroad were the least of Henry's worries about international relations. While he always tried to punch above his weight, the king was painfully aware that England, then with a population of just under three million, was a second-rate power that could never match the military, industrial or financial clout of Spain and France.

Henry had three inviolate diplomatic imperatives. The first was at all costs to prevent military alliances between France and Spain; indeed, if possible, to set them at each other's throats. The king once frankly told a Spanish envoy that 'he had no fear of being annoyed or troubled by anyone in the world, so long as a perfect amity did not exist' between these countries.[41] The second was to weaken or destroy the centuries-old Franco-Scottish 'Auld Alliance' and stymie French adventures north of the English border. Finally, Calais and its immediate hinterland had to be retained and protected at all costs because of the Pale's importance to the wool trade with Flanders and its symbolism as the last English toehold on the continent of Europe.

There were also the 'nice to have' rewards from diplomatic endeavour such as the advantageous marriages of his offspring with the royal families of Europe, never for love, but solely for political advantage. This was always possible, although he was constrained by only having to offer as prospective spouses young Edward and his two daughters Mary and Elizabeth, both of whom had unfortunately been declared illegitimate by statute.[42] Finally, the arrest or repatriation of a handful of English traitors exiled in Europe – first and foremost Cardinal Pole – would always gladden Henry's cankered old heart. Where diplomacy or the protocols laid down by international treaties failed him on this score, the king would hire his own assassins, as we shall see later.

No doubt these all were matters which Henry, as God's deputy on earth, discussed regularly with the almighty during his prayers, soliciting divine intervention on his and England's part. Henry, in his sublime arrogance, naturally believed that when he spoke during his pious devotions on his knees, God listened attentively.

Age and ill-health was also wearying the king and, always a pragmatist, he was only too well aware that time was running out for him to achieve all he wanted before handing over a safe and secure realm to his cherished son and heir. So in the aftermath of the 1539 crisis there was a growing determination to settle scores and realise outstanding ambitions of military glory. Out of this was born an audacious plan to exert Henry's suzerainty over what he saw as the vassal kingdom of Scotland – or at least to neutralise it as a threat – tame his unruly dominion of Ireland and, best of all, to assert the English monarchy's ancient right as kings of France.

The huge construction programme of defences around England's east and south coasts, the Scottish borders and in the Pale of Calais was broadened and accelerated and the Navy Royal's strength was increased by purchase or lease of Hanseatic merchant vessels, domestic shipbuilding and modernising existing warships. England had to be transformed into a secure fortress before Henry could embark on the fulfilment of his grand strategy.

The defences eventually consisted of seventy-three castles, forts, towers, bastions and bulwarks in England, Jersey in the Channel Islands and in the Pale of Calais, built between 1539 and 1547. Total expenditure on this project was £376,500 or £231 million at today's prices, with the costs met by the new courts of First Fruits and Tenths (set up in 1540 to collect monies from clerical benefices previously sent to Rome) and Augmentations, the bureaucracy that oversaw the legalised pillage of the religious houses.

Some fortifications were paid for by loyal subjects or local corporations. In Hampshire, Sir William Paulet, Lord St John, built, at Henry's personal request, a rectangular stone tower with two bastions at Netley to defend Southampton Water in 1542–5. Due to Tudor bureaucratic processes worthy of some ridicule, he had to be pardoned in 1547 for building it without possessing a licence to crenellate, or fortify a structure.[43]

Despite the disposals of monastic property, it was thought prudent to appeal to Parliament in 1540 to grant a subsidy, or tax, to pay for the 'great charges for the preparation of an army by the sea ... [and] his majesty's navy for the defence of his loving subjects and realm against enemies [in] the pretended invasion'. There had also been the 'extreme costs and charges' for the new fortresses. Parliament of its 'own free will, liberality and assent, like true natural, faithful and most loving subjects', agreed to grant payments equal to four-fifteenths and tenths of all 'moveable goods, cattle and other things' payable over the next four years.[44]

Huge teams of construction workers were recruited for this monumental project. For several years, it was impossible to contract a mason to build your family monument in your local church, as all were working on the so-called 'Device Forts'. Everyone was paid their five or six pence a day – plus travel expenses – although there were two strikes for higher wages at Guisnes[45] in the Calais Pale in 1541 and at Deal in Kent two years earlier, when nine troublemakers in this 'mutiny' were imprisoned in Canterbury Castle and at Sandwich Gaol.[46] At Guisnes, the Welsh ringleader, Morris ap Powell, appeared before a special commission of Oyer and Terminer[47] in the market place and, within hours, was hanged outside the town. His body was left on the gallows as a grisly warning. 'Since then the labourers have been doing their job more quietly,' Sir John Wallop tersely reported.[48]

The Thames Estuary forts controlling the river approaches to London were completed in March 1540, the blockhouses at East and

West Cowes on the Isle of Wight that summer and by the autumn, building work had finished on the circular artillery forts in 'The Downs' (the strategic anchorage off the Kent coast) and at Calshot at the entrance to Southampton Water. Construction on the castles at St Mawes and Pendennis guarding the port of Falmouth, Cornwall, had begun in April and October.[49] Later, stone structures replaced some of Cromwell's hastily erected earth bulwarks of 1539, because many had decayed beyond any defensive usefulness.

'Ship-killing' artillery defences had been around for some time, as at Dartmouth Castle in Devon, designed in the late fifteenth century. Henry's larger fortresses sprang phoenix-like from the dying embers of the medieval castle. These were a group of rounded bastions surrounding a central tower, allowing artillery to cover a wide arc of firepower on all sides from three to five tiers of embrasures. Some were designed to operate independently; others could provide crossfire for mutual defence. At Sandgate in Kent there were more than sixty gun ports and another sixty-five loopholes for hand-guns.[50]

The coastal fortifications were designed to deter a landing but if this failed, to delay the progress of an invasion to allow time for defending forces to concentrate and hurl the enemy back into the sea.

Later modifications to the 'Device Forts' included the latest military innovations, based on Italian experience, such as flanker bastions and the first arrowhead bastion at Yarmouth Castle on the Isle of Wight that would pour enfilading fire on attackers trying to force an entrance at the main gate.[51]

Sandgate and Camber in Sussex, together with the earth bulwarks linking the castles protecting The Downs off the Kent coast, were apparently the brainchild of the surveyor and architect Stefan von Haschenperg, a 'gentleman of Moravia'.[52] By July 1541, he was building an artillery platform on top of the keep at Carlisle Castle and a new semicircular stone bastion. A year later, he was in disgrace for having 'behaved lewdly and spent great treasure to no purpose' and had to provide surety for his performance. He was suspended in May 1543 and in August 1545 complained of having received no pay 'these two years'.[53]

Giovanni (or John) Portinari, an Italian engineer, was recruited to take charge of building operations at Sandown Castle, Isle of Wight.[54] Portinari was a man of many talents; he was paid £25 for building scenery for one of Henry's grand court masques in 1538 and worked on the king's tomb at Westminster in the late 1540s. At Sandown in 1545, he was 'captain' of 284 labourers on four shillings a day and plainly operated in some splendour as he employed a standard bearer at twelve pence a day and his fifes and drums were paid eight pence each.[55]

Across the English Channel, the frontline defences of the Calais Pale were not forgotten. The Beauchamp tower on the north-east corner of the walls of Calais was rebuilt in 1540–1 with two bastions, and a massive trefoil bulwark erected on the south. When Henry's commissioners saw the work there in May 1541, they noted approvingly that 'not a cat could stir' without detection within range of its guns.[56] At the Rysbank fort, two new towers were constructed, one facing seaward and the other, D-shaped, protected Calais harbour. Henry had ordered that the latter be built further west but this would incur 'great expense in removing the sandhill where the tower should stand and its removal would endanger the haven'.[57] So the location was shifted and by August 1542, the work was completed and ordnance installed.

Henry had a deep fascination with military and naval science, whether it be new fashions or developments in the design of fortifications, warships or artillery, and he delighted in showing off his knowledge and expertise.

Rather like some twentieth-century politicians who had been serving officers in their youth, he had no hesitation in sending meddlesome advice to his military commanders in the field about how they should conduct operations. During the siege of the French town of Landrecy by English and Imperial troops in late 1543, he had carefully studied a map of the town (probably the one still held by the British Library)[58] and sent instructions to build two huge earth mounds from which guns could 'beat the houses and scour the streets'.[59] Sir John Wallop, his general on the spot, showed the royal advice to his allies and, with predictable sycophancy, announced 'both of them liked your grace's opinion marvellously and had already minded the same'.

Wallop also reported a new and alarming weapon being used by the besieging Imperial forces: a giant mortar firing 'artificial' shells with forty or fifty bullets 'every one able to kill a man' – patently an early form of shrapnel. A few days later he graphically described its terrifying effects: 'It was a strange and dreadful sight to see the bullet fly into the air, spouting fire on every side. At [its] fall ... [it] leaped from place to place, casting out fire and within a while, burst forth and shot off guns out of [it] – an hundred shot, as loud as a hackbut. What hurt it has done I know not yet.'[60]

Wallop believed this 'fantasy' would intrigue his master and asked if the inventor could work for Henry.[61] The king was indeed fascinated by this sixteenth-century weapon of mass destruction. Wallop reported that Charles V was happy that the inventor could work for Henry for twenty days, generously charging his brother king for only five or six for his services.[62]

In April 1541, a venerable Italian, 'aged about seventy years', demonstrated another new invention to Henry – a device, probably an early telescope, that enabled ships to be observed from great distances.[63] The French ambassador thought it was a mirror which, if placed on the highest tower of Dover Castle, could allow an observer to see 'all ships that leave Dieppe. Although it seems incredible, he has persuaded this king to provide money to make it and left yesterday for Dover to fulfil his promise.'[64] Sadly, history is silent as to whether he succeeded.

The other major plank in England's defences was Henry's Navy Royal. He had inherited seven warships from his father and had added twenty-four more by 1514.[65] In 1536, the *Mary Rose* and the *Peter Pomegranate* were rebuilt, followed by the *Great Bark*, the flagship *Henry Grace à Dieu* and several smaller warships.[66] Their firepower was increased by adding 'great guns' and both cannon and ammunition were manufactured by the Sussex Weald iron foundries which started production in 1543.

His warships had become floating artillery platforms, grouped in 'battles', with each ship tasked with crippling or destroying an adversary at close quarters. English captains were ordered to sail between enemy vessels to enable broadsides to be fired by both port and starboard batteries and to aim their shots low to hole below the waterline, rather than damaging masts and rigging.[67]

Henry also built the 300-ton *Galley Subtle* in 1544, its banks of oars manned by slaves. A proclamation announced that convicted felons should suffer such dangerous hardship for their crimes and, at one point, the idea of using Scots prisoners of war for this purpose was also considered. In the event, the oarsmen were free men, not for humanitarian reasons, but probably because they were stronger and better fed than the dregs of the prisons.

Other new-builds included carracks, the 450-ton *Pansy* in 1543, *Anne Gallant* and *Grand Mistress*, two galleasses of the same displacement with a single bank of oars, and the 300-ton *Greyhound*, all in service by 1545. The *Antelope*, built in 1546, was operational right through to the Armada campaign in 1588 before being rebuilt in 1618. She was eventually blown up by Parliamentary dry forces off the Netherlands in 1649.

The king also acquired three ships, captured in action: the 300-ton *Salamander* and the 240-ton *Unicorn*, seized as prizes from the Scots at Leith in 1544 and the *Galley Blanchard*, taken from the French two years later. The carrack *Matthew Gonson* was purchased (doubtless at a cheap price) in 1545 from the family of William Gonson, paymaster of the navy, who committed suicide the year before.[68] Henry also hired large merchant vessels from the Hanseatic League in 1544 to convert into warships – *Jesus of Lubeck*, *Christopher of Bremen*, *Mary of Hamburg*, and *Struse of Danzig*. These were purchased the following year, together with the *Morion of Danzig* and the *Great Christopher of Danzig*, the latter bought for £550.

He may well have designed the thirteen 'row barges' – undecked oared vessels of twenty tons, armed with seven guns and designed to harry attacking enemy warships, as well as scouting, or interdicting small pirate vessels. These entered service in 1546 and had names taken from elements of the Tudor royal heraldry such as *Portcullis*, *Three Ostrich Feathers*, and *Double Rose*. The king's enthusiasm for his row barges foundered on their poor sea-keeping and endurance; most were decommissioned within a year of his death and sold off.

Finally, the administration of the navy underwent a major reorganisation in 1545. The 'Council of the Marine' or the 'Chief Officers of the Admiralty' was created, the forerunner of the Navy Board that exists today. Truly, Henry VIII was the father of the Royal Navy.

The clarion call of patriotism was always an effective distraction from the problems of internal dissent. By 1542, Henry was happy to be persuaded by a war party within his court that this was the right time for a foreign conflict which, like a 'potion of rhubarb', could cleanse 'choler from the body of the realm'.

With England now a safe base, protected by its navy and those expensive fortifications, plans were now being made for an overseas military adventure bringing glory, honour and lustre to Henry VIII's reputation as a warrior king.

3

Death of a 'Most False and Corrupt Traitor'

Early on the morning of Wednesday, 28 July 1540, a brooding Thomas Cromwell, until recently Henry VIII's chief minister, ate a frugal last breakfast in the Tower of London. His restless wait was soon over. A sharp rap on the door announced the arrival of Sir William Laxton and Martin Bowes, two Sheriffs of the City of London, come to escort him to his execution on Tower Hill.[1]

The prisoner had been warned that he was to die that morning.[2] However, by the king's special grace, he would be beheaded rather than hanged, drawn and quartered – the barbarous penalty for traitors that turned the scaffold into a bloody abattoir. The former Lord Privy Seal was doubtless grateful for this minor act of royal clemency.

He also learnt that he would not be alone in sampling the sharp taste of Henry's justice on this bright summer day. Accompanying him to the scaffold would be Walter, baron Hungerford, a former beneficiary of Cromwell's patronage. He had been condemned for treason – having paid magicians and the witch 'Mother Roche' to predict the king's death – and his chaplain, William Bird,[3] sympathised with the rebels who had threatened Henry three years before.[4] Hungerford was also found guilty of sodomy with 'William Maister, Thomas Smith and some of his other servants'[5] and raping his daughter Eleanor (or even more appallingly, possibly her eleven-year-old half-sister Mary).[6]

This was a terrible litany of ignominy and shame, but you can only execute a miscreant once. Although the main charge against him was high treason, Hungerford would also become the first to die under legislation drawn up seven years before by Cromwell that outlawed 'the detestable and abominable vice of buggery, committed with mankind or beast'.[7]

Thomas Howard, third duke of Norfolk, the most malevolent of the minister's many enemies at court, had earlier bragged to his cronies that Cromwell's death 'would be the most ignominious in the country'. Hungerford's appearance on the scaffold that morning was a callous attempt to humiliate Cromwell in his last hour by associating him with a felon guilty of the most scandalous of crimes.

The minister's downfall had occurred almost seven weeks earlier. Norfolk had ordered Sir Anthony Wingfield, Captain of the King's Guard, to come with his halberdiers to the Palace of Whitehall on Saturday, 10 June, to arrest Cromwell during a Privy Council meeting. The officer was stunned by the news of his mission, but the duke told him peremptorily: 'You need not be surprised. The king orders it.'[8]

The Lord Privy Seal had arrived late and was startled to find his usual chair at the head of the table occupied. As he sat down, Norfolk snapped: 'That is no place for you. Traitors do not sit amongst gentlemen.'

The palpable contempt and hatred in his words hung menacingly in the tense, crowded room. Right on cue, Wingfield and his six men burst into the room and the captain seized the minister's arm.

Astonished, Cromwell hurled his cap on to the floor and cried out: 'This, then, is all the reward for all my services?' His embittered, uncomprehending question was followed by a hapless plea to his fellow councillors: 'On your consciences, I ask you, am I a traitor?' Their answer came swift and brutal. Some shouted 'Yes, yes!' Others pounded their fists on the council table and, in time with the reverberating thumps, chanted: 'Traitor! Traitor! Traitor!' Like predatory animals, they scented Cromwell's blood, knowing that the imminent river journey to the Tower was a sure sign of his demise.

Norfolk stepped forward. 'Stop, captain!' he barked. 'Traitors must not wear the Garter.' The duke ripped off the silver-gilt St George chain, with its enamelled white and red Tudor roses, from around the minister's neck, while angrily accusing him of many 'villainies'. Sir William Fitzwilliam, earl of Southampton, ripped the jewelled Garter from around his former friend's leg. Cromwell was pulled about like a rag doll, as the symbols of power and authority were torn from him. As the councillors stepped back, panting from their exertions, he was bundled out, still yelling protests, and taken to the river stairs and the waiting wherry.[9]

Within the hour, Charles de Marillac, the French ambassador to London, had learnt of Cromwell's downfall and the king sent 'a gentleman of the court' to the envoy to explain what had happened. Henry had 'wished by all means to lead back religion to the way of truth' but Cromwell, who supported the German Lutheran Protestants, had 'always favoured the doctors who preached such erroneous opinions'. The minister planned to suppress the old religious beliefs and 'the affair would soon be brought to such a pass' that Henry 'with all his power could not prevent it'. Cromwell's faction would become so strong 'that he would make the king descend to the new doctrines, even if he had to take arms against him'. Marillac was unconvinced that this was the entire truth and in his dispatch to Paris, posed the question: 'How great was Cromwell's crime that he had so long been able to conceal it?'[10]

Henry wasted no time in appropriating his fallen minister's wealth. Two hours after the arrest, Sir Thomas Cheney, Treasurer of the Royal Household, was sent, with an escort of fifty archers, to Cromwell's palatial home at Austin Friars in the north-west quarter of the City of London.[11] A large rowdy crowd outside cheered as treasure to the value of £7,000 (more than £4 million in today's money) – coin, gold and silver plate, crosses, chalices and other loot from monastic churches – was carted away to the secret royal jewel house, pursued by a jeering rabble.[12] Low-value items were given to his now unemployed servants, who were ordered to stop wearing his livery badge.[13]

The king must have inspected this booty, as eleven of Cromwell's possessions appear in an inventory of royal goods compiled after Henry's death in 1547. Three – a pair of large glass gilded flagons; a pair of chased silver-gilt pots weighing 206oz (5.8kg) and a needlework cushion with the initials 'T.C.' – must have been recently acquired by a preening Cromwell, as they bore his arms as earl of Essex, the title bestowed upon him in April 1540.[14] Seldom has egotism taken such a swift and dramatic tumble.

None of Cromwell's friends lifted a finger to help or defend him, with the exception of Thomas Cranmer, archbishop of Canterbury. He wrote bravely to Henry saying that the minister had been a 'servant... in wisdom, diligence, faithfulness and experience, as no prince in this realm ever had'. Cranmer added: 'Now, if he be a traitor, I am sorry that I ever trusted him and am very glad that his treason is discovered in time... [but] to whom shall your grace trust hereafter, if you might not trust him?'[15]

That night, the citizens of London lit huge bonfires in the streets to celebrate Cromwell's fall. From his window in the Tower, he must have seen the red glow of the fires flickering on the church towers and steeples above the dark streets and heard the jubilant shouts of the mob exalting his fate. Edward Hall, the partisan chronicler, recorded that among those rejoicing were the monks turned out of their monasteries who 'banqueted and triumphed together that night' – although some, fearing his escape, 'could not be merry'. The clergy had detested him, as he could 'not abide the snuffling pride of some prelates... [but] others, who knew nothing but truth by him, both lamented him and heartily prayed for him'.[16]

Letters were conveniently discovered in Austin Friars that allegedly had been sent by German Lutherans to Cromwell. Their content triggered one of Henry's notorious tantrums. 'The king was so exasperated against [Cromwell] that he could no longer hear him spoken of, but rather desired to abolish all memory of him as the greatest wretch ever born in England,' reported Marillac. Henry 'proclaimed that none should call him by any other title but only Thomas Cromwell, shearman' – a deliberately wounding reference to his humble origins.[17]

Southampton replaced him as Lord Privy Seal and Sir John Russell became Lord High Admiral. Lord Chancellor Thomas Audley took charge of judicial affairs, even though he did not understand the legal languages of French or Latin. Audley also bore the unenviable reputation of 'being a good seller of justice whenever he can find a buyer'. The bishop of Winchester, Stephen Gardiner, an arch-enemy of Cromwell, was recalled to the Privy Council.

Henry's brother monarchs in Europe were elated at the downfall of a minister who had frustrated their diplomatic designs. Charles V of Spain sank to his knees, offering up prayers of gratitude to the Almighty. Francis I of France shouted gleefully at the arrest, and instructed his ambassador in London: 'Tell [Henry] from me that he has occasion to thank God for having let him know the faults and malversations [corruption] of such an unhappy person as Cromwell, who alone has been the cause of all the suspicions against not only his friends, but his best servants ... Getting rid of this wicked and unhappy person will tranquilise his kingdom, to the common welfare of church, nobles and people.'[18]

Cromwell had known full well that he would survive and prosper if he always gave his monarch everything he wanted, when he wanted it. For once, he had failed in that mission and had become scapegoat for the king's disastrous marriage to his fourth wife, Anne of Cleves. Furthermore, he had trespassed into areas that impinged heavily on royal pride and vanity and committed the unpardonable sin of making the sovereign look ridiculous. He would therefore lose his head.

The minister had good cause to complain that fate had dealt him an unlucky hand of cards. After all, everything had looked so promising.

Henry had willingly acquiesced in the quest for a new bride after the death of his beloved third queen, Jane Seymour, in October 1537. He may now have 'God's Imp', his longed-for son Edward by Jane, but in the uncertainties of the Tudor world with its political dangers and sudden epidemics, a 'spare heir' – a duke of York – was needed to safeguard his dynasty. After much toing and froing around Europe for a suitable bedfellow, Anne of Cleves emerged as the front-runner in the royal marriage stakes.

She was the twenty-four-year-old sister of Duke William who ruled a group of duchies on the Lower Rhine, today part of Holland and Germany. Although the ducal family were not Lutheran, they shunned papal authority.[19] As Cromwell must have pointed out, such a union had considerable diplomatic advantages in the dangerous cockpit of European politics.

Hans Holbein the younger, the king's painter, was packed off to Düren[20] in 1539 to paint a likeness of the princess to help Henry judge her fitness as his bride. Holbein's painting, now in the Musée du Louvre, Paris, shows a demure and shy young lady, her hands clasped at the waist, with a high forehead and heavily lidded eyes cast modestly downwards. Despite her rather bulbous nose, the king was delighted by this portrayal and by early October, the marriage treaty was concluded.

Looks are not everything. Unfortunately, Anne was uninterested in Henry's favourite pursuits – gambling and hunting – and spoke only a guttural Low German that the English found nasal and unappealing to the ear.

She eventually departed Calais on the noon tide on 27 December 1539. Despite the icy weather, her ladies worried that she would become unfashionably sunburnt during the hazardous five-hour voyage to England.

Travelling at a sedate pace, Anne arrived at Rochester, in Kent, four days later to rest before the journey to London to meet her bridegroom. Henry, both impetuous and careless of protocol, donned a disguise of a multicoloured hooded cloak and rode helter-skelter with five cronies from court for an early glimpse of his latest wife-to-be. His intention, he had told Cromwell, was to 'nourish love'.[21] This madcap journey epitomised romantic chivalry and as the party clattered, laughing, down the twenty-five miles (40km) of frozen roads from Greenwich Palace, the years seemed to roll back for the king. Henry may have imagined that he was once again a passionate, virile young lover, rather than a portly forty-eight-year-old, growing increasingly infirm with ulcerated legs.

His bride was languidly passing the time chatting with her ladies in the bishop's palace at Rochester, overlooking the River Medway. On the afternoon of New Year's Day, she sat at the window watching the sport of bear baiting in the courtyard below.[22] Amid the roar of the crowd and the barking of the hounds harrying the brown bear, she was startled by the sudden appearance in her apartment of a clean-shaven man with a thin face and arched eyebrows. By his clothes and deportment, he was a gentleman.

Her surprise visitor was Sir Anthony Browne, Henry's Master of the Horse, and one of the king's merry companions on that reckless ride from Greenwich, who had come to announce his sovereign's imminent arrival. Bowing low, he glanced up at her, sitting sedately amid her

German ladies, all prattling in their grating dialect at this stranger's sudden interruption.

What he saw cut him to the quick.

'I was never more dismayed in all my life [and] lamented in my heart ... to see the lady so far and unlike that was reported,' he observed later. In that instant, he realised 'the king's majesty should not content himself with her'. Recovering quickly, he politely explained his mission and received Anne's permission to usher in her bridegroom. He returned to the eager Henry waiting impatiently outside, but 'dared not' reveal his impressions of the new queen of England.[23]

Bursting with romantic bravado, Henry, with Sir Anthony and another courtier, entered the room. When the king 'tried to embrace her and kiss her', Browne 'saw and noted' in Henry's face 'such a discontentment and misliking of her person as he was very sorry of'.

Romance took flight and swiftly flew the room.

Henry was aghast, if not mortified. What had happened to the stunning beauty of Holbein's portrait? Anne looked older than her years. Her complexion was sallow and her face disfigured by pitted smallpox scars. She looked bored and worse still, frumpish and dowdy. For someone with an ego the size of Henry's, it was galling that Anne shyly 'regarded him little but always looked out of the window at the bear baiting'.[24] His face betrayed that he was 'marvellously astonished and abashed'.[25]

The king 'tarried not to speak with her twenty words' and grumpily stumped out, taking with him gifts of a partlet[26] of richly decorated sable skins and a new bonnet. He left behind a perplexed German princess, wondering whether this was some arcane English courtship ritual that nobody had warned her about. The next morning, a bashful Browne delivered Henry's presents, together 'with a cold and single message as might be' from her deflated and discontented bridegroom.[27]

As far as Henry was concerned, she had become the 'Flanders Mare', that mean epithet that poor Anne of Cleves has been saddled with down the centuries.[28] Back in London, he told Cromwell with some asperity that if he had known how his bride looked, she would never have come to England. 'What remedy now?' he demanded. His sheepish minister knew of none and was very sorry. 'I think she has a queenly manner,' he added feebly.[29]

Their wedding was scheduled twenty-four hours after Anne's

triumphant arrival at Greenwich, but this was postponed for two days while the king hunted desperately for a way to escape the marriage. Diplomatic necessity stood as a rock-like obstruction to any chance of him evading the union.

Charles V was in Paris, en route to the Netherlands to quash a rebellion in Ghent, and had been fêted by Francis I during eight days of lavish feasting in the French capital. Friendship between the Catholic powers of Spain and France was always a danger signal for Tudor England, with the risk that Henry could become friendless and isolated in Europe. An alliance with Cleves was better than no European ally at all, as Cromwell probably pointed out. The king ruefully admitted: 'If it were not that she is come ... into England and for fear of making a ruffle in the world and driving her brother into the emperor and the French king's hands ... I would never have her. But now it is too far gone, wherefore I am sorry.'[30]

Henry and Anne's restrained wedding went ahead at Greenwich on Tuesday, 6 January – the feast of Epiphany. The last echoes of the Christmas festivities were stilled and any merry japes were rare in the corridors of the palace that year. Just before the unwanted nuptials, the reluctant and resentful bridegroom – 'nothing pleasantly disposed' – complained to Cromwell: 'My lord, if it were not to satisfy the world and my realm I would not do that I must do this day for no earthly thing.'[31]

After the short ceremony, conducted by Archbishop Cranmer, there was a Mass and banquets, elaborate masques and 'diverse sports till the time came that it pleased the king [and the queen] to take rest'.[32] The traditional public bedding ceremony of royal weddings was scrapped and eventually the couple scrambled up onto a specially made great bed, Henry swathed in a voluminous linen nightshirt and wearing a jaunty nightcap. The bed's gilded oak headboard, bearing the initials 'H' and 'A' was decorated with carvings of a man with bulging codpiece and a woman with meek, downcast eyes holding the phallic symbols of a sword and a serpent.

Beneath these graphic embodiments of carnal pleasure and fecundity, Anne had to suffer the fumbling, groping and grunting attentions of her obese and probably flatulent bridegroom. It was a calamitous wedding night.

The next morning Cromwell pruriently asked the king: 'How liked you the queen?' He must have flinched at the vehemence of his master's rejoinder: 'Nay, my lord, much worse, for by her breasts and belly, she should be no maid; which when I felt them, struck me so close to the heart that I had neither will nor courage to prove the rest'. Henry felt constrained to leave her 'as good a maid as he found her'.[33]

The royal physician Dr John Chambre was consulted about this 'indisposition' and the king was comforted by his advice not to 'enforce himself' because of the danger of 'inconvenient debility' to the royal genitalia.[34] After four nights of dutiful effort, Henry had not consummated the marriage and did not intend to. When he did sleep with his queen, on alternate nights, the main activity was a quiet hand or two of cards.

Henry discussed the most intimate problems of the marriage bed with the senior Gentlemen of his Privy Chamber. It may be, as some have speculated, that the king was aroused by the sensual perfume of a woman's body. Unfortunately, Anne suffered from a persistently sour body odour, perhaps caused by the food she ate, her sweating from wearing heavy clothes or poor personal hygiene.

In direct man-to-man talk, the king told his most intimate servant, Sir Thomas Heneage, Groom of the Stool, that he could have no appetite for Anne 'as a man should do with his wife, for such displeasant airs as he felt with her'. Anthony Denny, another Privy Chamber confidant, heard that Anne's body, with her 'slack breasts', was of 'such indisposition ... that he could never ... be provoked and stirred to know her carnally'. Frustrated, both sexually and diplomatically, Henry lamented to Denny that the marriage of princes was a 'far worse' business than those of poor men. 'Princes take [what] is brought them by others' but the poor could have wives 'of their own choice and liberty'.[35]

On 2 February, the lavish plans for Anne's coronation at Westminster Abbey were abandoned. As word spread of royal displeasure with the latest queen, those venal nobility and gentry who attended her court in hopes of generous patronage drifted away in search of fortune elsewhere.

Anne meanwhile spent her days playing at cards and dice with her ladies and embroidering cushion covers; she was an excellent needlewoman. Some of her countrymen remained in her household. Master Schulenburg, her cook, and Englebert, her footman, were reminders of what she had left behind in Cleves. Anne also had a pet parrot to help while away her hours of boredom.

The queen's accounts show her to be kind and thoughtful, with rewards given to those who had done some small service, such as the servant who brought her a greyhound or the twenty pence given to 'a poor man' who delivered 'certain household stuff'. Tumblers who performed for her on 20 January received five pence and the same amount was paid to an 'old man' working in the garden at Greenwich. Each page of payments is signed 'Anne the Quenen' with a bold, Teutonic flourish.[36]

Understandably, the tedium tried her patience. During Lent, Henry was angered by a conversation with her about Mary, his daughter by his first wife Katherine of Aragon. He told Cromwell that Anne began 'to wax stubborn and wilful' and he 'lamented his fate that he should never have any more children if he so continued'. He declared before God that the queen was not his lawful wife.[37]

Anne of Cleves lived in an untroubled world of naive innocence. Lady Jane Rochford, one of her ladies, boldly raised the subject of the lewd gossip circulating at court: 'I think your grace is still a maid.' Startled, the queen replied: 'How can I be a maid and sleep every night with the king? When he comes to bed, he kisses me and takes me by the hand and bids me "Goodnight sweetheart" and in the morning, kisses me and bids me "Farewell darling". Is not this enough?' He may have become a tyrant but at least Henry was polite in bed. Eleanor Manners, countess of Rutland, commented archly: 'Madam, there must be more than this, or it will be long before we have a duke of York, which all this realm desires.' But the queen had not yet grasped the essentials of procreation. 'Is not this enough? I am contented with this, for I know no more.'[38]

The king must have been aware of the sniggering about his marriage in the palace corridors. He told his favourite physician Dr William Butts that he had experienced *duas pollutiones nocturnas in somno*, 'two movements during sleep' (colloquially, 'wet dreams') and he firmly believed himself 'able to do the act with others, but not with her'.[39] Such evidence could be used to quash any ribald chatter about the king's capability to sire another son.

Cromwell was the obvious victim to suffer for this embarrassment. In early April, Marillac reported that the minister was 'tottering' in his hold on power[40] so it was a surprise that on Sunday, 18 April 1540, Cromwell was created earl of Essex. He was also appointed Lord Great Chamberlain of England, while remaining Lord Privy Seal.[41] His duties as secretary to Henry were taken over jointly by his long-standing protégés, Thomas Wriothesley and Ralph Sadler, who were both knighted.

Cromwell's ennoblement was facilitated by the death of sixty-eight-year-old Henry Bourchier, second earl of Essex, who broke his neck when thrown by a frisky young horse on 12 March, with no sons to inherit his title. The office of Lord Great Chamberlain had been vacant since the death of John de Vere, fifteenth earl of Oxford, a week after Bourchier's reckless demise.

To many at court who loathed Cromwell – some paid exorbitant interest on his loans to them – this royal generosity suggested that the minister still enjoyed Henry's protection and confidence. For others, who detested the upstart minister for his lowly birth and his unshakeable grip on the levers of power, his ennoblement and new office (hitherto enjoyed by the oldest families in the realm), added fresh fuel to the burning fires of their hatred.

Chief among his enemies were Norfolk and his son, Henry Howard, earl of Surrey. Another dangerous adversary was Stephen Gardiner, bishop of Winchester, who with the duke, led the religious conservative faction at court. Gardiner's zeal in hunting down heretics made him the chief target of evangelical vitriol. His successor in the Winchester diocese, the staunch Protestant John Ponet, described the bishop as having frowning brows, deep-set eyes, a 'nose hooked like a buzzard' and 'great paws [like the devil]'.[42] More than 120 years later, Thomas Fuller claimed 'his malice was like what is commonly said of white [gun]powder which surely discharged the bullet, yet made no report, being secret in all his acts of cruelty'.[43] His quick anger was feared both for its venom and bite. Recently, more balanced views of his personality have emerged,[44] suggesting that Tudor reformers may have found it wiser (and safer) to vilify the bishop rather than reviling the king over his brutal persecution of religious agitators.[45]

Gardiner and Norfolk were instrumental in passing the draconian Statute of Six Articles or, in Protestant eyes, 'the whip with six strings', in June 1539,[46] a measure that stopped religious reform dead in its tracks and reflected Henry's personal obsession with spiritual orthodoxy. The first article, targeted at heretic 'sacramentaries', decreed that the Body of Christ was present within the consecrated bread and wine during Mass. Denying this would bring death by burning at the stake, even after recantation. The other measures were affirmation of the vows of celibacy for nuns and monks; a new prohibition against priests marrying; the continuation of private Masses and a restatement of the importance of the sacrament of confession and the administration of Holy Communion. Taken together, they made heresy a secular offence for the first time. Penalties for transgression, like the crime of treason, were death by hanging, drawing and quartering and forfeiture of estates and goods.

There were probably 300 married priests in England.[47] Cranmer had illegally married in Nuremberg in 1532 (a year before being consecrated archbishop of Canterbury) and he prudently sent his wife and daughter back to her old home. He enjoyed a close personal relationship with the king and Cromwell had once ruefully told the archbishop: 'You were born in a happy hour ... for do or say what you will, [Henry] will always take it well ... He will never give credit against you, whatsoever is laid to your charge.'[48]

As far as the king was concerned, not only did this new legislation rein back accepted religion to a doctrine he was more comfortable with, but it also yielded diplomatic and political benefits. The Six Articles presented a more traditionalist face to his Church settlement, which would appease the Catholic powers that had become so threatening in 1539. Legal powers enforcing the old religious tenets also reduced the risk of new insurrections by supporters of the old faith in England.

Cranmer had been allowed to dispute the terms of the Six Articles during the torrid three-day parliamentary debate on the legislation, attended throughout by Henry who had personally corrected the draft Bill.[49] He was comforted by the king's furious reaction to criticism of him bandied about by Sir John Gostwick, knight of the shire for Bedfordshire. Henry branded him a 'varlet' and warned that if he did not apologise to Cranmer, 'I will make him ... a poor Gostwick and otherwise punish him to be the example of others.'[50]

The new law spawned widespread arrests of religious reformers, but was not a licence for wholesale slaughter, probably because Cromwell sent potential victims overseas, out of harm's way. Five hundred were freed in a general pardon 'of all heresies, felonies committed before 1 July 1540'.

However, three evangelical priests – William Jerome, vicar of St Dunstan's, Stepney, Robert Barnes and Thomas Garret – were arrested in 1540. Garret had escaped execution for heresy seven years before in Oxford.[51] Barnes had returned from exile in Antwerp and preached against Gardiner, punningly referring to him as a 'gardener setting ill plants in a garden'. In religion, Gardiner's views were as unyielding as much as his sense of humour was lacking. When Barnes was forced to seek Gardiner's pardon, the haughty bishop, with basilisk glare, 'being twice desired by him to give some sign that he forgave him, did lift up his finger'.

The trio were hauled up before Henry and Garret acknowledged that the king 'had so disputed with him that he was convinced of his rashness and promised to abstain from such indiscretions'. Barnes also acquiesced, but Henry limped to the altar in his chapel, painfully genuflected, and told him: 'Submit not to me. I am a mortal man, but yonder is the Maker of us all, the author of truth.'[52] The priests had to demonstrate their return to orthodox doctrine in Easter sermons.[53] Gardiner remained remorseless in his pursuit of them, and despite his denials, it seems likely that he instigated their subsequent imprisonment in the Tower. Once behind bars and aware of their impending fate, they withdrew their recantations.

Meanwhile, the scandal of the king's loveless marriage could not continue unresolved. In early June, Thomas Wriothesley found Cromwell alone in the first-floor gallery at Austin Friars, morosely staring out of the window. The minister told him: 'One thing troubles me... The king likes not the queen, nor did he ever like her from the beginning. I think she is as good a maid for him, as she was when she came to England'. Wriothesley urged him: 'For God's sake, devise how his grace may be relieved by one way or another... for if he remains in this grief and trouble we shall one day smart for it.' Cromwell, verging on desperation, could only answer: 'Yes. How?'[54]

The Lord Privy Seal decided that his best chance of recovering Henry's favour was by filling his Exchequer. He introduced legislation to dissolve the last religious Order in England, the Knights of St John of Jerusalem, and appropriating their substantial lands, property and wealth for the king's use. When Cromwell ran into parliamentary resistance, he accused the Order of denying the royal supremacy over the Church. The Act was passed at the end of May[55] and sizeable quantities of gold and silver plate and £588 6s 8d in cash (£360,000 in 2019 money) were removed from their church at St John's, Clerkenwell. Sir William Weston, last Grand Prior, died on the day the Act of Dissolution took effect.

Cromwell was not yet done. On Friday, 3 May, he introduced a new taxation Bill into the Lords, the Subsidy of Fifteenths and Tenths. After he warned that Henry would be vexed by Parliament's disloyalty if the measure was rejected, it was passed in just five days, granting the king four-fifteenths and tenths of personal income, payable over four years, and secondly, one shilling (5p) in the pound levied on property values, payable annually for two years.

These measures failed to safeguard Cromwell. The minister, like a cornered animal fighting for its life, furiously lashed out, arresting Gardiner's allies, Richard Sampson, bishop of Chichester and dean of the Chapel Royal, for denying Henry's supremacy, and Dr Nicholas Wilson, one of the king's chaplains, for helping 'certain traitors which denied the supremacy'.[56] Arthur Plantagenet, viscount Lisle, Lord Deputy of Calais, who had been plotting against Cromwell for months,[57] completed this round-up of religious conservatives. Lisle was the illegitimate son of King Edward IV and because of the latent threat of the Yorkist 'White Rose' faction to the Tudor crown, was always vulnerable.

Marillac believed the Lord Privy Seal's credit with the king was 'so shaken' that 'he was very near coming to grief… Things are brought to such a pass that either Cromwell's party or that of the bishop of Winchester must succumb'.[58]

The beleaguered minister had gravely underestimated his enemies' muscle.

An audacious plan by Norfolk and Gardiner would finally sweep him from power, in the pleasing shape of the duke's teenage niece, Katherine Howard. That March, the bishop had staged a magnificent banquet at his palace in Southwark and Henry had graciously accepted an invitation to attend. As the king watched the dancers, he noticed a giggling girl, stylishly dressed in the French fashion, among the strutting young bucks of the court. Henry was immediately attracted by her vivacity and beauty.

The meeting was not accidental. Norfolk and Gardiner, unashamedly acting as pimps, were using the girl as bait to attract Henry. As the king grew more infatuated with her nubile charms, so his demands to escape from his loveless marriage with the malodorous Anne of Cleves grew more vociferous. Their plan's strength lay in its simplicity and virtual certainty of success. If Cromwell won a divorce and the king married Katherine, both duke and bishop could exert influence on Henry through his new bedfellow, as the Howard family had done with another niece, Anne Boleyn, Henry's unfortunate second wife. On the other hand, if the minister failed to free the king from his unwanted marriage, he would fall and face execution.

Some time on Thursday, 8 June, the king gave Lord Chancellor Audley secret instructions to draw up a parliamentary Bill pronouncing that Cromwell had undermined his sovereign lord's objective of a religious settlement. His arrest came two days later.

Many more venomous allegations about Cromwell's crimes were whispered by his enemies. Foreign sources suggested he intended to make himself king and marry Henry's daughter Mary.[59]

Audley's Bill never saw the light of day. The attainder that condemned Cromwell for treason and heresy was short on facts but long on invective. The preamble bore Norfolk's unmistakable snobbish stamp, as it described the minister as being raised from a 'very base and low degree' to the status of an earl, but who had become the most detestable traitor, as proved by 'many personages of great honour, worship and discretion'. Furthermore, Cromwell had 'held the nobles of the realm in great disdain'. Other charges – that he had freed those guilty of treason, sold export licences, was involved in bribery and extortion, granted passports and drawn up commissions without Henry's permission – were mere make-weights.

The meat of the attainder had Gardiner's fingerprints all over it. Cromwell was a 'detestable heretic' who had licensed heretics to preach and freed them from prison. Worse still, he had claimed in March 1539 that the imprisoned evangelical preacher Robert Barnes taught true religion and if Henry rejected this truth, 'I would fight in the field... with my sword in my hand against him and all others'. Cromwell had brandished his dagger, saying, 'This [will] thrust me to the heart if I would not die in that struggle against them all. I trust that if I live one year or two, it shall not lie in the king's power to resist'.[60]

The attainder was passed, without dissent, on 29 June.

Five days earlier, Anne of Cleves had been sent to Richmond Palace, Surrey, for 'health, open air and pleasure', as an epidemic of the plague afflicted the capital. In reality, the king wanted her out of London so he could end their marriage without histrionics or petulance on her part.

The king, as Supreme Head of the Church, saw no problem in his bishops agreeing an annulment. The decision to avoid sex with Anne was more cynical than mere physical repulsion. Henry had been forced into a marriage which was an abomination and so he deliberately did not consummate it until due process could establish the truth of the matter. This was the crux of his case.[61]

Cromwell's testimony would be key. Probably, some kind of deal was struck to grant indemnity to his family in return for his co-operation. In a letter to the king, the prisoner 'on his knees' begged Henry to 'be a good and gracious lord to my poor son [Gregory], the good and virtuous woman [who is] his wife and their poor children and also to my servants'.[62]

He underwent forceful questioning in the Tower on at least two occasions by Norfolk and his two erstwhile friends Audley and Southampton. They were all skilled interrogators; Southampton had tricked George Boleyn into confessing incestuous adultery with his sister the queen in 1536 and Audley, with Cromwell, had questioned Sir Thomas More two years before that. Norfolk, to the prisoner's surprise, was kindness personified, hearing him out 'without any interruption, with such gentleness I could not desire more'.[63] That was all part of the 'softening-up' process in interrogation techniques.

Cromwell's alleged heresy was that of a sacramentary who denied the presence of Christ in the holy wafer and wine of the Mass. His undated letter to Henry, written from the Tower, refuted the attainder's heresy charges. He felt grief 'that I should be noted a traitor when I always had your laws in my breast and that I should be a sacramentary. God knows the truth; that I am of the one and the other guiltless.'[64]

One of his last letters is stripped bare of the polite veneer of official correspondence. Abject fear, despair and a wretched hopelessness overwhelmed Cromwell. He ended: 'Frail flesh incites me continually to call to your grace for mercy and grace for my offences and thus Christ save, preserve and keep you ... Written at the Tower this Wednesday, the last of June with the heavy heart and trembling hand of your highness' most heavy and miserable prisoner and poor slave.' There is a long gap, almost half a blank page, then a pathetic *cri de cœur* scrawled on the bottom edge: 'Most gracious prince, I cry for mercy, mercy, mercy!'[65]

Henry commanded his new secretary Sir Ralph Sadler to read this letter three times and was reported to have been visibly moved, even blubbing like a child. But even royal crocodile tears did not save Cromwell.

His evidence to the Clerical Convocation investigating the marriage pointed out that Cromwell would confirm what Henry declared to him after that wild ride to Rochester. 'As he is condemned to die, he will not damn [his] soul but declare what the king said, not only at the time but continually after [till] the day of marriage and many times after, whereby his lack of consent will appear and also the lack of the will and power to consummate.' Henry ended: 'I never consented to marry for love to the woman, nor yet, if she brought maidenhead with her, took any away from her by true carnal copulation.'[66]

The Convocation of two archbishops, sixteen bishops and 139 learned academics, meeting in the Westminster Abbey chapter house, ended Henry's fourth marriage on 9 July after two days of deliberation.[67] Their collective wisdom, that the marriage was anulled by Henry's unwillingness to marry and its subsequent non-consummation, was distilled down to a twelve-page volume bound in red velvet.[68] Their decision was ratified by Parliament four days later.[69]

A group of courtiers, led by Charles Brandon, duke of Suffolk, informed Anne that not only was her marriage ended but she was no longer Queen of England. They gave her a letter from Henry, together with a 'token of money' and left her with an interpreter to digest its contents. It listed the properties and manors that would be given her ('Where's Bletchingley?' she asked) and other details of the king's settlement. There were reports that she fainted at the news, but if she did swoon, it probably was with relief that she would not face the same fate as Anne Boleyn.

Behind that stolid exterior, Anne of Cleves was no fool. She had been offered an elegant way to escape a nightmare marriage, with her dignity (and virginity) intact. She would be the premier lady in all England, keep her fifteen-strong household of German servants and receive an annual payment of £500, or more than £300,000 at 2019 prices. This was the generous reward for her acquiescence and silence.[70]

She wrote to Henry, now her 'most benign and good brother': 'Though this case [is] most hard and sorrowful unto me for the great love I bear your most noble person, yet, having more regard to God than to any worldly affection... I hereby accept and approve that the pretended matrimony between us is void and of no effect... My lords and others of your majesty's council, now being with me, have put me in comfort and that your highness will take me for your sister, for which I most humbly thank you.'[71]

Furthermore, she told her brother, Duke William, she had 'suffered no wrong or injury' and that her body was 'preserved in an integrity which I brought into this realm'. The king 'whom I cannot now justly have as my husband, has adopted me as his sister and, as a most kind and loving brother, uses me with as much or more humanity and liberality as you...'. She begged him not to make trouble over the settlement and announced she would stay in England.[72] The letter's contents must have been approved in advance by Henry.

After the six bitter and dangerous years that the king had endured in ridding himself of Katherine of Aragon, it had taken him six days to oust Anne of Cleves from another loveless marriage. Only one legacy of this tedious episode remained to be resolved.

On 28 July, Cromwell emerged from the Tower of London under heavy guard and walked the short distance up the slope to Tower Hill. A thousand halberdiers were drawn up along the route and around the narrow scaffold, because of fears of a rescue attempt by his former retainers in the huge waiting crowd.

On the way, the condemned man met the deranged Hungerford, gibbering and muttering, as he waited, restrained by his guards, to follow Cromwell to his death. He tried to comfort the frenzied baron. 'There is no cause for you to fear. If you repent and are heartily sorry for what you have done, there is mercy enough [from] the Lord who, for Christ's sake, will forgive you. Therefore, be not dismayed and though the breakfast which we are going [to] be sharp, yet trusting in the mercy of the Lord, we shall have a joyful supper.'[73]

After mounting the steps to the wooden scaffold, Cromwell turned to the crowd. 'Good people, I have come here to die and not to purge myself as some may think that I will. For if I should do so, I [would] be a wretch and a sinner and a [miserable man]. I am by the law condemned to death and thank my Lord God that has appointed me this death for my offence... I have offended my prince for which I ask him [for] hearty mercy.'

He was anxious to dispel the popular belief that he was a Lutheran. 'I pray you that be here to bear record [that] I die in the Catholic faith, not doubting any article of my faith – no, nor doubting any sacrament of the church. Many have slandered me and reported that I have been a [supporter] of [those who] have maintained evil opinions, which is untrue. But I confess that as God, by his Holy Spirit, instructs us in the truth, so the devil is ready to seduce us, and I have been seduced.'

Cromwell spied some courtiers in the crowd and offered them some advice: 'Gentlemen, take warning from me, who was from a poor man made by the king into a great gentleman and I, not content with that, not with having the kingdom at my orders, presumed to a still higher state. My pride has brought its punishment.'[74]

His words may have been interrupted by poor mad Hungerford who repeatedly and piteously called out for the executioner to get on with his bloody business.

Cromwell knelt before the low block and told the headsman: 'Pray if possible, cut off the head with one blow so that I may not suffer much'. His hope went unfulfilled. The executioner was called Gurrea, 'a ragged and butcherly miser', who some claimed was chosen because of his incompetence. The former minister 'patiently suffered the strokes of the axe by the hands of him who ill-favouredly performed his office'.[75] Was this Norfolk's final revenge?

Watching was the duke's son, the earl of Surrey. He sneered: 'Now is that false churl dead, so ambitious of other's [noble] blood. These new erected men would by their wills leave no noble man a life.'[76]

Hungerford was quickly beheaded and the two corpses were carried back to the Tower where they were buried in the Chapel of St Peter ad Vincula. The heads were parboiled and set up on pikestaffs above London Bridge.

That same day, Henry married Katherine Howard in a private ceremony at his new palace at Otelands, near Weybridge in Surrey.[77]

On 30 July, the priests Barnes, Jerome and Garret were burnt at Smithfield for heresy. Hall, the chronicler, could not understand why they were executed 'so cruelly although I have searched to know the truth. If I may say the truth, most men said it was for preaching against the doctrine of... Gardiner who chiefly procured their death'.[78]

Three others were executed at St Bartholomew's Gate in Smithfield for treason.[79] Richard Featherstone, Thomas Abel – who had been kept in a filthy cell and was 'almost eaten up by vermin' – and Edward Powell were hanged, drawn and quartered for denying the king's supremacy and maintaining that his marriage to his first queen was still valid.[80]

There is little doubt that the three reformers were sacrificed to continue the pretence of Cromwell's apostasy. These and the other deaths also demonstrated that Henry was determined to preserve the integrity of his Church, while treading a narrow, precarious path between Catholic beliefs and liturgy and evangelical reforms.

The German Lutheran theologian Philip Melanchthon was horrified by Cromwell's death and demanded: 'Let us cease to sing the praises of the English Nero.' He added that this 'English tyrant is contemplating other outrages'.[81]

4

A King Besotted

On 28 July 1540, fifteen days after the annulment of Henry's union with the ill-starred Anne of Cleves was ratified, the king married his fifth wife, nineteen-year-old Katherine Howard[1] in the chapel of the new palace at Otelands, Surrey. Henry had hobbled along a familiar stony path to secure his new spouse. She was yet another of Norfolk's nieces: a first cousin both to the king's one-time mistress Mary Boleyn and her sister, Anne, his second wife.

Katherine was the daughter of the feckless Lord Edmund Howard and his first wife Joyce (née Culpeper), who had died when she was about seven. Her father was appointed Comptroller of Calais in 1531 and the child was foisted on his irascible stepmother, Agnes, dowager duchess of Norfolk, to be brought up as her ward at Chesworth House, near Horsham in Sussex, and after October 1536, at Norfolk House in Lambeth, across the river from Westminster.[2]

Edmund was the black sheep of the powerful Howard clan. His career began brightly enough as captain of the English right wing in the stunning victory against the Scots at Flodden in September 1513. Then he became an inveterate gambler who squandered his wife's estates and more besides. The ne'er-do-well was forced to borrow considerable sums at grossly excessive interest rates and to don outlandish disguises to outwit those clamouring for repayment, before he fled England's shores.[3]

As his creditors dogged him, so did ill-health, particularly the dreadful pain wreaked by kidney stones. In 1535, he wrote to Honor Lisle, wife of the Lord Deputy at Calais, to thank her for the diuretic she supplied him. The potion 'had done me much good', he announced, as he had excruciatingly passed 'some gravel'. His ordeal was far from over. Tudor medicine sometimes created unfortunate consequences

and this was especially true of Honor Lisle's potion. 'It made me piss
my bed this night, for which my wife has sore beaten me, saying it is
children's parts to piss their bed. You have made me such a pisser that
I dare not this day go abroad,' he added wretchedly.[4] He was unaware,
in his humiliating incontinence, that the medicine's main ingredient
was probably the leaves of the dandelion, a common yellow-flowered
weed, vulgarly known as 'piss-a-bed'.

Howard was dismissed as Comptroller in February 1539[5] having
achieved little of consequence and died, still burdened by debt, in
March that year at the ripe old age of sixty-one, leaving a third wife,
Margaret, three surviving sons and three daughters from his first marriage, as well as a host of frustrated creditors.

His eldest brother Norfolk – always keen to advance his family's
interest – secured Katherine's appointment as one of the twelve maids-
in-waiting to the new queen, late in 1539. Henry first saw her when
he travelled to Greenwich to await Anne of Cleves's state arrival in
London, perhaps on 19 December, when he took an immediate liking
to her.[6]

She was 'short of stature', vivacious and flirty, and following the
custom for unmarried girls, wore her luxuriant auburn hair hanging
down her back. Her eyes, beneath prominent arched brows, were hazel
and her face had high cheek-bones. Her only physical drawbacks to
modern eyes, perhaps, were the slightly hooked Howard nose and
her plumpness, although the Tudors would have thought her buxom
and comely. Politics and religious controversy were closed books to
her. Proud Norfolk praised his niece's unsullied virtue – her 'pure and
honest condition' – during a contrived conversation with the king.

The duke and his ally Gardiner had arranged social events when the
king could meet the teenage girl, hoping that love between them would
blossom and with it, their influence over Henry. Sumptuous feasts were
held at Gardiner's sprawling fourteenth-century palace in Southwark
in March 1540, and 'entertainments' at Lambeth were arranged by the
dowager duchess before Katherine left her household in April.[7] Henry
was seen 'crossing the Thames to visit, often in the daytime and sometimes at night'.[8] She was schooled in her dealings with the king, with
instruction on how to behave in the royal presence, what to wear and
what to say 'to entertain the king's highness'. New clothes were procured
so she would appear her brightest and best.[9]

Henry fell headfirst into the carefully baited honey trap. The king 'cast a fancy' to Katherine and she became a 'blushing rose without a thorn' and the 'very jewel of womanhood' in his rheumy old eyes.[10] This Howard girl, he convinced himself, would be his last true love and the passion was all the sweeter for arriving so late in life. During those spring evenings, as his barge was rowed across to Lambeth, the heady essence of romance must have honeyed the air for the deluded, besotted king. Inside his burgeoning body beat the heart of a young, potent man. His mammoth vanity whispered to him that he still could attract a girl of such beauty and charm, despite her being surrounded by admiring young courtiers much nearer her own age.

Ralph Morice, Cranmer's secretary, believed his sovereign's 'affection was so marvellously set upon the gentlewoman as it was never known ... to any woman' before.[11] And when Henry wanted something, Henry seized it, brooking no argument. As Imperial ambassador Eustace Chapuys shrewdly observed later: 'If this king's nature and inclination be taken into account, if we consider that whenever he takes a fancy to a person or decides for an undertaking, he goes the whole length, there being no limit or restriction whatever to his wishes.'[12]

True love is nurtured by thoughtful gifts to an intended spouse. On 24 April 1540, Katherine was granted the goods and chattels of two Sussex murderers, father and son,[13] and almost a month later, received a present of twenty-three sarsenet (or soft silk) quilts 'bought of Baptist Brown and William Latremoyal'.[14] These were hardly romantic love tokens, as they amounted to the humble possessions of a pair of bucolic footpads and what were probably cast-offs from the royal Department of the Wardrobe. Still, it was the thought that counted.

News of Henry's new passion reached the ears of his lonely and neglected wife Anne of Cleves, still busily embroidering her cushion covers. On 20 June, she complained to Carl Harst, the duke of Cleves' ambassador in London, about the king's fascination for one of her maids-of-honour. Harst informed the duke in Düren that the royal affair had been continuing for months.[15]

Anne's disquiet about her straying husband came too late. Four days later, she was exiled to Richmond Palace, as the Tudor legal machinery to annul her marriage shifted up through its gears. Henry had promised to follow her within forty-eight hours, but never kept his empty pledge.[16]

The French ambassador Marillac was slow off the mark in picking up gossip about the king's *amour* and when he did, his information was inaccurate and premature. On 21 July, he reported that it was 'commonly said that the king will marry a lady of great beauty, daughter of the duke of Norfolk's deceased brother. If permitted to write what I hear, I would say this marriage has already taken place but as this is kept secret, I dare not certify it as true'.[17] That same day in another dispatch to France, he asserted that 'the king has consummated marriage with this lady . . . and it is feared she is already *enceinte* [pregnant]'.[18] Ungallantly, he now considered Katherine 'more graceful than beautiful'.

Others knew more about what was going on. Joan Bulmer, who had been a lover to Francis Dereham, a former gentleman pensioner of the duke of Norfolk and once secretary to the dowager duchess, wrote to Katherine from York on 12 July. She was living in great misery and begged for a position at court – 'the nearer you, the better'. Joan plaintively sought a reply, 'for I trust the queen of Britain will not forget her secretary'.[19]

The Privy Council, ever the doyens of sycophancy, humbly begged their sovereign to 'frame his most noble heart to love' – even to remarry and to create, they coyly added, 'some more store of fruit and succession to the comfort of his realm'.[20] Henry could not deny their humble petition.

The king and his new queen consort made a grotesque couple. Henry was now aged forty-nine and being at least six foot one inch (1.85m) in height, he towered over his diminutive wife. Their mismatch was accentuated by his huge bulk and his fleshy, moon-like face. The pain from his ulcerated legs meant that he walked with the aid of a jewelled staff. It must have seemed a marriage between beauty and the beast. Katherine was more than thirty years younger than her husband and probably five years younger than Mary, her eldest stepdaughter.

The royal couple were sternly cautioned by the Privy Council to use the marital bed 'more for the desire of children than bodily lust' as their marriage was 'a high and blessed order, ordained of God in paradise'.[21]

On 8 August, Katherine made her first public appearance at a spectacular banquet at Hampton Court and was proclaimed queen.[22] A week later, prayers were ordered to be said in the parish churches for her, Henry and Prince Edward.[23]

One might have thought that Anne of Cleves would be jealous over

Katherine's usurpation of her place as queen, even though she remained the king's beloved 'sister'. Perhaps the thought that the trials of those long nights in the creaking marriage bed were now being exacted on another wife came as *schadenfreude*, a malicious enjoyment of another's misfortune. Anne was 'as joyous as ever and wears new dresses every day', reported Marillac, 'and takes all the recreation she can, in diversity of dress and pastime'.[24]

The old ogre was beside himself with joy over his tender young bride. Marillac considered he was 'so amorous of her that he cannot treat her well enough and caresses her more than he did the other [Anne of Cleves]. She and the court ladies dress in the French style and her device [motto] is "*Non autre volonte que la sienne*"' – 'No other wish but his own' – embroidered in gold thread around the sleeves of her gowns.[25]

This may have seemed a dutiful expression of wifely endearment, but in practice it was more a case of no other wish but *her* own. Some courtiers realised that Henry 'had no wife who made him spend so much money in dresses and jewels'. Every day, the queen desired 'some fresh caprice', which the love-struck king eagerly fulfilled.[26]

An inventory of Katherine's jewellery catalogues 127 items given by Henry, from their wedding to his New Year presents of January 1541. For example, there was a gold and white enamelled brooch with a 'very fair diamond' held by a tiny man with blue enamelled coat and the image of a king, holding a sceptre. There were seventeen girdles of gold to wear around her waist, as well as twenty-three pairs of beads for the neck 'with crosses, pillars and tassels attached'. Katherine gave away four as gifts to Princess Elizabeth, her cousin Lady Elizabeth Carew (for her marriage), her lady-in-waiting Lady Eleanor Rutland ('for a token') and the final one to Lady Margaret Douglas, the king's niece. Another piece was a gold pomander (containing perfume to ward off the stench of the Tudor great unwashed), fitted with a clock garnished with twelve rubies, with a gold chain decorated with sixteen of these stones. This was later given by Katherine to her stepdaughter Mary, but she retained its elaborate chain for herself. The inventory extends to twenty-four pages, a revealing testimony to royal largesse and abject infatuation.[27]

The king thought little about the expense of these exquisite baubles. His new love, after all, was priceless. Married life with Katherine suited

Henry and made him feel younger and carefree. The French ambassador noted: 'The king was never in better health'.[28]

Henry's regal sun shone warmly upon the House of Howard, with honours and offices heaped into their welcoming arms. Norfolk 'nowadays has the chief management of affairs' in the realm, reported Marillac. Surrey, the duke's son, was installed as a Knight of the Garter, appointed cup-bearer to the king, and in September succeeded Cromwell as Steward of the University of Cambridge. On 8 December, he was granted manors in Suffolk and Norfolk, most of which he subsequently sold. His sister Mary, duchess of Richmond,[29] became a member of the queen's household and Katherine's brother Charles was made a Gentleman of Henry's Privy Chamber.

The summer of 1540 was the hottest in living memory. The herald Charles Wriothesley recorded that 'no rain fell between June until eight days after Michaelmas [29 September] so that in [many] parts . . . the people [drove] their cattle six or seven miles (9.7–11km) to water them and . . . [many] cattle died. There [were] strange sicknesses among the people [such] as laskes [dysentery] and hot agues [fevers] and also [the] pestilence where many people died'.[30] Henry ordered prayers to be said in every parish for divine assistance to end the drought, before hastily fleeing the plague in the capital for the green fields of rural England.

He decided to show off his new queen in a whirlwind royal progress through the Thames Valley and on to Northamptonshire and Bedfordshire that sweltering summer, hunting, feasting, dancing and singing all the way. The honeymoon was truly pastime with good company and a period of rare contentment for Henry. A new daily regime was imposed after the royal party reached his house at Woking, Surrey: 'To rise between five and six, hear Mass at seven and then ride [hunt] till dinner-time which is ten a.m. He says he feels much better thus in the country than when he resided all winter in his houses at the gates of London'.[31]

The Privy Council followed the king in his peripatetic progress, holding regular meetings, attended by between six and twelve councillors, at royal residences along the route. At one session, at Grafton Regis, Northamptonshire,[32] on 29 August, they heard a complaint from the dean of Windsor about a priest and others in the Berkshire town who had spoken 'unfitting words about the queen's grace'. As the plague was raging in Windsor, the Privy Council preferred to investigate from a safe distance. A week later, the king was content that the Windsor priest should 'reside in his benefice' but should first receive a 'lesson to temperate his tongue hereafter, under [the threat] of further punishment'. A spell behind bars for the loud-mouthed parson was ordered.[33]

In mid-September, Henry fell ill at Ampthill, Bedfordshire, as revealed in a letter from Cranmer. The archbishop avoided raising 'heinous rumours about the king in far countries', until he was 'recovered [from] his disease',[34] probably a bout of malaria. After convalescing, Henry was back at Hampton Court in early October.

There he discovered, to his fury, that his 'beautiful and esteemed' niece was having an affair with the queen's brother, Lord Charles Howard. Lady Margaret (daughter of his sister Margaret and her second husband, Archibald Douglas, sixth earl of Angus) had probably met Charles during her duties as a senior lady-in-waiting in Katherine's Privy Chamber.

This was the second time that Lady Margaret's romances had piqued the king, each time involving a Howard. Five years earlier, she had fallen for Thomas, a half-brother to Norfolk, and was secretly engaged, if not married, to the courtier. After the bastardisation of the Princesses Mary and Elizabeth by Acts of Parliament in 1534 and 1536, Margaret was in line for the crown. Henry was enraged, believing that Thomas Howard could eventually claim the throne by marrying a royal bride.

The king had then wanted to execute his niece. But at that stage, he was woefully short of legitimate heirs and her life was spared because the affair had not been consummated. The lovers were clapped in the Tower – Howard was sentenced to death for treason – but Margaret was released after suffering a recurring fever. She was sent to live a more chaste life at the Bridgettine nunnery at Syon, Middlesex,[35] under the supervision of the abbess, Agnes Jordan, who grumbled about her servants' behaviour and her disruptive visitors. Margaret was released on 29 October 1537, but Howard died in the Tower two days later, probably from disease.

After her latest affair was discovered, Margaret was returned to Syon for a year 'for much over lightness' in her behaviour and then confined at Norfolk's palace at Kenninghall, Norfolk, where Cranmer later warned her grimly to 'beware the third time'.[36] It was then back to Syon, until Henry allowed her return to court.

When he had embarked on his progress, Henry left behind dangerous problems in London, aside from the plague's mounting death toll. His Privy Chamber was a hotbed of evangelical reformers, still brazen in their fervency despite Cromwell's death. One of them was John Lassells, who had worked for the stricken minister as a messenger in 1538–9, before becoming a 'sewer', or an attendant at the king's table.

That September he and three colleagues called Jonson, Maxey and Smethwick met in Henry's great antechamber at Whitehall. Lassells sought news about the spread of 'God's Holy Word, seeing we have lost so noble a man [Cromwell] who did love and favour it so well'. He doubted that Norfolk and Gardiner, ringleaders in bringing him down, truly loved the Holy Bible's teachings. Maxey claimed that the duke unashamedly declared 'that he never read scripture in English, nor ever would. Only yesterday I overheard him say: "It was merry in England before this new learning came up."'

There were rumours that Norfolk had angrily reproved an Exchequer official who had married a nun after her religious house was dissolved. Her husband had explained to the duke: 'Well, I know no nuns or religious folk, nor such bondage, seeing God and the king made them free'. Norfolk had ranted: 'By God's sacred Body, that may be, but it will never be out of my heart as long as I live,' and stalked off.

Lassells believed that Henry remained committed to religious reform and urged his comrades 'not to be rash or quick in maintaining the scripture, for if we would let [Gardiner and Norfolk] alone and suffer a little time, they would, I doubt not, overthrow themselves, standing manifestly against God and their prince'.[37]

Some were already dying for their campaign to reform religion or for defending the old faith. On 7 July, a lawyer called William Collins, who lived in Southwark – then part of Gardiner's Winchester diocese – was burnt at the stake for 'heresy against the sacrament of the altar'. At his death, 'he confessed his error and died very penitently'.[38]

Collins had objected to the idolatrous worship of a wooden statue of Christ in a chapel used by Spanish sailors to pray for a safe passage home. He loosed an arrow at the statue, striking it in the foot, and loudly called upon it 'to defend itself or punish him if it could'.[39] He had been imprisoned for two or three years and his execution was popularly believed to have been contrived by Gardiner.

On 4 August, Thomas Empson, a monk from the Benedictine monastery at Westminster (suppressed seven months earlier), appeared before the Newgate justices after having been imprisoned for treason in denying the king's religious supremacy. He still adamantly refused to seek the king's pardon, nor swear the oath acknowledging his governorship of the English Church. His black monk's habit and cowl was ripped off his back and he was returned to his cell 'until the king knew of his malicious obstinacy'.[40] A contemporary chronicler noted: 'This was the last monk that was seen in his clothing in England'.[41] Empson probably died later in prison.

Henry's fifth queen now had a reminder of her own vital role in the royal marriage – producing a duke of York to safeguard the dynastic line. Young and healthy she might be, but there must be every likelihood that Henry could no longer cut the royal mustard, as he had probably become at least intermittently impotent. Furthermore, in the privacy of the bedchamber, Katherine must have found her man mountain of a husband physically repugnant.

In November, Richard Jones, high master of St Paul's School, London, dedicated his translation of a tract on childbirth called *The Byrth of Mankynde, Otherwise Named the Woman's Book*, to the queen. It would have been an unedifying read, as it recounted a process of unremitting suffering and repeatedly referred to the mortal dangers of labour, illustrated by alarmingly graphic woodcuts. Helpfully, it also included suggested remedies for infertility.

An increasingly confident Katherine began to flex her muscles as queen. In early December she tried to have two of Mary's maids-of-honour dismissed, after taking umbrage that the king's daughter showed less respect to her than her two predecessors. One maid was removed two months later, at the king's demand, and the girl apparently died of grief at her lost livelihood.[42]

The first difficult meeting between reigning and discarded queens came on 3 January 1541. Katherine had apparently become jealous over mischievous gossip that Henry was about to take Anne back.[43] Anne of Cleves' New Year present to Henry of 'two fine and large horses caparisoned in mauve velvet', did nothing to ease Katherine's suspicions.

She was invited to Hampton Court but kept waiting while Lord Chancellor Audley and Robert Radcliffe, Lord Great Chamberlain, instructed the new queen in how 'she was to receive and treat her visitor'. Anne of Cleves was eventually admitted to Katherine's presence and sank humbly to her knees in front of her, despite 'the prayers and entreaties [of the queen] who received her most kindly, showing her great courtesy', according to Chapuys.

Then the king entered, bowed to his 'good sister' and then embraced and kissed her. All three sat down to supper, Anne pointedly seated near the bottom of the table. This stilted, rather contrived jolly time *à trois* continued the following day. As was his wont, Henry sent his queen gifts of a ring and two small dogs – which she immediately presented to Anne as a token of her goodwill.

Further examples of Henry's largesse followed. Six days later, he confirmed her marriage jointure which included properties once belonging to Queen Jane (Seymour) and estates formerly owned by the attainted traitors Cromwell and Hungerford. He also allotted more than £4,600 (£2.6 million in modern money) a year for her household, which now included girlhood friends from her days at Norfolk House, like Katherine Tylney.[44]

In late February, Henry fell dangerously ill again at Hampton Court, initially with another dose of malaria. He seems to have eaten little and as Marillac unkindly observed, this should 'have profited [more] than hurt him, for he is grown very stout' and 'marvellously excessive in drinking and eating'.[45] The fistulas in one of his legs, 'formerly kept open to maintain his health, suddenly closed to his great alarm, for five or six years ago, in like case, he thought to have died. This time, prompt remedy was applied and he is now well and the fever gone.'

Then a black cloud of melancholy and depression pressed down on the king – a '*mal d'espirit*' according to Marillac – which triggered furious rages against his churlish subjects and his fawning Privy Council, some of whom he held in 'sinister opinion'.

Henry grew mercurial; 'people worth credit say he is often of a different opinion in the morning than after dinner'. Shrovetide was spent 'without recreation, even of music, in which he used to take as much pleasure as any prince in Christendom' and he sent away many courtiers. 'He stayed at Hampton Court with so little company that his court resembled more a private company than a king's [retinue].' Visitors to the palace were turned away 'as if to hide... the king's indisposition'[46] and even Katherine was kept away from him.[47]

Henry's temper must have improved because later in March, substantial land and properties owned by the former Benedictine priory at Hurley, Berkshire, were granted to Charles Howard, now restored to favour after his affair with Lady Margaret.[48]

On 19 March, Henry escorted his queen down the Thames from Westminster to Greenwich Palace in a stately procession of vessels led by his great gold and red barge, propelled by twenty-four oarsmen, with music played by fifes and drums in an accompanying boat.[49]

Between London Bridge and the Tower, the royal party were welcomed by the Lord Mayor of London and the masters and wardens of the city's forty-eight livery companies, their craft flying brightly coloured heraldic banners. As the cavalcade rowed sedately past the Tower, a salute of 'great guns' boomed out from its ramparts, echoed by salvoes fired by ships moored all the way to Greenwich.

The queen, probably at the instigation of Norfolk and Gardiner, now took her first tentative steps in meddling in state business.

Richard Pate, Henry's departing ambassador to Charles V, had defected to Rome because of his opposition to the religious reforms in England. In the early hours of 28 December 1540, he fled Namur (in today's Belgium) with his chaplain Seth Holland and 600 crowns (£150) in cash.[50] His servant Richard Attown believed his master had sought sanctuary in the bishopric of Liège, where 'he may remain at liberty for any treason or other offence'.[51] In reality, Pate travelled to Rome, later to gratefully accept the nugatory appointment of bishop of Worcester from Pope Paul III.[52]

Henry's titanic vanity was punctured by this diplomatic humiliation and he became taxed by doubts over the loyalty of his other ambassadors. How far had this poison of treachery spread?

Sir John Wallop, the former royal envoy in France and captain of the fortress of Guisnes in the Calais Pale, was known for his religious conservatism. He was summoned home early in March and placed under house arrest. During his interrogation, he 'stood very stiffly to his truth, not calling to remembrance what he had written and said, contrary to the duty of a good subject'. But when shown his letters to 'that traitor' Pate, Wallop's defiance collapsed and he appealed for mercy, protesting he had done nothing malicious and that his denials were caused by forgetfulness. He refused to be tried by law, relying instead on Henry's clemency.[53]

The king also harboured suspicions about the diplomat and poet Sir Thomas Wyatt the elder, despite his personal affection for him. Wyatt had been caught up in the investigation of Anne Boleyn's alleged adultery and incest in 1536 and had spent more than five weeks in the Tower before being freed, probably on Cromwell's orders. Sir Thomas was now back behind the walls of the fortress.

Chief among the latest accusations against him were claims by Edmund Bonner, the acerbic bishop of London, that Wyatt had communicated with Cardinal Pole, writing that 'By God's Blood, you shall see the king, our master, cast out at the cart's tail'.[54] These foolish words could be construed as treasonably predicting the king's death or overthrow. Wyatt denied this, saying his contacts with Pole enabled him to spy on the cardinal and his treachery in Europe. 'God alone knew' the torment he had suffered in trying to remember everything he had said or done, 'whereby a malicious enemy might take advantage by evil interpretation', the envoy told the Privy Council.[55]

Katherine persuaded Henry to show mercy to both. Wallop was pardoned 'on his spontaneous submission and at the intercession of Queen Katherine'. He was reinstated as captain of Guisnes and two years later appointed commander of English forces in France. Wyatt also received royal absolution, 'though on hard conditions'. He was required to confess his guilt and also take back his wife Elizabeth after fifteen years of separation following her adultery.[56] He also had to resume conjugal relations with her 'on pain of death and confiscation of property, if he be untrue to her henceforth' by maintaining 'criminal relations with one or two other ladies that he has since loved'.[57] Henry, always prudish about other people's marital behaviour, was an unorthodox, combative marriage counsellor.

Katherine's uncle, Lord William Howard, another half-brother to Norfolk, was also appointed Henry's ambassador to Francis I of France.

The king departed for a short visit to Dover, on the Kent coast, to review progress on the shore fortifications overlooking the narrow seas between England and France, leaving his young wife behind at Greenwich.

Her nemesis now entered her life.

Thomas Culpeper, one of Henry's special favourites among the Gentlemen of the Privy Chamber, began seeking her favour. He was a distant kinsman to the queen on her mother's side, as they shared a common ancestor in the reign of Edward II.[58] He probably began at court as a page to Henry but by 1537, he had attained his current position after years of unrelenting ambition.

The following year the king reprieved one of Culpeper's young servants on the gibbet 'to the great comfort of all the people' crowding around the scaffold in the tiltyard at Whitehall Palace. The boy had stolen his master's purse, containing a jewel of the king's, plus £11 in cash. 'He was brought to the place of execution . . . and the hangman was taking down the ladder from the gallows [when] the king sent his pardon for the boy and so he was saved from death.'[59]

This eleventh-hour act of clemency suggests the king's fondness for Culpeper and how much he valued his roguish company and his tender ministrations to his painful legs. Rewards continued to be heaped on the twenty-seven-year-old's head in 'consideration of his true and faithful service': grants of former monastic land in Yorkshire, Essex, Kent, Gloucestershire and Wiltshire from 1537; sinecure appointments at Penshurst Place, Kent, and as Clerk of the King's Armoury, Lieutenant of Tonbridge Castle, Kent, and Steward of Ashdown Forest, Sussex. The last grant, signed at Hampton Court on 20 December 1540, was of properties once owned by Cromwell in Sussex.[60]

But Culpeper had a sinister side. About two years before, he had brutally raped a park-keeper's wife in a wood, while 'at his bidding', three or four companions held her down. As villagers tried to detain the assailants, they were fought off and Culpeper murdered one during the brawl. He and his cronies were arrested but Henry pardoned him.[61]

Undaunted, Culpeper remained arrogantly in the limelight, competing on the fifth day of a grand tournament at Westminster in May

1540. He fought on foot at the dividing barrier, probably with pole-
axes, against Cromwell's newly knighted nephew Richard. But he was
knocked to the ground, with only his pride injured.[62]

In mid-March 1541, William Brice, another of Culpeper's servants, was
questioned about a violent affray in Southwark with those employed by
Thomas Paston, another Gentleman in Henry's Privy Chamber. Three
days later, John Hurley, John Cousins and John Hubbard, servants of
both courtiers, were thrown into the Fleet Prison for their part in the
fight.[63]

The fight was probably triggered by their masters' rivalry in winning
the queen's attentions. Culpeper certainly sought an attachment and
patronage from her – and much more besides. Marillac was later to
declare sarcastically that the courtier who had shared the king's bed
now 'wished to share the queen's too'.

In early April there was gossip that Katherine was pregnant. 'The
queen is thought to be with child,' reported Marillac, 'which would be
a very great joy to this king who, it seems believes it and intends, if it
be found true, to have her crowned [queen] at Whitsuntide.'[64] Despite
all the excitement, it was a false alarm.

Henry returned to Greenwich and on Maundy Thursday performed
the traditional ceremony of washing the feet of poor men and giving
them purses of money in the Chapel Royal. Katherine, wearing an
apron over her gown, bathed the feet of pauper women.[65] Later that
day, the queen gave Culpeper an expensive velvet cap.[66]

On Easter Sunday, 17 April, Chapuys informed Charles V of the discovery of a new conspiracy against the king in Yorkshire, involving a
plot to assassinate Robert Holgate, bishop of Llandaff and governor
of the northern counties.[67] 'About fifty persons, among whom were
six or seven priests, had determined to kill the bishop ... intending to
take possession of a fortress of the king where [the bishop] resides.'[68]
The conspirators were 'perhaps emboldened and encouraged in their
undertaking by the fact that for some time, there has been a rumour
that the Scots were stirring on the border ... [They] have been nearly
all arrested and ... there will be no grace for them.'[69] Ten days later,
Marillac reported that some 'eighty or 100 gentlemen and priests'

planned the rebellion but after it was foiled, some fled to remote areas or to Scotland.[70]

Chapuys believed the conspiracy was dangerous because Henry's subjects in the north resented the 'cruelties and executions' that had followed the northern rebellions in 1536–7. Henry's grim vengeance – the horrible sight of corpses swinging from trees – remained fresh and vivid memories. 'There was going to be a great fair at Pontefract [Yorkshire] where the last rising took place, and the conspirators... would have attended... with [more than 300] retainers. Their plan was to [win] over as many people as they could, then openly denounce the king's tyranny and slay all who would rise in [his] defence. They had hopes of assistance from the king of Scotland, who would not nowadays meet with much resistance if he were to make war on this king.'[71]

The 'Wakefield Plot' in actuality involved only eight or nine priests and a handful of laymen, the only gentleman being William Leigh of Middleton while the others included the clothier Thomas Tattershall and the yeoman Gilbert Thornton. They were hanged, drawn and quartered at Tyburn, as was Thomas Green, former prior of the Premonstratensian abbey at Croxton, Leicestershire, dissolved in 1539.[72] Sir John Neville, scion of a minor branch of the noble family and a former member of the king's bodyguard, had failed to disclose his knowledge of the conspiracy and may have passively supported it. He was executed at York on 15 June together with a 'poor man' of Wakefield called James Diamond, two chantry priests from Trinity College, Pontefract, and a chaplain. Fifteen died for their roles in the plot.[73]

Henry decided to resolve the problem of the restive north once and for all. A royal progress to the region had been planned since February 1537, but repeatedly postponed.[74] Now it had become imperative.

The king had not forgotten nor forgiven its inhabitants for their rebellions that threatened his crown. He intended to remind them of the authority, majesty and awesome military might of the Tudor monarchy. He was also eager to receive publicly their homage and submission, down on their bended knees in the dust. Henry had exclaimed angrily that he had an 'evil people to rule' and promised 'to make them so poor that they would never be able to rebel again'.

Before he departed for the northern capital of York, there was a piece of unfinished business to transact. Cardinal Pole's mother Margaret, after being accused of perpetrating 'sundry detestable and abominable treasons',[75] had been incarcerated in the Tower since the White Rose Yorkist faction was eliminated in 1538. The countess of Salisbury, her grandson Henry and Edward Courtenay, son of the beheaded marquess of Exeter, had been exempted from the general pardon in 1540.[76] The two boys had not faced trial, nor appeared in the Act of Attainder, so their imprisonment had no legal justification.[77] Reginald Pole, still nimbly dodging Henry's revenge in Europe, castigated this 'Western Turk' for his tyranny that 'began with priests, then [went on] to nobles... and at length it has come to women and innocent children... including the son of my brother, a child, the hope of our race'.[78]

Henry paid out £13 6s 8d (£13.33) a month for food for these three prisoners, as well as 18d (8p) a week in wages for a serving woman for Margaret. She had complained that her old bones were suffering from the dankness and cold of the Tower. So in March 1541, the Privy Council instructed the queen's tailor, John Skutt, to make the countess a parcel of warm clothes, made up of a furred nightgown, a worsted kirtle, a furred petticoat, another nightgown of say (a fine-textured cloth, like serge) lined with satin. A bonnet, four pairs of hose, four pairs of shoes and slippers were also provided, costing £11 16s 4d (£11.82).[79] A further 66s 8d (£3.33) was spent on necessaries for her the following month.[80]

Two months after this expenditure, Henry decided to execute her.

The motivation for his spur-of-the-moment decision remains obscure. Was it the involvement in the Wakefield conspiracy of Sir John Neville, a man 'of mediocre ability and wit' and member of a cadet branch of the White Rose family? Was it driven by Henry's instinctive need to neutralise any threat while absent from his London power base – like the secret execution of Edmund de la Pole, earl of Suffolk, back in 1513, before the king's embarkation for war with France? Was it merely sweet revenge on her exiled son, Reginald Pole?

The cardinal may also have been seeking to organise his mother's escape, as suggested in his letter to the bishop of Lavaur in southern France: 'As to what you write of my affairs, both what was lovingly planned for my mother's release and about that friend of yours who procured this... Afterwards,... [he] was kept in custody, although he has since been liberated...'[81] This 'friend' was Gregory Botolf, former chaplain to Viscount Lisle (himself still imprisoned in the Tower), who had defected to Rome and had briefly been imprisoned at Diest (in today's Belgium), following diplomatic pressure by Henry.[82] Had his spies revealed this plan to rescue her?

As preparations for the northern progress accelerated, the king ordered that the Tower be emptied of prisoners, some to be executed and others pardoned.

Margaret, countess of Salisbury, was the first to die, at seven o'clock on the morning of 27 May 1541. Such was the unseemly haste, that only a small wooden block was available in the Tower precincts for the headsman's grisly work. Even the usual executioner was absent, exacting Henry's justice on the Yorkshire plotters. Instead, 'a wretched and blundering youth' was hired. After commending her soul to God and offering up prayers for the royal family, she was told 'to make haste and place her head on the block, which she did'. The tyro headsman managed only to 'literally hack her head and shoulders to pieces in the most pitiful manner'.[83] Marillac observed wryly that 'those here are afraid to put to death publicly those whom they execute in secret'. Her body was buried, not in the magnificent chantry chapel she had erected in Christchurch priory, Dorset, but only yards from where she was slaughtered like an animal, in the chapel of St Peter ad Vincula.

When he heard of his mother's death, Pole was surprisingly sanguine. 'Till this day I thought myself highly favoured of God, as being descended from one of the best and noblest women in England... but it has now pleased the Almighty to honour me still and increase my obligation, since he has made me the son of a martyr, whom the king of England has brought to the scaffold for her perseverance in the Catholic faith.' The cardinal told his 'thunderstruck' secretary: 'Let us rejoice together, for we have now one advocate more in heaven.' With that, Pole retired to his office for about an hour and emerged 'as cheerful as before'.[84]

In 1886, Margaret Pole was beatified by Pope Leo XIII because she and many other English martyrs had died for the dignity of the Holy See 'and for the truth of the orthodox faith'.

Marillac learnt of the condition of the two imprisoned boys in mid-July. He reported to Francis I that Edward Courtenay had more freedom within the Tower's walls 'and has a preceptor [teacher] to give him lessons – a thing which is not done towards the little nephew of Cardinal Pole who is poorly and strictly kept and not desired to know anything'.[85] Henry Pole died in the Tower the following year, probably from disease, and Courtenay was eventually freed in August 1553, after the accession of the Catholic Mary I.

Others had been taken from the Tower to die under Henry's laws. On the day of Margaret Pole's beheading, some of the Wakefield conspirators suffered traitors' deaths at Tyburn.[86] A month later, Lord Leonard Grey, a kinsman of the Poles, and formerly Lord Deputy of Ireland, was executed at Tower Hill for a veritable litany of treasons, including leaving 'all the king's artillery in Galway ready for the bishop of Rome or the Spaniards if they landed, as a report [suggested] that Cardinal Pole with an army would land about that time.'[87] The heads of those executed were briefly impaled on pikes at London Bridge, 'in order that the people may forget those whose heads kept their memory fresh.'[88]

On 30 June 1541, the royal couple, with 2,000 courtiers and an escort of 1,500 soldiers, set out from Whitehall on the long-promised progress to the north. This was not a benevolent visit, nor one of celebration, but more an army of occupation on the march. Trouble was clearly anticipated; normally 1,000 riders took part in a progress. As well as his 250 'very tall and strong' Yeomen of the Guard and the fifty 'Spears' or gentlemen pensioners with their armed retainers, the king had reinforced his bodyguard with 'gentlemen of Kent, whom he trusts most'.[89] His artillery train was also shipped north by sea and unloaded at Hull, ready to quell any insurrection.

A draft *gest*, or itinerary, for the progress suggests that Henry originally planned to travel to York from Sheffield via Monk Bretton, Chevet, Wakefield and Hazelwood, but this included the West Riding, scene of the recent conspiracy, and the plan was dropped, probably because the king feared local hostility.[90]

The journey north was painfully slow, with cold, wet and stormy weather delaying arrival at Lincoln until 9 August. Hunting also proved an enjoyable distraction from the already circuitous route; more than 200 stags and does were killed by the royal party at Hatfield, south Yorkshire, alone. The queen may have become bored by the continual joys of the chase, if not the unwelcome sexual attentions of her corpulent husband. On 27 August, she appointed Francis Dereham, an old flame from her teens and lately returned from Ireland, to be her secretary and an Usher of her Privy Chamber.

Henry and his enormous retinue eventually entered Yorkshire through Barnsdale, where he was met by '200 gentlemen in coats of velvet and 4,000 tall yeomen and serving men, well horsed, [who] on their knees made submission, by the mouth of Sir Robert Bowes [who] gave the king £900'. The formal submission was not quite the popular outburst of loyalty that it seemed, as it was written by the king's Council of the North and its contents amended by Privy Councillors in the royal party.[91] Those who had remained loyal in the 1536 rebellion were greeted separately and rewarded by a smiling regal countenance.

Edward Lee, the conservative archbishop of York, together with more than 300 priests 'made a like submission and gave the king £600'.[92] The gift was generous but it did nothing to appease the king. Just to remind the clergy who was the supreme governor of the Church in England, the archbishop was instructed that 'all the [saints'] shrines be taken down in all his province and that the place where they stood to be made even and plain'. That of St William, a predecessor of Lee's as archbishop, in York Minster, was included in this act of iconoclasm.

The king continued to employ confrontation rather than conciliation in dealing with his northern subjects, deliberately humiliating York by his entry into the city on 18 September, three weeks late. Henry approached the northern capital through Fulford, rather than the planned route at Micklegate with its grandstand, decorated with the arms of the king, queen, Prince Edward and the city, and its anxiously waiting choirs. Instead, York's leading citizens and local gentry had to kneel ignominiously around the cross at Fulford while their humble submission to the king was laboriously read out.[93]

Plans to meet James V of Scotland for a diplomatic summit at York were finalised in July and 1,500 men worked around the clock to refurbish the Benedictine abbey of St Mary, dissolved in November 1539, as the meeting venue.[94] The abbey, occupying a fifteen-acre (6 hectare) site outside the city walls was repaired, painted, and adorned with hanging tapestries sent up from Whitehall, to house Henry and the Scottish king for discussions on border tensions.

Henry's diplomatic objectives were that Scotland should break with Catholicism, declare its own 'true religion' and stay neutral during any war between England and France.[95] His Privy Council had pointed out reassuringly on 27 August that James 'might with a great deal less danger repair hither than [when] he lately went into France, having no sea to pass ... nor going to a stranger but his natural uncle who cannot but love and tender him.'[96]

James V never came.

An impatient Henry waited nine days for him to arrive but thoroughly shamed and angered by his nephew's snub, departed York on 27 September for London, his petulance fuelled by a Scottish raid into England nine days earlier.

Worry was heaped upon the king's peevishness when he arrived at Hampton Court in late October. His precious son and heir was stricken with a 'quartan fever', a form of malaria that creates paroxysms every fourth day. Panicking, Henry 'summoned all the physicians of the country to advise and after long consultation, they agreed,' as one told Marillac privately, 'that the fever placed him in danger.'

The ambassador's informant gloomily pointed out that apart from this affliction, 'the Prince was so fat and unhealthy as to be unlikely to live long'.[97] The doctor's pessimism was happily unfounded: the four-year-old prince recovered.

But worse was now in store for Henry.

5

Deadheading the 'Blushing Rose'

The king returned to Hampton Court on 29 October 1541 and told his chaplain, Bishop John Longland of Lincoln, that on Tuesday, 1 November – All Hallows' Day – there should be special prayers for 'the good life he led and trusted to lead' with his queen, who had given him such 'very perfect love'. His great happiness had grown ever stronger because of the absence of the 'troubles of mind which had happened to him [in earlier] marriages'.

Earlier that month, the evangelical John Lassells had requested an interview with Archbishop Cranmer to impart some dangerous information. Lassells had talked to his married sister Mary Hall, once employed by the Howard family at Horsham and Lambeth and now nurse to a child of Lord William Howard. She had known Katherine when chamberer to Agnes, the sixty-four-year-old dowager duchess of Norfolk, so Lassells urged his sister to exploit this old relationship by seeking a lucrative position in the royal household.

Mary had no interest in working for the queen and felt sorry for her, because 'she is light both in living and in conditions'. After Lassells asked her to explain, scandalous revelations about Katherine's nocturnal shenanigans in the Howard household tumbled out.

She breathlessly disclosed that the queen (one of the 'more forward virgins') had an affair with Francis Dereham in 1538, who 'had lain in bed with her in his doublet and hose between the sheets a hundred nights. There had been such puffing and blowing between them' that a girl who slept in the same dormitory 'said she would lye no longer with her'. Moreover, Henry Monox, a lute player who had taught Katherine to play the virginals[1] when she was fourteen, 'knew a privy mark [a birthmark] on her body'.[2] Mary was dumbfounded that the king had taken as his queen a girl who had 'lived so incontinently before marriage'.

Possession of such incendiary information about the monarchy was a frightening dilemma in Henry's England. The threat of gaol for misprision of treason – failure to disclose the crime – concentrated even the most bovine of minds.

Cranmer, as the spiritual head of the Church, was the obvious man to hear these prurient disclosures. Afterwards, Marillac noted that 'The brother, knowing that it would be high treason not to reveal such a thing within twenty-four hours, consulted a friend and revealed all to the archbishop.'[3] Any conspiracy theorist worth their salt would feel justified in believing that Mary's revelations were a carefully planned trap for the Howard clan. Surely Lassells was acting maliciously to defeat his rival religious faction at court? However, there is no evidence that her accusations and their *exposé* was anything other than happenstance; an accident waiting in the wings to destroy the royal marriage.

Lassells, like a triumphant school sneak, ran hotfoot to pass on the poisoned chalice of knowledge about Katherine's lurid past. Cranmer was both aghast and 'marvellously perplexed' at these lewd disclosures and felt that he alone could not accept the responsibility for deciding what action to take. He sought counsel from Edward Seymour, earl of Hertford (who oversaw government business in London during the king's progress) and Lord Chancellor Audley about how to handle the matter. Not relishing involvement in the problem, nor its horrendous implications, they all 'weighed the matter and deeply pondered [its] gravity'. Predictably, while 'greatly troubled and disquieted' at the news, they resolved, cravenly, that Cranmer himself should tell the king.[4]

The archbishop unsurprisingly 'could not find it in his heart to express [the allegations] to the king's majesty by word of mouth'. Cranmer, 'sorrowfully lamenting', left a sealed note in the king's pew in the Chapel Royal at Hampton Court, with his plea to read it in private written on its cover. His letter accused the queen of having 'lived most corruptly and sensually', far from the 'pure and honest condition' of Norfolk's voluble affirmations of Katherine's teenage innocence and chastity. When Henry arrived to pray for the souls of the faithful departed during Mass on the morning of All Souls' Day, Wednesday, 2 November, he picked up the letter and read its contents.

His pious supplications were instantly forgotten. Henry was more puzzled than angered by the allegations, declaring that 'he so tenderly loved the woman and had conceived such a constant opinion of her honesty, that he supposed it to be rather a forged matter, than of truth'. The king, a practising conspiracy theorist to his fingertips, may have suspected that a sinister plot was seeking to blacken his pretty wife's unblemished name. Nonetheless, he secretly summoned Southampton (Lord Privy Seal), John, Lord Russell (Lord High Admiral), Sir Anthony Browne (Master of the Horse) and his secretary Sir Thomas Wriothesley, to conduct a discreet investigation, 'as he could not believe it till the certainty was known'. Henry emphasised that no 'spark of scandal' should sully his queen's reputation until their inquiries concluded.

They wasted no time in turning over the stones of Katherine's past life to discover what unsavoury secrets lurked beneath.

Dereham was arrested by Southampton on charges of piracy.[5] Under interrogation at the Tower, he confessed he had known Katherine 'carnally many times, both in his doublet and hose between the sheets and in naked bed'. There had also been 'sundry women, one after the other, that had lain in the same bed with them when he did the acts'.[6]

Monox admitted being in love with Katherine and that she had reciprocated his feelings. He 'had commonly used to feel the secret and other parts of her body' and Katherine had promised to grant him 'her maidenhead, though it be painful to her'. The dowager duchess had discovered them together and after angrily giving Katherine 'two or three blows', charged them never to be alone together again.

Her bedfellows in the girls' dormitory were Katherine Tylney and the ambitious Joan Bulmer. All three were 'entertained by Dereham' and Edward Waldegrave, Monox's cousin, another regular nocturnal visitor to the girls' bedchamber.

Later, Katherine Tylney was cross-examined about events in the Howard houses and claimed that the dowager duchess only knew there was love between Dereham and the future queen. 'Once she found Dereham embracing Katherine in his arms and kissing her.' The feisty old lady 'gave Dereham a blow and also beat the queen and gave Joan Bulmer a blow because she was present'. When Dereham was required for some task, 'the duchess would say "I warrant if you seek him in Katherine Howard's chamber, you shall find him there."'[7]

Andrew Maunsay, former servant to the duchess, also testified about the three-in-a-bed romps at Lambeth. He swore that three times when

Dereham, wearing his doublet and hose, and Katherine were in bed, her friend Katherine Tylney 'lay in the bed at the time'.[8]

In jealous revenge for his lover's transference of her affections, Monox wrote an anonymous letter to the duchess, suggesting that if she were to rise half an hour after retiring to bed and visit the dormitory 'she would be displeased' by finding Dereham and Katherine together'.[9]

Mary Hall, interrogated by Southampton under the pretence of a hunting trip to Sussex, had remonstrated with Monox about his relations with Katherine, but they still secretly exchanged love tokens. The dowager duchess had the keys of the gentlewomen's chamber brought to her every night, but Katherine stole them for her trysts with Dereham. Alice Welkes, another servant, had whispered to her about Katherine's affair with Dereham but Mary had observed: 'Let her alone for [if] she [carries] on as she begins, we shall hear she will be nought within a while'. Mary acknowledged she had never told 'my lady of Norfolk, Lord William [Howard] or his wife' about what was going on'.[10]

The queen had 'denied all' during a fractious interview with her uncle Norfolk. Marillac recognised that the duke might well be vexed, 'for the queen happens to be his own niece and the daughter of his brother, just as Anne [Boleyn] was also his niece on his sister's side and his having been the chief cause of the king marrying her'.[11]

When Cranmer visited Katherine, he 'found her in such lamentation and heaviness [in spirit] as I never saw no creature, so that it would have pitied any man's heart in the world to have looked upon her'.[12] With clerical prolixity, he had planned to discuss the 'grievousness of her demerits', the justice of Henry's laws 'and what she ought to suffer by the same'. But when he saw the queen's desperation, the gentle archbishop tried to comfort her by talking about the king's 'benignity and mercy', fearing that 'the recital of the laws with the aggravation of her offences might have driven her into some dangerous ecstasy or else into a very frenzy'.

Katherine told the archbishop: 'Alas, my lord... the fear of death grieved me not so much as does the remembrance of the king's goodness, for when I remember how gracious and loving a prince I had, I cannot but sorrow. But this sudden mercy, and more than I could have looked for, showed to me [who is] so unworthy at this time, makes my offences to appear... much more heinous than did they before.'

Sir Edward Baynton, her vice-chamberlain, reported that the queen

insisted that 'all Dereham did to her, was of his importune forcement...
and violence, rather than of her free will and consent'. So it was not
promiscuity on her part; she had been the tragic victim of a series of
rapes.[13]

Within the next few days, the beleaguered queen confessed her
affairs with Monox and Dereham to Henry: 'I, your grace's most
sorrowful subject and most vile wretch in the world... make my most
humble submission and confession of my faults.' Down on her 'hands
and knees' she begged for mercy, although she was 'the most unworthy
either to be called your wife or subject. My sorrow I [cannot] by writing
express, nevertheless, I trust your most benign nature will have some
respect [for] my youth, my ignorance, my frailty.' She dared to hope
she might win 'your grace's pity and mercy.'

The queen then offered her version of those now infamous teenage
affairs. 'First, at the flattering and fair persuasions of Monox, being
but a young girl, [I] suffered him at sundry times to handle and touch
the secret parts of my body, which neither became me with honesty to
permit, nor him to require. Also Frances Dereham, by many persuasions, procured me to his vicious purpose and obtained first to lie upon
my bed with his doublet and hose and after within the bed, he lay with
me naked and used me in such sort as a man does his wife many and
sundry times, but how often I know not. Our company ended almost
a year before the king's majesty was married to Anne of Cleves and
continued not past one quarter of a year or little above.'

This was the 'whole truth' and she beseeched Henry to 'consider
the subtle persuasions of young men and the ignorance and frailness
of young women'. Katherine so desired 'to be taken into your grace's
favour and so blinded by worldly glory that I could not, nor had the
grace to consider, how great a fault it was to conceal my former faults
from your majesty, considering that I [always] intended during my
life to be faithful and true to your majesty after[wards]. Nevertheless,
the sorrow of my offences was ever before my eyes, considering the
infinite goodness of your majesty towards me from time to time, ever
increasing and not diminishing.'

The young queen's fate lay in the king's hands, 'with my life and death
wholly in your most benign and merciful grace, to be considered by no
justice of your majesty's laws but only by your infinite goodness, pity,

compassion and mercy, without which I acknowledge myself worthy of the most extreme punishment.'[14]

This was a shrewd and eloquent letter, designed to exploit any last vestiges of love that Henry might still feel for her. Can we detect the Machiavellian hand of Norfolk in her choice of words?

Her later relationship with Culpeper somehow slipped her mind. Was Katherine's letter written in desperate hope that the investigation would be stopped dead by her frank admission of past promiscuity? Allegations of adultery with the king's favourite would remain hidden. This was a breathtaking gamble on her part and perhaps symptomatic of the emotional turmoil which enveloped Katherine as her glittering world unexpectedly collapsed around her.

On Saturday, 5 November, Henry entered the council room at Hampton Court and remained in conference with his Privy Councillors until midday. In the early afternoon, he embarked on his barge and slipped away down the Thames, without pomp or show, to Whitehall Palace, leaving his council still in session.

The king had also deserted Katherine and was never to see her again.

The Imperial ambassador Eustace Chapuys soon discovered what was going on – both he and Marillac posted spies to note comings and goings at the palace – and reported that Cranmer had visited the queen 'two or three times – to interrogate and admonish her, as is supposed, on the part of the council, but he did not [find] much out'.

Despite Henry's insistence on discretion, news of the investigation reached the dowager duchess at Lambeth, perhaps via Norfolk. On Sunday, 6 November, she asked her servant: 'I hear... Dereham is taken and also the queen. What is the matter?' Gullibly, her retainer thought the Privy Council's action had been triggered by some harsh words that Dereham had uttered to a gentleman usher,[15] but the old duchess could scent disaster in the wind. 'Nay', she said, 'I fear there [will] be some ill [and the queen] shall come to my home again.'[16]

The Privy Council returned to London that evening and continued discussions through the night at Whitehall. After snatching some sleep and sustenance, on Monday they adjourned to Gardiner's palace at Southwark and, with much apprehension, laid out the evidence that

was accumulating against Henry's queen. The king was initially scep-
tical, but as the libidinous tale was recounted, his love for Katherine
was irrevocably extinguished.

The king's reaction to his betrayal over her past was so terrifying
that his councillors, Norfolk among them, cowered as he treated them
to the most fearsome of all his many furies. Stomping up and down,
he vengefully called for a sword so that he could kill Katherine 'that
he loved so much'. That 'wicked woman', he screamed, had 'never such
delight in her lechery as she [will] have pain and torture in her death'.
His rage and passion were so intense that his advisers feared his grief
had driven him dangerously insane. They shrank from his wrath, as he
blamed them for 'soliciting' him to marry the Howard girl and bitterly
reproached his ministers for 'this last mischief'.

Henry's frenzy at length subsided into tears and he blubbed like a
child, cursing his 'ill-luck in meeting with such ill-conditioned wives'.[17]
A more prosaic official account of the meeting described the king being
so 'pierced with pensiveness, that it was [long] before he could [utter
his sorrow] and finally with plenty [of tears] (which was strange in his
courage), opened the same'.[18] Henry then suddenly departed to forget
his injured pride by seeking solace in a few days' energetic hunting of
stags.

The councillors left the meeting 'very troubled, especially Norfolk,
who is esteemed very resolute and not easily moved to show by his face
what his heart conceives', Marillac commented.

It was agreed to discharge the queen's servants, seal all her coffers and
chests, and post guards on the doors to her apartments. Her brother
Charles was banished from court without explanation.[19]

The French ambassador initially believed the trouble lay in the
discovery that Katherine could not have children, then heard rumours
of her affair with Dereham. 'The way taken is the same as with Queen
Anne [Boleyn] who was beheaded. [Katherine] has taken no pastime
but kept in her chamber, whereas, before, she did nothing but dance
and rejoice and now when the musicians come, they are told that it is
no more the time to dance.'

On Friday, 11 November, the Privy Council ordered her removal
to the former nunnery at Syon, Henry's traditional domicile for any
royal lady accused of immorality. She would stay there 'in the state
of a queen, furnished moderately... with three chambers, hanged

with mean stuff without any cloth of estate ... with a mean number of servants'.[20] Sir Edward Baynton[21] was in charge of this tiny household, with his wife Isabel as one of the queen's four personal attendants. At least she was one friendly face for the queen, as she was her half-sister, having been born to her mother during her first marriage.[22]

The next day, Henry's councillors, both spiritual and temporal, and his senior judges were called to Whitehall to hear about 'the abominable demeanour of the queen'. No mention of her marriage pre-contract with Dereham was allowed by the king, but this august audience were to be made aware of his 'just cause of indignation and displeasure, so ... the world may know and see that [what has been] done [has] just cause and foundation'.[23]

Then Dereham, in the vain hope of mercy, stammered out to his interrogators that Thomas Culpeper had 'succeeded him in the queen's affections'. He also confessed that after being appointed to her Privy Chamber, she had warned him: 'Take heed what words you speak' and had given him a present of cash. This sounds like hush money. Dereham shamefacedly acknowledged boasting that if the king were dead, he would marry Katherine, who had given him 'special favour'.[24]

The timing of his dramatic admission can be established fairly precisely. On 12 November, the Privy Council wrote to Sir William Paget in France, to report 'a most miserable case which lately came to revelation'. Their letter described the Dereham and Monox allegations but mentioned nothing about Culpeper's later carnal activities. It added: 'Now you may see what was done before the marriage. God knows what has been done since, but [Katherine] had already got Dereham into her service and trained him upon occasion [to] send errands and ... to come often to her Privy Chamber.' One of her household, involved in a *ménage à trois* with Katherine and Dereham at Lambeth, had also been called to her room. The Council added pruriently: 'What this pretended [meant], it is easy to be conjectured'.[25]

The same day Norfolk visited Marillac and told him the queen 'had thought that after her free confession, they would not enquire further, but finding the contrary, refuses to eat or drink and weeps and cries like a madwoman, so that they must take away things by which she might hasten her death'. Evidence suggested 'that [the queen] has prostituted herself to seven or eight persons'. The duke spoke 'with tears in his eyes of the king's grief, who loved her much, and the misfortunes of his house in her and Queen Anne, his two nieces'.[26]

Katherine had not reckoned with the persistence of Tudor bureaucracy.

Henry's court was notorious for the promiscuous behaviour of its ladies, but this case struck too close to the crown. Much of what had been uncovered was idle gossip and hearsay, but other evidence already fatally compromised Katherine's reputation as queen or, indeed, a well-born gentlewoman.

Furthermore, the investigators, like questing hounds, sensed that conclusive evidence of the queen's 'incontinence' or adultery would be discovered. Any hopes of mercy she may have clung to, disappeared like a wraith at dawn, when Culpeper confessed that 'he intended and meant to do ill with the queen and [likewise] the queen [was] so minded with him'.[27]

Katherine's confession, with its blatant sins of omission, had become her death warrant.

Dereham's allegations about Culpeper must have emerged late on 11 November or early the next day, as on the 12th, Norfolk visited Marillac a second time and admitted that he had been deceived about how many lovers the queen had taken. Now he knew 'what was much worse'. During the progress to the north, 'she had made acquaintance with a young Gentleman of the King's Chamber named Culpeper who had been with her five or six times in secret and suspect places, [including] Lincoln, where they were closeted together five or six hours'.

Their words, signs and messages indicated that they had been lovers.

A proclamation deprived the queen of her title and announced that she would face the full rigour of the law. Henceforth, she would be known only as plain 'Katherine Howard'.[28]

Her wardrobe was restricted to six French hoods (or head-dresses), edged with goldsmith's work, 'so there be no stone or pearl in the same' and six gowns and the same number of kirtles[29] of satin damask and velvet, again without gems. All her jewels and personal belongings were brought to London.

Eleven Privy Council members, including Cranmer, Gardiner and a thoroughly abashed Norfolk, had questioned the queen at Hampton

Court earlier on 12 November. Katherine acknowledged giving Culpeper presents, but denied 'upon her oath' that Culpeper had ever touched her body, other than her hand.

Lady Jane Rochford had been a lady-in-waiting to Anne of Cleves and had retained this position in Katherine's household. She was thirty-six and was in some financial difficulties as the widow of George Boleyn, the executed brother of Henry's second queen.

She was now portrayed by Katherine as a wicked procuress in her relationship with Culpeper, who ironically may have bribed her chaperone to gain *entrée* to the queen. Lady Rochford many 'times [asked] her to speak with Culpeper, declaring him to bear her goodwill and favour, whereupon [Katherine] did at last [agree] he should speak with her'. She had promised 'that he desired nothing else but to speak with her and she would swear upon a [Bible] he meant nothing but honesty'.

Thereafter, Culpeper talked with the queen an hour or more 'in a little gallery at the stair head at Lincoln when it was late in the night, about ten or eleven of the clock' – then in her bedchamber at Pontefract and in Jane Rochford's chamber at York. She even promised Katherine that when they returned to Greenwich Palace, 'she knew an old kitchen' where the queen 'might well speak' with Culpeper.

Anxious about her reputation, the queen told Lady Rochford: 'Alas madam, this will be spied [discovered] one day and then we shall be all undone,' but her lady replied: 'Fear not, madam, let me alone, I warrant you'.

Katherine protested that she had tried to end this dangerous liaison, telling Culpeper to 'no more trouble me or send [messages] to me'. She called him a 'little sweet fool' when he refused to heed her injunctions. After the investigation began, Lady Rochford advised the queen 'in no way to disclose this matter, saying they would "speak fair to you, use all ways with you, but if you confess, you undo yourself and others. And for my part", said Jane Rochford, "I will never confess it [even if] torn by wild horses." '[30]

The next day, a Sunday, Wriothesley was sent to Hampton Court to dissolve the queen's household. They were assembled in the great chamber and there told 'openly [about the] offences that she had done in misusing her body with certain persons before the king's time'. The secretary then discharged them.[31] Maids of honour were to stay with friends (for questioning) but one, Anne Bassett (rumoured to have enjoyed a casual dalliance with Henry in 1538–9), was to have special provision at the king's cost 'in consideration of the calamity of her friends'.[32]

Katherine Tylney, the queen's companion in those bawdy nights in the girls' bedroom and later one of her ladies, was questioned at Westminster by Wriothesley, fresh from Hampton Court. When the royal party stopped at Lincoln, did Katherine leave her chamber late at night? Where did she go? Who went with her? The scribes' quill pens[33] scribbled away busily as the witness answered. Yes, the 'queen went two nights' to Lady Rochford's chamber which was 'up a little pair of stairs' by the royal bedroom. She and a servant called Margaret Morton accompanied her, but were sent back. Margaret later went up again and came to bed about two in the morning. 'Jesus,' exclaimed Katherine Tylney, 'is not the queen abed yet?' She replied: 'Yes, even now.'[34]

Sir Anthony Browne interrogated Margaret, who claimed that she had 'never mistrusted the queen until at Hatfield [on the way north, on 18 August][35] she saw her look out of her chamber window [at] Mr Culpeper [in such a way] that she thought there was love between them'. The servant also acted as an innocent bearer of messages between Katherine and Culpeper. At Pontefract, 'every night the queen, being alone with Lady Rochford, locked and bolted her chamber door on the inside'.[36]

Culpeper joined Dereham inside the Tower. He described his 'stolen interviews' with the queen at Greenwich Palace, and at other houses during the royal progress – trysts 'contrived' by Jane Rochford, who 'provoked him much to love the queen'.

At each place, Katherine would seek means of discreet entry. Once she feared the king had grown suspicious and had stationed a guard at the back door 'and Lady Rochford made her servant watch in the court [yard] to see if that were so'.

The queen ingenuously worried that the sacrament of confession might reveal all. 'She doubted not that [Culpeper] knew the king was Supreme Head of the church and [she] bade him beware that whenever he went to confession, he should never shrive [confess his sins] of such things as passed betwixt her and him. If he did, surely the king, being Supreme Head of the church, should have knowledge of it.'[37]

Even as Culpeper was being questioned, the goods and chattels in his room at Whitehall were being inventoried by John Gates, brother-in-law of Anthony Denny, an up-and-coming Gentleman of the king's Privy Chamber. As well as bedroom furniture, Gates found two velvet caps given to Culpeper by a doting king. He owed the king and six other courtiers a total of £195 2s 8d (£109,000 at 2019 prices) but was a creditor to others to the tune of £214 18s 1d (£122,000), much of which had been recovered.

Gates' search of Culpeper's chamber was thorough, as befits a man expert in these matters. It must have been in that small room that a letter written by the queen to her lover was discovered, much to the courtier's undisguised delight. It was only 300 words long on a single sheet of paper, but it finally sealed Katherine's grim fate.

It was full of love and tenderness. She had heard that Culpeper was sick, which had 'troubled me very much till such time that I hear from you, praying you to send word how you do. For I never longed so much for [a] thing as I do to see you and to speak with you ... which I trust shall be shortly now [and this] comforts me very much.

'When I think that you shall depart from me again, it makes my heart to die to think ... that I cannot be always in your company ... I ... pray you will come when my lady Rochford is here, for then I shall be best at leisure to be at your commandment ...'

The letter was signed: 'Yours as long as life endures, Katherine.'[38]

Henry must have believed that he was cursed in his wives. This all seemed horribly familiar, coming five and a half years after his second wife Anne Boleyn and her alleged paramours. Then, his love had been transformed into a burning hatred and he revelled in her death, even specially hiring a French executioner to expertly lop off her head with one graceful sweep of a sword. Then, of course, there was Jane Seymour, another wife already lined up, whom he joyfully visited within an hour of Anne's demise.[39]

His response to Katherine Howard's downfall was markedly different, as he lapsed into self-pity and melancholy. The king, said Chapuys, 'has wonderfully felt the case of ... his wife and he has certainly shown greater sorrow and regret at her loss than at the faults, loss or disgrace of his preceding wives.' The king, however, 'does not seem to have any plan of a female friend to fall back upon'.[40]

Anne of Cleves, 'greatly rejoicing at events', moved back to Richmond Palace to be nearer her former husband, perhaps cherishing hopes of a reconciliation with Henry.

Others had the same notion, but they should have been wary of being overheard. Jane Rattsey asked Elizabeth Bassett one day in London: 'What if God worked … to make the lady Anne of Cleves queen again?' Jane added: 'What a man is the king! How many wives will he have?' She was detained and during questioning, explained this was merely an 'idle saying suggested by her friend praising the lady Anne and dispraising the queen that now is'.[41] She ended up in the custody of Lord Chancellor Audley, when she confessed her crimes and 'seemed most sorrowful'.[42]

There was more talk about Anne of Cleves that exasperated the Privy Council, which was trying to focus on resolving the problem of Henry's fifth wife. In early December they heard of scurrilous rumours that the discarded queen 'should be delivered of a fair boy and whose should it be, but the king's majesty and gotten when she was at Hampton Court. [This] most abominable slander … [was] told to [Richard] Taverner, [one of the Clerks] of the Signet, both by his mother-in-law and wife who said she heard it [from] the widow [Frances] Lilgrave, who [in turn] had heard it from old Lady Carew'.[43]

Henry learnt of the gossip and demanded that the Privy Council inquire 'diligently whether Lady Anne … has indeed had any child or no, as is rumoured, for his majesty has been informed that is so indeed'. If that were true, Henry considered her household to be 'in great default' for not telling him.[44]

Of course, there was no truth in the rumour – the alleged confinement turned out to be just a stomach upset – but those involved in spreading such lies paid a heavy penalty. Widow Lilgrave could not remember who had told her this vile 'slander of the king's person' and ended up in the Tower in punishment for her unguarded words. So did Richard Taverner 'both for concealing of the said slanders heard from her and others and reporting also the same himself'.[45]

The Privy Council's attempts to quash this salacious rumour-mongering proved unsuccessful however, as Chapuys reported that Anne 'was known to have gone away [from London] in the family way from the king and had actually been confined [for the birth] this summer. The rumour of [this] confinement, real or supposed, has widely circulated among the people'.[46]

The ambassador of Cleves, with a catastrophically bad sense of timing, raised the futile question of a possible reconciliation between Henry and Anne. His interview with Cranmer was abruptly cut short by the archbishop, saying the matter was 'too important for him to discuss without the king's command'.[47] He persisted in pressing the matter and finally ended up with the bishop of Winchester (remember his quick temper?) who told him 'with every appearance of anger that the king would never take back the lady'.[48]

Jane Rochford joined Katherine's alleged lovers in the Tower. During questioning, she admitted that one night at Lincoln, 'she and the queen were at the back door waiting for Culpeper at eleven o'clock at night, when one of the watch came with a light and locked the door'. Shortly afterwards he came into the queen's apartments 'saying he and his man had picked the lock'. Since the investigation began, Katherine had 'daily asked for Culpeper', saying if her relationship with him became known, 'she feared not'. She firmly believed that he had 'known the queen carnally'.[49]

But on the third day of her incarceration Katherine's chaperone 'went mad, by which her brain was affected'. Chapuys told Charles V that she recovered her reason 'now and then and the king has sent her' into the custody of the wife of John, Lord Russell, the Lord High Admiral. The royal physicians visited her 'desiring her recovery that [Henry] may afterwards have her executed as an example'.[50]

The Spanish ambassador asked Southampton directly what Henry's intentions were about the queen. The Lord Privy Seal believed the king would 'show more patience and mercy than many would think – more than her own relations wished, meaning Norfolk, who said, God knows why, that he wished the queen was burned'.[51]

Henry meanwhile had to suffer Francis I's cloying sympathy about the scandal. The French king felt his grief deeply 'as his own', but 'his good brother should consider that the lightness of women cannot bind the honour of men and that the shame is confined to those who commit the crime'.[52] Those miscreants now faced the grim consequences of their felonies.

On Thursday, 1 December, Sir John Gage, Constable of the Tower, delivered Dereham and Culpeper to London's Guildhall to face trial on charges of high treason. Their twenty-four judges were led by Sir Michael Dormer, Lord Mayor of London, flanked by Lord Chancellor Audley and an uncomfortable Norfolk.[53] The indictment alleged that 'Katherine, Queen of England . . . before the marriage between the king and her, had led an abominable and base, carnal, voluptuous and vicious life, like a common harlot, with [many] persons, as with Francis Dereham of Lambeth and Henry Monox of Streatham, [while] maintaining the outward appearance of chastity and honesty.'

Katherine 'led the king by word and gesture to love her and (believing her to be pure and chaste and free from other matrimonial yoke) arrogantly coupled herself with him in marriage. The said queen and Dereham, being charged . . . with their vicious life, could not deny it, but excused themselves by alleging that they were contracted to each other by marriage . . . [which] contract they had falsely and traitorously concealed from the king . . . to his peril and [that] of his children to be begotten by her, and the damage of the whole realm.' After the marriage to Henry,

> the queen [and Dereham], intending to renew their vicious life . . . practised . . . [his appointment] in the queen's service and [Katherine] had him in notable favour above others and in her secret chamber and other suspect places, spoke with and committed secret affairs to him both by word and writing and for fulfilling of their wicked and traitorous purpose, gave him gifts and sums of money . . .
>
> The queen, not satisfied with her vicious life . . . on 29 August at Pontefract and places before and after with Thomas Culpeper, late of London, one of the Gentlemen of the king's Privy Chamber, falsely and traitorously held illicit meetings and conference to incite Culpeper to have carnal intercourse with her [and] insinuated to him that she loved him above the king and all others. Similarly, Culpeper incited the queen.
>
> And the better and more secretly to pursue their carnal life, they retained Jane Lady Rochford as a go-between to contrive meetings

in the queen's stool chamber [lavatory] and other suspect places and
so the said Jane falsely and traitorously aided and abetted them.[54]

Culpeper and Dereham pleaded not guilty.

'Sufficient and probable' testimony in support of the crown's case
was then delivered. Marillac recognised that it was only presumptive
evidence that supported allegations that Katherine and Dereham continued their affair after she became queen, although she had told Jane
Rochford that if Culpeper would not listen to her, there was 'behind
the door another, who would not ask for a better share' of her favour.

Norfolk behaved strangely during the six-hour trial. 'Even in examining the prisoners, [he] laughed as if he had cause to rejoice. His son,
the earl of Surrey, was also there and the brothers of the queen and
Culpeper rode about the town' in an ostentatious display of bravado.
Their behaviour mystified Maurillac and he sought explanation: 'It is
the custom and must be done to show they did not share the crimes
of their relatives'.[55]

Before the jury retired to reach their verdict, both prisoners changed
their pleas to 'guilty'. Accordingly, they were sentenced to be 'taken
back to the Tower and thence drawn through London to the gallows
at Tyburn and there hanged, cut down alive, disembowelled and (they
still living) their bowels burnt, beheaded and [their bodies] quartered'.[56]

Both were executed on 10 December, but the king offered one last
token of his regard for his former bedfellow Culpeper. By his 'most
gracious determination'[57] his former favourite was, at his petition,
spared the traditional traitor's death, the penalty being commuted to
beheading, although he was still dragged through the streets to Tyburn,
tied to a hurdle.[58] Dereham suffered brutal evisceration, as his sentence
demanded. Both men's heads were then displayed on pikestaffs on
London Bridge.

You will have recognised that much of the evidence supporting these
convictions was circumstantial or mere hearsay, the latter inadmissible
in modern court proceedings. Despite the threat or use of torture to
extract confessions, evidence of adultery between Culpeper and the
queen could not be produced in court. But in Tudor times, this would
not have mattered one jot. Evil thought must trigger treacherous act
and by eradicating this secret malice, the Privy Council believed it was
cutting off the head of the hydra of treason.[59]

Aside from this, Culpeper was a confirmed lecher and the queen was probably as flighty as she had been at Horsham and Lambeth. Just what happened during those nocturnal hours on the royal progress, once even in the cramped and noisome surroundings of the queen's lavatory? How did they pass the time? Card games? Chess? What could they find to talk about for so long? What would that legal talisman, the 'fair-minded citizen', believe to have occurred?

Under today's criminal law, there would have remained 'reasonable doubt' over their guilt. But in civil law, a jury's decision is based on the 'balance of probability' and this criterion might determine that the queen and Culpeper committed adultery, not just once, but on several occasions, amid malicious efforts to preserve the secrecy of their assignations. It is difficult not to believe that Henry was regularly cuckolded.

Culpeper's and Dereham's indictments were derived from the old 1352 Treason Act, coupled with the 1534 Treason Act (bodily harm to the king) or the Second Succession Act 1536 (deeds imperilling the king or his heirs). It may be that subsequent opposition by senior judges may have resulted in Katherine and Lady Rochford being convicted later by parliamentary attainder, instead of facing a trial based on doubtful legality.[60]

Some modern historians have suggested that Katherine was not the silly, capricious and immoral bimbo of more traditional opinion, but a naive girl who was subjected to serial sexual abuse. In their view, she fell into the hands of depraved predators and consequently, had behaved like many such tragic victims who, suffering from low self-esteem, felt driven to appease her abusers. Dereham and Culpeper may have blackmailed her into paying money, or providing expensive gifts, as a price for their silence over her past. The payments to Dereham, for example, hint of the queen's fears about her vulnerability. Additionally, she could have been coerced by the fear of exposure into granting anew her sexual favours.

Looking back almost five centuries, it may be problematic to apply the moral values and behavioural codes of modern society to those of the Tudors. This was an age when, under the thirteenth-century Statutes of Westminster, it was socially acceptable (and normal) for men to have intercourse with young girls. Those aged twelve could marry and sixteen was regarded as the appropriate age to begin childbearing, although Margaret Beaufort, Henry VIII's grandmother, experienced the dangerous birth of her son at thirteen. It was not until 1576 that legislation made sex with girls under ten a felony and a misdemeanour, if committed with those aged between ten and twelve. The Criminal Law Amendment Act of 1885 raised the age of consent to sixteen.

Equality of the sexes would be an alien concept in Tudor society. Moreover, in the mid-sixteenth century, women (believed to be influenced by the devil), were deprecated as more lustful than the men they inflamed. Married women would be fatally dishonoured if they secretly met men other than their spouses.

Today, we rightly throw our hands up in horror at such social norms, but that is the way it was in Tudor England. If all the facts were known to them, would Katherine be seen as a victim by her contemporaries, or the 'common harlot' of Culpeper and Dereham's indictment? Their answer was probably the latter.

Katherine's uncle, the duke of Norfolk was meanwhile in a much-deserved tight spot. He confided to Marillac that those 'who were jealous of him' at court had denounced him to the king 'as wishing to embrace all great affairs of state'. To avoid such suspicions 'especially at the time of this trouble', Norfolk dared 'not do all the good offices he intended'.[61]

Then his family became engulfed by this royal cause célèbre. The dowager duchess, Lord William Howard and his wife Margaret (who had returned to England eight days before) and Norfolk's sister Katherine, Lady Bridgewater, were among those arrested, on suspicion that they knew of Katherine and Dereham's 'naughtiness' but failed to disclose it. Lord William 'stood as stiff as his mother and made himself most clear from all kinds of mistrust or suspicion', Wriothesley declared after his arrest. 'I did not much like his fashion.'[62]

The intake of noble prisoners caused problems at the Tower. Its lieutenant warned the Privy Council there were not enough rooms 'to lodge them severally' unless the royal apartments in the White Tower were opened up. Henry agreed to this but 'could not remember [where] he had a double key' to these quarters, so all the locks had to be changed.[63]

Norfolk was a survivor in the cut-and-thrust politics of Henry's court. The moment had come to abandon his family to save his own neck. Soon after Culpeper and Dereham's trial, he departed London for his seventy-room palace at Kenninghall, a village midway between Thetford and Norwich, well away from his family's torments. Chapuys observed: 'It is presumed that he did not go of his own free will, but was sent on some pretence or other, to have him away from the Privy Council, now that business touching his own family must necessarily be discussed'.[64] Marillac believed that the duke faced disgrace. 'Of his future, many presume ill and none good. It looks as if the end of these tragedies will not be scandalous but pitiful.'[65]

With the objective of living to fight another day, on 15 December, Norfolk 'scribbled' an ingratiating, obsequious letter to his sovereign lord, while 'prostrate and most humble' at his feet:

> Yesterday [it] came to my knowledge that my own ungracious [step] mother, my unhappy brother and his wife, with my lewd sister of Bridgewater, were committed to the Tower.
>
> By long experience, knowing your accustomed equity and justice used to all your subjects, [I] am sure [this was] done but for some [of] their [faults] and traitorous proceedings against your royal majesty.
>
> Which, revolving in my mind, with also the most abominable deeds done by two of my nieces against your highness has brought me to [the] greatest perplexity that ever [a] poor wretch was in. [I] fear that your majesty, having so often and by so many of my kin been thus falsely and traitorously handled, might not only conserve a displeasure in your heart against me and all other of that kind but also . . . abhor to hear speak of the same.

Searching desperately for some much-needed kudos, the duke now sought to win credit for the discovery of his own family's crimes against the crown. He reminded Henry that much of what had come to light was contained in his own report after searching Dereham's coffers at Lambeth. The dowager duchess, as well as his 'two traitorous nieces', had not shown him any love and this rancour, together with his honest endeavours in the matter, provided 'hope that your highness will not conserve any displeasure in your most gentle heart against me'.

Still 'prostrate at your royal feet [and] most humble', Norfolk pleaded with Henry to tell him 'plainly' how 'your highness do weigh your favour towards me'. He assured the king: 'Unless I know your majesty [continues] my good and gracious lord as you were before their offences [were] committed, I shall never desire to live in this world any longer but [would] shortly... finish this transitory life, as God knows, who sends your majesty the accomplishments of your most noble heart's desires.' The two-page letter was signed 'Your most humble servant. T. Norfolk'.[66]

There are no signs of careful drafting in this letter. The duke's words spill off the pages, pleading, beseeching and grovelling for mercy, the appeals of a desperate man in jeopardy of losing everything he most cherished. In Norfolk's mind, the imprisonment or possible death of his immediate family mattered less than his own survival and another chance to achieve his ambitions at court.

On 22 December, Lord William Howard came to trial, pleading not guilty to knowing of the queen's misconduct, but falsely concealing it. He changed his plea after the evidence was produced and was sentenced to perpetual imprisonment and forfeiture of his goods. Some of the smaller fry – Katherine Tyler, Joan Bulmer and seven Howard servants, were similarly sentenced. Eventually, thirteen members of the Howard family would be thrown into jail for misprision.

Norfolk returned to the Howard house at Lambeth at the turn of the year, amid continuing doubts about his future. He had been ordered 'not to quit it or attend the Privy Council until the queen's case be investigated'.[67] But later, he returned to court 'apparently in his full former credit and authority'.[68]

There was speculation about the fate of the pugilistic dowager duchess of Norfolk. Marillac reported that 'some say she will die, others that she shall keep perpetual prison like her son Lord William. All her goods are already confiscated and are of marvellous value, 400,000 or 500,000 crowns, for ladies in this country succeed for life to the moveables of their deceased husbands. Norfolk is greatly interested, since the greater part came to her through his late father, yet the times are such that he dare not show that the affair touches him, but approves all that is done.'[69]

Parliament began a new session on Monday, 16 January 1542 and was addressed by Lord Chancellor Audley. He apparently did not mention the queen by name[70] but he did want to make one important point. 'An injury received from a friend or a familiar is heavier than one from an open enemy or an unknown person and for this reason, the crime of high treason ought to be more heavily punished.'

On the following Saturday, a Bill of Attainder was introduced into the House of Lords against Katherine, listing her heinous crimes. The dowager duchess and Lady Bridgewater also stood indicted for misprision of treason, and were condemned to perpetual imprisonment and forfeiture of their property and goods. To 'avoid doubts in the future', the attainder also contained clauses declaring that 'any lightness of body' of [future] queens must be revealed to the king and Privy Council within twenty days of acquiring that knowledge, on pain of prosecution for misprision of high treason. Furthermore, anyone inciting another to have 'carnal knowledge' of the queen consort or the wife of the monarch's son, 'shall henceforth die' for treason. Finally, 'an unchaste woman [who dared] to marry the king' and concealed her promiscuity 'shall also be guilty of high treason'.[71] Henry's successors, in their search for virgin brides, may well have cursed that clause in the centuries to come.

Given the king's anxiety for a swift end to his marriage, it is surprising that the Bill sank without trace for a week. Audley told the peers on 28 January not to make too hasty a judgement on a matter of such gravity. The queen should be given an opportunity to clear her name in a meeting with a small delegation, who might be able to calm 'her womanish fears'. Katherine was none too keen to explain herself, although she eventually met a small committee and acknowledged her great crime against her monarch. Henry urged both Lords and Commons to be unanimous in their verdict.[72]

By Saturday, 11 February, the Bill of Attainder had been passed and received royal assent,[73] not, as usual, by the king in Parliament, but *in absentia*, by letters patent under the Great Seal of England. This procedure was charitably introduced for the first time to spare the king further distress by having to hear recited the 'sorrowful story and wicked facts' and because his presence in the Parliament House 'might reopen a wound already closing in the royal bosom'.[74] Henry politely thanked the Commons who had 'taken his sorrow to be theirs'.[75]

Letters patent were also employed to give royal assent to a second Bill, introduced on 4 February, to inflict capital punishment on those 'who after the accusation, examination and confession or conviction of treason shall happen to fall mad or lunatic'. In such cases, four of the king's council could testify that such persons 'at the time of doing their treason and at the time of their accusation ... were of good, perfect and whole memory' and thus faced the penalty for treason, if found guilty.[76]

This legislation was intended to legalise the execution of Jane Rochford, still raving and gibbering within the Tower. Henry might have enjoyed absolute rule as a monarch and be able to act imperiously without parliamentary approval, but he knew his history of England and valued her traditions and framework of laws. He was always careful to attempt nothing that superficially seemed illegal, but if a law was troublesome, he had it changed, or wrote a new one to fit his purpose; just one of the many conveniences of being a despot.

On 29 January, Chapuys reported the queen, still at Syon, to be 'making good cheer, fatter and more handsome than ever she was, taking great care of her person, well dressed and more adorned [with jewels], more imperious and commanding and more difficult to please than ever she was when living with the king. She believes her end will be on the scaffold, for she owns she has deserved death. Her only prayer is that her execution be in secret rather than in public'.[77]

Henry meanwhile was busily checking the inventory of the queen's jewels. He posted off some of his Privy Councillors to Anne of Cleves to reclaim a ring given to her by Katherine. It was not jewellery of high value – worth three gold crowns at most – but a stone in its setting was said have magical powers to protect against spasms.[78]

The king wasted no time in disposing of his troublesome young wife. On the afternoon of Friday, 10 February, Katherine was moved from Syon, downriver to the Tower, for her execution.

The cold light of reality – the horror of what was to come – finally hit her like a douche of icy water and she panicked, resisted and had to be dragged, screaming, into a small covered barge, manned by four oarsmen. Four ladies attended her on this last passage down the Thames.

The queen's boat was escorted by a larger vessel carrying the duke of Suffolk and a troop of soldiers, with Southampton and other Privy Councillors travelling in a third. This sombre little procession must have shot the narrows between the piers of London Bridge in the fading light of that grim afternoon and one can only hope that Katherine looked away quickly to avoid seeing the impaled heads of her lovers displayed above.

A few minutes later, resplendent in mourning black velvet, she stepped ashore at Traitor's Gate, those around her paying 'as much honour as when she was queen' before being taken to the comfort of the royal apartments inside the fortress.

On the evening of Sunday, 12 February 1542, Katherine was told to prepare herself for death 'by disposing her soul', as she would be beheaded the next day. That night, with a morbid curiosity, she asked to see the executioner's wooden block, 'pretending that she wanted to know how she was to place her head on it. This was granted and the block being brought in, she herself tried and placed her head on it by way of experiment', reported an astonished Chapuys.[79]

At seven o'clock the next morning, the disgraced queen was escorted to the small green within the Tower where Anne Boleyn had been beheaded six years before. Before her was a black-painted scaffold, its planks covered with a copious layer of straw to soak up her blood. In the small crowd watching, she must have recognised her cousin Henry Howard, earl of Surrey, come to see the final demise of his father's dreams and machinations. Suffolk was away sick and Norfolk must have considered it more prudent to stay away.

Marillac told the French king that Katherine was 'so weak that she could hardly speak but confessed in a few words that she had merited a hundred deaths for so offending the king who had so graciously treated her'.[80]

With one blow from the axe, her giddy head was severed cleanly from her young body.

Her corpse was wrapped up in a black cloak by her ladies, placed in a plain, rough coffin and carried the few yards to the church of St Peter ad Vincula, inside the Tower's walls. There Henry's fifth queen was buried before the altar, a few feet away from the grave of his second.[81] Two Howard cousins lie together who lived, loved and died as his queens.

Lady Rochford knelt to pray on the bloodstained straw. Her madness had deserted her immediately she learnt of her impending execution. She stood and recited 'a long discourse' of 'several faults she had committed in her life'. She too was beheaded with one blow of the axe and was buried alongside her mistress.

Among the silent crowd was the prosperous merchant Otwell

Johnson, who next day reported on the executions to his brother in Calais: 'I saw the queen and Lady Rochford suffer... whose souls (I doubt not) be with God, for they made most godly and Christian ends that ever was heard tell, since the world's creation.' They had spoken of 'their lively faith in the Blood of Christ... and with goodly words and steadfast countenances, desired all Christian people to take regard of their worthy and just punishment... against God heinously from their youth, in breaking all His commandments and also against the king's royal majesty very dangerously'.[82]

The king claimed to be always aware of the need 'to do justly... have mercy and walk humbly with thy God'. Accordingly, he suddenly decided to release Arthur Plantagenet, viscount Lisle, who had been incarcerated in a narrow little room in the Tower since his arrest for treason during Cromwell's last struggle for power in May 1540.

Lisle's Garter insignia had been returned to him in January but on 2 March 1542, Wriothesley arrived with the happy news that he was a free man, carrying 'a ring bearing a rich diamond' as a goodwill token from the king. He told him to be 'of good cheer, as it was proved he was void of any offence'. The excitement and rejoicing caused by this announcement unfortunately triggered a massive heart attack and Lisle died the following night.[83] His wife Honor (she of the powerful diuretic) was left 'distraught of mind' at his death, and died, still insane, in Cornwall in 1566.

The dowager duchess of Norfolk and Lord William Howard were eventually freed in August 1542 after Henry finally came to believe they had learnt a hard lesson.

His unhappy queen dispatched, the king's spirits seemingly improved.

During the last three days before Lent there was much feasting at Henry's court. A banquet was arranged for its ladies and in preparation, the king 'did nothing but go from room to room to order lodgings to be prepared for these ladies', wrote Chapuys.

It was all of 'great and hearty cheer' but the ambassador doubted that any lady would want to take on the dangerous duty of being Henry Tudor's next queen, particularly in the light of the new legal requirement for chastity and virginity.

'Few, if any, ladies at court nowadays [are] likely to aspire to such an honour of becoming one of the king's wives or to desire that the choice should fall upon them,' he reported wryly.[84]

6

The 'Rough Wooing' of Scotland

Amid all the furore about the fate of Queen Katherine Howard, a pro-clamation was published on 23 January 1542, declaring that Henry VIII had graciously consented to add 'King of Ireland' to his Imperial style and title, for the greater tranquillity of that island 'and at the instant request of his subjects there'.[1] An Irish parliamentary Act decreed it would be high treason to disturb or interrupt the dignity of 'his crown of Ireland . . . as united and knit to the imperial crown of England'.[2]

There must have long been debate about the Irish crown, as suggested by a curious document, its contents half-legend, half-legal statement. This listed Henry's seven separate lawful titles to his suzerainty over the troublesome Irish, derived from ancient chronicles. It claimed that the Irish race had originated in 'Bayon' (Bayonne in Gascony), part of the lordship of 'King Burgomyn . . . king of Britain, which is now called England'. Henry's claim to the French throne implied that he remained lord of Bayonne and, therefore, the Irish 'should be his men and Ireland his land'.

Apart from evidence based on fictitious British kings, there was a more tangible precedent supporting the king's right to sovereignty over Ireland. The Irish chiefs had submitted to his predecessors Henry II and Richard II. Furthermore, Pope Adrian IV – the only Englishman thus far to wear the papal tiara – had published a Bull in 1155 granting the lordship of Ireland to Henry II 'to increase the Christian faith and holi-ness and to set the people . . . in governance of good laws and virtues, [their] vices to eschew'. This had been confirmed by Adrian's successor Pope Alexander III in 1172. After listing Henry VIII's other claims, the document concluded: 'Therefore, from the beginning to the end, good is our king's right to the lordship of Ireland and therefore, hold them [in] shame that will say the contrary.'[3]

The Irish proclamation had followed the imposition of English laws and justice in Wales in 1536,[4] an administrative measure that transformed the Welsh into English subjects in everything but name. Seven years later, another Act established Welsh counties and redrew parliamentary representation in Wales.[5] Was the king implementing a master plan to unite the British Isles into one sovereign entity, with the crowns of all three kingdoms worn by Henry and his Tudor successors? Was Scotland his next target to achieve an ambition to become the first British *Rex et Imperator*, more than 250 years before the Act of Union[6] was passed, creating the United Kingdom?

In 1512, three years after Henry's succession, the English claim of feudal lordship over Scotland, dormant since 1482, was reasserted in an attempt to intimidate the Scots into keeping England's northern frontier quiet while the king invaded France.[7] This attempt at coercion proved fruitless and the Scots army rampaged across the border the following year, only to be humiliatingly routed at Flodden. In 1523, Thomas Cromwell, as a tyro Member of Parliament, had argued that Henry 'should join the same realm unto his, so that both they and we might live under one... law and policy for ever'.[8] His foresight was ignored and the English claim on the Scottish crown forgotten.

Forging a dynastic union with his neighbour reappeared as an important ambition on the king's agenda in the early 1540s.[9] After all, his eldest sister Margaret had been queen of Scotland[10] and her surviving son, James V, born in April 1512, was now king and these family ties encouraged hopes that he could annex his nephew's kingdom.[11]

Scotland had proved an irritating and painful thorn in his side throughout his reign. There was the dangerous 'Auld Alliance', the Scots' mutual defence treaty with France of 1295, renewed in 1492 and again in 1512. Before the birth of Prince Edward, Henry was also troubled by fears that James himself might claim the throne of England after his death. His anxieties were increased by pernicious Scottish proposals in 1524 that their young monarch be declared Prince of Wales and granted royal lands in England. Henry angrily dismissed this plan as 'haughty and covetous'.[12]

It was not as though James had displayed much interest in diplomacy as a youthful king. He had sired nine illegitimate children in his lifetime (all by different mothers), at least three of them before he was twenty. Perhaps he should not be overly blamed for his overactive libido. Early in his reign, he was said to have been encouraged in his amorous adventures by his guardian, Archibald Douglas, sixth earl of Angus, to distract him from meddling in Scottish politics.[13]

Scotland remained firmly closeted in the French sphere of influence, with James marrying Francis I's consumptive daughter Madeleine on New Year's Day in 1537. After her death, seven months' later, he agreed to wed the tall, voluptuous widow Mary of Guise.[14] Henry found this second marriage particularly galling because Mary was briefly his most fancied candidate for a bride after the death of Queen Jane Seymour, as 'he was big in person and had need of a big wife'.[15] He ended up, of course, with Anne of Cleves.

Then there was the problem of Scotland's resolute adherence to the Catholic faith. In 1537, James had received a consecrated cap and sword from Pope Paul III and been encouraged to root out all heresy. One of the Scottish king's chief advisers, Cardinal David Beaton, archbishop of St Andrews, had enthusiastically followed papal instructions to rally James against the heretic Henry VIII. Hence the repeated failure of English demands for the repatriation of rebels and criminals, as required by the preposterously named Anglo-Scottish Treaty of Perpetual Peace of 1534.[16] James had told Henry in March 1541 that he could not repatriate good Catholics as he knew they would be persecuted.[17]

Finally, James V's apparent snub of his 'dearest and well-beloved uncle' in not turning up for the summit meeting at York in 1541 still rankled with Henry. There are many theories about why James did not journey south. His two sons had died in infancy within hours of each other in May and the Scottish crown appeared vulnerable. It is suggested, for example, that his council would not allow him to travel because of fears that he would be made hostage. Henry had apparently conceived an audacious plan to kidnap his nephew on Scottish soil and carry him off to London and English servitude.[18]

It seems astonishing that a Christian king, professing himself an enlightened Renaissance prince, might conspire to abduct a brother monarch (and kith and kin) but Henry was no respecter of tiresome diplomatic protocol, or accepted standards of kingly comportment. To him, the end always justified the means, however unorthodox and contrary to civilised behaviour. The plot, if plot there was, symbolises the rank deceit, malice and perfidy that darkened much of his dealings with the Scots – his 'rough wooing' to persuade them to come to heel, on his terms. So the rumoured threat of kidnapping might well have shaped James's decision to stay at home.

The more likely reason for James's absence was more mundane. The Scottish king had promised Francis I that he would not meet his uncle as this 'could never be to his honour'. He knew if Henry wanted to invade Scotland, the French king would then declare him his 'incontinent enemy and [would] use all his forces against him'.[19]

Henry's wrath and humiliation at being stood up by his nephew at York was made more galling by reports of a Scots raid sixteen miles (26km) into England on 20 September 1541, killing seven Englishmen, burning a house and stealing cattle. The king told Sir William Eure, governor of the frontier town and fortress of Berwick upon Tweed, that he took this incursion 'in most displeasant part, [particularly] for that they have lately pretended a fervent love and amity towards Us'. The Scots might not 'desist until they feel the smart of their doings', he added ominously.[20] All Scots living in the county of Northumberland were forcibly repatriated.[21]

Brimful of righteous indignation, Henry complained to James about the raid that showed 'an open hostility between us, which is greatly to Our marvel, [rather] than ... friendship as you have lately expressed. Wherefore dearest brother ... We require you to cause speedy redress to be made, as the lack thereof should [make] Us enforce by other means to provide that Our subjects and country should not be misused'.[22] A month later, the Scottish king belatedly replied, promising that 'sharp charge' had been given to his officials to pay compensation and bring the miscreants to justice. Then it was his turn to complain about border incidents: 'Your subjects in great number have come within Our realm, raised fire and made much slaughter.' After the customary tit-for-tat demand for redress and punishment, James pledged that his ambassadors would convey his thoughts on the border and 'other matters' after their arrival in England.[23]

Raids in search of booty were part of the warp and weft of life on the frontier between England and Scotland. Cattle stealing had formed an important slice of the local economy for both sides since time immemorial. As a consequence, fortified 'Pele' towers, used as look-out points or places of refuge, had dotted the border country since about 1200.

These border tensions, however, could provide a convenient excuse to deliver a knock-out blow to the Scottish army, or at least, by employing fire and devastation, teach this unruly nation a brutal lesson that it was unwise to meddle lightly with Henry VIII.

Diplomacy still had some minor role to play. The king wanted to demonstrate publicly that he was prepared to negotiate a peace with Francis I – while simultaneously and duplicitously seeking an ally for an invasion of France.

On 29 January 1542, wise old Eustace Chapuys reported to Charles V that Henry wished 'a closer alliance with Your Imperial Majesty, which he has more or less urgently solicited at various times'. But he warned:

> It seems to me as if the chief cause for this king's urgent solicitations is [nothing] other than his jealousy of the king of France, and the fear he has of Your Imperial Majesty becoming the latter's friend and ally.
>
> All his efforts have been, and are still, directed towards sowing discord and mistrust between you two, so that you may never realise that union and alliance of which he is mostly afraid ... Should [war] break out between you two, his plan is to temporise with each of the belligerents, and deceive you both with fine words, until, when you are tired and exhausted by the contest, he may reap greater advantage.
>
> [By staying neutral, Henry would avoid expense] ... which is what he dislikes most nowadays – and then will play his cards to advantage and profit by the game.[24]

Chapuys' cynicism was entirely justified.

For some months, there had been much diplomatic toing and froing over proposals for the marriage of Henry's eldest daughter Mary to Francis I's favourite son, Charles, duc d'Orléans, now second-in-line to the French crown after the death of the Dauphin Francis in 1536. Such a union would forge an Anglo-French alliance that could pour oil on the troubled waters of Scotland. Twenty-year-old Charles was handsome, extravagant, frivolous and fond of practical jokes. His only physical drawback was the blindness in one eye, caused by smallpox. However, matters were complicated by French attempts to marry Charles off to Maria of Spain, the fourteen-year-old daughter of Charles V, again for diplomatic advantage, offering to renounce claims to Milan and Savoy[25] if the wedding went ahead. Once married, they could inherit the Netherlands, Burgundy and Charolais.[26]

The negotiations between England and France over the marriage began with discreet inquiries about Mary's prospects for healthy child-bearing and continued in earnest early in 1542. They immediately hit the stumbling block of Mary's illegitimacy, as declared by Henry's Acts of Succession. Marillac was the luckless ambassador charged with the detailed discussions. The first meeting was hardly propitious; the English delegates waxed so lyrically about the honour of taking part in the proceedings, that the envoy 'might have been lulled to sleep' by their tedious ramblings.

The second day also failed to achieve anything substantive, as Marillac's formal authorisation mentioned Mary's illegitimacy. This should be struck out, the English insisted, as 'by Act of Parliament, it was treason for them to confess her legitimate'. If that word was erased, they could discuss the marriage terms 'and then speak of the illegitimacy. Otherwise, they could not proceed.'

After some delay, Henry agreed that negotiations could continue if the word '*légitime*' was struck out in Marillac's diplomatic papers, but it would be absolute anathema for the annulment of his first marriage to Katherine of Aragon to be questioned. When all else was agreed, he 'would declare his intention upon this and would do much for Francis' for whom he had 'most affection' in all the world.[27] For his part, the French king, who understood the most persuasive arguments to use with Henry, promised full payment of all the arrears of cash due him under treaty, together with a 'large dowry assigned' to Princess Mary for life 'to the perpetual extinction of the [king's] pensions and arrears' owed him by the French.[28]

But this tempting offer and Mary's marriage to the playful French prince came to nought. The princess, six years older than her would-be bridegroom, was an expendable pawn in a game of farcical diplomatic posturing. Mary understood this and confided to one of her ladies that 'it was folly to think that they would marry her out of England, as long as her father lived'. She would remain 'only Lady Mary, the most unhappy lady in Christendom'.[29]

How right she was. Her devious father was conspiring concurrently with Charles V for an alliance with Spain that would launch a joint offensive against France.

The emperor, fearing his diplomatic couriers could be intercepted in France, sent instructions to Chapuys by sea, carried by 'a discreet and trusty person, with particular orders that should he be in danger of being taken prisoner, he is to cast all the papers into the sea, so that they should not fall into the enemy's hands'.[30] He hastily sent another note that same day, authorising his ambassador to show his first letter to Henry or his Privy Councillors, but not to let it out of his hands 'for fear of the English turning it to their profit with the French, or Francis saying that we were first to break the truce and contravene the treaties between us'.[31]

Marillac, impatient at the delays and impediments in arranging Mary's marriage, was becoming suspicious about Henry's true intentions. There were, he told Francis, some worrying straws in the wind that suggested 'that war is to be guarded against'.

Norfolk remained in disfavour in April 1542. He had spent some months 'languishing' at Kenninghall, being 'very ill in body, besides being mentally worried'. Now, he rose phoenix-like from the ashes of his family's disgrace.

By June, Marillac reported that he was 'so received and caressed, that presumably there is need of him. To lead a host, there is no person in England like him' and army veterans had been calling at his Lambeth home, 'reckoning to be soon employed'. Besides, 'ten great ships of war' were being equipped with artillery and munitions and 'nothing is done in the Tower [of London] but dress bows, iron arrows and pikes, mount artillery [and] prepare wagons'. Money was being coined 'day and night' from the gold and silver spoils from the dissolved abbeys.[32]

That month, Henry sent Thomas Thirlby, bishop of the new diocese of Westminster,[33] as an emissary to Charles V to finalise plans for an invasion of France by English and Imperial forces in 1543. In his pouch was the draft of an Anglo-Spanish treaty, envisaging each nation's invasion force to number at least 25,000 men 'for the honour of the same and terror of the enemy'.[34]

On 4 July 1542, Francis declared war on Charles V over their conflicting claims to the duchy of Milan, exacerbated by the French king's anger over the murder of one of his ambassadors at Pavia, Lombardy, by Imperial troops. France's 'Most Christian King' also now had an unlikely ally in Suleiman I of the Ottoman Empire.

Throughout that spring and summer, the English tried to provoke the Scottish king into taking military action, but he procrastinated, hoping that the cross-border wrangling could continue until the onset of winter, when bad weather would rule out an English invasion.[35]

In late August, Henry heard that Scottish forces were being moved closer to the border, as if James V 'minded some sudden exploit'. Urging vigilance against any incursion, he ordered the garrisons at Berwick and Carlisle to be reinforced 'to cut off the Scots from their victuals and keep them waking by nightly alarms'. The militia near the borders should be ready to march 'at an hour's warning' and if the Scots entered England, 'some men should be sent to unguarded places in Scotland to burn, spoil and destroy all they possibly can'.[36] The Privy Council that day ordered the shipment to Berwick of 1,500 longbows, 300 hackbuts,[37] and 1,000 sheaves of arrows, 3,000 bills and gunpowder for artillery and hand-guns.[38]

Henry fired off another threatening letter on 23 August to James V, expressing mystification at 'the great attempts and entry into Our realm' by Scottish marauders. The king was convinced this latest incursion did not demonstrate his deceit – 'you being a prince of honour' – but believed it was instigated by the 'evil disposed minds' of some Scottish councillors, according to 'certain letters sent from some of them which, by chance, have come [into] Our hands'. It would be more convenient to all parties, if his subjects and councillors followed his declared policy of friendship with England, Henry added tartly. If this was not to be, there was 'a short and speedy remedy provided in this matter between us'.[39]

The time for polite diplomatic exchanges had ended. Even as this letter was heading post-haste to Scotland, Henry recalled Norfolk to the colours. The duke was appointed 'Lieutenant and Captain-General of the North', charged with not only 'defend[ing] his majesty's realm ... but also invad[ing] ... Scotland'. He was to tarry [there] for the most annoyance of the Scots, for the destruction of their country, [and] to give them battle'. Norfolk's commission was to be written 'by some very honest man, sworn to secrecy'.[40]

But the Scots struck first, inflicting a small-scale, yet humiliating, defeat on the English, almost by accident. Sir Robert Bowes, Vice-Warden of the Middle March, had been ordered to guard the border, not to initiate hostilities. However, the temptation of plunder proved too compelling and he launched a foray into the Scottish border country. On 24 August 1542, his 3,000 troops were ambushed at Haddon Rig, three miles (5km) from Kelso, by a smaller Scottish force under Sir Walter Lyndsay.[41] After being more concerned to protect their captured livestock than fight a set-piece action, the English broke and around 500 prisoners were taken in the rout, including Bowes and his brother.

After all Henry's threatening bluster, this was insufferable and vengeance was demanded. Scotland had meddled 'with the most noble prince and father of wisdom of all the world' who would not 'be trifled with'.[42] His, and England's, dishonour must be purged by the copious shedding of Scottish blood. Norfolk was sent north to the borders, gathering troops on the way, his efforts galvanised by the king's fresh fury over the murder of two of his heralds returning from the Scottish court. These 'abominable and so barbarous' murders, he fumed, were an outrage on civilised society.[43]

James V's ambassadors arrived in York for negotiations in mid-September. Marillac believed the conference was little more than an English sham: 'By the preparations they have made secretly, it is plain enough that they go more with the intention of displaying their ensigns in war than telling their opinions in a friendly council.' Before departing to the meeting, a Scottish diplomat in London had seen 'great preparations' for war which 'quite frightened him'.[44]

Henry demanded that the Scottish envoys immediately pledge that James would come to London or York at Christmas to sign a new treaty of friendship. His queen's latest pregnancy would not be accepted as an excuse for delay – a date should be set 'without ifs or ands of his wife, considering the common error of women in reckoning their time'. English prisoners held in Scotland must also be released forthwith.

'If, on the other hand, they will not fully agree, but seek new delays, you shall assemble the army and set forward' into Scotland, he instructed his representatives in York. The English force should undertake 'some notable exploit', burning and pillaging the Scottish borders, while his warships should sail to Orkney and Shetland and 'devastate the corn and cattle there'. The Scots should pay for their faults 'and make Us think your pains and Our money well employed'.[45] But the Scots still prevaricated and six days later, the English army was mobilised.

Norfolk could never be described as a sunny general, happy in his work. Charisma was unaccountably missing from his personality and he did not suffer fools gladly. He also was an unlucky military commander, as events in Scotland and later in France were to prove. His letters in both campaigns are full of complaints, gripes and grievances, which must have proved extremely tedious reading for officials in London.

There were undoubted shortcomings in logistical support for his hastily assembled army, but the duke's dispatches suggest not only anger and impatience over poor planning but also an instinctive desire to create excuses to vindicate any future failure on his part. Such anxiety was born out of his bitter experience of Henry's unpredictable temper and the certain knowledge that Norfolk's many enemies at court would be only too pleased to point accusing fingers at him for military blunders.

Shortages of beer loomed large in his mind – more important than it sounds, because in Tudor times, drinking water was frequently contaminated and likely to cause a dysentery outbreak that could incapacitate the troops. To avoid such infection, soldiers drank low-alcohol 'small beer' instead of water, transported in 'tuns' or barrels.[46] The duke told the Privy Council: 'I wrote . . . to send 1,000 tuns of beer to Berwick and also wrote to Sir George Lawson [Treasurer of Berwick] to [discover] what he could [supply]. His answer shows that he could do nothing towards furnishing so great an army for eight days going towards Edinburgh. Hull and York should be written to, [and told] to brew as much as they can.'[47]

Norfolk's misgivings about the expedition were not eased by more bad news from Lawson a week later. 'There are no tents or pavilions within this town, nor elsewhere that I know in these parts,' he reported. It was impossible to bake the required quantities of bread in time for the army's arrival. He hoped to 'provide forty or fifty bullocks and 100 wethers [castrated rams] against your coming', and had set 'workmen to prepare 100 spears in readiness and have sent to Newcastle for the making of spearheads with all speed'.[48]

One hundred spears do not equip an army. It was all far too little and threatened to be far too late. Exasperated, Norfolk and Sir Anthony Browne, Master of the Horse, pausing at York on their way north, decided to speak frankly about the lack of means to feed and arm their troops. They told the Privy Council on 20 September that scarcely any food from East Anglia and London had arrived in Berwick – one ship en route with a cargo of malt sank at Hartlepool – and the navy's warships were delayed by bad weather in the North Sea. 'My Lord Privy Seal [Sir William Fitzwilliam, earl of Southampton] ... has been ill all night, which we think is for melancholy, because the victual ships are not arrived. We are likely to lack bread and drink at Berwick for lack of foists [large casks] and mills to grind wheat.'

Despite all these adversities, the king's generals wisely sweetened their dismal news with a pledge of their own fortitude: 'It is impossible to invade Scotland or ever pass Newcastle without victuals, although never men would more gladly accomplish the intended journey than we would.'[49]

Henry was daily becoming restless and ever more cantankerous over the delays in launching military operations against Scotland. He was astonished that his artillery had not yet arrived at Berwick, but nurtured forlorn hopes that 'God will frame things prosperously in time'. He was irritated that his advisers had urged the abandonment of plans to lay waste to the northern isles. 'Shetland is so distant that Englishmen who go yearly to Iceland dare not tarry on these coasts after St James' tide [25 July]. They must pass through the Pentland Firth, the most dangerous place in Christendom and Scottish men who know it best, dare not pass it at this season. Orkney is also very dangerous and full of rocks. The people live by fishing and have little to devastate save oats and a few beasts, which are so wild that they can only be taken by dogs.'[50] No 'shock and awe' military operations there then.

To Henry, Scotland was a heather-covered land of mystery. He knew little of its mountains, rivers, roads, castles and towns and failed to understand its people, culture or society. One of his doctors, the Scot Walter Cromer, was seconded from his medical duties to brief the king on his country's topography. Conveniently, he possessed a map of Scotland to assist him in this royal geography lesson. Another Scottish doctor, banished by Cardinal Beaton for his Protestant beliefs and exiled in London, was also asked to draw a more detailed map or 'platte'.[51] One doubts whether Henry was a receptive pupil.

The king was also enraged that the Scottish ambassadors had finally agreed that James would meet his uncle at York on 15 January next, with the significant proviso that 'we have ample safe conduct' under Henry's Great Seal. They also promised that the 'English gentlemen who are prisoners in Scotland shall be delivered, ransom free'. However, their horses and equipment could not be returned 'because in the ruffle [at Haddon Rig] these were carried off by Englishmen of Tynedale and Redesdale as [well] as by Scotsmen'.[52]

Henry was not to be diverted from vengeance. The Scottish concessions were dismissed as mere 'accustomed dissimulation' and despite his 'natural inclination to avoid war with his nephew', he told his representatives not to agree to anything until his 'notable exploit to purge the dishonour which the Scots caused his realm' had been successfully completed.

A formal declaration of war was unnecessary, as the Scots had been told of the 'readiness' of the English army, 'yet for declaration of the matter to the world, a proclamation shall be devised containing such causes, as for the king's honour, shall be thought convenient'.[53] Every leader of a totalitarian state needs plausible grounds to justify his aggression against another sovereign nation. A legal document asserting Henry's sovereignty over a vassal Scottish king who owed him homage and allegiance, would be an ideal 'convenient cause'.

The Privy Council wrote to Edward Lee, archbishop of York and Cuthbert Tunstall, bishop of Durham, asking them to search, 'with all expedition', their archives for 'anything that may be found for the clearer declaration of the king's title' to the Scottish crown. Several documents came to light in the Durham priory archives, showing 'the dependence of the kings of Scotland upon the crown of England' between the years 1093 and 1189, as well as a statement proving Edward I's suzerainty over Scotland in May 1291.[54]

Invasion preparations were still not going well. Norfolk, labouring under 'a great agony of mind', was keen to protect his back in London. He hoped his allies Gardiner and Wriothesley would become his 'buckler [shield] of defence, if the king is not content with the doings here. I cannot rule the waves and without the ships of war with their provisions from London, it would be folly to set forth'.[55]

He was beginning to doubt his chances of success in this campaign. '[The earl of Southampton] has been ill these eight or nine days and came this day on a litter. The fear of not being able to [take] this journey troubles him and God knows, I would rather have one of my arms broken than to miss his company, for without him I [would be] all naked.'

The duke, who arrived at Newcastle just in time for Southampton's death from kidney stones, was also fretting about longer-term issues. He begged Gardiner and Wriothesley to intercede with the king to prevent him being appointed Warden of the Scottish Marches after hostilities had ended. 'In my old age [he was sixty-nine] the winter here would kill me. I would rather lose the small substance of goods I have, than lie this winter in any house this side of Doncaster, save only Leconfield [Yorkshire] where the air is nothing so vehemently cold as it is here.'[56]

His plea was successful. Six days later Henry wrote, a trifle sniffily, that he did not intend 'in any way to trouble' [Norfolk] with the Wardenry and on 26 October appointed Edward Seymour, first earl of Hertford, temporarily to the post.[57] Norfolk's relief at being spared a harsh winter on the Scottish borders was tinged by irritation that this appointment enabled the Seymour clan to continue their inexorable advancement within Henry's government.

It was not as if the general did not relish fighting the Scots, which had become a tradition for the Howards. He and his father, the second duke, had been the glorious victors at Flodden almost three decades before and he believed fervently that his family had been 'appointed by God to be to the Scots a sharp scourge and rod'.[58] Now, with his son Surrey and his half-brother Lord William Howard riding beside him, Norfolk was determined to bring steel and fire to punish the hated Scots. He promised the Privy Council: 'We shall do, as much as is possible to do, to make the enemies speak according to the king's pleasure, or else make them such a smoke as never was in Scotland these hundred years.'[59] Despite the use of the duke's typically cautious caveat – 'as much as is possible' – these were brave words indeed.

But a serious dearth of carts and wagons to transport beer and food had forced the curtailment of a full-scale invasion of Scotland. The army could not be fed simply by scavenging for victuals in the bleak border country. Norfolk's expedition was reduced to the status of a *chevauchée*, a fast-moving military column inflicting harsh punishment on an enemy by killing, burning and destroying everything in its path – the origin of the modern 'scorched earth' military tactic.

The duke and his 20,000-strong army of levies from the northern counties of England finally crossed the Scottish border on 22 October 1542 at Berwick. His departure was not auspicious. As the soldiers tramped across the town's stone bridge over the River Tweed, it collapsed, abruptly halting their triumphant march into Scotland. When they all finally got across the river, 'five men [had] drowned and many were sore hurt' and as night fell, the English column had penetrated only four miles (6km) into enemy territory.

Charles Brandon, duke of Suffolk, and Bishop Tunstall heard from Norfolk on 24 October from near Coldstream, close to the border and still complaining about the lack of food. His note, brought by a hard-riding messenger, urged Suffolk to 'warn all Northumberland to bake and brew as fast as they could' in preparation for the troops' return. Shortage of supplies meant the army 'could not tarry past four days longer in Scotland, [during] which time he would [cause] the most annoyance of the enemy that he could'. Local reports suggested that Norfolk's army had marched off in the direction of Kelso, nine miles (15km) away, 'from whence much gunshots were heard and the saying of the borders is that they have done very great harm to Scotland'.[60]

Progress, while slow, seemed encouraging. The reality was very different.

Norfolk's incursion galvanised the Scots into action. A spy in English pay reported that the duke had captured two fortified pele towers 'and destroyed man, wife and bairn'. But the Scottish army was being mobilised, with the highland clans ordered to send more soldiers. Gibbets were set up in four counties to execute those who did not volunteer. The nobility were urged not to allow James V to fight on the battlefield, in order to safeguard the Scottish crown.[61]

Four days later, on 28 October, Norfolk reported that 'we are forced to turn homewards towards England and this next night shall be the last . . . we intend to lie in Scotland'. Food shortages demanded his retreat 'for few of the army after their departure from York found any bread or drink between there and Newcastle where they were somewhat refreshed. Since coming into Scotland, most have drunk nothing but water these five days and eaten no bread since coming from Newcastle.'

His troops may have been starving but the duke had 'never seen Englishmen endure with so little victuals . . . and yet well willed to go forward, if it had been possible to have furnished them with any reasonable portion of bread and drink'. But within the last forty-eight hours, twenty-nine had died from 'drinking puddle water' and he feared that 'no small number of this army are like to follow the same way'.

The poor Scottish roads had made moving the artillery difficult and had broken the axles of his carts, forcing them to jettison beer supplies. Some soldiers had 'broken [off] the heads of the vessels and let the drink run out'.

Norfolk continued his tale of military woe. 'Tomorrow or the next day, we will dissolve the army, which is not a little to our displeasure. If God had not sent us fair weather and if the River Tweed had risen, we should have been forced to return the way we came, which would not have been done without leaving behind us the most part of our carriages. Where we thought to have marched seven or eight miles (11–13km) a day, the greatest journey we have made has not been five miles' – despite setting out each day at dawn.

The previous day, Sir Anthony Browne had led a cavalry force six miles further into Scotland 'and there did burn eleven towns and villages... and devastated the country all about, [with] as plentiful of corn as was possible to be, and thanks be to God, returned to the camp without loss of any man'. Norfolk had burnt Kelso and its twelfth-century Tironensian abbey, overlooking the confluence of the Tweed and Teviot rivers. Surrounding villages were also torched, 'utterly devastating all the corn... [so] they shall not be able to recover [from] this displeasure [for] many years hereafter'. He had hanged eight Scots for horse-stealing but had not encountered the Scots army. The duke had also spotted two French ships, 'laden with ordnance', steering for the Firth of Forth. Seven or eight hours later, he saw English warships, led by Vice-Admiral John Carey, following the same course: 'We be in good hope they have done some good exploit there.'[62]

In his heart, Norfolk knew his accident-prone expedition had failed, but he presented a brave face, boasting to Gardiner and Wriothesley, of the 'great hurt we have done in Scotland' and that 'this is the goodliest army that I have seen'. However, if it had invaded two months earlier with sufficient food supplies, 'we might have done what we would without great resistance'. He sought help in winning the king's permission for him to return home, 'for surely if I should remain in these parts you shall never see me alive'. Norfolk was suffering from his 'old disease of the lax [dysentery, which] is now marvellous sore upon me... and if I escape this time, I trust only to serve his majesty to his contentment'.

Now comes an example of the charmless duke's insensitivity and avarice, if not his penchant for bad timing. He wanted to snap up one of the choice properties in the king's gift that had belonged to his old comrade-in-arms, the barely cold Southampton. These were being distributed during Norfolk's absence in the north and he told his fellow Privy Councillors: 'I pray God [that] the house of Bath Place may light upon me, who has no house in London. [Lambeth was across the Thames.] All other noblemen be well served, save I only.'[63] He added: 'If any man has had cost and pain this journey, mine has been treble, as I doubt not all my fellows will say.'[64]

Safe behind the walls of Berwick, Norfolk wrote again to Wriothesley, worrying that 'his highness does not take our proceedings here in good part. Assuredly, we have travailed [laboured] at all times and hours no less than all our powers would extend to, to accomplish everything to the king's satisfaction.'[65]

On 2 November, a disgruntled Henry wrote a caustic letter to the duke which must have made him blanch when reading it. 'We wish that such a costly and notable enterprise had been more displeasant to [our] enemies. We marvel you have not [told] Us the names of the towns, villages and castles which you have overthrown, burnt and destroyed, with an estimate of the cattle and other things which you have taken and destroyed.' This information would be useful for propaganda purposes, although Henry grumpily observed there would have to be some exaggeration, as the destruction 'was not of such sort as We did trust and desire'.[66]

The old soldier and his fellow discomfited generals could only plead that no fortresses had been destroyed because 'they were thrown down by Norfolk twenty years past and as for the towns and villages, we do not know their names...'[67] Miraculously, the duke managed to conjure up a list of razed Scottish settlements. He bragged about the twenty 'towns' he had destroyed around Kelso, but most were mere hamlets, or single dwellings, too small to appear even on modern large-scale maps of the area.

Henry remained deeply frustrated – he had expected the sack of Edinburgh – and believed the expedition was bungled. Accordingly, a second, smaller force sallied forth to smite the Scots, this time commanded by Hertford, who crossed the border on 16 November to ravage Teviotdale with 2,000 cavalry drawn from English garrisons in the East and Middle Marches. On his return, he took especial care to list the nine towns and villages and thirteen homesteads he had laid waste, together with the harvest, six miles into Scotland. However, much of this 'remained in stooks or shorn in the fields, whereby it was so wet with the snow that fell the same night, which was a foot deep, that some part of it would not burn'. He would have been more successful, if the Scots had not been warned by 'their country men and women inhabiting these borders'.[68] Henry, however, 'accepted the doings of my army' and commended Hertford's 'execution of affairs'.[69]

James V had not been slow in organising retaliation. He mobilised a 20,000-strong army to attack England near Carlisle, but also appealed to Pope Paul III for assistance against Henry who 'rages so against him, only because he refuses to desert the Holy See and will not join him in a war against the French king'. His uncle had greater resources and would use them to compel James to 'follow his impiety or else devastate' Scotland. Could the Pope convince 'the Christian princes to send speedy succour – for if this fire is neglected it will shortly pervade all Christendom'?[70]

After all his disappointments, some good news awaited Henry.

Sir Thomas Wharton, Warden of the English West March, had reported the appearance of a Scottish army that outnumbered his defenders by at least five-to-one. The Scots had divided into two wings, with James waiting with a small force at Lochmaben, four miles (6.4km) west of Lockerbie in Dumfries and Galloway, intending to attack England across the Solway sands at ebb tide. The larger portion, numbering 18,000 and concentrated at Langholm on the River Esk, was ostensibly under the command of Lord Maxwell, but he was absent at the crucial time and they were eventually led by James V's favourite Oliver Sinclair.

The Scots engaged a hastily mustered 3,000-strong English army under Sir Thomas at Solway Moss on 24 November 1542.[71] The battle was over soon after it began. After a cavalry chase at Oakshaw Hill, the Scots found themselves trapped south of the Esk, between the river and a treacherous peat bog. After intense fighting, there was a disorderly retreat over the tidal estuary in which several hundred Scots drowned after the weight of their armour dragged them down in the filthy mire. Panic-stricken, they abandoned their horses, baggage and artillery and fled back pell-mell into Scotland.

More than 1,200 prisoners were taken, including two earls, five barons and more than 160 'gentlemen of inheritance'. Three thousand horses were taken by the triumphant English, together with twenty-four 'great' field guns, four cartloads of booty and thirty standards – including the personal banner of James V. Only seven Englishmen died in the action.

Henry was cock-a-hoop at the news of the English victory 'which it has pleased Almighty God to give unto Us against Our enemies'. A triumphant grin spread across his moonlike face and Chapuys noted that for the first time, the sadness and dejection that had cursed him 'since he learnt of the conduct of his last wife' had vanished. The king felt so chipper that the ambassador suspected that he was toying with the idea of finding a sixth wife and he began to invite ladies to lavish court entertainments.[72]

He offered his 'condign thanks' to Sir Thomas Wharton, assuring him that 'We shall so impart in Our heart this your service and consider it shall be to your singular comfort hereafter'.[73] As Norfolk no doubt wryly noted, to the victor comes the spoils, although Wharton had to wait until March 1544 to be created first baron Wharton, with generous grants of lands in Durham, Westmorland and Yorkshire.

Hertford resumed his despoliation of the eastern borders six days later, burning Coldstream and its Cistercian nunnery and taking eighty prisoners, together with sixty horses, 280 head of cattle, 3,000 sheep, and 'the best booty that has been got [within] any man's remembrance in these parts'.[74]

James V had watched the disaster at Solway Moss, probably from the safety of Birrenswark Hill, between Lockerbie and Middlebie. He returned to Scotland's east coast and spent five days with his queen at Linlithgow before moving on to Falkland Palace, Fife, on 6 December, via Edinburgh. He took to his bed with fever the next day, 'all the time raging, crying out and speaking but few wise words'.[75] His courtiers believed him to be sick in mind over the defeat and reported he was for 'ever moaning' over the loss of his royal standard. Two days after his arrival, his queen gave birth to a baby girl, who was to become Mary Queen of Scots.

Frustration and disappointment over the lack of a male heir was the last nail in his coffin. James died at midnight on 14/15 January 1542, aged thirty. His last words were reportedly: 'It came wi' a lass, it'll gang wi' a lass' – meaning 'It began with a girl and it will end with a girl', probably a reference to his dynasty's accession to the Scottish throne in 1371 by Robert II, son of Walter Stewart and his wife, Marjorie Bruce, daughter of Robert the Bruce.

His death occurred before the arrival of a letter from Pope Paul III, dated 9 January, which referred graphically to Henry as a 'son of perdition and of Satan'. Paul granted James 60 per cent of the Church's income in his kingdom to help him 'fight bravely in the cause of God'. Rather apologetically, the Pope added that if the Holy See's powers had not been so exhausted, he would have sent some hard cash for James's campaign.[76]

The Solway Moss prisoners were sent to the Tower of London but were back home in Edinburgh by the end of January 1543, having promised to work for a renewed treaty of friendship, to be sealed by the marriage of baby Mary and Prince Edward.[77] The king regarded them as the cadre of an 'English party' within the governance of Scotland and made them swear to bring the infant Mary to England and to seize some of the country's strongholds. Ten also swore a secret oath that Henry would be offered the Scottish crown if Mary died.[78] This, of course, constituted high treason as far as the Scots were concerned, but if challenged, the hapless prisoners could plead, with some justice, that their oaths were made under duress.

Fate had seemed to have dealt Henry a winning hand in his war of nerves with Scotland. France was at war and unlikely to come to Scotland's defence. The Scottish nobility, still reeling from the defeat at Solway Moss and their king's sudden death, seemed in total disarray.

Could he exploit these advantages to finally secure his northern borders and have a Tudor as king of Scotland?

7

The Sixth Wife

In January 1543, Henry VIII was aged fifty-one and, despite his massive ego and brash public bravado, had probably recognised that his increasingly poor health made the chances of his begetting a second son and heir ever more remote. More tellingly, he was also probably suffering from a reduced libido, possibly an erectile dysfunction[1] and, unknown to him, a low sperm count.[2]

The king, even with all his Imperial power, could not halt or vanquish the advance of geriatric decay, nor could he come to terms with its existence. Old age, with its innate limitations and frustrations, had suddenly and unexpectedly crept up on the once athletic Renaissance prince, like a furtive thief in the night.

Katherine Howard's licentious betrayals had also destroyed any lingering pretensions to youthful virility and vigour that he might still have clung on to in his wildest fancies. After ridding himself of his coquettish fifth wife, for the first time in more than thirty years of tempestuous wedlock, the king had no plans for another bedmate, whether wife or paramour, to keep him warm at night. Some ladies at court were mentioned as still sparking a gleam in the king's eye, like twenty-two-year-old Anne Basset, rumoured to have enjoyed royal favour in 1539, but it was obvious that Henry had nobody immediately lined up to replace his disgraced and executed queen.

Eustace Chapuys had reported totally unfounded rumours circulating in the Low Countries that Anne of Cleves had not been as chaste as everyone had thought and what was more, had now grown too fond of a glass or two of fine Gascon wine. He conveyed this unkind gossip to Sir William Paget, Clerk to the Privy Council, who asserted that Henry would not remarry her, nor take yet another spouse, 'until Parliament positively forced him to do it'.[3] Despite this unwavering declaration, the Spanish ambassador felt compelled to expend some silver-tongued effort to persuade Henry not to seek a sixth wife in France, after the king mischievously bragged to him that the French 'were continually presenting Us with ladies to marry'.

It had become unhappy reality that Henry now required a kind and considerate consort, rather than a nubile lover, to share his autumn years. A companionable woman's soothing touch was needed to regularly dress his debilitating and agonising legs, to divert him from the daily trials of kingship and to comfort and cheer him in his declining years as he slumped ever deeper into dotage. She could also care for his brood of three children by three different mothers, who lived with their own households in various royal properties in the Home Counties, safe from the fatuous distractions of court and the king's irascible temper.

Mary, now nearing her twenty-seventh birthday, was still without a diplomatically advantageous husband, her hopes of a match apparently stymied by her illegitimacy, as decreed by her father's laws. However, Chapuys reported in mid-January 1543 that the French had resumed negotiations about her projected marriage to Charles, duc d'Orléans, as his French counterpart (with characteristic Gallic sophistry), claimed 'they were not so scrupulous in France [and] would take her for a bastard'. Such issues merely 'made them yawn'.[4] Her half-sister Elizabeth was aged nine and a half and the precocious and somewhat starchy Edward, the apple of the king's eye, would become six years old that October.

The crushing victory over the Scots had gladdened Henry's heart and swept away his enduring melancholy, and with it, the sombre gloom that had been draped like a giant pall over the royal court. Since the queen's execution almost a year before, there had been little talk within its echoing galleries about 'banquets and ladies' nor any plans for masques and other dazzling amusements.

But time can become a great healer, even if it was you who beheaded your wife. Chapuys observed before Christmas 1542 that 'all has changed and order is given that [Princess] Mary shall come to court' to act as hostess for the seasonal festivities, 'accompanied by a great number of ladies. They work night and day at Hampton Court to finish her lodgings'.[5]

The princess travelled in some style to the riverside palace from her home at Hunsdon, Hertfordshire, arriving four days before Christmas.

She was affectionately greeted by her father, who had raided one of his amply stocked jewel houses to find appropriate gifts for his daughter: silver plate and jewels, including 'two rubies of great estimation'. The Spanish ambassador speculated: 'Many here think that before the end of these feasts, the king may think of marrying again, but hitherto, there is no appearance of it.'[6]

One of Mary's ladies was Lady Katherine Latimer, who had secured her position in the household the previous winter, perhaps because she may have been a godchild to Mary's adored mother, Katherine of Aragon. It is very probable that she was a member of the princess's entourage that December, and it was then that she caught the king's attention during the feasts and dancing at Hampton Court during the twelve merry days of Christmas.

Katherine was born in 1512, probably in August, the elder daughter of Sir Thomas Parr, of Kendal in Cumbria, and his wife Maud. Her brother William was born the following year and her sister, Anne around 1515. The Parrs' family seat had been Kendal Castle since the fourteenth century, but its poor repair and lack of facilities forced them to abandon it for more salubrious accommodation in the town. Katherine may have been born at their London home, near the Dominican friary at Blackfriars, in the south-west corner of the City.

Her father became a courtier after Henry's accession to the throne in 1509 and had fought at the Battle of the Spurs during the invasion of France four years later. He was appointed Master of the Wards and briefly Comptroller of the Royal Household. Maud was also a lady-in-waiting to Katherine of Aragon and their daughter was probably named after the queen in those early happy days of the royal marriage.[7] Sir Thomas died in 1517, probably one of the many casualties of that year's epidemic of Sweating Sickness, and was buried in the Blackfriars church, He left £800 to be shared equally between his daughters as their marriage portions. Thereafter, his family estates were managed by his capable widow who was aged about twenty-five at his death. She also ensured her children received a sound classical education. Suggestions that Katherine hated the traditional feminine skills of sewing (telling her mother that her hands were 'ordained to touch crowns and sceptres rather than spindles and needles') are probably apocryphal.[8]

When she was twelve, there was an attempt to pair Katherine off with Henry, a scion of the powerful northern family of Scrope, but this match foundered after failing to meet the conditions for her marriage laid down in Sir Thomas's will and disagreements over the scale of her dowry.[9] She was eventually married in May 1529 to twenty-two-year-old Sir Edward Borough (or Burgh), who was five years older than her. He was the eldest son of the fearsome and vituperative Thomas Borough, baron Borough of Gainsborough, Lincolnshire, once Lord Chamberlain to Anne Boleyn. His notorious fervent temper kept his six sons and six daughters in mortal fear; two of the daughters unsurprisingly became nuns to escape the rigours of family life. Maud Parr's will records her indebtedness to him for her daughter's marriage, as the dowry had not been fully paid.[10]

Sir Edward's grandfather had been declared a lunatic in 1510 and was held under restraint at Gainsborough Old Hall until his death in August 1528, and there were unsavoury rumours suggesting that a strand of insanity ran through the family genes. It certainly was not a peaceful household. Elizabeth, née Owen, married to Borough's second son Thomas, was forcibly expelled from the house in 1529[11] and after his death, her father-in-law obtained a private parliamentary Act declaring her two children bastards.[12] Significantly perhaps, when Maud Parr visited her daughter in the summer of 1530, she chose to stay at her own manor of Maltby rather than in the toxic atmosphere of Gainsborough Old Hall, eighteen miles (29km) away.[13]

After eighteen months of tension and strife living with her in-laws, in October 1530, Katherine and her husband moved to the manor of Kirton-in-Lindsey, another family property 12 miles (19km) away in north Lincolnshire. The scale of relief for the young wife must have been indescribable. The couple's happiness was short-lived, however. Edward, who had suffered from frail health and 'a distracted memory', died suddenly before April 1533.

Katherine's mother had passed away in December 1531, leaving her daughter 'a cross of diamonds, with a pendant pearl, a cache of loose pearls' and, prophetically, 'a jewelled portrait of Henry VIII'.[14] The childless widow moved in with her cousins, the Stricklands of Sizergh Castle at Helsington, Cumberland, who were near-neighbours to her old home four miles (6.4km) away in Kendal.

During the summer of 1534, she married forty-one-year-old John Neville, third baron Latimer, who lived in the fifteenth-century castle at Snape, near Bedale, north Yorkshire. Latimer was a second cousin to her father and a relative of Catherine Neville, dowager Lady Strickland, and she may have arranged the match. He had been married twice before and had two young children by his first wife. One wife may have died in childbirth, the second quite soon after her wedding.

Their marriage was not uneventful. Two years later, Katherine was caught up in the violence and mayhem of the two rebellions that broke out, one after the other, in the north in protest against Henry's dissolution of the monasteries and what was seen as the malign influence of Cromwell and Cranmer on the king's religious policy. A group of insurgents attacked Snape and forcibly carried off Latimer to join their ranks. He served unwillingly as captain of the rebel contingent from the bishopric of Durham and Richmond in north Yorkshire and acted as one of their representatives during negotiations with the duke of Norfolk at Doncaster in October 1536.

Latimer found himself in an impossible position. Uncertain of his loyalty and convinced that he would betray them to Henry, the rebels returned to Snape in January 1537 and seized Katherine and her two stepchildren as hostages after breaking into the undefended castle. They were freed unharmed after her husband interceded with their captors.

When the revolt was mercilessly crushed in March 1537, Latimer faced Henry's reckoning for his apparent treachery. Pleading for mercy, he claimed his involvement with the insurgents had been under duress and declared: 'My being among them was a very painful and dangerous time to me.' Norfolk, that enthusiastic instrument of royal revenge, unexpectedly supported Latimer's appeals, telling Cromwell that he could not discover any evidence against him, other than that he was 'enforced, and no man was in more danger of his life'.[15] When all else fails, corruption can provide the key to unlock liberty. After a judicious bribe of a £20 annuity to Cromwell and the probable gift of his London house to the avaricious Lord Privy Seal, Katherine's husband escaped the scaffold.

The couple moved to their manor of Wick, two miles (3.2km) from Pershore, Worcestershire, in the summer of 1537 to begin a new life and Latimer was rehabilitated in royal favour. The following year, he purchased former monastic properties in Yorkshire, possibly to demonstrate his rejection of the rebels' manifesto. In 1542, he campaigned on the Scottish borders and attended Parliament in London that winter, but his health began to deteriorate.

He died on 2 March 1543 and was buried in St Paul's Cathedral, London, under an impressive tomb, which was recorded as being 'broken all in pieces' seventy years later.[16]

Henry probably already knew Katherine Latimer, who had frequently visited her siblings at court. Her handsome and elegant younger brother William, created baron Parr in 1539, was one of the king's favourite courtiers. He had been a playmate of Henry's bastard son Henry Fitzroy, duke of Richmond, in his youth and after he came to court, the king nicknamed him 'His integrity'. He was appointed captain of his elite bodyguard, the gentlemen pensioners, in November 1540.

But a whiff of notoriety surrounded William Parr. By April 1543, his marriage of sixteen years to Anne Bourchier, daughter of Henry Bourchier, second earl of Essex, had long lost all affection, but remained legally valid. His estranged wife had scandalously borne a child by her lover, John Lyngfield, alias Huntley, former prior of the Augustinian monastery at Tandridge, Surrey (dissolved in 1538). The child and her future progeny were declared bastards by Parr's private Act of Parliament[17] to protect the legal descent of his lands and titles. During 1541–3, Parr had enjoyed an affair with Dorothy Bray (a maid-of-honour to Anne of Cleves and then Katherine Howard), soon after his wife had eloped with her irreligious prior, who seems to have mis-laid his solemn vows of chastity.[18] Parr went on to fall for the vivacious fifteen-year-old Elizabeth Brooke, daughter of George Brooke, ninth baron Cobham (yet another of the former queen's maids-of-honour and the niece of his former mistress), whom he later married. One can begin to understand why the haughty foreign ambassadors in London snuffled so disapprovingly at the morals of Henry's court.

Katherine's younger sister Anne had been appointed, at the age of thirteen, a maid-in-waiting to Henry's first queen in 1528 and went on to serve in the households of Henry's successive queens. She was clearly a model of propriety and discretion. Ten years later, Anne had married the hot-headed William Herbert, a rising figure at court. Known as 'Black Will' (but not to his face), Herbert, in his youth, had murdered a man in Bristol, fled to France to escape Tudor justice and joined Francis I's army. He had later served in the gentlemen pensioners, and had laboriously clambered up the greasy pole of royal favour to become an Esquire of the Body in 1535 and a Gentleman of the Privy Chamber in 1540.

Latimer's will was quickly proved on 15 March 1543, which provided adequate, but not overly generous provision for Katherine, his two children from his first marriage, and bequests to his servants.[19] It stipulated that his estates at Nunk Monton and Hammett in north Yorkshire should go to his widow, provided she brought up her stepdaughter Margaret.

The previous month Henry had cautiously begun to pay her court.

Katherine was thirty-one, slim, quite short – around 5ft2in (1.6m) in height[20] – auburn-haired, with light brown eyes and a fashionably pale complexion. She was attractive rather than beautiful, with a vibrant and spirited personality, who enjoyed intelligent conversation and was well educated – she could speak fluent French and Italian, had a smattering of Greek, and later could read and write excellent Latin. She was also a dignified and graceful dancer and enjoyed wearing fine clothes (her favourite colour was a bright crimson) and jewels, particularly sparkling diamonds.[21]

The widow was also experienced in the ways of the sick-room and was known to be kind and gentle. Her personal motto – 'To be useful in all I do' – carried the responsible ring of a modern sensible, practical and dutiful Girl Guide leader.

Beneath that dependable exterior, Katherine was known to be cursed with a hot temper, although she could suppress it most of the time. In later years, as queen, she could be commanding, a trifle conceited, and certainly not someone to cross lightly.

On the political front, she was known to be pious, holding moderate Protestant beliefs[22] like her sister Anne. Katherine was not overtly linked with the evangelical group still inexorably warring with the religious conservatives for dominance and influence at Henry's court, which made her a safe candidate to be his sixth wife. Additionally, a marriage to the daughter of such a respectable northern family could also bring Henry a measure of public approbation in that troublesome far-flung corner of his kingdom.

Unlike her predecessor, as the childless widow of two dead husbands, there also could be no question of disagreeable surprises skulking in Katherine's past – indeed, her obvious virtue was one of her most praised and prized assets. She may possibly have become pregnant during her marriages and this provided the improbable hope that another son and heir could be provided with Henry. On the other hand, her history of not having children could protect the king's doubtful virility from prurient gossip about the lack of new progeny. His much vaunted reputation as a lusty and powerful monarch could remain unblemished.[23]

All in all, therefore, she was the ideal choice to become the king's wife and consort and kindly stepmother to his children. He told his Privy Council: 'Gentlemen, I desire company, but I have had more than enough of taking young wives and I am now resolved to marry a widow whom you know, the wife that was of Lord Latimer.' His advisers nodded sagely and all said 'that his majesty had chosen well and they knew of no more honourable widow in the realm'.[24]

There was just one troublesome fly in this soothing ointment prescribed for Henry's dotage: Thomas Seymour, the thirty-four-year-old darkly handsome younger brother of his dead queen Jane and of his general, Hertford.

In July 1538, Norfolk had proposed that the rakish Seymour should marry his daughter, Mary, widow of Henry Fitzroy, in a blatantly political move to unite the two most powerful families at court. Norfolk humbly approached the king for permission for her marriage, mentioning two suitors, Seymour – 'to whom his heart is most inclined' – and another, whose name the king unfortunately could not remember afterwards. Henry, 'answering merrily', predicted that if the duke was minded to bestow his daughter to Seymour, he would be coupling 'her with one of such lust and youth as should be able to please her well at all points'.[25] One can imagine the leer creasing his bloated face as he uttered this lewd quip. Despite Henry's salacious assessment of Seymour's physical attributes, the alliance was wrecked by Mary's rejection of him as a bridegroom and the arrogant contention of her brother, the earl of Surrey, that her suitor's lineage fell a long way short of the stringent lines of noble blood and ancestry demanded by the House of Howard.

Sir Thomas had returned to court in January after eight months away in Vienna where he had served as a military observer, studying the tactics and weaponry used in the war against the Ottoman Empire in present-day Hungary.

Almost immediately, Katherine Latimer had fallen deeply and hopelessly in love with him. Like her sister Anne, she plainly had a penchant for hot-headed and dashing men of action, with an exciting streak of unreliability and danger in their personality.

Throughout the early spring of 1543, her clandestine but still chaste relationship had continued with this bearded Lothario with such piratical good looks. After her two socially advantageous marriages to sick or older husbands, she had sampled the sublime joy of true love for Seymour, whose charisma and magnetism positively dazzled all the giggling ladies of the court. Her prim heart was excited and captivated by his unashamed glamour and his colourful tales of derring-do, yet failed to be deterred by his infamous quick temper, strutting pride and overt sexual aggression. She still was married to an ailing husband but eagerly anticipated her blissful wedding to Seymour after, of course, a decent interval of mourning following Latimer's death.

The king was certainly aware of Katherine's passion for Seymour and because of this, his psychology would have quickened his yearning to possess her as his wife. Any betrothal to his brother-in-law, in one sense, would constitute her a sister to Henry. Such a match recalled his first marriage to Katherine of Aragon: both women had the same Christian name and in both cases, he took, or would take, the place of a brother, so his unconscious craving for an incestuous union was satisfied. Ironically, therefore, Katherine Latimer's discreet but boundless passion for the heroic Seymour became the pivotal factor in her suitability as the king's new wife.[26]

It was custom and practice for a widow to retire from public life during the period of grieving for her deceased husband. This did not seem to apply to Katherine, whose constant presence at court seems to have been demanded by Henry. By the end of March 1543, she had become a permanent fixture.

When rumours of his desire to marry her reached Katherine's ears, she was horrified, reportedly exclaiming: 'Better to be his mistress than his wife.'[27] Who can blame her? After all, Chapuys had pointed out that February that 'Few, if any ladies now at court would aspire to such an honour.'[28] Their reluctance would be magnified by the knowledge that any hint of promiscuity in their past could bring them a one-way ticket to the Tower. The ghost of Katherine Howard still haunted the darkened corridors of Hampton Court.

But the king's own past had demonstrated that he was not a man to be gainsaid by anyone, particularly in matters of the heart. Henry realised he would have to act quickly to stop his would-be bride consummating her love with Seymour, or becoming a party to a betrothal or pre-marriage contract, thus negating his own wedding plans.

As a lame and sick man with a frightful track record of five unfortunate marriages behind him, Henry resorted to his exchequer and powers of patronage as fitting ways and means to woo Katherine. On 16 February, he placed an order with the royal tailor John Skutt to make gowns in the fashionable French, Dutch, Italian and Venetian styles and French head-dresses, at a total cost of £8 9s 5d, or £4,630 in today's spending power. The order is headed: 'My lady Latimer'.

On 23 April, her brother William was elected a knight of the Order of the Garter[29] and the same month appointed Lord Warden of the Western Marches on the Scottish borders. This was probably an unwelcome appointment, as Parr would have preferred the comforts of life at court, rather than that of a soldier stationed on a remote and unstable frontier. By these appointments, Henry, revelling in his autocracy, was signalling that his mercurial power could raise up those enjoying his favour, coupled with the implicit threat that he could instantly break them too. These were cynical ploys to apply family pressure on his reluctant bride to agree to marriage.

To emphasise his absolute power as king, on 30 April Seymour was hastily posted off to Brussels as joint resident ambassador, with Nicholas Wootton, to Mary of Hungary, governor of the Netherlands. Throughout the next few years, Henry made certain sure that Katherine's would-be lover was always conveniently out of the country. For example, although recalled in mid-July, Seymour was immediately appointed marshal of the English forces being sent to the Low Countries under Sir John Wallop. Later, Seymour was kept at sea, as captain, successively, of the king's warships *Peter Pomegranate* and *Sweepstake* in the fleet under John Dudley, recently created Viscount Lisle and appointed Lord High Admiral from January 1543.[30]

Katherine's resistance to marrying Henry was impossible to sustain. She was like a bird trapped in a gilded cage, unable to escape what fate had unkindly decreed her. Four years later, safely after Henry's death, she admitted to Seymour: 'For as truly as God is God, my mind was fully bent the other time I was at liberty to marry you before any man I know... God withstood my will... most vehemently for a time and through His grace and goodness... made me renounce utterly my own will and to follow His will most willingly.'[31] After quashing understandable fears for her life, driven by the fate of previous queens, she must have sensibly considered how long Henry would last and calculated that if Seymour could remain patient, their love might not have to wait too many years before being sanctified by marriage.

On 8 July, the king apparently sent for Katherine and said bluntly: 'Lady Latimer, I wish you to be My wife'. Katherine fell humbly to her knees and meekly answered: 'Your majesty is my master. I have but to obey you.'[32]

Henry was in great haste to marry his widow woman. On 10 July 1543, Cranmer issued a special licence, written in Latin, to Henry 'who has deigned to marry the lady Katherine, late wife of Lord Latimer deceased . . . to have the marriage solemnised in any church, chapel or oratory without the issue of banns'.[33]

The wedding followed two days later, in the Queen's Privy Closet, above the west end of the Chapel Royal at Hampton Court. Twenty-one people crammed into the small space, which must have become airless and close on that sunny day.

Among those witnesses supporting Henry were John, Lord Russell, now Lord Privy Seal; Sir Anthony Browne, Master of the Horse; Hertford; Sir Thomas Heneage, Chief Gentleman of the Privy Chamber, and others of his gentlemen, including Sir Richard Long, Anthony Denny and, of course, William Herbert. Of these, only Russell, Browne and Heneage were adherents to the religiously conservative faction at court, while the remainder were firmly in the reformist camp. Katherine's witnesses were the king's daughters Mary and Elizabeth; his niece Lady Margaret Douglas (now happily forgiven for her two affairs with the Howards); the bride's sister Anne; Jane Dudley Lady Lisle; Anne Stanhope, countess of Hertford, and Katherine Willoughby, duchess of Suffolk. Again, these last three ladies of the court were supporters of the evangelical cause.

Not so Bishop Gardiner, who performed the short marriage service in English, who, as we know, was a determined and fervent religious conservative. He put the usual questions to bride and groom and Henry, with *hilari vultu*, a 'smiling face', answered each one with a loud, impatient cry of 'Yea'. Grasping Katherine's right hand in his, he repeated, after the bishop, the marriage vows, which are not so different in wording to those of today. 'I, Henry, take thee, Katherine, to my wedded wife, to have and to hold, from this day forward, for better for worse, for richer for poorer, in sickness and in health [did Katherine inwardly groan at this point?], till death us do part and thereto I plight thee my troth.' While holding the king's hand, Katherine then made her vows, adding after the phrase 'sickness and in health' her additional pledge to be 'bonair and buxom in bed [another bridal shudder here perhaps?] and at board, till death us do part and thereto I plight thee my troth.'[34]

The wedding ring was then slipped on Katherine's finger and gifts of gold and silver proffered in celebration of the marriage. Gardiner said a short prayer and blessed the union. Henry, always with an eye for legal niceties, ordered his notary, Richard Watkins, to make public the legal attestation of the marriage.[35]

Later that day the new queen presented Mary with a pair of gold bracelets, set with rubies, together with £25 in cash as a token of her thanks for welcoming her into Henry's family. Another thoughtful gift was sent to Elizabeth.[36]

The morning after the wedding night, the new queen ordered her apothecary to supply 'fine perfumes' for use in her bedchamber at Hampton Court. As Anne of Cleves (she of those 'displeasant airs') discovered to her cost, Henry was sexually aroused by the scent of a woman, and his new wife was making some carefully chosen purchases to ensure her husband's physical interest in her. A month later, there was another order for three pounds (1.4kg) of pouches of potpourri 'to make sweet the queen's bed'. There may, however, be a more mundane reason behind these purchases. The queen's bedchamber and her other private apartments in Hampton Court were on the first floor of the eastern range of buildings on the palace's inner court. Her privy kitchen was located immediately beneath. In winter, the heat rising up from the ovens and open fires down below would have warmed the bedchamber above. The kitchen smells would be less welcome and may explain the requirement for perfumes and her repeated orders for sweet-smelling herbs.

Other articles bought soon after her wedding included eleven yards (10.1m) 'of black damask for a nightgown' and the making of a 'night-gown of black satin with two Burgundian gardes [sleeves] embroidered and edged with velvet'.[37] Henry liked his wives to wear black nightgowns; Anne Boleyn is known to have possessed one. Katherine understood how to handle an older husband and was not going to make the same mistakes as Anne of Cleves.

On 20 July, the bride, now at Otelands, wrote to her brother, serving on the English border with Scotland, to tell him of her marriage. 'It has pleased God to incline the king to take me as his wife, which is the greatest joy and comfort that could happen to me,' she declared valiantly, well aware that the letter might be read by others. In a sharp reference to the pressure William had clearly applied on her to marry Henry, she told him with a *soupçon* of bitterness: 'You are the person who has most cause to rejoice.' However, she asked him to 'let her sometimes hear of his health... [and visit her] as if she had not been called to this honour'.[38]

Her letter was enclosed with one to Parr written by Wriothesley, the king's secretary, who, concerned about his haughty and disputatious behaviour with his fellow military commanders in the north, warned him testily that he should shape himself to be 'more and more an ornament to her majesty' his sister.[39] The reprimand failed to have any effect; two months later, Parr was recalled to London.

As with Katherine Howard, the king showered gifts of stunning jewellery upon his new queen, many of them adorned with Katherine's favourite gem, the diamond. Henry always had good taste in jewellery and his presents eloquently symbolised his new-found love.

Three items particularly catch the eye. The first was a brooch with an image 'of King Henry the Eight with the Queen, having a crown of diamonds over them, and a [Tudor] rose of diamonds under them'. The second was a gold tablet, having on one side 'an H and K [and] a rose all of diamonds with ostrich feathers and five small rubies and on the other, a fine diamond held by an image with four other diamonds'. Finally, there was another gold tablet with the 'King's picture painted... with a rose of five diamonds and six rubies' on the obverse and on the reverse, 'two men lifting a stone, being a diamond with [a border of] twenty-two diamonds, two rubies and a fair emerald'.[40] Other jewellery was inherited from Katherine's predecessors as queen, like the T-shaped *tau* cross of diamonds that once belonged to Jane Seymour.

Edmund Harvel, Henry's ambassador to Venice, naturally rejoiced at the king's marriage to 'so prudent, beautiful and virtuous a lady, as is by universal fame reported'. The Doge and his council, he added, had offered 'no mean congratulations on the marriage'.[41] Chapuys reported the royal wedding to the crown prince of Spain (later to marry Princess Mary to become Philip I of England): 'May God be pleased that this marriage turns out well and that the king's favour and affection for the princess [Mary] continue to increase.'[42]

Wriothesley told Charles Brandon, duke of Suffolk, about the wedding: 'Last Thursday to my Lady Latimer, a woman in my judgement for virtue, wisdom and gentleness most meet for the king's majesty. I am sure his majesty has never had a wife more agreeable to his heart than she is. Our Lord send them long life and much joy together'.[43] His words indicate the reaction of Henry's ministers and courtiers who, given his previous marriages, must have heaved a collective sigh of relief at the king's sixth union with a decent, respectable widow who would cause no trouble or heartache to her increasingly peevish husband.

The only prominent nose to be put out of joint belonged to Anne of Cleves, still living in comfortable royal oblivion at Richmond Palace or at another of the manors granted her after her marriage annulment. Almost three weeks after the wedding, the Spanish ambassador heard 'from an authentic quarter' that Henry's fourth queen would 'greatly prefer giving up everything that she has and living... in Germany [than] remaining in England, treated as she is, and humiliated and hurt as she has lately been at the king marrying this last lady, who is by no means so handsome as she herself is. Besides which, there is no hope of [Katherine] having children, considering she has been twice a widow and has borne none from her deceased husbands.'[44]

There were reports that Henry had courteously invited his 'beloved sister' Anne of Cleves to attend the wedding ceremony but she was not present – probably a blessing, considering the crush within the Queen's closet at Hampton Court.

Anne was officially reported 'very pleased' at the king's latest marriage but this was merely her bowing, with a cordial public face, to the inevitable. In reality, Chapuys believed she had 'taken great grief and despair at the king's espousal of this last wife', rather than realising his great mistake in failing to appreciate her bewitching Germanic charms.[45] In direct contrast to her public utterances, Anne's reported private comments oozed with resentment and spleen. Here was a woman spurned and finding her umbrage very difficult to conceal. 'A fine burden Madam Katherine has taken on herself!' was one scathing exclamation. 'The king is so stout that such a man has never been seen. Three of the biggest men that could be found could get inside his doublet,' she added maliciously.[46]

One of the reasons behind her private pique was the failure of an obscure plan to better her status. The duke of Cleves' ambassador, whom Henry's council believed, in reality, to be Anne's agent, had been living miserably in foul squalor in a room above a disreputable tavern in London, with just one manservant to look after his daily needs. He had been called to court two or three times during early 1543, probably on matters connected with the cast-off queen. Nothing came of it, and he continued to live in abject penury, as he received no money from Düren to meet his living expenses. Chapuys tried several times fruitlessly to obtain an exit passport for him, so he remained stranded in diplomatic limbo, eking out a wretched existence. 'The poor devil... must very much wish to be out of this country for he does nothing here,' the ambassador told Charles V.[47]

The plague was raging yet again in London and Henry revealed his monomania about the disease by publishing a proclamation on 15 July from Hampton Court forbidding citizens of London from entering any house occupied by the king and queen and banning any royal servant or courtier from visiting the infected capital.[48] The court beat a hasty retreat from the threatening pestilence six miles (9.5km) westwards up the Thames to Otelands and then embarked on the traditional summer progress through the Home Counties – staying at royal houses in Buckinghamshire, Bedfordshire and Hertfordshire.

Such itineraries were an expensive business for the courtiers involved. On 17 July, Sir Thomas Heneage, one of the witnesses at the marriage ceremony, wrote to a moneylender as he 'desired a loan... to go on this progress'. Heneage had received no cash from his usual lender and dared not ask him because 'they die so sore' from the plague. He promised to repay the loan at Michaelmas (29 September).[49]

Unfortunately the weather for the progress was less than clement. Archbishop Cranmer asked the bishops to have special prayers said in the parish churches for 'seasonable and temperate weather' after the long periods of rain that had caused flooding and 'great hurt to the corn and the fruit now ripe'.[50]

Two weeks after the wedding, there was another trial of sacramentaries – those who heretically refuted that the consecrated communion wafer represented the physical presence of Christ – under the Statute of Six Articles. This case hit close to home – the court at Windsor – as it concerned John Marbeck, the organist of St George's Chapel within the castle walls; Robert Testwood, 'a singing man' or chorister there; Anthony Pearson, a priest and popular preacher from nearby Winkfield, Berkshire, and Henry Filmer, a tailor and churchwarden of St John the Baptist's Church, New Windsor. A fifth local man called Bennett had also been charged with heresy and imprisoned in the dank and verminous Marshalsea Gaol in Southwark, where he remained because he had been struck down by the plague.

Four appeared in court at Windsor on Thursday, 26 July, before John Capon, a former Benedictine abbot and bishop of Salisbury since 1539, William Franklyn, dean of Windsor, and a jury of their peers, drawn from the Chapel Royal's own tenants. Testwood was so ill that he could barely stagger into the dock with the aid of crutches. Bennett's plague incongruously saved his life, as he recovered and was eventually freed after his accusers were convicted of perjury.

The other four defendants were all found guilty in a contentious trial in which the case against Testwood included the vacuous accusation that he avoided looking at the Host when it was raised at the climax of the Mass, instead of acknowledging it devoutly. Pearson, as a priest, could expect no mercy, having told his congregation blasphemously that 'you shall not eat the body of Christ . . . gnawing it with your teeth that the blood run about your lips'.

Marbeck had claimed that the 'Holy Mass, when the priest consecrates the body of our Lord, is polluted, deformed, sinful and open robbery of the glory of God' but was surprisingly reprieved in October.[51] His royal pardon, signed at Woodstock in Oxfordshire, may have been granted because of his perceived 'innocence and honesty', but rumour suggested it was more a result of Bishop Gardiner's pleas for his life, because he enjoyed him playing organ music so much. The other three were burnt at the stake at Windsor for their heresy on 28 July 1543.[52] The active Protestant Richard Hilles wrote afterwards that 'our king has burnt three godly men in one day and he is always wont to celebrate his nuptials by some wickedness of this kind'.[53]

Katherine meanwhile was tasting the first lavish and luxurious fruits of being a queen. A new household was created for her, including Lady Margaret Douglas, the king's niece, but the queen's sister Anne was appointed chief lady-in-waiting. Margaret, her stepdaughter, was one of her maids of honour. Her uncle Sir William Parr was named her Lord Chamberlain. She also chose the Protestant reformer and Merton tutor John Parkhurst to be her domestic chaplain. She had met him during her visit to Oxford with Henry during the royal progress, when he penned some elegant Latin verses in their honour. He had been chaplain to her close friend Katherine, duchess of Suffolk.[54] The queen was also granted her own Great Seal, with Henry's royal arms impaling her own.[55]

Katherine's early purchases of clothes displayed an unadventurous taste, ordering black and purple gowns that were far from showy.[56] She appointed a Dutch goldsmith, who had anglicised his name to Peter Richardson, as her own jeweller shortly after the wedding. She had a pet dog, a small spaniel named 'Rig', which wore a collar of crimson velvet embroidered with gold.[57] Her parrots were fed on hempseed.[58]

Those around her joined a citadel of culture. The new queen recruited the playwright and convicted sodomite Nicholas Udall[59] and the Flemish artists Susanna Horenbout and Levina Teerlinc into her household and patronised the leading portrait painters of the day, as she enjoyed presenting tiny miniatures of herself and Henry as gifts to family and friends.[60] Katherine also maintained her own troupe of actors and took on the Bassano brothers, a group of six Venetian lute players once patronised by Anne of Cleves. She delighted in the merriment provided by her fool, or jester, Thomas Brown, for whom clothes of grey and red are recorded as being purchased from a draper in 1545/6.[61] She kept a kindly eye on Princess Mary's fool, Jane, an unhappy innocent, who in March 1543 had contracted some awful kind of skin infection that required monthly shaving of her head by a barber who was paid a groat (1.5p) each time for his pains. In September 1544, she paid sixteen pennies (7p) for three geese for 'Jane Fool' with which she could amuse herself in a quiet corner of the Privy Garden at the Palace of Westminster.[62]

The new queen immediately took up the unspecified responsibilities of home-maker to Henry's children. With the exception perhaps of Edward, parental love for the Tudor children had been as rare as hen's teeth, and even for the prince it was supplied at arm's-length. Mary, who was only four years younger than Katherine, had suffered years of isolation and rebuffs from her father. The princess grew very close to her, becoming more like a friend than a stepdaughter. Both Mary and Elizabeth went on the summer progress and when Mary fell ill on a journey between the royal houses of Grafton and Woodstock, Katherine sent her own litter to convey her to Ampthill in Bedfordshire where she and the king were staying.[63] The queen also involved herself closely in the education of Edward and Elizabeth.

Later that year the queen brought all three of the king's children together under one roof in her efforts to forge a distinct royal family. Richard Layton, Henry's ambassador to Paris who later moved to Brussels, wrote enquiring after their health that December and asked whether the king and his children 'continued in one household'.[64] No wonder the letters to her from Henry's children demonstrate real affection and warmth.

Two days before Christmas, her brother William Parr was created earl of Essex (vacant since the execution of Cromwell) and her uncle Sir William was made Baron Parr of Horton, Northamptonshire, in a ceremony in the presence chamber at Hampton Court.[65]

Like everyone else before them, the Parrs were exploiting the king's love to reach up and snatch the dazzling prizes of status and wealth – while they could.

8

Fie on You, Traitor!

On 9 May 1540, the Chapter of the Most Noble Order of the Garter, meeting after their annual feast at Windsor, faced an uncomfortable item on their agenda. Membership of the Order was (and remains) in the personal gift of the sovereign. But three of the twenty-four Knights had been executed for high treason and expelled.[1] Should these traitors besmirch the Order's register of members, or should they be 'blotted out, as they deserved?' Some thought their beautifully illuminated book would be 'made ugly' by such erasures, so the Chapter sought the Solomonic wisdom of Henry VIII, who had donated the volume in 1534.[2] He decided that the register should remain untouched, save for the derisive phrase *Vah proditor!* – 'Fie on you, traitor!' – being inserted above or alongside the offender's name.[3] The entries for Thomas Cromwell, elected a Garter knight in August 1537, but executed for treason on 28 July 1540, were among the first to be annotated by this mark of signal dishonour.[4]

The Order's rules had been revised by Henry, the last time in 1531, and he included in his amended statutes the 'Points of Reproach' that required expulsion of those members being found to be 'heretical, traitorous, or cowardly in battle'.

This process, known as 'degradation', was ceremonial of high drama and vivid symbolism. Garter Principal King of Arms and his fellow heralds would process into the choir of St George's Chapel, the spiritual home of the Order within Windsor Castle. Garter would then read out the 'Instrument of Degradation', whereupon a colleague would clamber up a ladder placed in the stall of the 'convict' knight and remove his coat of arms. At the words: 'Expelled and put out from the arms' the herald would 'violently cast down' the coat and its crest onto the floor, followed by the malefactor's sword and banner.

In a grotesque parody of a game of soccer, these would be contemptuously kicked out of the chapel through the Great West Door. The traitor's knightly accoutrements would then be punted through the castle's lower ward, out by the nearest gate and finally dumped in the surrounding ditch as testament to the disgrace of the expelled knight.[5] The metal plate bearing his arms, fixed to the back of his stall, would be destroyed. Bah! Traitor!

Because of the precarious security of his dynasty, the king abhorred treason as the most heinous of crimes committed against him and the Tudor state. To root out all treachery, penal measures were introduced to sharpen powers to punish those who defied the king's ecclesiastical supremacy, as well as protecting his uncertain succession to the throne.

The pre-eminence of the old Treason Act of 1352 had remained unchallenged until the 1530s when new legislation extended the scope of statutory treason in law. It was no longer just a question of planning their sovereign's death, or levying war against him. The law of the land would now adjudge them traitors simply if they did not follow Henry's predilections in religious liturgy and beliefs, or refused to support changes made in his choice of wives, their status, or that of any royal offspring.[6]

Murder by poisoning, counterfeiting or clipping the coinage, marrying the king's sister, niece or aunt without royal consent, or 'defiling or deflowering' them, all became treason. As Jane Rochford discovered to her cost, insanity would now fail to provide the means to escape the lonely walk to the scaffold.

The Act of Proclamations, passed by a supine Parliament in 1539, enabled Henry to govern England and Wales by personal decree rather than having to seek legislation to authorise every measure, decision or action that he and his Privy Council wanted enacted.[7] This stealthy government power remains with us today and is used for administrative expediency under measures known to Whitehall mandarins since the 1930s as 'Henry VIII clauses'.[8]

Cromwell's Treason Act of 1534 introduced the legal principle that slandering the monarch was punishable by death. It was now treason 'maliciously to wish, will, or desire by words or writing... to imagine, invent, practise, or attempt any bodily harm' to the king or queen or their heirs apparent. Depriving them of their 'dignity, title, name or of their royal estates', or 'slanderously or maliciously to publish and pronounce, by express writing or words that the king, our sovereign lord, is an heretic, schismatic, tyrant or usurper' now fell into the same legal trap.[9]

The legislation also denied fugitives the perpetual safety in designated sanctuary places, such as the whole of the county palatine of Durham, where they could live without fear of arrest, in contrast to the forty days allowed them if they sought shelter in a church. These ancient rights were removed because 'treason touches ... both the surety of the king's ... person and his heirs and successors'.[10]

It is probable that Henry himself determined the nature and content of this draconian legislation. His personal and political creed was easily understood, even if it was autocratic and intimidatory. Those subjects who were not explicitly for him must therefore be his enemies and should be destroyed.[11]

The green shoots of free speech were ruthlessly scythed down. Fear and suspicion stalked Henry's realm, like the grim reaper in the most virulent of epidemics. A few ill-chosen words uttered while in drink, or in a moment of anger, could take anyone to the gallows. Malicious accusations of treacherous statements could provide a potent weapon to settle any scores against a neighbour or rival in business. Add to this the other laws against heresy and it was obvious that England had become a totalitarian state, ruled by tyranny.

With our twenty-first-century liberties, we might assess the evils of 'Bluff King Hal's' regime based on memories of the rule of despotic dictators in Europe during the last century, with their secret police, show trials, book-burnings and mass political and ethnic persecutions. Perhaps looking at Henry's own authoritarian state in a contemporary context may create a more balanced view. For example, in Venice, carved *bocca di leone* (lion's mouth) letterboxes were inserted in the exterior walls of public buildings to enable informers to post anonymous denunciations of friends and neighbours. Then there were the cruel operations of the Inquisition in Catholic countries, efficiently rationalised by Pope Paul III in 1542.[12]

But there is no denying the terror that the new legislation created in Henry's England. Even as the Act was being drawn up in London, Stephen Vaughan, Henry's agent in the Low Countries, was alarmed by the Tudor state's sudden interest in his utterances. In letters to Cromwell, he denied accusations that he held Lutheran beliefs and complained about inquiries into 'my manners, my opinions, my conversation, my faith'.[13]

In London, the Protestant reformer Richard Hilles feared the oppression of Henry's police state. It was no longer a novelty to 'see men slain, hung, drawn, quartered or beheaded, some for trifling expressions which were explained or interpreted as having been spoken against the king, others for the Pope's supremacy, some for one thing and some for another'.[14] Marillac observed in 1541 that when 'a man is a prisoner in the Tower, none dare meddle with his affairs, unless to speak ill of him, for fear of being suspected of the same crime'.[15] One example of the new law's severity came on 1 July 1541, when a wretched Welsh minstrel was hanged, drawn and quartered for singing playful ditties 'which [were] interpreted as prophesying against the king'.[16]

In practice, this law against free speech was more difficult to impose than Cromwell had planned because of the evidential fragility of allegations, or the tainted motives of accusers. Another problem was that if the conversation was in private, there could only be one witness against the defendant; a flawed case of one man's word against another's. Of the 404 cases alleging treasonable words or writings during 1532–40, at least 230 were found not to be treason at all, or the charges never came to court. Conversely, sixty-four people were probably executed, another ten died in prison, thirteen were pardoned, nine were reprieved and six fled the country for speaking or writing felonious words.[17] Those found guilty had commented disparagingly on Henry's sex life or procreative abilities; criticised the talents or actions of his ministers; seditiously misrepresented government policies or spread rumours about popular dissatisfaction or unrest.[18]

If we lived today under the iron fist of Henry's laws, I would be guilty of high treason for flagrantly writing unflattering statements about the old despot. If you read these perilous words aloud, or lent this book to a friend, so would *you*. Luckily for all of us, these punitive measures have long been repealed.

Finally, in 1543, three further Acts were passed, again widening the definition of treachery. The first deemed it high treason to refuse to swear an oath of loyalty to the king against the Pope.[19] The second stated that any treasons or misprisions of treason committed outside Henry's realm could be tried *in absentia* in England.[20] The third declared that it was high treason to plot to 'deprive the king, queen, prince or the heirs of the king's body... of any of their titles, styles, names, degrees, royal estates or regal power annexed to the crown of England'.[21] Henry left no legal stone unturned in his pursuit of traitors.

The road to the scaffold was a terrifying journey for any doomed victim of Tudor justice. Torture was employed to persuade (*sic!*) suspects to reveal incriminating evidence or induce confession. The use of such methods during interrogation was illegal under common law, with its perpetrators ostensibly becoming criminals themselves. However, it *was* permitted in treason cases or other offences against the state, if approved by the Privy Council. Between 1540 and 1640, there were 101 such licences granted and these sanctioned the use of torture 'for the better boulting out of the truth' – an obscure reference to the milling machinery that separated flour from the bran.[22]

Thomas Cromwell was a keen advocate of torture during questioning and Henry enthusiastically approved its use, as shown by his demands in 1543 that the duke of Suffolk should 'by good means or otherwise by tortures... to get out the very truth' from a prisoner.[23]

The mechanics of torture were sired by the most diabolical human ingenuity. First and foremost was the engine called the rack, an iron frame about six feet (1.8m) long, with wooden rollers or toothed windlasses to which the prisoner's hands and feet were secured by ropes.[24] When these capstans were turned, his body was excruciatingly stretched, dislocating the joints of the limbs or tearing apart the ligaments and sinews. Just a glimpse of the rack, or hearing a victim's piercing screams of agony, was enough to make some prisoners blurt out information to escape the ordeal. This fearsome machine may have been invented by John Holland, second duke of Exeter, when he was Constable of the Tower in the 1440s – hence it being known to apprehensive Londoners as the 'Duke of Exeter's daughter'. There was only one rack in England and this was in the Tower of London; the remains of one survived there at the end of the nineteenth century.[25]

Another member of this unholy family of pain and terror was the 'Scavenger's Daughter' or, as the Protestant author John Foxe called it, 'Skevington's Gyves'. Traditionally, this was named after Sir Leonard Skevington, who invented it around 1545 while Lieutenant of the Tower, although his name does not appear as a holder of that post during Henry's reign.[26] This monstrous device was the direct opposite of the rack, as it compressed the victim's body rather than stretching it. It consisted of a metal frame with iron shackles or hoops that were secured around the prisoner's hands, neck and feet while in a sitting position. The body was squeezed into a tight ball, with the head forced down, the lower limbs pressed into the thighs and the legs up into the stomach. As the pressure increased, blood spurted from the nose, ears and the tips of the victim's fingers. The agony of the 'Scavenger's Daughter' was administered in bouts lasting no more than ninety minutes. There were also sturdy iron gauntlets, fitted with screws, which crushed the fingers.

If none of this nightmare paraphernalia was available, fiendish resourcefulness could also achieve the required result. In July 1543, Suffolk and Cuthbert Tunstall, bishop of Durham, described how they loosened the tongues of two prisoners ('one a very simple creature') while investigating what transpired to be unfounded rumours of a 'new commotion' or rebellion in County Durham. They fitted the prisoners with new leather shoes, well saturated with pig's grease, and set them in stocks, their feet held fast, close to a blazing hot fire. Basically, they fried their feet.[27]

There were other techniques that relied on extreme discomfort, or denying revitalising slumber or food to the suspect, similar to the sleep or sensory deprivation of modern interrogation methods. This form of duress was graphically known to Tudor torturers as 'pinching' the victim, a deadpan phrase that hides chilling connotations. In 1535, three Carthusian monks were chained upright by the neck, arms and legs to vertical posts for thirteen days in the Tower before they appeared in court.[28] A small cell, known vividly as 'Little Ease' – a tiny, dank room that did not allow the prisoner to stand, sit or stretch out prone – was reportedly located in the crypt of the chapel of St John the Evangelist on the second floor of the White Tower, although the present structure is quite roomy.[29] There was another 'grisly dungeon' called 'Whalesbourne', where sunlight never penetrated, perhaps part of the Coldharbour gate that once stood at the south-eastern corner of the White Tower, where rats supposedly tore 'flesh . . . from the arms and legs of prisoners during sleep'. The central keep also contained 'The Pit', an airless underground room or *oubliette*, twenty feet (6m) deep that held up to three prisoners.

When those accused of high treason came to trial, more than one in four pleaded guilty because they realised the judicial odds were stacked heavily against them. By rule of law, they were denied lawyers to defend them on matters of fact, in the vain belief that the judge was the prisoner's best counsel. They were also refused advance knowledge of the indictment against them, denied copies of depositions by prosecution witnesses, or even a list of those who would testify against them. Moreover, the crown alone could compel the attendance of witnesses by *subpoena*. The uncorroborated confessions of alleged accomplices were freely admitted as evidence, as was hearsay.[30] After 1542, the prisoner also lost the right to object to a member of the jury hearing his case.[31] The state was determined that the defendant would only leave the court as a condemned man.

If the legalities of such trials became inconvenient, there was a Parliamentary Attainder, an expedient deftly employed by Cromwell to destroy Henry's enemies. As this was a legislative procedure, these Acts could be passed without any defence being offered. The methodical minister had consulted Henry's learned judges about whether they believed condemning a traitor without hearing any evidence or mitigation on the defendant's behalf could be overturned at law. They told him it could not.[32]

The traitor's death was the ghastly culmination of these proceedings of state vengeance. For his last journey, he was roped spread-eagled to a wooden sheep hurdle which was dragged by a horse, bumping across the cobbles and through the stinking mud, from the Tower up to the old Roman road to Tyburn, via Holborn and what is now Oxford Street, a route later nicknamed 'The Devil's Highway'. Awaiting the traitor were two wooden gallows and the executioner, armed with the implements of his evil trade to fulfil his bloody business.

This barbaric form of capital punishment was vividly described by the chronicler Charles Wriothesley in recounting the executions of two priests in Calais on 10 April 1540. 'After they were hanged and cut down, [they] arose and stood on their feet and helped the hangman put off their clothes. So living, [they] were laid on a board, fast bound, and then dismembered, their bowels burnt before them and spoke always till their hearts were pulled out of their bodies, which was a piteous death.'[33]

The sins of the father were visited on the sons. A key deterrent of the law of treason was not only the forfeiture of the traitor's goods but also the disinheriting of his descendants. The victim's blood was legally branded as 'stained and corrupt', his lineage disgraced and therefore, his shamed children could not enjoy his estates and property. This corruption of his bloodline was symbolised by his castration, as part of the disembowelling.[34]

Treason cases totalled 979 from 1532 to Henry's death, in which 336 defendants suffered death, or just over 34 per cent of those accused. Of these executions, 216 had been involved in open rebellion against the king in the north in 1536–7 and fifteen in the Yorkshire conspiracy of 1541.[35]

While surviving Privy Council registers fail to supply much information about those under suspicion, it seems that after Cromwell's downfall in 1540, fewer people fell foul of the penal treason laws, perhaps because the population had become thoroughly downtrodden, or merely that the surviving data is incomplete. During July 1540–January 1547, around a hundred people were prosecuted for such treachery, indicating an average of roughly fourteen cases a year, compared with about seventy per annum when the Lord Privy Seal was proving such an effective chief of secret police for Henry. However, during the last years of his reign, twenty-eight out of ninety-six prosecutions were successful – a higher proportion than Cromwell managed to achieve, perhaps indicating that legislation had closed former loopholes to defendants.[36]

One class of traitor escaped Henry's vengeance but not his wrath – those who fled overseas to escape justice and those renegades who defected to the papal cause. Henry always insisted on their immediate arrest and extradition to answer for their crimes in an English court. When this failed (as mostly it did), he was happy to encourage covert attempts to kidnap or murder the fugitives.

The mammoth Attainder Act of 1539[37] was the largest of the Tudor period, covering a third of all those condemned by Parliament throughout the sixteenth century.[38] Twenty-six names referred retrospectively to those executed in the northern rebellions, a further six were involved in the alleged 'White Rose' conspiracy, but the remaining fifteen were exiles, or had been detained while fleeing England. Henry and his advisers believed that if such fugitives were 'left unharried, such men would have the opportunity to work their feats of treason' in Europe. Banishment was merely shifting sedition and treachery overseas and this could store up trouble later.

Heading the list of those attainted who had fled the country was Reginald Pole, whom the king truly reviled and publicly castigated as England's arch-traitor, together with his steward Michael Throckmorton, chaplain Thomas Goldwell and John Hillyard, a priest associated with him.

William Peto, Provincial of England of the Observants order of Franciscans, also featured. He showed considerable nerve in preaching against the divorce with Katherine of Aragon in Henry's presence on Easter Sunday, 1532. Peto also warned that if the king continued to behave like Ahab (an Old Testament monarch of Israel), dogs would lick his blood after his death, just like they had Ahab's.[39] Because Peto was canny enough to describe only what *could* happen, he avoided prosecution for predicting the king's demise. Still, he spent the next six months in prison and, after his release, fled England and was now in Italy. In 1543, Pope Paul III named him bishop of Salisbury, but clearly he could not take up the appointment.

Sir Adrian Fortescue, a distant relative of Anne Boleyn's, had also committed unspecified 'detestable and abominable treasons'.[40] He was beheaded at the Tower in July 1539. Like the clerics, he probably had 'adhered to the bishop of Rome, the king's enemy and stirred seditions in the realm'.

Henry had ample justification for loathing Pole. He was the third son of Sir Richard Pole (d.1504), chamberlain to Prince Arthur, and his wife Margaret, née Plantagenet, countess of Salisbury, who, you will recall, was suddenly and brutally executed on the king's orders in May 1541. The young Pole was recognised as a scholar of considerable merit and received an annual annuity of £12 from the king in 1512–13. Eight years later, he was off to Padua with a £100 royal stipend in his purse. In October 1529, Pole was sent to Paris and successfully (and ironically, as events turned out) secured a favourable opinion from the Sorbonne's erudite doctors on the legality of Henry's divorce from his first wife.

Cardinal Reginald Pole (1500–58). His efforts to defend Holy Mother Church and despose the 'schismatic and heretic' Henry made him the 'arch traitor' in the king's eyes. Pole survived several assassination attempts by agents of the Tudor monarch. Under Mary I, he became the last Catholic Archbishop of Canterbury.

Then in early 1532 came the beginnings of the great rift between king and theologian. He had warned Henry rather too forcibly about the political and diplomatic dangers in pursuing the divorce from his Spanish-born queen. Tact was never Pole's forte and he paid the price for his temerity. He had been tipped as the next archbishop of York but his chances of royal preferment disappeared like incense in a draughty church. Pole departed England to write his vehement attack on the king's supremacy over the Church. Created a cardinal just before Christmas 1536, he embarked on a mission of sedition and diplomatic manoeuvring against Henry as he championed the sacred cause of Holy Mother Church, despite repeated and determined attempts to abduct or assassinate him by English agents.

About 130 clergy or laymen with conservative religious beliefs probably escaped from England between 1533 and 1546. In addition, there is a long list of English and Irish rebels who were forced into exile to save their necks, like the 'traitor boy' Gerald Fitzgerald, who fled Ireland for Brittany with thirty men in March 1540.[41]

A more bizarre case was that of the fantasist priest Gregory Botolf, whom we met earlier in that improbable plot to spring Pole's mother from the Tower. Known jocularly as 'Gregory Sweetlips' for his eloquent skill in preaching, he was chaplain to the unfortunate Viscount Lisle and concocted a madcap scheme in early 1540 to capture Calais (with the aid of 600 mercenaries), and surrender it to Cardinal Pole and Pope Paul III. Botolf was, according to a fellow chaplain, 'the most mischievous knave that was ever born'.[42]

Henry devoted considerable energy and resources to seek the arrest and extradition of any fugitive, while seizing property they left behind in England. So it was with Botolf. He fled to Louvain in modern Belgium, disguised as a student at the university there, but soon Tudor justice reached out to clutch him. The king suggested that a trap should be set for him – the bait of a profitable clerical benefice inside the Pale of Calais, required his 'immediate repair thither'.[43] The offer, although written (under duress) by one of his imprisoned accomplices, was hardly subtle and predictably proved untempting. The mayor of Louvain then received a letter from the Privy Council blithely requesting him to arrest and imprison this troublesome priest for stealing church property – the plate he had drunkenly admitted filching from the chantry house of St Gregory in Canterbury, Kent, some years before. Botolf was thrown into the bishop of Liège's jail at Diest for a few months while strenuous diplomatic efforts were made to extradite him.[44] These failed; Botolf never came to trial and papal influence soon ensured his release.[45] 'Sweetlips' then disappears from the historical record.

Not so lucky were two others caught up in Botolf's flights of treasonable fantasy, probably wholly innocently in both cases. Edmund Brindholm, parish priest of Our Lady's Church in Calais, and Clement Philpot, one of Lisle's gentleman servants, were attainted later in 1540 for allying themselves with 'the king's enemy, the bishop of Rome and assisting Raynold [*sic*] Pole, an abominable and arrogant traitor, compassing the surprise of the town of Calais'.[46] Botolf had earlier assured Philpot: 'You shall have plenty. Whereas we now be inferiors, we shall be superiors. The world shall be our's.'[47] His promises proved as far-fetched as his hare-brained schemes. Brindholm and Philpot were executed at Tyburn on 4 August 1540.[48]

Others were more fortunate. Robert Brancetour, a London merchant and one of Pole's associates, was named in the Act of Attainder as being 'now in Italy, devising the king's destruction [and] having knowledge of the [northern] rebellion ... moved princes to levy war against the king'. In March 1539, Henry wrote to the French king demanding his arrest and that of Pole, once they had entered his dominions.

That December, the English ambassador to Spain, Sir Thomas Wyatt, was tipped off about Brancetour's presence in France, as a member of the visiting emperor's entourage. He assured Henry 'it [would be] for your service greatly to have him' and urged the king to write to his brother princes, Francis I and Charles V, to extradite him to England. Meanwhile, Wyatt would secretly entrap him. 'If your majesty commands ... he shall never escape my hands,' he promised.[49]

In early January 1540, Wyatt had secured an audience with the French king about Brancetour, who was living at a Paris address, under close surveillance by English agents. The envoy described him as 'a man of small quality that had been a merchant's factor and robbed his master and since ... had conspired against [Henry] ... In his heart, there was no one that bore more malice to [Henry's] person than he.' Pompously, Francis observed that he could not be a 'good French [man] and false to [his brother king] and that was certain'. He ordered his *prévôt*, or provost, to accompany Wyatt when arresting Brancetour.

Two hours later, ambassador and provost went 'without light' to the traitor's lodgings. Unfortunately, in his anxiety to force an entry, Wyatt fell and hurt his leg badly. 'I told him that since he would not come to visit me, I came to seek him. I showed him what pain I had taken at the door, I had hurt my leg and that I feared that [it] would not be [healed] this month.' (Was he really expecting sympathy?)

Wyatt's sudden appearance, like a pantomime villain, stunned Brancetour. 'His colour changed as soon as he heard my voice. And with that, in came the provost and set hand on him.'

The envoy tried to snatch up the letters on Brancetour's table but 'he caught them before me and flung them backwards into the fire. Yet I overthrew him and caught them out [of the flames] but the provost got them.'

After this struggle, Brancetour insisted that he was a servant of Charles V and charged the provost to deliver him and his papers into the emperor's hands. He produced a cerecloth[50] bag from inside his doublet, containing more papers. These he handed to the provost, who, finding himself in diplomatic waters that ran uncomfortably deep, departed to seek fresh instructions from the French Chancellor.

In his absence, traitor and would-be arresting officer stood staring at each other in an uncertain stand-off. Breaking the silence, Wyatt 'used all my soberness' to convince Brancetour to surrender himself into Henry's mercy. He rejected this, saying that he had heard that the king had 'long hands – but God has longer'. As if to mock Wyatt, the wanted man admitted he had seen Cardinal Pole three months before, 'that he had come with him to Avignon and at Rome' and now he was leaving for Spain.

The provost returned, rather embarrassed, to whisper in Wyatt's ear 'that he must carry the man to his lodging, not to mine, nor [could he] deliver me the writings but keep them safe'. So Brancetour was taken away with the 120 or 140 crowns (£30–£35) that he had with him.

Further efforts to lay hands on the traitor failed, but Wyatt managed to win an audience with Charles V on the evening of Twelfth Night. He told the emperor that Brancetour 'seemed to hang about your court, that was both vassal and rebel to his good brother [Henry] which, according to the treaties [between England and Spain] should have no refuge at your hands'. Charles acknowledged that Brancetour had served him for ten or twelve years – once in Persia, where he deputised for an ambassador who had fallen sick in Turkey and then died. He had also worked for the emperor 'in Africa, Provence, in Italy and now here... Since that time, I know not that he has been in England whereby he has done offence to the king, unless it be for going with Cardinal Pole...'

This was plainly disingenuous and the emperor prevaricated over agreeing to extradite Brancetour, saying he would consider whether the treaties applied in this case after he returned to Spain. Then he went on the offensive. 'I will speak frankly with you,' he told Wyatt with some asperity. 'You have [caused] him to be taken here, whereof I have no little marvel, seeing that you knew him to be a follower of my court. I promise you now it was evil done [by] you without telling me [of it] before.'

Charles swept aside Wyatt's objections. Why should he agree to the destruction of a faithful follower? 'I tell you plain, I will speak for his deliverance both to the Constable [of France] and to the [French] king and I trust they will not do me so great a dishonour as to [allow] one that [serves me], to suffer damage. [Even if] your master had me in the Tower of London, I would not consent to change my honour and my conscience.'

Brancetour was freed by the French the following morning.[51]

Francis wrote to Henry almost three weeks later, huffily complaining that the overbearing Edmund Bonner, the English ambassador in Paris since 1538, had been crass and insulting in accusing him of acting 'against God, reason and [his] duty' in releasing the wanted man. This was a charge that was 'infamous, unjust and contrary to the treaties' between England and France. He could not believe that such words had been spoken on the instructions of Henry and, hence, Marillac, his ambassador in London, would demand Bonner's immediate recall, 'to be replaced by a more prudent and wiser diplomat'. In an abrupt change of tone, he told Henry that he was enjoying excellent health.[52]

Marillac sought an audience with Henry on 1 February and found the king 'astonished that his [ambassador] should have used [such] terms [to Francis] and sorry that he had so badly understood his duty'. But if his brother king was so 'ill-pleased at hearing words so unseemly for the ears of a prince, so [Henry] had still more reason to be displeased', because of the implication that he would act in such an 'uncivil or barbarous' way 'to any prince in Christendom'. He would recall Bonner immediately.

Then the king pointed out that Brancetour's initial detention 'had been very agreeable evidence to him of Francis's goodwill and no doubt, he was much displeased that, on the Emperor's warrant, the prisoner had been released'. If Bonner, his ambassador, knowing 'the wrong done to his master, had in sudden anger exceeded the terms of his charge, then he begged Francis to pardon it, as he desired always to remain a friend'.[53]

The diplomatic wrangling over Brancetour continued with increasing heat.

Charles V, now in Brussels, received Wyatt again. The ambassador taxed him about the traitor's release, claiming, as Henry had instructed, that this decision showed ingratitude for the English king's support and friendship. The word 'ingratitude' dropped like a rock into the murky pool of diplomatic dialogue. The emperor stopped the conversation immediately and made Wyatt repeat his words. Icily, he stated that he owed the English king nothing and the word 'ingratitude' could 'only be used by an equal or superior' monarch. Henry, he declared angrily, would never have dared to use such language 'were it not for that broad ditch [the sea] between him and me'.[54]

As far as he was concerned, it would be 'unreasonable to deliver him to the hangman without knowing why'. Wyatt, struggling manfully to control his temper, asked quickly whether Charles was calling Henry a 'hangman'. The emperor ignored his riposte, saying if he understood the legalities of the case correctly, 'it only remains to execute' Brancetour. Therefore, he intended to send him away from his court for a time but 'he was not bound to do more, even if all the king of England charged Brancetour with was true'.[55] In the event, Charles sent the fugitive to Rome to stay with Pole and await further orders from the Imperial court.[56]

If Henry's brother monarchs were proving perverse and obstinate about extraditing his traitors, the fugitives themselves were just as slippery in escaping from the king's grasp.

Gregory Dudley, son of John Sutton, seventh Lord Dudley, had fled England because of his religious beliefs, but strangely, had decided to hide himself in Calais, where the king's writ ran, as in all his dominions. There he lived on just 6d a day (2.5p or £6 at today's prices), probably disguised as a labourer, but later went to Paris, where Sir William Paget, on a mission to the French court, found him in February 1543. Dudley was preparing to travel to Rome to meet Cardinal Pole, a powerful religious magnet to all dissident Englishmen.

Paget obtained a blank warrant from the French for his extradition and promised Henry that he would 'either send him, or bring him back on my return' to England.[57] He kept 'this miserable fool' in safe keeping and two days later scribbled down his confession. It seemed a cathartic moment for the traitor. 'He begged for mercy with more tears than I ever saw distil from any creature's eyes,' Paget reported. Dudley had been starving in Calais and was 'driven to work with a mattock and shovel and if there be no greater malice in him than appears, he might be pardoned'.[58]

Unusually for a Tudor official, the quality of mercy was not strained. His compassion evaporated nine days later when Dudley escaped. Paget was gravely embarrassed to lose the one traitor who looked certain to be repatriated. He wrote to the king at some length, seeking pardon for the escape of 'this false traitorous boy Dudley' who, while Paget was consuming his well-deserved supper, 'whipped out [through] the door and was out of sight [in the street] before that beastly fool, his keeper, could open the door and follow'.[59]

Dudley went to ground but re-emerged at the end of April in Italy, when two English agents, Edward Raleigh and John Brant, spotted him in Milan. They had noticed a stranger, accompanied by four Frenchmen, who obviously was making every effort to avoid them. Enquiries confirmed their suspicions that this was Gregory Dudley en route to see Pole, now in Bologna, carrying letters to him in the panniers of his mule.

Raleigh and Brant faced a dilemma; should they try to arrange his detention or just kill him on the spot? Murdering him could be 'unprofitable', since they might lose his correspondence and the prize of its vital intelligence, as well as the chance of a confession, damaging to the popish cause. There again, seeking his arrest could be 'difficult in a free country where papists bear much rule'.

They asked the local governor to detain Dudley until the arrival of diplomatic support. He willingly agreed but before Dudley could be arrested, he slipped away, heading for the safety of papal territory. Fortunately, they tracked him down again and he was imprisoned in the castle at Milan, his letters retrieved by the agents and sent back to the Privy Council in London.[60] His time behind bars was short-lived. Before the end of August, Brant was the bearer of bad news: 'that naughty person Dudley [was] suffered to escape out of Milan castle'.

Aside from Pole, there was one fugitive traitor that fed Henry's neuroses more than any other, the so-called 'Blanche Rose', who was hiding in France. His *nom de plume* is the clue to the king's apprehension. In reality, this mysterious figure was one of Henry's subjects called Dick Hosier, the son of a cobbler or tailor. His adoption of this nickname suggested that he claimed to be a long-lost member of the royal House of York – the 'White Rose' threat to the Tudor crown that the king believed had been finally destroyed in that bloody persecution of 1538.

That name 'Blanche Rose' also held inherited dread. This was also the sobriquet of Edmund de la Pole, third duke of Suffolk, secretly executed by Henry in 1513 to neutralise his claim to the throne. The appearance of a possible new pretender, after the dangers and insecurity that Henry's father had suffered from such upstarts, was enough to make the king hobble with fury. Was this a spectre risen from the grave, a portent of evil events to come? The claim to be of the Blood Royal alone made him a traitor.

Blanche Rose had made his debut in France in 1531 after fleeing from England for reasons now unclear. He had been arrested after a request by Sir Francis Bryan, then Henry's ambassador in France, and had spent eight years in a stinking Parisian prison. He was now free and wasted little time in making himself known. In July 1540, he 'accidentally' accosted the steward of Sir John Wallop, the new ambassador to France, in a street market in Rouen and identified himself, saying he had been imprisoned and now wanted help to return to England. Wallop, blessed with a long memory, told Norfolk: 'This is he that calls himself "Blanche Rose", of whom Mr Bryan can tell you enough.'

Hosier had fallen down on his knees, humbly begging Wallop to win him pardon from Henry and confessing to having been born in Wales 'where his father and mother live'. They were 'of base estate and artificers, which is plain declaration that he is English [sic] born'.[61] What should the envoy do about him?[62]

Henry demanded that Francis I should return this latest traitor to England and, to expedite matters, Wallop should apply pressure on the French king to fulfil his treaty obligations. 'If you obtain him, We require you to send him surely hither', he told his ambassador, more in hope than expectation, after his experience of French dilatoriness.[63]

The French insisted that he was not an Englishman, but had been born in Orléans, sixty-nine miles (111km) south-west of Paris. Then they shifted their ground to admit that his mother, then his father, were both English and that she still lived in Orléans. He was, however, a French subject. Wallop argued that after hearing him speak, it was plain that he was not French-born, 'as he spoke very ill French and as good English as I'. He assured Francis that 'Blanche Rose' was a 'very naughty fellow and full of words as can be possible'[64] and his parents' origins made his claim for the traitor's extradition irresistible.

Henry was growing ever more piqued by the French procrastination. He asserted that Hosier was his subject 'but of too base parentage for [Francis] to care anything about the matter. He had only demanded him in order to prove [Francis'] inclination towards the treaty and he now saw how little they [worried about its] violation'.[65]

On 18 October 1540, Henry sent yet another formal demand for him to be repatriated to England, adding, in support of his case, a lengthy discourse on how *he* had fulfilled his treaty obligations with the French and other princes.[66]

It was to no avail; both sides had reached an impasse as to the citizenship (and thus jurisdiction) of the alleged traitor and to reinforce their case, the French had freed Hosier, deliberately, to provoke Henry.

The king, who had invested much emotional energy in the matter, was not prepared to let it drop. The 'Blanche Rose' reappeared in his written instructions to Lord William Howard, briefly ambassador to France in 1541 before the downfall of his niece. Howard was briefed on 'how to speak and answer [about] a certain detestable traitor and common murderer remaining there, naming himself the Blanche Rose, [alias] Dick Hosier. In case he shall hear anything spoken of him, he shall take with him certain writings and depositions ... whereby he shall well perceive from whence he is come, what he has been and is'.[67]

Remarkably, the fate of the Blanche Rose appears prominently in the

ultimatum of demands delivered to the French ambassador as a prelude
to war between England and France on 22 June 1543.

The reasons given for hostilities begin with the French refusal to pay
Henry's tribute of 102,104 crowns (£25,526) annually for nine years –
wealth was always uppermost in the king's thinking. 'Meanwhile, your
master has maintained our sovereign's rebels, as namely the son of a
cobbler who boasted he was of the blood royal and called himself *la
Blanche Rose*.' Only then come complaints about the French incitement
of Scotland to invade England, their treatment of English merchants
and Francis' new alliance with the infidel Turks. France was given
twenty days to fully satisfy Henry's demands before England and Spain
declared war.[68]

Even this ultimatum did not deliver the traitor into the king's eager
hands.

Diplomacy had failed Henry. To his intense frustration, the European
monarchs had refused to live up to their treaty obligations to extradite
those vile traitors and rebels that had escaped his retribution and who
were now busy plotting against him in Europe.[69] Diplomatic letters and
courtly conversations were clearly not the best way to neutralise the
threat these exiles posed Henry and his dynasty. It was time for more
direct action.

The means to achieve this came from an unexpected quarter.

In mid-June 1544, when Henry's army was fighting in northern France,
Ralph Fane, one of Henry's gentlemen pensioners and another soldier,
Richard Wyndebank, received letters recommending an Italian mercenary, Colonel Ludovico da l'Armi, for the king's service.[70] He turned up
at the English siege of Montreuil a few days later and then moved on
to the English lines surrounding Boulogne, where he created great suspicion 'by every day viewing the trenches and the camp, condemning
the king's doings ... [and not hiding] the affection he bears to France
or, at the least, that he cannot like his grace's good successes'.

Knee-deep in the foul mud of their siege-works, no one liked this
know-it-all, particularly as he was a handsome, dashing foreigner. This
tactless, impolite visitor was also a constant irritant to Sir William
Paget, now Secretary of State, who was attending the king at the siege

of Boulogne. He told John, Lord Russell, serving with the English forces investing Montreuil, that da l'Armi was 'a subject of the bishop of Rome' born in Bologna, and was a nephew to Cardinal Lorenzo Campeggio, 'who you knew how well he minded his grace's affairs'.[71] The Italian had been brought up in France, where he had been in government employment. 'The king therefore requires you to send me word at whose recommendation he came to your acquaintance and what you think of him.'[72] Russell thoroughly mistrusted Italian mercenaries. '[Neither he] nor any other Italian, should have tarried [here] and seen our doings, for I know their natures and treasons.'[73]

Yet Henry recruited him as his agent, supposedly to hire mercenaries in Venice, but more pertinently, to murder Pole or anyone else in southern Europe who had fallen into the king's bad books. Da l'Armi was 'Henry VIII's gangster', the 'perfect criminal type: vain, violent, plausible and impudent'.[74] He was brash, swaggering, bursting with Italian charm and brio – and utterly ruthless.

When he arrived in Venice in January 1545, da l'Armi made a bad impression on Edmund Harvel, Henry's ambassador there. 'He pretends great devotion to you', he told the king, 'but I have observed him to have great familiarity with the [papal] legate and others of the French faction. I esteem this as done for some policy but must report it.' Even the papal legate held 'him in great suspicion'.[75]

The mercenary must have felt safe and comfortable in the crowded city with its confusing network of narrow canals. Even today, a nocturnal (and expensive) gondola ride through the badly lit back canals provides a vivid impression of the continued mystery and anonymity of the city, coupled with an atmosphere verging on the sinister, as the moon strikes a sparkling path on the water. Here in the darkness lurked ample opportunity for the assassin to plan equally dark deeds.

In 1545, the three Venetian magistrates commissioned the Veronese painter Bonifacio de' Pitati (1487–1553) to paint four religious masterpieces[76] to hang in their headquarters in the Palazzo dei Camerlenghi, by the Rialto Bridge. One painting was *The Slaughter of the Innocents*, depicting the New Testament story of the pitiless massacre of the infants by Herod's soldiers.[77] The arch-shaped picture, now in Venice's Gallerie dell'Accademia, shows a tall, bearded figure, standing in the lower right-hand corner, nonchalantly watching the carnage and mayhem going on around him. Next to him is another figure holding a shield bearing a coat of arms. These are of the da l'Armi family and the dandy's clothes resemble those worn by the assassin when he was later arrested. This must be Henry's gangster who had arrived in Venice that year. If so, this painting could be considered the most expensive 'Wanted' poster in the history of criminology.[78]

Meanwhile Colonel da l'Armi began to prove his worth to Henry. Diplomatic reports from Brussels suggested that he was 'much spoken of in Italy and may have 6,000 Italians to serve the king if he will'.[79] Even Harvel had changed his mind about him, reporting in March 1545 that he 'evidently loves and esteems his majesty'.

His father, Gasparo da l'Armi, lived in Bologna in the Papal States. That his son was in Henry's pay 'much pleases his father and all his friends in Bologna', but the authorities in Rome took a dim view and summoned da l'Armi senior to explain himself, on pain of losing a surety of 50,000 crowns (£12,500). However, the Vatican's intimidation of the father failed to curb the son's covert activities.

It was reported (wrongly, as it later turned out) that Pole refused to attend the Church's council at Trent (Trento in north-east Italy) with other cardinals, for 'fear of his life, doubting such captains as have been rumoured to serve your majesty, whereof the fame is very great in all Italy'.[80]

In Rome, Cardinal Niccolò Ardinghelli, newly appointed Prefect of the Apostolic Signatura, with involvement in the secret services of the Holy See, had grown worried about the clandestine operations of Henry's agent. He was probably behind the abortive plan in late March to murder da l'Armi, when Piero Maria de San Secondo, a mercenary captain in French pay, had been sent with twelve men to kill him.[81] On 5 May, Ardinghelli summoned Francesco Venier, Venetian ambassador to the Vatican, for a confidential chat over a goblet or two of good *vino*. He disclosed that the king of England 'kept a number of persons in his pay in diverse places for some purpose' which must be 'considered sinister, his character being such as it is'. Chief among Henry's motley crew of ruffians was da l'Armi, and Pope Paul III himself believed that his presence in Venice 'was not in accordance with the good understanding between him and the Signory, nor, for the respect and honour of the Apostolic See, ought it to be tolerated'.

The Doge and Signory should immediately expel him from Venice and her territories 'lest it appear that he enjoys your Serenity's favour'.

The envoy warned Ardinghelli that many Venetian merchants lived in England with valuable investments, so they would have to 'proceed somewhat moderately with that king'. The cardinal brushed aside such caution: 'His Holiness does not require the Signory to do as *he* would do, [if] he could get hold of da l'Armi, who is his rebel and has committed so many crimes'. Instead, he 'demands his [expulsion], lest through the Signory's protection, he may find an opportunity for perpetrating some enormous outrage'. Da l'Armi was being paid fifty crowns (£12.50) a month by Henry, seemingly for nothing, which 'induces a suspicion of some mischievous design'.

The Venetian understood very well what Ardinghelli was talking about. He had heard whispers in the Vatican's corridors that da l'Armi was plotting 'some mischief and among other things, he has some treacherous design against Cardinal Pole who is now at Trent'.[82]

Three days later, the ambassador was kneeling before the seventy-seven-year-old grey-bearded Pope Paul III, who was anxious to learn what the Venetian government was planning about da l'Armi.

The issue was very close to the pope's heart and he told Venier that the mercenary and his accomplices were preparing to undertake some terrible crime and were only waiting for a Gentleman of Henry's Privy Chamber to arrive with the king's commission. He was expected in Venice within the next twelve days.

'We see this villain near at hand. He is our rebel and on many accounts would deserve a thousand deaths. We perceive that the king of England, who is a heretic, has no other enmity [hostility] in Italy than ours ... and in several quarters he is plotting I know not what mischief ... Should any disturbance arise, it would be unfitting for it to have originated in Venice.' The pope added: 'The council is sitting [at Trent]. We do not know what direction [Henry's] thoughts may take. There is the particular [case] of Cardinal Pole, whom these ruffians may have been ordered to kidnap, or take some other sinister action against him.'[83]

After the Venetian Council of Ten had been honoured by a visit from the papal nuncio (a diplomatic envoy from the Holy See) with a similar message from the Vatican – delivered with 'some warmth' – da l'Armi was summoned by them to answer some hard questions.

But the bird had flown. Harvel's secretary said that da l'Armi was away on the king's business. Alarmingly, the Venetians received intelligence that he had gone to Trent.

Whatever his mission was, it apparently remained unfulfilled. The mercenary colonel had returned to the city, as in early August 1545, he was involved in a fight with the Venetian night watch, commanded by Zuan dalla Moneda, captain of the Council's boats.

Da l'Armi was one of eight or ten armed men who lived in a house fronting one of the narrow back canals. The building was surrounded, and when challenged, the desperadoes cried warning shouts of 'Arms!' and drew their weapons. During the running battle that followed, a member of the watch was badly wounded. The penalty for this crime in Venice was death.

As investigations into the incident continued, it was discovered that da l'Armi had hired assassins to murder an army officer, Count Curio Bua, in Treviso. They had stabbed and slashed at him two or three times with knives or swords (which he survived) before clambering over the city walls to escape on their horses, left at a taverna about a mile (1.6km) away. One assailant had been captured later, rather stupidly hiding in da l'Armi's house in Venice.[84]

Harvel had explained to the Signory that during the night-time fracas, da l'Armi had mistaken the watch for a gang of his enemies. They believed this glib explanation and were prepared to show him favour to please Henry, whom they held 'in great reverence'. His latest outrage, however, changed everything and they planned to proceed against him and his accomplices.

Although now a wanted man, with a price of £100 on his head, dead or alive, da l'Armi brazenly called at Harvel's house 'and confessed the deed', saying that he had paid Curio Bua fifty crowns as a down-payment on his mercenary fee, but had been defrauded. The assault was only an act of hot-blooded vengeance.[85]

That night da l'Armi fled Venice post-haste for Brussels and he saw some fighting against the French in late September 1545.[86]

Da l'Armi then turned up at Henry's court where he spent a few months, successfully building the persona of a loyal servant, wrongfully treated. Paget told his colleague Sir William Petre in December that the mercenary thought himself 'cast out at the cart's tail. He had a vengeful wit and [is] naturally disposed to work mysteries. Such a man, at such a time, is to be cherished.'[87] It was therefore decided that he should return to Venice to continue as Henry's agent.

The Venetians were rightly suspicious. A motion to agree to Henry's request for a five-year safe conduct for da l'Armi was unanimously defeated by the city's Council of Ten on 4 December, 'for the peace of the inhabitants of Venice and to avoid disturbing the peace of their towns'. Five days later, the motion was put again, and this time it was passed with a majority of eighteen, with two abstentions, 'for his majesty's gratification by reason of our ancient friendship with him'.[88]

Da l'Armi had lived to fight another day. '*Guaio*' – 'Trouble' in Italian – must have been his middle name.

The killing continued.

9

The Last Chance of Military Glory

On Tuesday, 3 August 1543, a proclamation was published in London declaring that England and Spain were now at war with France. Francis I had become a mortal enemy to Henry and Charles V (indeed to all Christian monarchs), through his unholy alliance with Suleiman the Magnificent, sultan of the mighty Ottoman Empire.[1] Following chivalric custom, Henry's chief herald, Christopher Barker, Garter Principal King of Arms, and his Imperial counterpart, François de Phallaix, Toison d'Or, were instructed to 'deliver their defiance' in person to the French king.

The protocol was that the Imperial herald would require Francis to disown forthwith his alliance with 'the Great Turk', compensate Charles V for injuries inflicted upon him and pay the tribute arrears due to Henry. If he met all the allies' demands, they would graciously make peace with him. Unfortunately, Francis neatly avoided this traditional ceremony by refusing Toison d'Or entry into France. Barker, unable to execute his mission alone, had to return to England.

His boorish behaviour only fuelled the king's enthusiasm for his invasion of France. Like an old warhorse, Henry could scent the acrid reek of spent gunpowder and longed for the martial beat of the drums and fifes, the billowing banners and all the grim paraphernalia of disciplined military slaughter.

During his childhood, Henry had listened spellbound to thrilling tales of old battlefield triumphs over the despised French. The old English claim to the throne of France was never far from the forefront of his mind. But those juvenile dreams of bravery and victory in combat that would linger famously in the annals of English history, had gone unfulfilled down the years, either by him or his generals – save for the routs inflicted on the Scots at Flodden and latterly at Solway Moss.

Henry had savoured just one fleeting moment of personal military glory: the Battle of the Spurs against the French on 16 August 1513.

So sweet was this victory, that soon afterwards, Henry commissioned a huge oil painting celebrating his personal triumph. At the centre of the action, the king is seen on horseback, gallant in shining black armour, receiving the surrender of the Chevalier Bayard,[2] kneeling at his charger's feet, as the killing continues in a furious mêlée around them. The painting was one of the first acquired by what later became the Royal Collection and it was displayed for public admiration, probably in one of the audience chambers of Henry's privy apartments at Whitehall.[3]

In truth, the fighting was far from the decisive, all-conquering victory that Henry, or his dramatic painting, boasted of. It was more skirmish than full-blown battle. French cavalry were escorting horsemen, carrying sides of bacon to resupply the besieged city of Thérouanne, when they were ambushed by English archers and artillery, together with Imperial forces. The leading elements turned tail and cannoned into their comrades coming up behind. Chaos ensued and the panic-stricken French fled, discarding their weapons in their haste to escape. The speed of their flight, as they spurred their horses to safety, led to the mocking name for this brief clash.[4] Henry captured nine standards and 250 prisoners, some of noble birth, but the fighting hardly constituted a crushing victory – except in the king's eyes.[5]

Battle or no, this was three decades earlier. The trumpet calls of triumph had long since fallen silent. His last offensive against France in the autumn of 1523 had ended in humiliation, when a 10,000-strong English army, commanded by Suffolk, came within fifty miles (80km) of Paris, before extreme weather – it was so cold that the troops suffered frostbite – and the desertion of their Imperial allies forced retreat to the safety of Calais.

Twenty years on, Henry was conscious that his advancing years and the medical conditions afflicting his increasingly obese body threatened his chances of enjoying battlefield glory again, let alone asserting his right to the French crown.

One physical manifestation of his problems was the garniture, or suit of armour, made for him possibly in 1540, by Erasmus Kyrkenar, who had become Master of the Royal Greenwich Armoury the previous year.

As in bespoke tailoring, armour could be adjusted or 'let out' to allow room for growth in the owner's chest or stomach. Two pieces of steel, each two inches (5cm) wide, were riveted on either side of the backplate to accommodate the king's increasing girth. The armour for jousting on horseback weighed a mighty 110lbs (50kg). The burden of the foot-combat version, at 88lbs (40kg), suggests that only a fit, agile man could fight with a sword or a poleaxe while wearing more than six stone of metal – particularly on a hot day.[6] Henry was that warrior in his fantasy, but reality dictated that instead of fighting alongside his knights, he should sit out any battle as a frustrated spectator.

Such physical difficulties did not deter his plans to invade France for the third time, nurtured since 1540, nor his unquestionable determination to lead the English army into battle. But first, he still had to secure his frontier with Scotland, which, despite the victory at Solway Moss and the death of James V, continued to appear vulnerable.

After the invading Scottish army had fled in November 1542, Henry should have seized this rare chance to invade a demoralised, politically divided and militarily weak Scotland before the French could intervene. If he had, the running sore of insecurity on his northern borders would have been healed once and for all. But lack of resolve, poor communications and inadequate intelligence allowed the opportunity to slip through Henry's podgy fingers, mainly because his attention was focused on preparations for the all-important war with France.

The king was indignant when, on 3 January 1543, James Hamilton, second earl of Arran, was appointed Governor and Protector of Scotland, ruling as regent for the baby Mary Queen of Scots during her minority. Arran also secured the succession in the event of Mary's death. Henry, who believed himself feudal overlord of Scotland, felt the choice of who governs this vassal state should have been his, and his alone.

This slight on the king's perceived rights did not dissuade him from sending reams of advice to Arran in his new role. The regent would profit by imposing a Scottish version of the English Reformation, sweeping aside those popish clergy, monks and friars and dissolving the religious houses to the great benefit of his exchequer in Edinburgh.

After all, the clerics and monks lived 'an abominable life... to the high displeasure of God', but had also caused damage to the country's economy by 'spending their time in all idleness and filthiness with such a face of hypocrisy and superstition as is intolerable'.

If the regent followed this sensible policy, his young son could marry Henry's second daughter, now aged almost ten. 'The Lady Elizabeth [is] endowed with virtues and qualities agreeable to her estate', wrote the king. 'We have determined in Our heart, [that] if We see [you] sincerely to go through with Us in all things, to condescend to a marriage to be celebrated between your son and Our daughter.' After the wedding, Henry would allow his new son-in-law to live at his Renaissance court and be 'brought up and nourished' within its splendid precincts.[7]

It would not take a genius to recognise that Arran's son would be a hostage guaranteeing his father's good behaviour, rather than a son-in-law welcomed into the disparate Tudor family. The king's generous offer was not accepted. The regent did agree to a three-month truce and imprisoned Cardinal David Beaton for conspiring with the French power-broker Claude de Lorraine, first duke of Guise, against him. In retaliation, a papal interdict suspended the rites and services of the Catholic Church in Scotland, so her population was denied Christian burial, marriage or baptism.

Events were unfolding rapidly in Scotland, sometimes to Henry's advantage, at others to his detriment. With wild swings in allegiances amid the turmoil of Scottish domestic politics, it became impossible for the king to know whom to trust.

Beaton was unexpectedly released from prison in mid-April 1543, the interdict lifted, and later, Pope Paul III sent his papal nuncio, Mark Grimani, patriarch of Aquileia, to Scotland; he landed safely, despite Henry's best efforts to intercept his ship and seize him. Arran pretended to disown this papal envoy but, duplicitously, had already placed Scotland under the pope's protection.

He wrote to Pope Paul III on 14 May about Scotland's 'incredible trouble' after James V's death. 'On the one hand is grief for a Prince dead in his prime, leaving only a daughter and heir; on the other, the English king, with a numerous army, is threatening again to invade Scotland.' To demonstrate his devotion to the Holy See, Arran committed 'the kingdom to the protection of Your Holiness, whom I beg to undertake the defence of its liberty and privileges...' In another letter, to the former diplomat Cardinal Rodolfo Pio da Carpi, he pointed out that hostilities between England and Scotland were caused by their refusal to join Henry's campaign against the pope's authority. His Holiness could best help with money, as well as an edict to defend the privileges of Scotland.[8]

Physical, rather than just spiritual, aid had arrived in Scotland. Matthew Stewart, fourth earl of Lennox, landed on Scotland's west coast in April 1543, with French military advisers and generous quantities of gold. With him was an emissary who would pledge French assistance in an English invasion.

Henry was exasperated by the Scots' machinations. On 25 April, he wrote to Sir Ralph Sadler, his ambassador in Edinburgh, urging that if Arran 'had not swerved too far from the king' he should be frank with him. Sadler, Henry instructed, should ask: 'Sir, what will you do? Will you now wilfully cast yourself away? Can you think otherwise but that the clergy... will seek all the ways possible for your destruction, though they give you now fair words?'[9] This was hardly the nuanced language of diplomacy and hint at the king's desperation.

A week later, he suggested that the tasty carrot of a rich English bishopric should be dangled in front of Cardinal Beaton as an inducement to betray Rome and his French loyalties. Sadler should meet Beaton in Edinburgh and remind him 'of the advantage of [deserting] France and uniting these two realms. If it is hard to persuade him to leave France because he has a bishopric there, you may say that the king's kindness is such that if he [were to] show more regard for the commonwealth... he may count on getting a better bishopric in England.'[10]

After all those missed opportunities, Scottish prevarication and breathtaking duplicity by both parties, Henry persuaded the hitherto intractable Scots to toe his line. On 1 July 1543, two treaties were signed at Greenwich. The Treaty of Greenwich declared peace between Scotland and England 'during the life of either Prince and for one year after'. Neither 'party should make or procure war upon the other or his confederates, or do anything to the hurt of the other'. Furthermore, neither prince 'upon pretext of any ecclesiastical sentence or censure, shall violate any article of this treaty'.[11] Significantly, it did not commit the Scottish government to renouncing its alliance with France, a clause that Henry had demanded as keenly as the others.[12]

He was also thwarted by the second Anglo-Scots treaty signed that day, this time agreeing the marriage of Prince Edward, now almost six, with the infant Mary Queen of Scots. The Edinburgh government resisted every attempt to have the king's grand-niece sent immediately to England. Both sides knew that whoever held the child also grasped the Scottish crown.

Henry could not allow this requirement to become a deal-breaker so reluctantly agreed that by the end of her tenth year, Mary would be delivered into English hands at Berwick, providing that the marriage had been sealed in a proxy ceremony. Meanwhile, Mary could stay in Scotland. After the marriage was consummated, the king would assign lands worth £2,000 a year, a sum doubled at his death. Scottish hostages would be sent to England as guarantors of her delivery.[13]

Despite these disappointments, Henry managed to convince himself that the threat from Scotland had been finally neutralised and that he could now concentrate on defeating his paramount enemy, Francis I of France.

Henry had fondly imagined that his invasion could be launched that summer of 1543, but the wearisome distraction of Scotland had caused delay. There had also been unexpected problems in his negotiations for an alliance with Charles V, who had been at war with France for a year.

The first difficulty arose over the problem of the king's self-appointed title of Supreme Head of the Church in England. The emperor was shamefaced about being the military ally of the heretic Henry. His diplomats considered it impossible to include the title in a treaty, or being bound to defend England against attack, including that by 'spiritual persons', a euphemism for the pope. The English insisted that the king should receive his full title (after all, his subjects could die for treasonably denying it) and his realm should have protection from papal-inspired invasions, as in 1539.[14]

Henry saw such issues in simple terms. He considered it strange that Charles should prefer Paul III as a friend, particularly, as he pointed out, 'this pope, being very frail, might die tomorrow and be succeeded by one of the French faction'. He marvelled at the emperor's new scruples about the papacy; did not his own mutinous troops sack

Rome in 1527 and hold Henry's old adversary Pope Clement VII hostage in the Castel Sant'Angelo for six months, before he escaped, disguised as a pedlar?[15]

After weeks of haggling, the negotiations were concluded. The alliance treaty, agreed by Henry on 11 February 1543, described him as 'Defender of the Faith etc', the title bestowed on him by Pope Leo X in October 1521, before his breach with Rome.[16] The use of 'etcetera' proved an expedient sidestep away from diplomatic pitfalls. The treaty and its terms were kept secret until the end of May and the following month, the allies' ultimatum was delivered to Marillac in London.

The allies' grand war plan ruled out a major English invasion until June 1544, when England and Spain would each field an army numbering 35,000 infantry and 7,000 cavalry. Charles would invade France from Flanders, through the Champagne region, while Henry would land in Calais and lead his troops eastwards along the River Somme through Picardy, as 'strategy, victuals and the enemy shall permit'. These were the very same lanes trodden by Henry V's heroes of Agincourt, 129 years before. The strategic objective of both armies was the poorly fortified French capital of Paris.[17]

Eager for military action, the king dispatched Sir John Wallop, now governor of Guisnes, and 5,000 English troops from Calais to assist in the emperor's defence of the Low Countries and, more importantly, to land a telling 'first buffet' or blow on the French.[18] They merrily burnt their way through the villages of north-east France without opposition, but then came one of those incongruities of Tudor warfare, dictated by the doctrine of chivalry. Wallop challenged the captain of Thérouanne to send out six of his officers to 'run with six gentlemen of our army for life and death'. The war immediately stopped and the English army sheathed their swords to watch and cheer the impromptu tournament, refreshed by looted wine and food. The contest, fought with deadly pointed lances rather than the blunt versions of peacetime, probably ended in a draw. One Englishman was 'hurt in the head to the death' and a Frenchman was wounded.[19] Chivalric honour satisfied, the English force pressed on and were assigned to the Imperial forces' siege of the Hainault town of Landrecy, captured earlier by the French.[20]

Noble chivalry was supplanted by the hard graft of war. From 12 August to the end of October, they dug trenches, carefully following

Henry's meddlesome advice on the construction of the siege-works and the firing of their mortars. Wallop reported that the 'town is so [well] trenched that no one can enter or issue out, yet [the French] boast they will re-victual it'.[21] When the French resupplied the town and an approaching enemy force became threatening, a discouraged Charles V decided to break off the siege. Wallop pulled back to Calais, having achieved little of any strategic value.

That June, a French fleet of sixteen ships had landed men at Aberdeen, in north-east Scotland, and delivered letters to Cardinal Beaton. On their way home, the French ships were intercepted off Orfordness, on the Suffolk coast, by an English flotilla commanded by Vice-Admiral Sir Rhys Mansel who, in a ten-hour action, tried to board her flagship, the *Sacre*, with men from his warships *Primrose* and *Minion*. Two French ships were captured, for the loss of one English. The enemy ships were scattered and eight headed back north to the Firth of Forth, where they berthed at Edinburgh's port at Leith to repair their battered hulls and tend more than sixty badly wounded crewmen.

The French sailed for home again on 9 August, this time sheltering amid a fleet of Scottish merchant ships, as the Anglo-Scottish peace treaty had not yet been ratified by Arran. Again they were intercepted by Henry's navy and four more were captured, with another chased back to Dundee by the English warship *Sweepstake*. Five or six Scottish vessels were arrested on Henry's orders after docking at Great Yarmouth, Norfolk, on suspicion that they were carrying Beaton's letters to France.

News of the ships' impoundment enraged the good citizens of Edinburgh, especially the ship-owning merchants, whose fury turned the city against Sadler, the resident English ambassador. 'They swore great oaths [that] if their ships are not restored they would have amends of me and mine and would set my house here afire over my head, so that not one of us should escape alive,' he reported in great agitation. Their reaction demonstrated 'the unreasonableness of the people who live here in such beastly liberty that they neither regard God nor [Arran]'. Sadler pleaded that unless the Scottish ships were released, he could not stay in Edinburgh without endangering himself and his family.[22]

The tumult had not subsided four days later. He reported that the city's provost had 'much ado to [stop] them assaulting me in my house and keeps nightly watch [outside] ... He prayed me to keep myself and my folks within, for it is scant in his power to repress or resist the fury of the people. And they say plainly that I shall never pass out of this town alive except [when] they have their ships restored. This is the rage and beastliness of this nation, which God keep all honest men from.'[23]

One of his servants, clearly claustrophobic, unwisely left the residency to sample the sweet air of Edinburgh. A 'Scottish villain' called him 'an English dog' and spoke 'such spiteful words about the king's majesty, as no true Englishman could bear ... Indeed, my man, having a good Englishman's heart in his body ... drew his dagger and struck the [Scot] about the face ... Whereupon, there were twenty drawn swords about my servant, whom they have sore wounded in sundry parts of his body ... [and] I am in doubt whether he shall escape death.'[24]

Sadler and his family were smuggled out of Edinburgh and safely ensconced in Tantallon Castle, East Lothian, overlooking the Firth of Forth.

Arran suddenly and unexpectedly overcame his hatred of Cardinal Beaton and defected to his pro-French party. On Sunday, 9 September, Mary was crowned Queen of Scotland at Stirling Castle in their presence.

Henry ordered Suffolk to launch an attack on Edinburgh with 8,000 cavalry and light artillery to seize Arran and Beaton, burn the city 'and as much of the countryside' as possible. Warships docked in Newcastle and Berwick should sail north and block their escape by sea. This offensive was retaliation for the damage caused to 'Our honour; the Scots and especially the [Regent] having deluded Our expectation' and failing to meet their treaty obligations.[25] Dishonour and disobedience to the king of England could not go unpunished.

Suffolk made excuses. Although his troops were held at twenty-four hours' readiness, he could not possibly mount such an expedition in late September when the uncertain weather militated against fighting in hostile territory. Moreover, his quarry had escaped; both Arran and Beaton had moved out of reach, up the coast to St Andrews, fifty-three miles (85km) north of Edinburgh.

The confusing drama turned rapidly into a crisis, with no firm ground yet found in the shifting quicksands of loyalty in Scottish politics. In

October, Jacques de la Brossé, cup-bearer to Francis I, arrived as the new French ambassador with seven ships in the River Clyde carrying £7,500 in gold crowns and war supplies. His immediate problem was that the money and weapons were out of reach in Dumbarton Castle, held by the earl of Lennox, who had decided to switch allegiances and support Henry's cause. He was motivated by the alluring prospect of marriage to the king's niece, Lady Margaret Douglas; a comfortable income to replace what he would lose in France, and promises of English assistance in overthrowing Arran so he could take over the regency.

Grimani, the papal legate, had come with the usual Vatican armoury of 'Bulls, faculties and pardons to get money' but found the Scots 'so wild, he wishes himself at home again', scoffed a cynical Sadler.[26] Grimani had escaped another desperate attempt to kidnap him, ordered (of course) by Henry. Three hours before dawn, he fled Glasgow in disguise for the safety of Stirling Castle. The legate admitted later that he was 'in great trouble and danger, not knowing who to guard against and, but for the Queen [Dowager] and the cardinal, who ... have saved my life, I would now be in the power of the king of England'.[27]

The following month, it was rumoured that Arran, at Cardinal Beaton's prompting, was determined to fight England, bolstered by la Brossé's pledges that 6,000 mercenary cavalry from Denmark would arrive, together with enough French gold to pay 10,000 Scots soldiers. Beaton bragged that Henry 'should not have the honour to begin the war [with Scotland] for they would begin [first]'.[28] The regent accused Sadler of forfeiting his diplomatic privileges by his conspiracies to suborn faithful Scots and demanded his expulsion from his sanctuary at Tantallon.[29] Suffolk sent Sadler his letters of recall and an escort of 400 cavalry, provided by one of Henry's few embattled allies in Scotland, conveyed him safely to Berwick on 11 December.[30]

The final blow to Henry's pride came that same day when the Scottish Parliament annulled the peace and marriage treaties signed in Greenwich five months before. They followed this up on 15 December by renewing all former treaties between Scotland and France. The 'Auld Alliance' was stronger than ever.

If Henry ever had a coherent policy in Scotland, it was now in tatters. He tried to convince Charles V to treat the Scots as enemies[31] but the emperor had his hands full in fighting the French.

Impotently, the king could only rage and bluster against the Scots government: 'You have covenanted with a prince of honour that will not suffer your disloyalty unpunished and unrevenged, whose power and puissance by God's grace, is and shall be sufficient against you to make you know and feel your faults and offences.'[32]

His ally Charles V had been following events in Scotland with alarm. He feared that war on Henry's northern borders would distract both him and his military resources away from the agreed campaign in northern France. In early December, he sent a special envoy, Férrante Gonzaga, viceroy of Sicily, to London with specific instructions to discover the king's plans.[33] 'We cannot make preparations for the invasion of the enemy's territories next year ... [if] the king suddenly withdraws his army ... to employ in Scotland,' the emperor emphasised. Would Henry change his mind at 'the eleventh hour and leave Us single-handed to fight the French'?

If Henry's ministers saw their priority was war with Scotland, Gonzaga should argue that Henry's Scottish problems were 'the very reason why the king should assist, with all his power, the undertaking against Francis ... because [he was] the abettor and ally of the Scotch'. Invading France would stop further French military assistance to the Edinburgh government.[34]

Henry, who fancied himself as an old campaigner, was unlikely to swallow this tortured military logic; did the quickest route to neutralising Scotland really lie in the green fields of Picardy? So the emperor, who long before had grasped how to influence the king, cunningly backed up his arguments with a little persuasive flattery to massage Henry's already gargantuan ego.[35]

Gonzaga was instructed to praise Henry's 'great wisdom, long experience, singular and clear understanding ... [of] military affairs. We not only defer to his judgement, but will approve any course he may suggest, the better to annoy, offend, harm and destroy the common enemy ... Such is Our trust in him that We have no doubt that whatever plan of campaign he fixes on, that will be the best.' The envoy should also remind the king of just what kind of enemy they would defeat. God had deprived Francis 'of his senses and reduced ... him to such terms that he may be punished and chastised for the innumerable injuries that Christendom has had to suffer at his hands'.

Then came the real clincher.

We have no doubt that Our brother the king of England would wish to attend personally the proposed invasion. We firmly believe that [this] step would be a very important one and contribute greatly to the success of the war, not only on account of [his] personal qualities, magnanimity, reputation and experience in military affairs, but [also] because it would undoubtedly terrify the king of France and his subjects. Yet, on the other hand, considering the present state of England and everything else concerning Our common affairs, We should not dare to propose it.

Chapuys was then to casually toss into the conversation with the king that Charles himself 'intends leading Our army in person'.[36] In all honour, Henry could not now back out from taking part in the invasion. He had been neatly boxed in by his own pride and vanity.

Detailed planning for the French adventure was proceeding rapidly. A report drawn up by Norfolk in March 1544 suggested the Army Royal's best route to the French capital was to cross the River Somme, north-west of the town of Nesle in Picardy – the very same ford used by Suffolk and his troops back in 1523. Enough food and animal fodder for twelve to fourteen days should be carried by wagons 'by which time, his majesty may be very near to Paris and shall pass by many good towns, not fortified... in [this] most plentiful country of France'. The old general proposed that the army's three formations – the vanguard, rearguard and battle – should land at Calais by 12 June, in readiness for the king's own triumphant arrival.[37]

The Tudor bureaucracy's plan for the invasion is a comprehensive fifty-four page document that detailed the costs, manpower, animals, weaponry and munitions needed for a successful campaign. Suffolk was appointed lieutenant-general of the 'Army Royal' on a generous salary of £5 a day, or almost £2,500 in today's money. In contrast, one of his foot soldiers received daily pay of 6d.

Total cost of a three-month invasion of France was estimated at £200,000 (£102 million today) with £10,000 for naval operations and another £12,000 for English forces on the Scottish borders. Add various additional charges and a £10,000 contingency budget and the final bill would amount to £250,000.

Funding would come from the revenues of the Court of Augmentation, taxes and other sources like the £40,000 produced by the sale of royal lands and £50,000 in short-term loans by foreign bankers and merchants at 12 per cent interest. However, this income fell short of the required budget by £116,000. Therefore, further properties would be sold, as well as lead from the roofs of dissolved monasteries. More loans would also be extracted from merchants in London and Antwerp.

The logistic support for Henry's military operations was itemised in great detail, describing the roles of the 2,328 people who milled flour, baked bread, brewed ale, butchered meat, drove cattle and the 724 wagons needed to carry their equipment, including those fitted with mobile ovens. Other carts carried 'several [flour] mills which go on milling and turning' as the wagons trundled along[38] and sections of prefabricated wooden forts for temporary protection. Additionally, 1,382 carts were to carry rations for the three army divisions, and ninety-seven wagons were to transport boats which, lashed together, were used for bridging rivers. To pull all those 'carriages', a total of almost 6,000 horses, seven to each vehicle, were to be provided by the English shires.

England had insufficient draught horses, so a request for 11,000 more to haul the artillery, munitions and baggage wagons was made to Henry's new allies in Flanders. They could supply only 4,000, because of demands by Charles V's army and the harvest needs of local farmers.

As well as a substantial artillery train (with 5,820 cannon shot and 84 lasts[39] of gunpowder for the vanguard alone), the minutiae of Tudor warfare is laid out in the officials' shopping lists for military hardware. These included 6,000 horseshoes and 300,000 nails; 1,000 shovels and spades, 500 pickaxes and mattocks and 200 felling axes. For lighting, there were fifty cressets (fire baskets), 150 lanterns and five barrels of tallow candles. Spare weaponry, to replace that lost or broken in combat, was listed as: 1,000 morris pikes, 200 demi-lances, 1,000 polearms, 3,000 yew bows and 6,000 sheaves of arrows (each with twenty-four shafts) and 28,800 silk or hempen bowstrings, in twenty barrels.[40] The bureaucrats did not forget the need for thirty skins of parchment and one ream of 'paper royal' for recording and distributing information generated by the invasion.

Proverbially, an army marches on its stomach, so there are estimates for the quantities of wheat, beer, malt, cheese, sheep, cattle and flitches of bacon that would be consumed during the fighting in France.[41]

Of course, there were also the soldiers to undertake the fighting. Henry, like the Tudor monarchs after him, could not afford to maintain a standing army, so, following the old medieval feudal tradition, looked to his court, the aristocracy, the Church and the gentry in England and Wales to fill the ranks. The southern counties alone would recruit 71,098 men, fitted out with 18,552 harnesses of armour. Most were untrained and ill-equipped levies and Henry hoped that he could stiffen the sinews of his army by hiring veteran German and Italian mercenaries to fight for England's cause.

Heading the list of those providing troops were the members of his Privy Council and the Lord Privy Seal, Sir John, Lord Russell, who contributed the largest contingent of 100 cavalry and 1,200 infantry. Suffolk certified that he could supply '300 of his tenants in Lincolnshire, able men and meet to serve, and with his household servants, he could make 100 horsemen with demi-lances and javelins, either on good horses or good geldings, [with] 100 archers and 300' armed with pole weapons. Norfolk and his son, the earl of Surrey, contributed 100 horse and 500 cavalry and Wriothesley, who became Lord Chancellor on Audley's death in April 1544, offered forty horsemen, fifty archers and 110 other infantry. Gardiner, bishop of Winchester, supplied 100 cavalry and 200 foot soldiers.[42]

Despite careful planning, war is a very uncertain business. The use of unreliable foreign mercenaries and the burgeoning cost of the war were to prove a disaster for the king and the economy of his realm. The estimated monthly cost of 1,500 German mercenary cavalry and 6,000 infantry was more than £8,200, including pay for standard bearers, priests and the four halberdiers who were bodyguards for each captain.[43]

The king's well-known fascination with military technology attracted offers of help from unexpected quarters. Giovani Battista, a painter of Ravenna in northern Italy, had plans for new-fangled weaponry. These included terracotta hand grenades, fire bombs that could 'burn the decks of ships' and 'round shields ... with guns that fire upon the enemy and pierce any armour'. He also offered gunpowder that exploded noiselessly 'which serves very well for ambuscades'. If these inventions were not alluring enough, Battista's wife was 'adorned with all womanly virtues, who can play the lute and sing, read and write, so as to teach girls'. Sadly, he had insufficient funds for them to travel to England.

One hundred steel and oak gun-shields were purchased for the king's personal bodyguard and others were manufactured at Greenwich to Battista's design. Several were found in the wreck of his warship *Mary Rose* that sank off Portsmouth in 1545; these were fixed to the gunnels and fired in salvoes by tugging a lanyard.[44]

Henry had not forgotten or forgiven his humiliation in Scotland and was hell-bent on punishing the Scots for their effrontery in their dealings with him. Hertford was sent north as his new general.

Regular raids across the border were ordered to keep the Scots off-balance and Paget briefed Hertford that Henry wanted to leave behind a spiteful message, amid the destruction and pillaging. 'It shall be well done ... to leave upon the church door or some other notable place within ... towns ... where [you] shall fortune to make spoil, these ... words: "You may thank your Cardinal for this. If he had not [lived], you might have been in quiet and rest ... He has travailed [worked] as much as [he] can to bring you sorrow and trouble."'[45]

Mere propaganda and plundering were wholly inadequate chastisement in the king's eyes. On 10 April 1544, Henry's orders for the smiting of Scotland were sent to Hertford. These were malicious, malignant and indeed, murderous. Today's humanitarian values would condemn them as the organised genocide of innocent Scottish civilians, but in Tudor times, such slaughter was thought legitimate during a *chevauchée*, that hard-hitting punitive expedition. To the king, these actions represented a suitably Biblical punishment on the Scots for their shameless behaviour towards him and God's own laws. Doubtless he discussed them fully with his Maker during his prayers and was certain he had received God's approval.

For this journey, put all to fire and sword [ordered Henry], burn Edinburgh town, so razed and defaced when you have sacked and gotten what you can of it, as there may remain forever a perpetual memory of the vengeance of God lightened upon [them] for their falsehood and disloyalty.

Do what you can out of hand and do not tarry to beat down and overthrow the castle, sack Holyrood House and as many towns and villages about Edinburgh as you may conveniently [attack]. Sack Leith and burn it and all the rest, putting man, woman and child to fire and sword without exception, where any resistance shall be made against you.

This done, pass over to Fife and extend like extremities and destructions in all towns and villages [which] you may reach conveniently.

Henry then commanded dire vengeance upon a particularly hated foe – Cardinal Beaton.

Spoil and turn upset down the cardinal's town of St Andrews as the upper stone [of the buildings] may be the nether and not one stick stand by another, sparing no creature alive within the same, specially [those] either in friendship or [in] blood allied to the cardinal. If you see any likelihood of winning [his] castle ... and if you fortune to get it, raze and destroy it piecemeal.

The Wardens of the English East and Middle Marches, who were to support the expedition by striking north with a 4,000-strong cavalry force, should also 'burn and destroy to the uttermost'. A paragraph added by Paget noted that it was the season for sowing grain and other crops but the Scots 'may be not suffered to sow their ground, [so] they shall, by the next year be brought to such penury as they will not be able to live nor abide the country'.[46]

Hertford was given Henry's proclamation explaining why Scotland should suffer at his hands. It related how Arran 'by the sinister enticement of the cardinal' had 'swerved' from his agreements with England. Those earlier taken hostage had falsified their promises' and shown only 'fickleness and unfaithfulness in return' for Henry's 'gentleness and clemency'. To 'revenge these dishonourable proceedings, the king has sent me to persecute this realm ... Nevertheless, my sovereign, minding not to extend the extremity of his sword to all men alike, has commanded me to publish that when the prescribed punishment of your disloyalty is executed, all who submit to the king's mercy shall be taken to mercy.'[47]

He was warned to postpone issuing it until he had gained the upper hand over the Scots in battle. It would be importune if, unprovoked, he wreaked destruction on the fair land of Scotland after proclaiming Henry as the 'chief governor' of Mary Queen of Scots and 'protector of that realm'. The king told Charles V that it was 'more convenient for a lieutenant to spoil and waste a country' than his monarch.[48] If Hertford failed to subdue the Scots army, 'he may fall to burning' the countryside, in a scorched-earth retreat, the Privy Council advised him on 27 March 1544.[49]

Lord High Admiral Lisle had assembled 103 transport ships supplied by the ports of London, Ipswich, Yarmouth, King's Lynn and Hull, together with another eleven hired from the merchants of Antwerp, Hamburg and Lubeck,[50] to embark Hertford's 10,000-strong army at Newcastle. Waiting impatiently there, Hertford realised that the old Tudor problem of paucity of funds to pay his soldiers and sailors had cropped up again, like an unwelcome genie. Sir Ralph Sadler, now Treasurer of the Scottish expedition, had a £30,000 budget, but after unexpected costs (including replacing rotten bread and herrings), this was insufficient for the back pay owed to the 'officers and mariners of the fleet' since 21 March.[51] Three days later, Henry sent £6,000 in cash and promised another £4,000 within twenty-four hours.[52]

Bad weather in the North Sea delayed the fleet's passage north and it was not until 26 April that the troops boarded the ships. Chapuys reported their sailing and prayed 'God grant them success, in order not to delay the expedition against France.'[53] After another delay caused by 'contrarious' winds, the fleet arrived off Inchkeith, an island in the Firth of Forth, on Saturday, 3 May 1544, protected by seven of Henry's warships.

The army were ferried ashore at nine the next morning at Granton Crag, two miles (3.2km) west of Leith. The unopposed landing took less than three hours to complete and then the troops formed up into three battalions to march on Leith, where the artillery, tents, horses and food were to be unloaded. After about a mile, the vanguard spotted about 6,000 enemy infantry and cavalry barring their route, drawn up with two lines of artillery along a small stream running through a valley.

Arran and Cardinal Beaton were prominent among their leaders, 'utterly determined to keep the passage', according to Hertford's dispatch. The English troops 'marched towards them with good speed' under galling artillery fire, both from the Scots' artillery and the guns defending Leith. Lisle was almost satirical in describing events. The 'stout cardinal... like a valiant champion, gave his horse the spurs and turned his back and was [happy] to leave his [guns] behind. Yet he tarried until we came within shooting distance of our hackbuts. He was [dressed] in a frock [cassock] of yellow velvet, cut and pulled out with white tinselled sarsenet.'[54]

The Scots retreated back to Edinburgh and the English stormed across the 'great trenches and ditches' protecting Leith. The port was captured shortly before nightfall with the English butcher's bill for the day totalling only three dead and six wounded. That night they encamped there 'and found such richness as they thought not to have found in any town of Scotland'.[55] As well as a store of grain and loot valued at £10,000, two Scottish warships, *Salamander* and *Unicorn*, were seized as prizes and taken into Henry's navy. A blockhouse on the tiny island of Inchgarvie[56] was destroyed by the *Galley Subtle*.[57]

After all the heavy equipment was landed, Hertford led 1,500 men towards Edinburgh the following Wednesday. Under parley, he warned the city's representatives that he was to inflict vengeance upon them for their 'detestable falsehoods. Unless they yielded up the town without condition and cause man, woman and child to depart into the fields, he would put them to the sword and their town to the fire'.[58] The general's suspicions about its citizens' pledges to surrender were justified by two houses in its suburbs being set alight. He also had received intelligence suggesting 'they would withstand us to their power'.

Lisle led an attack on the city's great iron-shod Canongate and a fierce battle ensued. 'The Scots shot out of the windows... of their houses so fast with handguns that our men [were] astonished [and] shot [at random in their panic, which] did more hurt to their fellows than to the enemy.' Lord William Howard was hit by an arrow above his cheek 'but the stroke was so faint and weak... that it did him little or no hurt at all'.[59] Artillery was called up, the gate blasted away, and the English stormed into Edinburgh, killing at least 120 or 140 defenders. A feeble attempt to assault the castle failed, so Hertford contented himself with ordering the city to be set ablaze 'in sundry places' causing a 'jolly fire'. The castle guns continued to fire into the smoke, panicking the English soldiers who fled out of the city, some being crushed in the panic. Hertford withdrew, having lost only twenty men.

A new provost had overnight hastily thrown up earth ramparts around the city's main gate 'and stood somewhat stoutly to their defence'. Reinforced by the 4,000 cavalry that had arrived from the borders, Edinburgh was assaulted again and the English broke through the gate, killing 400 or 500 Scots.

The city was 'wholly burnt and desolate' as was Holyrood House, in a huge, cataclysmic blaze that lasted two days. Watching the conflagration from a nearby hill, Hertford could hear 'the poor miserable creatures of the town ... crying out "Was it worth the Cardinal?"'[60]

On 15 May, Leith was razed to the ground, its pier destroyed and Lord Seton's castle, orchards and gardens, 'the fairest in Scotland', ruined. This rough treatment was explained because 'he was the chief labourer to help their Cardinal out of prison, the only author of their calamity'.

Three days later, the English army reached the safety of Berwick, having destroyed three castles, one abbey and a nunnery, and thirty-two towns and villages, aside from Edinburgh and Leith.[61] Henry was delighted and sent his commanders 'hearty thanks for their manly and discreet handling of their charge', for the loss of just forty men.[62]

He was less pleased by a news-sheet circulating in London that claimed the expedition was a total failure, 'to the slander of the king's captains and ministers'. A proclamation issued on 18 May 1544 ordered those 'having such books' to 'bring them in to the Lord Mayor ... within twenty-four hours' for burning.[63] These rumours spread to Europe and news of the supposed English defeat was greeted in Rome 'with incredible rejoicing'. Truth is always the first casualty in war and Henry's jubilant enemies had the smiles wiped off their faces as the facts emerged. They understood at once that France would be next to feel his military might. In unconscious confirmation, the king ordered Hertford to send 4,000 of his army to Calais 'for the wars against France'.[64]

More worrying was the arrest of a Scot who planned to set London ablaze and had 'procured all the ways and means [to achieve] the burning and devastation' of the capital.[65]

Henry's health was endangering his French adventure. In March 1544, the ulcers on his legs had flared up again, confining him to bed with a fever for at least eight days. His convalescence was painfully slow; on 12/13 April, he had not recovered sufficiently to attend to state business and admitted to Chapuys that he was 'not feeling quite well'. His doctors urged him not to lead the Army Royal, as Chapuys reported in April: 'Those about the king [do not] wish him to be personally in the enterprise, [for] fear for his person and that his presence would retard all affairs. It would be necessary to march much more slowly, on account of his weight and ill-health and also ... not to put him in hazard.'[66]

A month later, he warned Charles V of possible delays to the invasion, caused by the king's 'desire and inclination – no, obstinate resolution – to personally attend the expedition'. He went on:

In order to ensure safety, it is ... necessary to provide so many things [which] will be impossible to get ready in a short time. I venture to say that the king will be acting imprudently if he persists in his determination of crossing the Channel and taking command of his army. However stout-hearted he may be, his age, his obesity and weight and the state of his legs are such that those who have seen him of late wonder how it is that he does not keep his bed. [They] think he will not be able to stand any fatigue without actual danger to his life.

And yet no one here dares remonstrate with him about that or dissuade him from the resolution he has taken. There can be no doubt that his presence in the field will be of great use, if only he can recover the use of his limbs but ... in his present condition, his voyage is fraught with danger and may turn out a serious inconvenience for your majesty's campaign.[67]

Later, Chapuys returned to this gloomy theme. He believed Henry 'has the worst legs in the world ... [He will] not be able to endure the least exertion without danger of his life, yet no one dare tell him so ... As he now is, [this] will be a danger.' Rather than campaigning, it would be better that Henry stayed in Calais.[68]

Ironically, Charles V was in no great physical shape either. He was a martyr to gout, having suffered eleven attacks in sixteen years, but these were now so frequent that he had stopped counting them. The gout may have been triggered by his liking for inappropriate food: oysters, pickled eels and spicy sausage, all washed down by German ale and Rhenish wine.[69]

Their enemy, Francis I, was also suffering from what St Mauris, the Imperial ambassador to Paris, graphically described as 'a gathering under the lower parts': an 'ulcerated bladder' or 'the French disease' – the euphemism for syphilis. The envoy added: 'As the wound is incurable the patient cannot last long, and he follows no regime, but lives according to his fancy... All agree that the king's body must be very corrupt.'[70]

The French king's personal challenge to the gouty Charles 'to meet in mortal combat' began to resemble more old men's toothless posturing than a symbolic chivalrous action.

The English army crossed the Channel to Calais under Suffolk and Norfolk with no clear idea of their military objectives. More than a week after marching out of the port and into enemy territory, Norfolk declared he was well-placed to attack Ardres 'and a little out of the way to besiege Boulogne and in the highway towards Montreuil'. He complained rather bitingly to the Privy Council that by now, he had expected to know his military objective.[71]

True to form, this bastion of pessimism was bursting with complaints. This was no way to run an army. 'There is a marvellous scarcity of hay and oats and no new hay yet cut because... of the great rains... I fear that the baking in the carts will fail because the ovens being heated, the mortar will fall out from the bricks and small shaking will cause the bricks to fall under and break.'[72] Food prices were too high: 'The soldiers will go hungrily to bed or else spend more than their wages if such prices continue.'[73] Small wonder that the Privy Council found his letters monotonous and depressing. 'I forbear to molest you, fearing that I have troubled you with too many things, because I have received no answer to any part of them,' he acknowledged sheepishly.[74] At last, on 20 June, he was ordered to besiege the town of Montreuil, south-east of Boulogne, which he believed, in a rare flash of optimism, could be won in four to five days – if not reinforced.[75]

This walled town, with its eight churches and a castle, sits atop a 135-foot (41m) chalk hill dominating the surrounding flat fields which provided little cover for a besieging force. Its fortifications had been strengthened after an unsuccessful siege in 1537 and it was garrisoned by 4,000 seasoned troops, many of them foreign mercenaries.[76]

Norfolk made slow progress towards his objective, escorted by his Imperial allies. 'We might have been at Montreuil three days past but we, knowing no part of the country, nor having no guides but such as they gave us, have been brought such ways as we think never [an] army passed – up and down the hills, through hedges, woods, marshes and all to cause us to lodge on French ground and save their own friends from [English looting].'[77]

On arrival, he had reconnoitred Montreuil's defences and complained that he 'had never seen so evil a town to approach'. The River Canche was impassable without his pioneers building plank bridges across boats 'which are not so easily set up as the king was informed'. It had taken 'all day to make just four of them'.[78]

The duke's despondency deepened yet further. Montreuil could not be surrounded 'considering the puissance [power] of the enemy ... I have not yet heard of any town won which was not besieged [all] round abouts!' What was more, the beer supplies were so sour that 'no man can drink it' and Norfolk's soldiers 'have been fain to drink water since yesterday morning'.[79]

On 7 July, the Council told him the king had now abandoned his plan to march on Paris and instead would besiege Boulogne, the French town and port south-west of Calais. These plans 'were to be kept secret'. They added tartly: 'Now that you are before Montreuil, his majesty expects you will do what you can to win it.'[80] Suffolk had received intelligence about the Boulogne defences and had discovered that 'instead of the ground around the town being earth, as the king was informed, it is rock and there is no earth there a foot deep'. Siege-works and mining beneath its walls would consequently be very problematic.[81]

Back at home, financing the war was already becoming difficult, despite hardly a shot being fired in anger. Chapuys reported at the end of June that Henry had borrowed a large sum in Antwerp 'and was speaking in great secrecy to many merchants for 40,000 or 50,000 crowns or more, to be repaid at Christmas, the interest for which will amount to much'.[82] He had also approached London merchants for further loans at 12 per cent. In addition, the king was mortgaging monastic lands to raise money from the leading citizens of London. This had yielded £7,500 from the corporation and another £7,000 from numerous prosperous traders – haberdashers, fishmongers, skinners, grocers and ironmongers, among them John Skutt, the king's tailor (£200) and Morgan Wolf, the royal goldsmith (£200).[83]

Henry, like all responsible soldiers about to go on active service, prudently made a new will and appointed his queen as regent to rule in his absence, with Hertford as commander of all homeland forces. The Commission of Regency, signed on 7 July 1544, instructed that Prince Edward should be moved to Hampton Court for greater security and decreed that Katherine should use the 'advice and counsel of the archbishop of Canterbury, Lord Chancellor Wriothesley, Hertford, the bishop of Westminster and Sir William Petre, Secretary of State, in her judgements'.[84]

Anxious to take to the field, the king was becoming impatient at his generals' negativity. It was time to stiffen their resolve to win the war. Paget wrote to them on 12 July as the royal entourage paused at Gravesend in Kent en route to Dover and the Channel crossing. Suffolk's concerns about the siege of Boulogne were dismissed out of hand. Yes, the town and castle did stand upon 'a rock, yet it is better to be mined, although more painful to the pioneers'. Anyway, the plan was 'not to win by mining but to shoot [at the walls] with ordnance and mortars and make some terrible frays against those within and so stun and torment them' into surrender.

As far as Montreuil was concerned, 'As the enemy study their defence, so men of experience must devise how to invade, as the king doubts not but they will. As for the 4,000 within [the town], Norfolk knows how Frenchmen count their numbers which always [boasts] two for one. Even if there be so many, they are mostly but Frenchmen and Norfolk has Englishmen with him'. Ominously, Paget stressed that if Henry returned home without a stunning victory, this 'shall be neither to his honour, nor to the reputation of those in charge under him'.[85]

This call to arms did not impress Norfolk. His investment of Montreuil was no siege at all for 'two gates are left open and a third may be used freely at night'. His fellow general, Russell, lies 'in a little hole', two arrow shots off the town, 'continuously visited [by] their ordnance'. The duke was based half a mile (805m) from the Abbeville gate and the enemy 'often shoots into my camp'. There was only enough powder and shot left for eight days' firing. Yet, he hastily assured Paget that 'never men were more desirous to win'.[86]

After several postponements, Henry crossed the English Channel and landed at Calais in the evening of 14 July 1544 for the second time in a war against France. His dreams had finally come true.

At the head of his host, he proudly rode a great courser, or armoured warhorse, with the Tudor battle flag of England – green and white horizontal bands with the red flag of St George in the canton – flying bravely before him.[87] His great helm and lance were borne by William Somerset, son of the second earl of Worcester, riding ahead of the king.[88] On either side marched 500 men of the Yeomen of the Guard, commanded by their captain, Sir Anthony Wingfield.[89] After leaving Calais, the column passed the town's place of execution, the gallows frequently having the mouldering remains of a traitor, spy or common thief, left as an awful warning of Henry's justice. It then marched past the square fortress of Newnham Bridge and through the villages of Peuplingues, Boninges and Pytham, en route for Boulogne.[90]

It was the first time that Henry had worn armour in the field since 1513; indeed he may not have donned a harness since his jousting accident in 1536. He had probably ordered two new field armours to be made for him at Greenwich, but settled on an imported design by the Milanese Francis Albert. This beautifully etched, blacked and gilt three-quarter armour[91] was almost certainly the one Henry wore on his march from Calais.[92]

The violent thunderstorm and torrential rain that greeted him and his column of troops as they arrived at Marquison (now Marquise), twenty miles (32km) from Calais on 25 July, was an uncomfortable reminder of the realities of campaigning.

But where was the glory?

10

Fortunes of War

On 18 July 1544, Charles Brandon, duke of Suffolk, the commander of Henry's Army Royal, arrived outside the walls and seventeen towers of Boulogne, perched on a hill overlooking *la Manche* – the Engish Channel. After a brief skirmish, in which three English cavalrymen had their horses killed under them, the French were beaten back to the town's gates. Suffolk identified a safe site for the English camp 'in such a place as they shall not much annoy us with their ordnance', and his pioneers discovered, despite his earlier gloomy reports, that there was nine feet (2.7m) of earth, available to make 'fair and large trenches, sufficient to carry our munitions and artillery through' without coming under fire.[1]

That same day, Sir William Paget told Suffolk of Henry's approval for plans to summon Boulogne to surrender, save for one major change. The king's demand that the French should 'lodge their allegiance' to him as their true sovereign, was pared back to only those 'within Picardy, the county of Boulogne and Guisnes', a region south of the Calais Pale. In return for their sworn loyalty, their property would be kept 'without impairment' and they would enjoy life 'more quietly and with more liberty than ever they have done hitherto' under Francis.[2] One wonders what the king's downtrodden subjects back home would make of this invader's promise.

This decision was another important and unexpected change in English war aims. Henry had rebuffed Imperial complaints about him wasting time in besieging Boulogne and Montreuil (rather than marching on Paris) by pointing out that unless both were seized, an advancing army could not be safely supplied with food and munitions. Despite all his martial swagger, it was becoming clear that the king was unwilling to allow his army to manoeuvre too far from his supply depots and his ships. If he did undertake a major campaign, it would be directed at Normandy, rather than against the French capital.[3] He told Chapuys stonily that 'there was no earthly way of marching forward without the capture of Montreuil, as otherwise it was impossible to get victuals for his army, which even at the very threshold of the emperor's [territory] had suffered extreme want'. Noting Henry's stern 'look and resolution', the ambassador wisely decided not to pursue the subject.[4] He dared not voice his misgivings about the king being 'too heavy to be able to move hastily', even without his armour.

Henry had unilaterally discarded the grand war strategy agreed with Charles V and was now content to only enlarge the Pale of Calais and destroy the French strongpoints on its borders. What had prompted this sudden volte-face in English military planning? First, there was the war's escalating cost, which had been seriously underestimated. Henry's finances were beginning to feel the pinch and more modest objectives would prove cheaper than striking at Paris. Second, there was the inescapable question of Henry's health. Privately, he must have realised at last that he was medically unfit for arduous campaigning far from home in all weathers. His cherished dreams of battlefield glory evaporated in the dawning realisation of his age and infirmities. That cloudburst at Marquise was both a salutary lesson and a defining moment. Standing round in a quagmire of mud wearing soaking-wet clothes was one thing, but watching your expensive armour rust about you was quite another.

Suffolk had suggested that Henry delay his arrival at Boulogne 'till the camp be in order' and to allow time to organise the necessary horses and supply wagons.[5] The king could not resist interfering in the organisation of the siege, probably after studying his own map of Boulogne.[6] Paget and Bishop Gardiner required that Henry should lodge in a lawyer's house on the outskirts of the lower town of Base Boulogne. It was important to capture or destroy a nearby watchtower as its guns could threaten Henry's planned accommodation. (This was the 'Tour d'Ordre', a Roman clifftop lighthouse, but in salacious allusion to its phallic appearance, the English called it 'The Old Man'.) 'That done, and note taken how far the [guns] of the town may reach, the king will [travel] through in one day'. As some of the French bastions could fire on Windmill Hill, on the opposite side of the town, 'Suffolk should not approach without a good trench for his safeguard'. Finally,

Henry approved the incursion of English troops into the low-lying suburb of Base Boulogne, 'but they should lie on the further side and in such number as to resist the power of the town'.[7]

Lisle had ridden towards Base Boulogne 'where [Suffolk] intends to place some of the ordnance which should annoy the town . . . There is great appearance of success if my lord's [plan] is followed which is to besiege the town [from] three places' which would block its gates and stop supplies coming into the harbour. However, artillery fire from the walls of Boulogne had proved accurate: 'They have their level and aim into so many places and valleys that no place is clear, but they shoot into our tents and have done much harm both to men and horses.' Counter-fire from the English guns nightly kept the Boulogne defenders awake 'for the battery pieces never cease and the stones of the walls fly about'.[8]

The besiegers' artillery had already battered the Tour d'Ordre, forcing its surrender on 22 July. Despite French boasts of invulnerability, the English guns had also damaged parts of the thirteenth-century Boulogne Castle. In response, the French burnt the houses of Base Boulogne but the suburb was swiftly reoccupied by English troops.

Meanwhile, Francis I was making eleventh-hour peace overtures to Henry. A letter was delivered to 'his good brother', promising to pay the arrears of the tribute or 'pension' owed him. If the fighting ended, Francis would 'stop the war of the Scots, so that England shall have no less amity with them than with France'. When friendship was re-established, Francis would 'show himself so reasonable' over payment of reparations that the king of England would be completely satisfied. A covering letter declared that 'I never desired otherwise than to continue the good and perfect friendship between us, which I cannot persuade myself to be diminished on your part, as I assure you it is not on mine . . . Pray God, my good brother, to have you in His care and guard'. It was boldly signed with a large signature, filling most of the page: 'Your good brother, cousin and ally, François'.[9] His earnest declarations of friendship had come too late and Henry refused to countenance any talk of peace without first securing his decisive military victory over the perfidious French.

Panicking over an epidemic of bubonic plague in Calais, Henry set out for Boulogne on 25 July, camping, as we have seen, in the rain at Marquise, just north of the town, where he was met by Sir Anthony

Browne, his Master of the Horse, with a cavalry escort. The king arrived at Boulogne the following day to assume command of the siege by the 10,000 infantry and 3,000 horse of this division of his Army Royal and set up his headquarters half a mile (805m) from the town's walls.

The English troops were governed by strict regulations prohibiting the rude soldiery's traditional pastimes in war of looting, pillaging and rape. Every soldier in Norfolk's force had been warned the previous month that 'no one should dare to leave the host to ravage or loot within the French land, on pain of death'. Some had already been hanged by the roadside, as a deterrent against further military misbehaviour.[10]

Demonstrations of resistance or defiance brought harsh retribution, as such perpetrators were regarded as forfeiting the protection of the laws of war. Civilians caught resupplying besieged towns would be killed. When a group of women smuggling food into Ardres were caught, they were told 'not to come there again under threat of having their hair and ears cut off, sewn in sacks, and thrown into the lakes near Guisnes'. Later, five men and twelve women were executed for this offence.[11]

Abbeys and churches were burnt and villagers died in the flames as they sought safety in their bell-towers. In the Boulonnais village of Audinghen, fourteen miles (23km) north of Boulogne, 101 men, women and children were slaughtered after fortifying their church and kill-ing several English soldiers. Similarly, eighty men and an unknown number of dependants were butchered after sheltering in their church at Petinghem, when cannon opened fire against them. Conversely, French peasants murdered an English scout and mutilated his corpse and other soldiers, caught stealing from an orchard, were killed and their bodies left hanging from the branches, their mouths stuffed with cherries.[12]

As in the punitive raids in Scotland, the English policy for their cap-tured territory was callous and brutal. The objective was to depopulate the Boulonnais region and put to the sword those peasants who fled into the forests, after destroying their homes and crops. Consequently, the spectre of famine haunted the area in the winter that followed. The invading troops brought with them the unseen slayers of bubonic plague and the Sweating Sickness that, together with starvation, killed perhaps as many as 50,000 in the Boulonnais during six months of 1544–5.[13]

Back in England, the queen was relishing her regency, attending to state business efficiently with an impressive eye for detail. On 22 July she wrote to Sir Ralph Evers, Warden of the Middle Marches of the Scottish border, to congratulate him on his 'right honest exploit' against the king's enemies – a raid into Scotland, when valuable prisoners were taken. 'Being appointed Regent', she offered her 'right hearty thanks, but also to require you to do the same to all such gentlemen and others who have served his majesty on the late journey in Scotland'.[14]

Three days later, Katherine sent a letter to Henry, thanking God for his 'good health and the prosperous beginning of affairs' in France. Prince Edward and Mary and Elizabeth were well. Then she turned to the business of state. Her Regency Council had ordered £40,000 (£21 million at 2019 prices) in cash to be sent to the king. Four thousand reinforcements were to be mustered, ready to depart at one hour's notice. The letter was signed: 'Your grace's most obedient and loving wife and servant, Kateryn the Queen. K.P'.[15]

On 31 July, she had news of the capture of a Scottish ship off Scarborough, Yorkshire, which was carrying 'certain Frenchmen and Scots ... with many letters to the French king and others'. The queen believed their 'apprehension much important' and that God had decided to reveal 'the crafty dealing and juggling of that nation'.[16]

During her regency, the queen signed five royal proclamations, mostly concerned with war-related issues, such as the cost of armour and the punishment of army deserters.[17] As plague was again raging in London and Westminster, she moved the court further west to the royal house at Woking, Surrey. A proclamation prohibited visits there by those from infected areas 'to avoid danger to the queen, prince and the king's other children'. In early August, Katherine was investigating 'a vain rumour' about French troops landing in England. 'Fearing that some seditious person had spread the rumour (for a landing of Frenchmen around Gloucester was unlikely)', she had ordered local magistrates to investigate the report and understood that all was well.[18]

Katherine's *Psalms or Prayers*, published anonymously in 1544, was based on a work by the Catholic martyr John Fisher of almost two decades before and portrayed Henry as an exemplary wartime monarch, in the mould of the Old Testament king David. It included a prayer for the king, drawing on Psalms two and twenty, with changes to emphasise Henry's religious authority, his obedience to God and his military prowess.[19] The sixty-page *Prayers and Meditations* followed in June 1545, with vernacular texts gathered together for personal devotions. This was the first book published in England by a woman under her own name.[20]

Like any anxious wife with a husband fighting in a war, the queen wrote a letter to Henry, still 'full of duty and respect' but earnestly hoping to hear from him. Although he had not been away long, Katherine declared that 'I cannot quietly enjoy anything until I hear from your majesty... Love and affection compels me to desire your presence'.[21]

The king, bursting with 'prosperous health', was far too busy to write to his wife. He was having the time of his life at Boulogne, supervising the siting of batteries to bring fire down on the town's formidable defences. Three were set up, each cannon protected by wickerwork-baskets packed with earth and stones, totalling 100 guns, with thirty mortars in reserve.[22] One battery was positioned on a huge mound of earth, thrown up to dominate the French defences between the castle and the Montreuil gate. Pioneers were also tunnelling to bring down sections of the town's walls to create a breach, through which the English could storm into Boulogne.[23]

In war, estimates of how much ammunition will be expended always fall well short of the reality of combat. The largest artillery – cannon and culverin – required thirty pounds (13.6kg) and twenty pounds (9kg) of gunpowder each time they fired.[24] The king, finding his reserve stocks running low, requested Mary of Hungary, regent of Flanders, to supply forty lasts of gunpowder 'or as much as you can spare. As you have the means of making within your government sooner than We have and your countries are protected by Our armies, you will not need much store of powder.'[25] Regretfully she could not comply, as Charles V had already taken all she had and 'still presses for more',[26] but fifty-five lasts were purchased from merchants in Antwerp.

Henry also needed 2,000 hackbuts (or muskets), but his agent there reported 'there are not 200 to be got in all this town, whereof part are... very slender gear, not meet to be sent to his majesty'.[27] In the end, the king was forced to empty the gunpowder magazines in his new fortresses at home and had to search ships moored in the River Thames to 'buy or borrow' more from their masters.[28]

Despite his readiness to pay hard cash for new supplies of gunpowder, Henry found himself in an increasingly parlous financial state that threatened the war's continuance. At the end of July, he sent a round-robin begging letter to the great and good back in England, soliciting immediate loans.

The pro forma missive begins with an explanation of his pecuniary problem. He had invaded France 'in Our own person with a puissant army and, having commenced the war with honour and likelihood of better success, We see occasion for greater charge than was... considered, both for tarrying longer than was determined and for... money to furnish the strongholds already taken.' Because time was pressing, Henry was 'bold of Our loving subjects, as We know will press themselves to satisfy Our desire and reputing the person addressed to be such, We require him to lend the sum of [blank] sterling and deliver it at London... within [blank] days... The king promises... assuredly to cause the same to be repaid within [blank] after this date.'[29]

Recipients of this imperious request for money numbered more than a hundred, including Henry's army commanders Suffolk and Norfolk. It also encompassed the clergy, who proved responsive. Loans received included the £1,000 offered by both the bishop of Lincoln and the archbishop of Canterbury and £500 apiece from the archbishop of York and the bishops of Durham and Ely.[30]

After receiving Henry's earlier admonitory letter, Norfolk had become a reinvigorated general, at least temporarily. The king's arrival, he servilely observed, would astonish the French and greatly advance the allies' cause. Frenchmen might boast that the English would never capture Montreuil or Boulogne, but the duke believed their bragging would soon stop. When his trenches at Montreuil were completed and they began firing on the town's defences, 'we hope to make them not so brave, as they are more in their words than they have yet shown in any great deeds'.[31]

Russell reported that '[A]fter closing Abbeville gate, we intend to [begin] a new trench and break through the old wall along which we will begin to make our mines.'[32] He was more frank in another letter to Paget. That night, the French had sortied out of the town at the dangerous moment when the besiegers were changing their sentries. Many 'were slain on both sides and young [John] Cheney [son of Sir Thomas Cheney, Treasurer of the Household] was stricken [by] a hackbut [bullet] beside his ankle bone and so into the flank [of his body] by reason thereof, his guts do come out and is in great jeopardy of death, as the surgeons say, albeit they say the best for his comfort.'[33]

Almost a week later, Russell, while admitting inexperience in siege warfare, had slumped into a slough of despond about their chances of capturing Montreuil. His troops and those of Norfolk were stationed 'so far apart that, on a sudden attack, they could not succour each other... As the gates are left open, the town cannot be won, for men and victuals go in at pleasure.'[34]

Six hundred men were labouring night and day constructing another huge earth mound, from which the besiegers' artillery could pour fire into Montreuil. Norfolk reported that 'lords and gentlemen' took their turn to 'labour in their own person to give example how the soldiers should travail'. The duke knew that his siege was ineffective, if not militarily preposterous, so was keen to point out that the town's defences were stronger than intelligence had suggested to Henry. 'There are quick men within, that spare not to visit us with not so few as a thousand shot of small pieces in a day and in the night, come and fight with our men hand-to-hand within our trenches.' He ended his letter with typical obsequiousness: 'The king's person here would be worth more than the presence of 20,000 men.'[35]

In early August, the old campaigner began to suspect he was a victim of scurrilous attacks about his poor generalship. Worried about these gathering clouds of recrimination, he wrote to Suffolk on 4 August, complaining that 'I am blamed by many... for remissness here and for not encamping nearer Montreuil. I am sorry in my old days to be thus spoken of... For the old love and acquaintance between us, I heartily desire you to procure the sending hither of some man whom the king trusts to report [on] what I have done and what more I might have done This will do me more pleasure than if you gave me £500.'[36]

Francis was still attempting to split the alliance and sign a separate peace treaty with Henry. He sent the sieur de Framozelles to the king at Boulogne who, in seeking an audience, had the excuse of requiring a passport to release his heavily pregnant wife, trapped inside Boulogne. The king condescended to see him and told him bluntly that if the French king were to offer him half his realm, he would never think of agreeing peace unless the emperor was first satisfied. Two days later, Henry wrote to Francis with much talk of his honour, 'which, as you know, We have hitherto guarded and will not have stained in Our old age'. However, Henry was prepared to be a mediator 'for the sake of Christendom and of our former amity'[37] – provided the French king make both allies 'reasonable and acceptable offers'.

The English bombardment of Boulogne began in earnest on Friday, 4 August and the next day, the king told his wife that its walls were already beginning to tumble and that he planned to capture the town within twenty days. All was going well; the English had captured Hardelot, Frank, Hubersent 'and three or four other castles' between Boulogne and Montreuil.[38] A week later, the queen's former sweetheart, Sir Thomas Seymour, Master of the Ordnance, agreed a contract with Robert Baker, master of the forty-ton Brighton ship *Trinity*, to bring over a further 3,965 iron cannonballs of various calibres from the Tower of London for the siege.[39]

Henry, always a pillar of moral rectitude as far as others were concerned, was annoyed by the flock of prostitutes who had crossed the English Channel to ply their trade among the 13,000 troops besieging Boulogne. His council wrote to the Lord Mayor of London on 5 September, complaining that the English camp was 'troubled with light women which daily repair out of England hither'. He was instructed to 'permit no woman to pass out of any [wharf] within the city' and to pass on this order to the mayors of Dover and other harbours on the south coast.[40]

Meanwhile, advance units of Charles V's cavalry had reached within thirty miles (48km) of Paris. The Imperial army had marched eighty-five miles (137km) along the left bank of the River Marne to Château-Thierry, which was sacked, as was Soissons. Its steady progress had been watched by French units manoeuvring on the opposite bank of the river, but the two armies never came to battle.

Later that month, the emperor was discomfited by a painful rebuke by Pope Paul III about his impious dealings with the heretical German princes and his 'league with a schismatic king who is the Church's enemy and [who] has injured him by the repudiation of his aunt' [the divorce of Katherine of Aragon in 1533]. Old memories lingered long in the Vatican. All this 'was evidence that [Charles] has gone over to the side of the enemies of the Church' and Paul exhorted him solemnly to return to the godly authority of Rome.[41]

Two days later, the emperor authorised his faithful diplomat Férrante Gonzaga (who had earlier confirmed Henry's commitment to the invasion of France) and his chief minister, Nicholas Perrenot, sieur de Granvelle, to negotiate a peace with Francis. They would seek an alliance, by marriage – offering as potential brides, Joanna, Infanta of Spain, or Anna, second daughter of Ferdinand, King of the Romans.[42] The Imperial army then turned homewards, even though military triumph hovered, mirage-like, only a few miles away.

Back in Boulogne, despite atrocious weather, Henry confidently expected a famous victory, as his batteries had 'enough cannons to conquer Hell'. For almost eight weeks, the English guns had fired more than 100,000 iron and stone shot at Boulogne's fortifications and its defensive outworks were regularly assaulted. Catapults also hurled 'balls of wildfire' into the town as terrifying incendiary weapons.[43]

The king, safely out of range of retaliatory fire in the north-east quadrant of the siege-works, excitedly told his queen on 8 September that 'the castle with the dyke [ditch] is at our command and not [likely] to be recovered by the Frenchmen again. [We do not] doubt [that] with God's grace, the castle and town shall shortly follow... for this day, We begin three [new] batteries and have three mines going, besides one which... has shaken and torn one of their greatest bulwarks. No more to you at this time sweetheart, both for lack of time and great occupation of business, saving [that] We pray you to give... Our hearty blessings to all Our children and recommendations to Our cousin Margaret [Lady Margaret Douglas, who on 6 July had married Matthew Stuart, fourth earl of Lennox] and the rest of the ladies and gentlewomen. Written with the hand of your loving husband, HENRY R[EX].'[44]

The English bombardment had left barely one house unscathed. On 11 September, the castle blew up in a spectacular explosion after gunpowder charges were exploded in a mine deep beneath its ramparts. Flying debris killed or wounded many of the besiegers. The decisive moment had arrived. There was no other option than the surrender of Boulogne. Its captain, Jacques de Courcy, sieur de Vervins, sought safe conduct for two of his gentlemen to negotiate a cessation of hostilities. This was granted by Henry the following day, with the strict proviso that no new fortification should be built, nor anyone be allowed to enter or leave the beleaguered town.[45]

A treaty signed by Suffolk and de Courcy[46] stipulated that the town and castle be delivered to Henry at 10 a.m. on 14 September, with 'all artillery, powder and munitions'. The captain and the 1,300 survivors of his garrison were allowed to depart unmolested later that day for the safety of French territory, as were the abbot of the Notre Dame monastery and his monks. The 2,000 inhabitants who chose to leave, 'with as much goods as they might carry',[47] were granted safe passage to Abbeville and Henry ordered his soldiers not to mistreat them – indeed, provided troops to guard them on the road.

It was a stormy day, with wind and torrential rain beating down on the straggling column of heavily laden refugees. They had not trudged more than a few miles before they were attacked, probably by the same English soldiers ordered to protect them. Their clothes were stripped off their backs and their possessions looted.[48] Norfolk later reported he had hanged many 'that have spoiled some of the Frenchmen'.[49] One Welsh soldier, Elis Gruffydd, said some French men, women and children collapsed (from hypothermia) 'because it was so wet [and] that there had not been one dry hour for ten days'. They sought refuge in the 'ruins of a church and village which we had burnt a short time before. Many, both old and young, died there of cold'.[50] Others drowned trying to wade across rivers swollen by the heavy rains.

On 18 September, Henry rode through one of Boulogne's battered gates to take formal possession of his prize of war. The sword of honour 'was borne naked before him by the lord marquess of Dorset, like a noble and valiant conqueror, [as] he rode into Boulogne. The trumpeters standing on the walls ... sounded their trumpets at the time of his entering, to the great comfort of all the king's true subjects', reported the ever-partisan chronicler, Edward Hall. Henry was met by Suffolk, his lieutenant-general, who offered up the keys of the captured town and the king rode on towards his lodgings in a hastily repaired house on the south side of Boulogne.[51]

Unfortunately, the king's taste of military glory was immediately soured by his ally Charles V. That same day, a separate peace was declared between France and the Holy Roman Emperor. Under the Treaty of Crépy, Francis abandoned his territorial claims on Burgundy, the kingdom of Naples, duchy of Savoy and suzerainty over Flanders and Artois. He agreed that his son, Charles, duc d'Orléans, (Princess Mary's would-be bridegroom) would now marry Charles V's daughter or niece, who would bring as dowries either the Netherlands or the city of Milan. To redeem his mortal sin of allying himself with the infidel Ottoman Empire, Francis promised 16,000 soldiers to fight the Turks in Hungary.[52] Following Pope Paul's reprimand to Charles V, a secret annexe to the treaty guaranteed French assistance in returning the German heretics to the Catholic Church. Those troops promised to fight Suleiman the Great could also be deployed to punish the Lutheran schismatics in Germany, 'at the Emperor's command'. The French king swore not to agree terms with Henry without including the Emperor and 'if, because of their treaty, the King of England should wish to quarrel with, or make war upon the Emperor' then Francis would provide military support.[53]

If Charles V was troubled about having Henry as an ally, he was just as uneasy about making peace with Francis, leaving England to fight on against France alone. This was an issue of honour rather than personal sentiment or morality. Helpfully, Granvelle, his chief minister, wrote him a lengthy justification for signing the treaty, replete with the stark words of *realpolitik*: 'As for saying that the King of England may be displeased and pretend that you have contravened [his] treaty... it is a maxim to regard the reality of treaties in conjunction with what is possible and not to run risks for the sake of groundless scruples.' Henry had breached the Anglo-Spanish treaty by arriving late in France 'and instead of marching in the common enterprise, he has halted with his entire army... to besiege some places on his frontiers, leaving you alone...'. Finally, '[T]here is no cause to fear the enmity of England and, as for joining with France against you... this success at Boulogne renders it the less likely.'[54] Charles's nagging conscience was thus placated.

Norfolk was elated by the news of Boulogne's capitulation, as he concluded that Henry's troops there would be freed to reinforce his faltering siege of Montreuil. He was running out of food and forage and his soldiers 'daily fall sick and the horses die'. At least the town's defenders were now suffering hardship; 'for many eat horseflesh and some of the Italian gentlemen are glad to eat a cat well larded and call it dainty meat'.[55]

Reinforcements of 5,000 men 'and certain [artillery] field pieces' belatedly departed Boulogne on 25 September after Norfolk made an unsuccessful attempt to storm Montreuil. His son Surrey led a hopelessly inadequate force to assault the Abbeville gate and after a 'right warm fight', broke through to the adjacent walls. Surrey was wounded and his troops forced to retreat to their flooded and muddy trenches, carrying their injured commander with them.[56]

Henry was preoccupied by rebuilding the defences of the captured French town, spending almost a week planning its refortification, including the demolition of the parish church to build a new artillery bastion. John Rogers, master mason at Guisnes Castle, was appointed to build the new ramparts, including an outwork in the north-east to protect the upper town and 2,660 yards (2,432m) of walls and bastions around Base Boulogne. A new citadel at the south-eastern corner, would command the harbour and the River Liane. At its mouth, the 'Old Man', the Roman lighthouse, was repaired and a large angular fortress would be built around it, protected, in the new Italian fashion, by arrowhead-shaped bastions.[57]

Some French inhabitants of Boulogne switched sides. By 26 September, a total of 155 had sworn allegiance to Henry and to 'renounce the obedience of all other princes and potentates and also the authority of the bishop of Rome'. They were then 'permitted to inhabit in his grace's county of Boulogne'. The list of those taking the oath was headed by nineteen-year-old Jehan le Vasseur.[58] Later, the English turned the depopulated Boulonnais into a colony, evicting French peasants and dividing up their lands as rewards for members of the Boulogne garrison, or renting them to settlers from the southern counties of England.[59]

Convinced he could safely hold on to his spoils of war, Henry secretly made plans to return home. Only twenty-four hours after he entered Boulogne, his ministers wrote to the Regency Council telling them to quietly arrange shipping: 'As many... ships as can be gotten at London, Dover, Rye, Harwich and other places... should be sent to Boulogne and Calais on pretence of bringing wheat or beer and other provisions'. Another ruse should be found to hide the means 'by which his majesty might safely, for sickness and most commodiously for his travail, return within the realm'.[60] Henry's hypochondria had resurfaced, sparked by the mounting death toll from the plague within Calais.

Yet the Army Royal was now exposed to the full force of French military might.

Some time before 23 September, Norfolk had intelligence that Henry, Dauphin of France, with a 50,000-strong army, many of them Italian freelances, was marching towards Montreuil to break the siege and was now only ten miles (16km) away. His vanguard included German pikemen, or *landsknecht* mercenaries, recently dismissed by Charles V. The king panicked, fearing that his 13,000 soldiers at Montreuil would be trapped and annihilated. He ordered that 4,000 reinforcements from England be immediately sent to Étaples, a port near the estuary of the River Canche. In addition, his fleet and some of the troops on the Scottish borders, 'should repair hither with as much celerity as the wind would suffer'.[61]

Norfolk was to withdraw to Boulogne, bringing back his artillery and equipment in good order. Disobeying orders, the duke burnt the mobile mills, the boat bridges and destroyed all the tents. They broke camp on 28 September and trudged wearily back to the coast. There were no tunes of glory for them nor, yet again, for their disgruntled general.

Henry, jealous of his new reputation as an all-conquering hero, was all for staying and deciding the matter on the field of battle. But Paget was concerned about the king's health and sought to convince him to depart as arranged, emphasising that he 'might with honour withdraw, having achieved the enterprise of Boulogne and that the king of France was not coming in person' to lead his troops against the English.[62]

Chapuys, tasked with disclosing Charles V's peace treaty to Henry, steeled himself to face the most terrible of Tudor rages. Surprisingly, the king's reaction was muted, although he 'found it strange that the Emperor should have concluded peace without concluding that which concerned him'. He also marvelled that Charles had not obtained at least a ceasefire 'so that he might more honourably withdraw his army . . . after offering battle to the enemy, if they would have it'. The envoy found the king 'silent and pensive, with none of his usual boastful manner' and believed that his sadness 'chiefly proceeds from fear that there may be shame and harm at the retreat of his army' from Montreuil.[63]

Norfolk and his starving troops arrived safely at Boulogne and Henry, pausing only to distribute some knighthoods among his gentlemen at his lodgings, quietly departed France for England on 30 September.

Then the duke and Suffolk disobeyed orders and quit Boulogne – leaving only 4,000 men as a garrison – for Calais, to defend it from a rumoured French attack. Many of the army then died from dysentery. Henry, now journeying to London, was amazed at his generals' wilfulness and stupidity, believing they were 'too well minded to come home'. The king's affairs at Boulogne were hindered 'by your so light coming away' and he believed matters were being 'very loosely handled [in] many ways'.[64]

The Dauphin launched a surprise attack on the port at Boulogne during the night of Tuesday, 7 October. Wearing white shirts over their armour to distinguish friend from foe in the darkness, 6,000 French troops infiltrated the battered streets of the Base Boulogne. They 'slew all they might, both men, women and children and went then to spoil the ships [in the harbour] but all who approached were killed'. Distracted by pillaging food supplies, the attackers faltered and were caught by 500 of the English garrison sallying out of the upper town. Six hundred were killed before the bloody-nosed French fled for their lives. Violent thunderstorms and floods prevented the Dauphin from renewing the assault and they departed, leaving a 'great fire where they lay last night'. His army withdrew to Guisnes where, after burning 'a few cottages' and two churches in sulky defiance, he retreated to Paris.[65]

As Boulogne had been saved, Henry felt able magnanimously to accept Norfolk and Suffolk's 'humble submission to have their late proceedings forgotten ... considering that God has so wrought that ... the victuals and ordnance at Boulogne [are] safe'. Their pleas [demonstrated] 'you being indeed penitent ... but this shall be a warning for you ... henceforth'.[66]

During the winter, peace talks with the French came and foundered. The king's joy at the capture of Boulogne remained – an exquisite hunting sword was specially made for him as a memento of his triumph[67] – but his triumph was not shared by some of his ministers.

Bishop Gardiner, now in Bruges, wrote frankly to Paget in mid-November about his disillusionment at events.

> I am very much troubled with the state of our affairs ... We be in war with France and Scotland. We have an enemy [in] the bishop of Rome. We have no friendship assured here [in Flanders]. Our war is noisome to the wealth of our own realm and it is so noisome to all merchants that must ... pass the narrow seas, as they cry out here wonderfully. We see at home a great ... lack of such things as the continuance of the war requires. [If] we show ourselves content to take a peace, we may have it, but [it would be] so miserable as the French ... offer it ... that thereby the king's noble courage should be so touched as we ought to fear the danger [to] his person.[68]

On 3 January 1545, Chapuys had an audience with Henry shortly after he had heard Mass in his oratory in Whitehall Palace. The king admitted he had felt 'ten times better' besieging Boulogne than he had since and the ambassador thought him 'evidently much broken [in spirits] since his return'.[69]

On the northern borders, a depleted English army had been making a dozen raids a month into Scotland to demonstrate their mastery of the region. The Scottish town of Kelso was burnt again and a garrison established to defend it.

Sir Ralph Evers, recipient of the queen's thanks for his exploits against the Scots, kept a meticulous 'bloody ledger', which gleefully catalogued the suffering he had inflicted on them during his career. This was a man happy in his work. His catalogue of devastation included 192 towns, villages, barns and churches destroyed; 403 Scots killed and 816 captured, as well as more than 22,000 cattle and sheep driven back to England.[70] In late February 1545, he crossed the border at the head of 5,200 men (mostly German mercenaries) and burnt and looted Melrose. During his withdrawal, he was ambushed on the 27th by a much smaller Scottish force at nearby Ancrum Moor[71] and was badly defeated. Evers was killed, together with 1,400 of his men. The Scottish regent saw Evers' body after the battle. 'God have mercy upon him,' Arran cried out, tears staining his face, 'for he was a cruel man and over-cruel, which many a man and fatherless bairn might rue. Wellaway [Grief] that ever such slaughter and blood-shedding should be amongst Christian men!'[72]

Gardiner's dejection was justified.

Henry's strategic mistake in unilaterally scrapping the allies' grand plan to march on Paris and focus instead on capturing Boulogne, failed to deliver a knock-out blow on French military might. Instead, like a small boy mischievously attacking a wasps' nest with a stick, he had left himself open to angry retribution. The tide of France's inexorable retaliation, planned since early January, was now in full flood and seemingly unstoppable. In April, Henry warned his commanders on the Scottish borders that 2,000 French infantry were to land on the west coast of Scotland, 'to encourage the Scots to invade this realm'. A second French force of 16,000 would 'also attempt to land in some [north-eastern] English port and pass towards the Scottish army, devastating the country'.[73]

The French king was assembling a fleet of between 150 and 200 ships in Normandy with an army of 60,000 men for an invasion of southern England, in addition to a probable offensive to recapture Boulogne. England and her monarch had not faced such dire peril since the dark days of 1539.

In the face of these threats, three armies in the field, totalling 90,000 men, were created to defend the northern borders, the south coast and reinforce Boulogne. This left few able-bodied men to maintain order in London, despite rumours about 'certain priests and strangers' planning to set the capital ablaze as a kind of French fifth column. Anxiety about undercover saboteurs increased when a ship called the *Hedgehog* blew up in the Thames at Westminster, although the explosion was in fact caused by the accidental firing of a gun, which set off a firkin of gunpowder.[74]

Hertford was sent to Rye in Sussex to repair the port's defences in case of invasion. The town's mayor and jurats were troubled by inhabitants who refused to pay for the work and the Privy Council directed them to 'constrain [such] persons to a uniformity with their neighbours, by imprisonment or any other lawful means'. Letters were also sent to the mayor of Bristol and the sheriffs of the western counties to 'call back all sailors from the sea' and recruit 'able mariners dwelling thereabouts' for naval service at Portsmouth, by the last day of June.[75]

In war, expect the unexpected. That summer, Francis ruptured a vein in his body and his doctors 'despaired of his life' as he was in danger of suffocation. However, he miraculously recovered and continued to haggle with Pope Paul III who had promised 6,000 men for the invasion,[76] supplied under the proviso that any peace negotiations with England would have papal involvement. Francis 'roundly refused' this, so no Vatican troops turned up, although one of his warships flew a papal flag.

The French planned that their armada, commanded by Admiral Claud d'Annebaut, should raid the southern coast of England before concentrating in the Solent. The fleet would defeat Henry's navy off Portsmouth and capture the Isle of Wight. If the landing was successful, the island would be exchanged for Boulogne.

In early July, forty or fifty English ships appeared off the invasion fleet's home base at Le Havre and bombarded the port, sparking panic in the town and its hinterland. Francis 'was in great fear for his own person as he was only three miles [5km] away from the English and his fleet was still unready for defence,' according to Spanish reports. 'He had all his baggage prepared for flight at midnight and, but for one of his captains, he would have fled in great disorder.'

Despite this alarum, by 15 July 1545, the invasion fleet was ready to sail for England, eager to avenge Henry's destruction wreaked upon the towns and villages of northern France. Francis, his wife and favoured courtiers boarded d'Annebaut's flagship, the 800-ton carrack *Carraquon*, for a splendid dinner to wish them Godspeed on their sacred mission. Unfortunately, just as they sat down to the feast, the ship caught fire, reportedly because the royal chef was careless with the galley ovens. The king and his party hurriedly disembarked, taking with them the expedition's gold and silver treasure, before the ship was steered back into port, where it exploded, scattering cannonballs into nearby vessels. More than 200 crew were drowned.[77]

Despite this accident, two days later the fleet departed. The admiral had transferred his flag into *La Maistresse*, 'the finest and strongest ship' remaining, but almost immediately, she ran aground and had to be sent back for repair. He must have begun to believe his mission was fated.

Across the English Channel, Henry's major naval base at Portsmouth was in a sorry state. Sir Anthony Knyvett reported in June that its turf-wall defences, dating from Cromwell's day, were 'much decayed'.

While he had sixty-one cannon, 'I have but eight gunners' and only about '100 able persons' to defend the port and town.[78] In the harbour, were sixty ships and a similar number were expected to arrive from the West Country. More than 4,000 troops were quickly mustered for its security.

In mid-July Henry inspected Portsmouth's hastily rebuilt defences. While there, he met the new Spanish ambassador, Francis van der Delft, who had succeeded the ailing Chapuys. His first audience was marred by the king's angry rejection of his suggestions to end the war by surrendering Boulogne.

After raiding the fishing village of Brighton, Sussex, the French fleet entered the Solent on Saturday 18 July, and concentrated off St Helen's Point, on the north shore of the Isle of Wight, looking for all the world like a forest of wooden masts. They came under ineffective long-range fire from English ships and shore batteries, although *La Maistresse* came close to sinking because of her earlier damage. Henry was dining in the great cabin of his 1,000-ton flagship *Henry Grace à Dieu* (alias *Great Harry*) in Portsmouth harbour, but as soon as the enemy fleet were sighted, drawn up in three squadrons, he hurriedly came ashore in one of his new row-barges.

The next day saw a flat calm in the Solent. Seventeen nimble French oared galleys pushed forward through Spithead to the shallow sand-bank area now known as 'No Man's Land'. They intended to lure the larger English warships into an area where they would run aground and, thus stranded, could be battered to pieces. The English fleet would be hampered by a lack of wind and the galleys enjoyed the advantage of a powerful tidal current which meant the English ships would have been held bows-on by the flood and unable to bring their broadside batteries to bear.[79]

By mid-afternoon that Sunday, Henry was on the upper ramparts of Southsea Castle, built almost on the beach to guard the deep-water channel into Portsmouth. With him was Suffolk, his land commander, to savour the grandstand view.

The tidal flow had reversed in favour of the English and a land breeze had sprung up, enabling the fleet to get under way. Lisle's flagship *Henry Grace à Dieu* led the fleet out into Spithead, followed by *Mary Rose*, 700 tons, flying the flag of Vice-Admiral Sir George Carew, appointed the previous day and now proudly wearing the symbol of office, a golden whistle, around his neck. His uncle, Gawen Carew, captain of the 600-ton *Matthew*, hailed the *Mary Rose* as they steered into battle and the vice-admiral yelled across from the quarterdeck 'that he had a sort of knaves [in the crew] whom he could not rule'.[80]

After she opened fire with a broadside, the *Mary Rose* suddenly heeled to starboard, as if caught by a freak gust of wind. Watched by the horrified spectators on land, the ship continued to lean precariously over, as ammunition and cannon broke free and rolled back across the decks, crushing some of the crew. Her massive port-side brick oven in the galley collapsed and its ninety gallon (409L) copper cauldron was thrown on to the orlop deck above.[81]

In an instant, naval discipline had vanished, replaced by a terrible chaos, panic and mortal fear. The sea rushed through the open gun ports in the ship's lower deck and within minutes, *Mary Rose* capsized and disappeared beneath the waves, just over a mile (2km) from Henry's vantage point. The ship's companionways (or stairways) linking the decks were jammed with sailors and soldiers desperately fighting to escape. If they managed to scramble up to the upper deck, they were trapped by the heavy rope netting stretched across the ship's waist to prevent enemies boarding the ship during close combat.

The piteous cries of the drowning men could be heard from Southsea Castle. Henry, his eyes starting with shock, cried out: 'Oh, my gentlemen! Oh, my gallant men! Drowned like rats!' Then, in a rare moment of compassion, he limped across to where Lady Mary Carew,[82] wife of Sir George, was standing, tears streaming down her face. The king tried to comfort her with halting phrases and inadequate words. She had just seen her husband go down with his ship.

Although small boats rowed out to rescue survivors, less than thirty-five of her crew of 400 were saved. Among those lost was the captain, Roger Grenville. A contemporary painting, once in the great parlour of Cowdray House, West Sussex, showed the immediate aftermath. The tops of two masts remain above water, one still forlornly flying the flag of St George. Three survivors cling to the masts, one frantically waving his arms to summon help. Around them are the bodies of drowned shipmates, floating near the foremast mainsail.

What had caused this disaster? One French account suggested that a cannon shot from one of the galleys holed the *Mary Rose* below the waterline, possibly near the stern on her port side. When a large portion of the hull was raised in 1982, this section had been lost to marine erosion, but there was shot damage to the muzzle of one of her cannon and shot fragments were found outside the vessel at her wreck site. If she was shipping water after being holed, *Mary Rose* may have been heading for the Spitbank shallows to be run aground to save the ship. At a speed of three knots, it would have taken just six minutes to reach safety, but the inrush of the sea compromised the ship's stability.[83]

Her refit in 1539, with extra guns added, made her top-heavy, which would have increased the risk of capsizing, especially in a sudden gust of wind. The problem would be compounded by not closing the lower gun ports before manoeuvring.[84] Russell, writing to Paget four days later, was 'very sorry [about] the unhappy and unfortunate chance of the *Mary Rose* which through such wretchedness and great negligence should be ... [so] cast away with those that were in her'.[85]

The Battle of the Solent continued. The Cowdray House painting showed a galley, flying a fleur-de-lis flag, settled low in the water by the bows, so it seems probable that a French ship also sank during the fighting.[86] Firing went on throughout the next day between the fleets but with little success on either side and for the next few days, the French galleys mounted attacks on English ships within Portsmouth harbour as 'the wind was so calm that the king's ships could not sail which was a great discomfort to them'.[87]

The French landed 2,000 troops at Bembridge on the Isle of Wight on the evening of Tuesday, 21 July, commanded by the Italian mercenary Pierre Strozzi. The new Spanish ambassador van der Delft reported that they burnt ten or twelve houses (at Nettlestone) but after several skirmishes with the local militia, fell back to 'take refuge in a small earthwork fort' – probably St Helen's bulwark – overlooking their fleet's anchorage.

There were other landings on the eastern side of the island, as part of a French strategy to attack Sandown Castle, still under construction, and other defences from the landward side. Their intention may have been to establish a bridgehead, protected by three prefabricated wooden fortresses. In Sandown Bay, the French, under the command of two galley captains called Marsay and Pierrebon, scaled the low cliffs on the beach but were met by the main body of the local militia. Intense fighting ended with both French commanders wounded and their troops taking to their boats.

The third landing was further south, at Monk's Bay, Bonchurch, under the command of the infantry general Seigneur de Tais. Today, his landing place must look very much like it did in 1545: a small shingle beach backed by steep, thickly wooded slopes reaching up to the chalk heights of Bonchurch and St Boniface Downs, 790 feet (241m) behind. Hidden up in the trees is the tiny eleventh-century church of St Boniface. A spring of clear water cascades out of a pipe down onto the beach.[88]

The 500-strong French force was unopposed and struggled up through the woods and undergrowth until they were halted by fire from the Hampshire militia positioned above the bay. The first French attack was driven back, but a second broke the defenders' line and their retreat turned into a rout as they were pursued by the French. A militia officer called Captain Robert Fisher was too fat to run, and (like Richard III) reputedly offered £100 for a horse on which he could escape. There were no takers and he was killed.

A follow-up landing of reinforcements at Whitesands Bay, south of Bembridge, was halted by a cavalry charge on Culver Down and de Tais was summoned from Bonchurch to take command. The English retreated and destroyed the sole bridge over the River Yar, isolating the French on the 'isle' of Bembridge, apart from resupply from the sea. With a stalemate in the fighting, they remained there unmolested for some days. Francis I fell victim to the fog of war when he boasted to Charles V that he had captured the Isle of Wight, Portsmouth and Southampton.[89]

Admiral d'Annebaut and his commanders decided in a council of war that it was too difficult to occupy the Isle of Wight, so the force there was recalled. However, the fleet still required fresh water and a party of soldiers, under another galley captain, Pierre de Blacas, Chevalier d'Aulx, filled their barrels from the spring in Monk's Bay. As the watering party laboured, d'Aulx and a company climbed higher through the woods to take up a defensive position. They were attacked by the militia and as his men fled, d'Aulx was wounded by an arrow in the knee, traditionally believed to have been fired by a woman. He offered to ransom his life, but was brained by a blow from a bill weapon. He was buried in an unmarked grave in the peaceful churchyard of St Boniface.[90]

The French headed for home having achieved nothing of military value, other than humiliating Henry. After another inconclusive engagement further east, off Shoreham, Sussex, a few days later, the appetite for naval warfare deserted d'Annebaut. He paused to sack the towns of Newhaven and Seaford on 25 July before his men were driven back to their ships. Lisle's pursuing fleet found themselves becalmed off Beachy Head and the French armada returned safely to their home ports.

Henry soon departed for London to escape the plague that had broken out in the fleet at Portsmouth. Once more, the opportunity for a decisive victory over the French had gone begging and he had suffered the mortification of enemy forces occupying English soil.

More bad news awaited him. His oldest friend Suffolk died suddenly at Guildford in Surrey on 22 August. The king paid for a sumptuous funeral for him in St George's Chapel, Windsor, where the duke was buried under a modest stone slab.

Money was to become an increasing preoccupation. The wealth of Henry's realm and exchequer were drained to pay for his wars against France and Scotland and repayments of his debts at exorbitant interest rates were falling due. Military glory had yet again eluded him.

His vainglorious ambitions had driven England towards bankruptcy.

11

'Old Copper Nose'

The prohibitive cost of war failed to smother Henry's ambitions. Over five years, he had been preparing for hostilities both militarily and diplomatically, but had not forgotten the economics. On 16 May 1542, his government began a secret debasement of England's coinage, in an unwitting first step towards conjuring up a fiscal storm that struck fatally at the economy of his kingdoms. This cynical money-making ploy, coupled with the runaway costs of the French and Scottish wars and rising retail and commodity prices, pushed his realm into humiliating bankruptcy. At times, Henry's Exchequer was bare of money.

It would take almost two decades for succeeding Tudor monarchs to repair the damage so carelessly and cavalierly inflicted by their father and to restore popular and commercial faith in the English currency.

For four centuries, the precious metal content of coins had been maintained in England at 92.5 per cent purity. During Henry's 'Great Debasement' that continued up to 1546, this was reduced to twenty-five per cent by adding base copper to the gold or silver melt.[1] Additionally, for sovereigns (worth £1), the constituent gold's fineness was reduced from twenty-three carats in 1544 to twenty-two the following year and to twenty in 1546. By reducing its diameter, its weight came down from 0.5 ounce (12.9g) to 0.44 ounce (12.4g) over this period.

A new coin, called the testoon, worth a shilling (5p), or one twelfth of a pound sterling, was introduced in 1544, with the head of the ageing king frowning on its obverse. Daily wear removed the thin silver coating to reveal its copper content hidden underneath. Henceforth, Henry was sneeringly nicknamed 'Old Copper Nose' by his cheated subjects. Loyal Sir John Rainsford, who had fought in France, complained angrily that his king now had a 'red and copper nose' and threatened to 'break the head' of whoever proposed the debasement.[2] In real spending terms, the testoon was worth nine pennies, not twelve, and later in Henry's reign this was slashed still further to five pennies (just over 2p).[3]

This audacious fraud inflicted on his subjects was of course cloaked by propaganda. A proclamation in May 1544 claimed the value of English money in Flanders and France was now 'so enhanced' that coin was 'daily carried out of the realm', despite attempts to enforce laws prohibiting exportation. The value of gold and silver in England was therefore increased by royal decree.[4] The official price of twenty-two carat gold was set then at 41s 10½d (£2.09p) an ounce (28g). However, merchants supplying the bullion for coining were paid at a rate seven pennies lower. An aide-memoire written by an Exchequer official predicted gleefully that by 'this alteration of the coin, the king's majesty shall have two gains, one by the proclamation of enhancement and the other by [lowering the precious metal content] of the coinage'.[5] Here was not one, but two monstrous state frauds, reminiscent of the fiscal policy of a modern banana republic.

These pernicious devaluations yielded a profit of £1.27 million (£627 million in today's money) from 1544 through to the early years of Edward VI's reign. Ironically, audits revealed that Henry was cheated out of almost £5,000 by crooked mint officials exploiting his arbitrary raising of the price of bullion.[6] The debasement was quickly spotted by the population and shrewd citizens hoarded the older coins with their greater precious metal content. Foreign bankers and merchants were reluctant to accept the devalued coinage and required repayment of Henry's debts in gold.

In addition to these problems, there were concerns about the circulation of counterfeit coins, some faked overseas beyond the reach of English law, under which the crime was treason. Paris became a centre for forging English money; a pair of die-stamps for striking Henry VIII four-penny pieces, or groats, turned up there in the nineteenth century. Was this a clue that clandestine economic warfare was being waged against England by France? This seems unlikely as the counterfeiting was hardly undertaken on an industrial scale and besides, the forgers were embarrassingly inept. A counterfeit groat made in Paris in the 1540s, in lightly silvered yellow metal, bore the name of 'Ferdinand' rather than Henry as king and had the lions of England facing in the wrong direction.[7]

Forgery also continued in England; on 20 December 1546, the Southwark ale brewer William Harpin, who had been convicted of counterfeiting testoons at Horsley, Surrey, was 'drawn from Newgate to Tower Hill and there hanged'.[8] Other criminal practices included clipping, filing and 'sweating' of the older coins to exploit their bullion content.[9] In February 1546, Joan Edling, the wife of the royal purveyor of oxen, was sentenced to be burnt to death for clipping gold coins, but was reprieved even as she was being tied to the stake at Smithfield.[10]

The harvests at the end of Henry's reign compounded the economic misery of debasement, taxation and inflation. Those of 1540–2 came early and had produced abundant cereals and fruit. The two succeeding harvests delivered only average yields, but those of 1545–6 were disastrous, with average produce prices rising 50 per cent, the highest then known at Exeter. In London, 'all manner of victuals were dear and at high prices' and wheat was sold at twenty-eight shillings the quarter (twenty-eight pounds or 12.7kg). The Lord Mayor, 'fearing great penury', imported cereals from Denmark and 'Bremberland' – Bremen in northern Germany – to feed the city's poor.[11] Four thousand quarters (51 tonnes) of corn were delivered to London in one month to provide the staple food of bread. Across England and Wales, rocketing food prices, exacerbated by further debasements of the coinage, caused starvation and distress.[12]

You will recall that the Army Royal crossed into France in 1544 amid strenuous efforts to overcome a £116,000 shortfall in meeting the forecast £250,000 cost of the wars. In the event, the fighting in France, defence against invasion the following year and expenditure on fortifications at home and in the Pale of Calais, blew away the budget as effectively as a salvo from the king's artillery during the two-month siege of Boulogne. Sixteen pages of careful accounts, drawn up in Edward VI's reign, estimated that £3,486,471 14s 5¼d had been expended from September 1538 to 1552 on fighting the French and Scots, more than £2.1 million of which was spent during Henry's last years.[13] In today's money this would equate to well over £1 billion. One has to admire the assiduity of Tudor accountants; who else would calculate the cost of hostilities down to the last farthing?

As we saw in Chapter 10, even as Henry was besieging Boulogne, he was seeking loans to augment his depleted war chest. At the same time, Vaughan, his overworked financial agent in Antwerp, was negotiating a loan of £20,000 from the German bankers Welser, as the English money market was struggling to meet the king's demands for more cash. Other loans were obtained from the Fugger and Schetz bankers as well as Italian merchants.[14]

Within three years, Henry had borrowed almost £1 million from the great Antwerp banking houses[15] and they began to worry about his ability to repay their high-interest loans. In March 1546, Vaughan reported that the Fuggers bank would not lend a further £250,000, 'unless all the king's subjects are bound to [repayment] by Act of Parliament'.[16] Henry could not stomach such interference in his domestic affairs, nor this slight to his prestige and honour. The Privy Council angrily rejected the terms, insisting that 'his highness will not, by entering such bonds as the Fuggers require, seem to the world to be brought so low as he should need, for that sum, to [give] them assurance by Act of Parliament'.[17]

Fewer banking houses were willing to lend huge unsecured sums to a big-spending king with unquantified or even dubious credit. Vaughan tried to educate Henry's ministers about the realities of the Antwerp money market. 'If you will have me press men overmuch, you shall discover too much [which] were better not known. Men here be wise, have many eyes [and] great intelligence out of all countries,' he explained. 'Think you that these men will disburse [such] huge sums before they be honestly assured to be repaid again? Think you that the merchants here will take the bonds of noblemen of England? No, I assure you.' He added: 'And as to our merchants, they be better known to strangers here than to ourselves. They will not all be taken for 30,000 crowns, no, though you lay them heaped all in one bond'.[18]

In the event, after providing loans to the crown, the London-based Italian bankers Bonvisi, Vivaldi and Cavalcanti could only offer the king their credit guarantees in support of his requests for further loans in Antwerp. Later, the foreign banks were prepared to accept the bonds of the English merchant companies – the Merchant Adventurers and the Staplers – or the Corporation of London itself as guarantors for the king's borrowing. This may have been patriotic, but it was also financially foolhardy. In case of default, Henry's backers enjoyed only marginal protection against confiscation of their members' personal assets through royal counter-bonds indemnifying them against losses.

Henry's debt burden was compounded by the financial idiosyncrasies of dealing with overseas bankers, aside from the unpredictable perils of fluctuating currency exchange rates. Then, as now, bankers were active in finding innovative means to boost their profits. Antwerp's financial strength was built on commodity trading and therefore loans were often offered not all in cash, but partly paid in kind, such as fustian cloth, copper and even gemstones. As the banks sometimes valued these commodities above their true market worth, this had the effect of driving up the interest rate from the agreed 12 per cent to an actual 14 per cent.[19]

In addition to foreign loans, Henry resorted to benevolences (compulsory gifts demanded from his over-taxed subjects) in 1542 and 1544 to 'raise a convenient mass of money'. In the latter case, all laity and clergy with lands or goods worth between £2 and £20, were charged at eight pennies (3p) in the pound, and twelve pennies in the pound if they owned greater assets. This benevolence brought in an estimated £120,000.[20] Forced loans and subsidies from Church and laity in 1543 and 1545, accrued another £180,000. A Bill in 1545 to enact the heaviest tax demand of Henry's reign was hailed by a browbeaten Parliament as merely 'a poor token of our true and faithful hearts' towards a monarch who had 'preserved us for almost forty years'.[21]

Not all his subjects displayed such a loyal disposition. The London alderman Richard Read unpatriotically refused to pay the 1544 benevolence and Henry ordered his forcible conscription into the army and immediate dispatch to the privations of duty on the wild Scottish borders. The Privy Council decreed in January 1545 that he should 'do some service... as soldier... at his own charge' to take part in 'any enterprise against the enemy. He is to ride and do as the other poor soldiers do... that he may know what pains other... soldiers abide, and feel the smart of his folly. Use him after the sharp military discipline of the northern wars.'[22] His unwanted military career was short and certainly not sweet. In February, Read was captured by the Scots and held prisoner, until being released in an exchange of captives at the end of the year.[23]

The king was also receiving income from a source that had come as a by-product of his break with the Vatican. The First Fruits and Annual Tenths of the Church, income that for centuries had been sent to Rome, was paid into Henry's exchequer from 1534. Clergy had to pay a portion of their first year's income (known as *annates*) and a tenth of their revenue annually thereafter.

The great sale of royal assets continued. By Henry's death, two-thirds of monastic estates had been sold, bringing £800,000 into the royal coffers, and a fifth of crown lands had been disposed of. This was pure short-termism, as these sales reduced future royal income and removed an important source of royal patronage to the crown's supporters.[24]

Based on the maxim that one cannot accumulate wealth without speculating first, it was suggested in 1544 that Henry's government should deal in the valuable commodity of alum, used to fix colours in dyeing. If wool, England's most important export, could be dyed effectively, its value increased considerably, thus also boosting foreign earnings. The alum would be acquired in exchange for monastery lead, which was failing to realise a good price because the English were swamping an already slow overseas market. Alum was 'a sweet merchandise', enthused Vaughan, 'and will be exceedingly well sold and that for ready money'.

Caveat emptor! Let the buyer beware! The alum speculation proved an unmitigated disaster. English pirates purloined one of the cargoes en route from Spain to England and the crown had to pay damages and return the captured ship. The alum suppliers suffered substantial losses because of falling lead prices, which led to unseemly squabbling over their compensation. It was also hoped that the Merchant Adventurers Company would buy large quantities, but 30,000cwt (1,524 tonnes) was far too much for the market to absorb in one bite. There was a sudden, terrible realisation that it would take seven years to sell the consignment at prevailing rates of consumption. Even when offered to foreign merchants at advantageous rates, little was sold. The deal, which cost the king more than £16,000 worth of lead, brought in only £7,000. He suffered a loss of £8,566 in cash.[25] Entrepreneurship had proved no solution to Henry's financial problems.

The fiscal crisis became desperate. The books stubbornly failed to balance, with excess of expenditure over income amounting to a frightening shortfall of around £1 million by the end of 1545.[26] Lord Chancellor Wriothesley tried calling in outstanding loans from debtors to the crown. 'We send out letters in great numbers [to] more debtors ... As for money, all the shift shall be made that is possible, but yet the store is very small. The contribution comes very slowly in.'[27]

The surviving left-hand section of Hans Holbein the Younger's preparatory sketch for the huge dynastic painting commissioned by Henry VIII. The picture was probably in the Privy Chamber of the Palace of Whitehall in 1537. It shows an imperious king with his father, Henry VII, like a regal ghost behind him. The lost right-hand section portrayed Henry's mother, Elizabeth of York, and his third wife, Jane Seymour. The painting, which served as a model for a number of propaganda portraits of the king, was destroyed in the fire at Whitehall in 1698.

Opposite page:

Henry's portraits were designed as propaganda to convince his subjects of his power and might. Later paintings showed the king descending into geriatric decay, as these examples suggest. Clockwise, from top left: Henry VIII, after Hans Holbein the Younger, painted 1542–7; portrait, perhaps seventeenth-century copied from one of 1542, showing the king massively increased in bulk and having to walk with a staff; portrait of the 1540s showing Henry's face falling away; and a line engraving by Cornelius Metsys of 1545, indicating just how far the moon-faced Henry VIII had deteriorated physically.

This page:

Henry VIII's sometime allies, sometime enemies. Right: Francis I (1494–1547) King of France, known to his subjects as François du Grand Nez – 'Francis the Long Nose'. Below right: The Imperial Emperor Charles V (1500–58), painted *c.*1515. His cap has the badge of the Blessed Virgin Mary with the Latin inscription 'Holy Mary. Pray for us'. Both monarchs needed all the help they could find to deal with Henry. This portrait was hung in the Presence Chamber at Whitehall and both paintings are now at Hampton Court Palace.

Love's labour's lost. This is the portrait, hurriedly painted in 1539 by Hans Holbein the Younger, that convinced Henry VIII that Anne of Cleves should become his fourth wife. Sadly, in the flesh, her appearance disappointed the king and in a flash, love had taken wing and fled.

The 'Blushing Rose' later sadly deadheaded. Portrait of a Lady, perhaps Katherine Howard, Henry's fifth queen, by Hans Holbein the Younger, *c.*1540. The attribution is based on the large ruby, emerald and pearl jewel worn by the sitter which belonged to Queen Jane Seymour and this, together with the jewelled band around her neck, may have been given to Katherine by Henry on their marriage in 1540.

Henry VIII's 'gangster' Ludovico da l'Armi is the nonchalant dandy standing lower right, watching the slaughter going on around him in this painting, *Massacre of the Innocents* by the Veronese artist Bonifacio de'Pitati. Da l'Armi is identified by the heraldry on the shield held by a retainer on his right and by his splendid attire. The painting was commissioned in 1545 by the Venetian magistrates to hang in their headquarters near the Rialto Bridge. Da l'Armi arrived in the city state that year.

Tempers began to fray among Henry's ministers as the Exchequer cash ran out and the demands of the war became ever more pressing. The Treasurer of the King's Chamber unashamedly hid himself from creditors after admitting he had been run out of town because he had no money with which to pay outstanding bills.[28] In August 1545, Wriothesley told Paget: 'If you had been as saving in laying out of the money as they here have travailed in getting it, there would have been a greater [amount of money] remain[ing].' There was no money left, so payments of bills and debts should be postponed until more cash 'arrived in ten or twelve days' time'.[29]

The following month Wriothesley received a Privy Council request for funds to pay for the uniforms and travelling expenses of 4,300 reinforcements for Boulogne. He was at his wits' end in coping with the financial emergency and his response was pointed.

I trust you will consider what is done already. This year and the last, the king has spent about £1,300,000, his subsidy and benevolence [bringing in] scant £300,000 and the lands being consumed and the plate [bullion] of the realm [melted down] and coined. I lament the danger of the time to come. There is to be repaid [from loans] in Flanders as much and more than all the rest...

Though the king might have a greater grant than the realm could bear at one time, it would do little to the continuance of these charges this winter – most of the subsidy being paid, the revenues received beforehand and more borrowed from the mint than will be repaid these four or five months – and yet you write me still, pay, pay, prepare for this and that. [You should] consider it is your [role] to ponder what may be done and how things may be continued.[30]

Seven weeks later, Wriothesley wrote to Paget after examining some calamitous reports from the king's under-treasurers: 'Now what I shall do or how I shall divide this matter that all may yet be saved... I cannot tell. I [wish] you would not write so often as you do, knowing the state of things as I, by the declarations of the treasurers. You [bid me] run as though I could make money. [I would that] I had that gift but one year, for his majesty's sake.'[31]

Having drained the financial pot of monastic property, there was one class of religious establishment that had somehow escaped the king's depredations: the colleges of priests, chantry chapels, hospitals and fraternities served by secular clergy. These were now dissolved in 1545 by parliamentary Act,[32] which alleged that income and property of some institutions had been misapplied by 'covetous persons' and this could be better spent by the king to meet his military commitments.[33] Unfortunately, the chantry chapels yielded little hard cash.[34]

The same year, Henry cast his greedy, acquisitive eyes over the silver and gold plate that adorned England's 10,000 parish churches – something that not even Cromwell had dared contemplate, let alone attempt, because of the high risk of popular anger and protest over the sequestration of these pious donations. Times had changed and needs must. After all, as Supreme Head of the Church in England, were not these sacred objects ultimately owned by Henry? The king began to ponder how he might 'borrow' the church plate[35] – not confiscating it, just temporarily utilising the precious resources of his Church to tide him over a sticky financial patch.

Hertford, full of religious reforming zeal and scornful of papist objects and liturgy, heartily approved of the bold plan when it was secretly disclosed to him by Paget in July 1545. 'I think it the readiest way of relief and the least chargeable to the king's subjects,' he commented. 'For God's service, which consists not in jewels, plate or ornaments of gold and silver, cannot thereby be anything diminished and those things better employed for the commonwealth and defence of the realm.' All that was necessary, suggested the general, was finding a way of selling the idea to the population: 'The worst that I see in it is a [rumour] may arise that the king's majesty is driven to shift for money, which nevertheless I think is much suspected and spoken of already in other parts.'[36] In the event, the king was persuaded that his government had more than enough problems to resolve, without the risk of another popular insurrection.

Despite this looming financial catastrophe, Henry was determined to retain Boulogne. He told the Spanish ambassador, Francis van der Delft, that he had seized the town honourably 'at the sword's point and he meant to keep it'.[37] At the end of August 1545, Norfolk's son, Henry Howard, earl of Surrey, was appointed Lieutenant of the captured town.[38] He proved an enthusiastic and eager commander, and like his geriatric monarch, yearned for victory and fame in battle. Unfortunately, his impatience for martial exploits did not chime with the Privy Council's mounting apprehension about the escalating expense of holding Boulogne and maintaining so many men under arms. The war in France cost £700,000 in 1544 and another £560,000 up to September 1545.

The writing was on the wall. Could Henry forget finally his narcissistic fixation with military glory and his place in history as a warrior king? No, he ignored the pleas of his men on the spot about the cost and suffering inflicted by his myopia to reality.

Sir Richard Rich, Treasurer of the Wars, was compelled to borrow money in October 1544 to pay the English troops the wages due them. 'The poor soldiers here die daily at Calais from the plague and are also weakened for lack of victuals,' he reported.[39] The cost of rations for the Boulogne and Calais garrisons for the period December–May 1544/5, totalled £180,000, but £44,000 of this still had to be found.[40]

Move on a few months, and the cost of defending Boulogne burgeoned to £133,000 for just two weeks in September/October 1545, £33,000 of which was unpaid wages to the garrison, the labourers working on the new fortifications and the commissariat. More than £11,000 was also written off by waste and loss of food.[41]

England's slide into bankruptcy gathered apace, as the scramble for funds from various government sources degenerated into a hand-to-mouth rummage for hard cash. Wriothesley told Sir William Paget in November 1545 that he had just been able to scrape together £20,000 to pay for some of the war costs: £15,000 in profits from minting currency ('our holy anchor'); £3,000 from the Court of Augmentations and £1,000 each from the Duchy of Lancaster and the Court of Wards. Elsewhere, the cupboard was practically bare. 'The Tenths and First Fruits have nothing, the Surveyors nothing, nor the Exchequer above £1,000', which was already earmarked for putting the Navy Royal to sea and repaying debts for artillery. 'I have faithfully promised Mr Cofferer [Sir Edmund Peckham, Cofferer of the Household] that we will borrow no more there until all be paid again.'[42]

Almost a week later, Wriothesley wrote again to Paget, desperation now creeping into his words. The daily strain of finding money was making him short-tempered: 'If you tarry for more money to be sent to Boulogne at this time, you may tarry too long before you have the sum desired . . . I assure you that I am at my wits' end [about], how we shall possibly shift for the three months following and especially for the next two. I see not any great likelihood that any good sum will come in until after Christmas . . . If ever I offend men in anything, I offend in this matter.'[43]

Norfolk, as Lord Treasurer, endorsed Wriothesley's fears about England's economic collapse and wrote sternly to his son, urging him to rein back his optimistic reports to the king about minor victories over the French and just how easy it was to defend Boulogne. 'Animate not the king too much for the keeping of Boulogne, for he who does so, at length shall get small thanks,' he cautioned. Paget had urged him to pass on this warning: '[U]pon what grounds he spoke it, I know not, but I fear [he] wrote something too much therein to somebody.'[44]

The Lord Treasurer, known proverbially for being tight-fisted and his bluntness, was aware that his son had incurred a crippling debt in building and furnishing an imposing Renaissance home on the site of a Benedictine priory at St Leonard's, on a commanding hilltop position outside Norwich. Named 'Mount Surrey', it was more a palace than a mansion, with magnificent furnishings to match. To meet the pressing demands of his numerous creditors, Surrey had been forced to borrow from his own steward, Richard Fulmerston.

You will remember the duke's alacrity in abandoning his family when his future became threatened at court. His son would now sample the same heartless ruthlessness.

Norfolk decided to employ his son's financial embarrassment as a bludgeon to knock some sense into his proud, patrician head and bring him sharply to heel over Boulogne. As a warning of what would ensue if his defiance continued, he tried to block the sale of one of Surrey's manors at Rochford, Essex, aimed at generating some much-needed cash.

Thomas Hussey, Norfolk's personal treasurer, also confided to Surrey that his father and the Privy Council were secretly planning to return Boulogne to the French, to end the fatal haemorrhage of England's wealth. But the earl's letters to the king hindered every attempt to pursue this policy: what they managed to achieve in six days was undone in six hours by Surrey's jingoism. 'My lord's grace [is] somewhat offended in seeing your private letters to the king . . . of such vehemence in animating the king to keep Boulogne . . . Every councillor says "Away with it" and the king and your lordship says "We will keep it".' However, Henry's ministers were too scared to raise the matter directly with him: 'There is not remaining in the council (my lord of Norfolk being absent, who will bark it to his dying day) a member that dare move [propose] the render [return of Boulogne].'

Hussey acknowledged 'there was no hope' that Surrey's expenses as Lieutenant would be repaid by the straitened Exchequer, but promised that if Boulogne were handed back, Norfolk would use his influence to ensure his son was appointed captain of Guisnes Castle or deputy governor of Calais. If Surrey did not accept this inducement, Hussey had heard his father declare that 'he had rather bury you and the rest of his children before he should give his consent to the ruin of this realm, not doubting that you should be removed, [because] of your [stubbornness]'.[45]

Surrey, in his arrogance, ignored this sage advice and continued to electrify Henry with breathless news of insignificant exploits against the French. On 4 December, in a nine-page letter, he reported the destruction of a church tower, used as an enemy observation post. Then the English had ambushed 700 French cavalry. 'In the charge, Mr Marshall broke his mace upon a Frenchman and Mr Shelley broke his staff [lance] upon ... a tall young gentleman ...' The enemy retreated, 'well dagged with arrows'. Surrey heartily wished that Henry could have witnessed his men's courage, indeed, urged him to take to the field again, so he could see how badly Francis had constructed his new fortifications facing Boulogne and just how easy it was to maintain the English-held town.[46]

The warlike earl soon brought disaster down upon himself. His spies told him on the evening of 6 January 1546 that the French were planning to resupply their new fortress of Chatillon, opposite Boulogne, with about 100 wagons, escorted by 600 cavalry and 3,000 mercenary infantry. The following night, Surrey attacked the French column at St Étienne with 2,500 men from the town's garrison. His men were in low spirits because of their mouldy food and overdue pay.

Surrey's mounted men-at-arms drove off the French horse and began to loot and burn the carts. His infantry charged the enemy mercenaries but the second English line suddenly panicked, broke ranks and fled for their lives, back to the gates of Boulogne.

Around 200 of his men were killed, including fourteen officers in the first infantry echelon. The French supplies safely entered Chatillon. The earl considered himself dishonoured and, in 'a frenzy', he urged Sir

John Bridges and other gentlemen to 'stick their swords through his guts and make him forget the day'.[47]

Dissuaded from suicide, that night he begged Henry 'to accept our poor service, albeit the success in all things was not as we wished, yet was the enterprise of our enemies disappointed [*sic*] ... If any disorder there were, [I] assure your majesty it was no [fault] in the [commanders], nor lack of courage on their part. It was the fault of a humour that sometimes reigns in Englishmen.'[48]

He was relieved of his command and replaced by Hertford. This was a heavy blow upon a painful bruise, as Surrey had long nurtured a deep contempt, if not hatred, for the Seymour brothers, whom he regarded as hardly of noble blood, if not uncultured parvenus.

Hertford stoked the fire of Surrey's resentment by not only accusing him of corruption during his Lieutenancy, but purging many of his appointees to offices in Boulogne. This he denied furiously, claiming that there were 'too many witnesses that Henry of Surrey was never for singular profit corrupted, nor yet bribe closed his hand, which lesson I learnt from my father'.[49]

He was recalled to London in March 1546, coldly received at court and forbidden an audience with the king. Norfolk's prophesy of 'small thanks' had proved all too true.

One of the biggest demands on Henry's dwindling resources was the cost of the foreign mercenaries, hired to fight the French. The English have always nurtured a deep antipathy for their neighbours in Europe. Sir John Wallop, commander of that expedition in support of Imperial forces in July–November 1543, had a low opinion of his Italian soldiers of fortune: 'It is evil meddling with them, having had good experience this year,' he told Paget.[50] Stephen Vaughan, Henry's agent in Antwerp, who toiled to find acceptable ready currency with which to pay the mercenaries, wrote: 'Happy is he that has no need of the Almains [Germans] for of all the nations under the heavens, they be the worst, most rudest and unreasonable to deal with.'[51]

Their xenophobia was quite justified. Foreign mercenaries became one of Henry's biggest headaches, as some never turned up to fight, while others, after being paid in advance, promptly absconded without drawing their swords on the battlefield. The German Christof von Landenberg, who was contracted to provide 4,000 infantry and a contingent of 1,000 cavalry, haggled over his conditions of service after arrival at Aachen and matters became so heated that the English officials Sir Ralph Fane and Richard Wyndebank fled his camp, fearing being murdered. Vaughan's life was also threatened.[52] The king had to write off the £9,266 paid to Landenberg.

The most irksome was the youthful and inexperienced Hessian captain Friedrich von Riffenberg, who, 'moved by [Henry's] pre-eminence in kingly virtues',[53] offered to raise 8,000 infantry and 1,500 cavalry to fight for England, in return, of course, for suitable remuneration. Beware a silver-tongued mercenary and his barefaced flattery. In June 1545, he signed the mercenary's standard articles of agreement, laying out his conditions of service.[54] Philip, Landgrave of Hesse, granted permission for him to enter the king's service and hoped, rather ominously, that Henry 'may have cause to be grateful'.[55] Riffenberg and his troops were hired for the equivalent of £15,500 a month for three months, for service initially in Boulogne, but later ear-marked for a planned month-long diversionary operation to burn and pillage the villages of Champagne, with the strategic aim of luring French forces away from the coast.

Unfortunately, the king's old ally Charles V refused to allow them to travel through his province of Brabant and complained that they had caused 'inestimable damage' in the Treves area and then 'forced their way into the bishop of Liège's town of Wesel'.[56]

The mercenary force reached the abbey at Florennes in today's Belgium on 28 October where the troops refused to march any further. Their English liaison officers, Fane, Thomas Chamberlain and Thomas Avery, were taken hostage and became convinced that Riffenberg and his lieutenant Wolf Slegher had masterminded the mutiny. Five hundred of 'the rascals' assaulted the abbey gate to drag the English out and negotiations began about how much had been paid to Riffenberg and whether the Germans would receive a month's pay to return home, which was owed under their *bestellinge*, or contract.

The English were led on foot – 'in the foulest way they could devise ... We were carried more like thieves than commissioners' – to the mercenary camp a mile away, escorted by 600 infantry. They were forced to enter an intimidating moot or 'ring' (the *landsknechts'* traditional assembly used to resolve disputes) and Riffenberg offered them a drum to sit on 'which we refused, as it was told us that the same [is offered] to them taken in derision'. The hostages protested that Riffenberg had already been paid and Chamberlain was threatened by 'these wilful beasts' with hanging, after insisting on a full account of the money already paid out. Eventually the hostages agreed to provide more cash and they were released after the intervention of an Imperial agent, in return for a safe conduct for Riffenberg.[57]

Back in England, Paget wrote to Riffenberg on 2 November in French, complaining of the 'disloyal and bad service' done to Henry and his 'strange use' of the English commissioners. He told him: 'I am grieved for the dishonour to yourself and the diminution of the credit of him who recommended you to his majesty.' Then he added a full-blown threat, bereft of bureaucratic niceties. Free the commissioners, he insisted, 'or else, be assured that wherever you be in all Christendom, it will cost you your life, even if his majesty pays 50,000 crowns for it.'[58]

Fane, Chamberlain and Avery, shaken but unharmed from their experiences, were free men again and Riffenberg, like many freelances, changed sides and served France. He is last heard of during the defence of Augsburg against Imperial forces in January 1547.[59] Philip, Landgrave of Hesse, was embarrassed by his soldier of fortune's outrageous behaviour. On 16 December, he wrote to Henry expressing indignation that Riffenberg and 'his fellow soldiers did not deal uprightly' with him and claimed to know nothing of the mercenaries' plans.[60]

These experiences did not daunt Henry, still hindered by the lack of trained and war-hardened troops. By the summer of 1545, he had hired mercenaries from a bewildering collection of European nations or regions: Scotland, Spain, Switzerland, Cleves, Gascony, Portugal, Italy, Greece, Turkey, Albania, Flanders and Burgundy.[61] The king even recruited some Tatar cavalrymen from the remote Russian steppes.[62] Spanish soldiers posted to Newcastle complained about the local food and resorted to cooking their own meals in the kitchens of their billets, causing friction with their landladies, who were unfamiliar with the joys of *paella* or other spicy Iberian dishes.[63] Italian freelances also served there for twelve months from April 1544.[64]

The Exchequer's chronic lack of funds also did not curb Henry's considerable spending on building, extending and beautifying his royal palaces. For example, more than £24,000 was expended on constructing the brand-new palace of Nonsuch, near Ewell, Surrey, deliberately built to rival Francis I's Château de Chambord in magnificence.[65] Work began there in 1538 and the Renaissance palace, with a separate banqueting house, was almost complete at Henry's death in 1547. A total of £28,676 was also spent at Whitehall during the 1540s[66] and £16,686 at Hampton Court between 1538 and 1547, mainly on new buildings erected in its park and privy gardens.[67]

Henry's reckless and profligate spending either had to stop, or its causes removed quickly. The intractable problem facing his ministers was Henry's vaunting pride in his war prize of Boulogne – he called it 'our daughter' – and the egomania and personal honour bound up in its continued occupation by the English.[68] Paget was given a sharp lesson for advocating the benefits of peace and he had to hastily and humbly assure 'his sovereign and most benign and gentle master' that all his knowledge of diplomacy had come from conversations with his monarch and that he would never favour a peace that was not to his satisfaction and honour.[69]

Time was against both protagonists in the war. If England was suffering the economic horrors of bankruptcy, France, in turn, was afflicted with crippling poverty. According to Spanish intelligence reports in June 1545, German mercenaries in Champagne were unpaid and 'committing all sorts of disorder'. The French cavalry and infantry were also owed back pay and 'the nobility [were] impoverished and the people ruined'. A French navy galley had been abandoned by its crew, 'most of its slaves having died of the plague'.[70] Vaughan in Antwerp passed on news that Francis I was 'exceedingly bare of money and his country pressed with misery and poverty'.[71]

On 9 September 1545, twenty-three-year-old Charles, duc d'Orléans, died on his way to join the siege of Boulogne, probably from influenza, although some thought the cause was bubonic plague and others that he had been poisoned. Francis himself was cursed with 'the French disease', suffering exhaustion and frequent fainting, and had to be carried around on a litter.[72]

Throughout that autumn and winter, Charles V toyed with the idea of playing the role of honest broker between his warring neighbours but he suspected and feared that a rapprochement between England and France would turn them against him.[73]

A frank briefing document, written by his officials, suggested that the emperor's good offices could be employed in arranging a truce, to prevent further 'weakening of the Christian cause, to the advantage of the enemy of the faith', the Ottoman Empire. The French might realise 'there is little [chance] of their taking Boulogne by force and a truce would be all in their favour as they would gain time by it ... [while] God ordained how the realm of England should fare after the death of the king.'[74] His diplomats bluntly pointed out that Henry was 'a prince of short life and on his death, the realm will descend to a child. For many reasons, the king of France may then obtain Boulogne cheaply.'[75]

Henry had not forgotten Charles V's craven desertion from his alliance with England. He now sought assurances that the emperor would honour his treaty obligations and sent Bishop Gardiner to Bruges to obtain these. After much prevarication, and delays caused by Charles's gout, he managed to achieve a partial clarification of the non-military clauses of the Anglo-Imperial treaty at Utrecht in January 1546.

At the same time, the king planned one last roll of the dice – a final military incursion into France, this time with Hertford, as Lieutenant of Boulogne, leading an army of 16,000 English soldiers, supported by 6,000 German and 4,000 Italian and Spanish mercenaries and 4,000 cavalry, to strike at Étaples and Ardres. On 23 March, Hertford landed at Calais and began to fortify the port of Ambleteuse, near Boulogne, as a base for the expedition.

Quite unexpectedly, Henry's last huzza on the battlefield was silenced, even before his troops had marched into enemy territory. The king was forced belatedly to recognise the financial disaster of destroying England's economy. His exchequer had been swept bare and the desperate shortage of food, caused by a calamitous harvest, had wrecked any chance of paying for munitions or supplying victuals to arm and feed Hertford's expedition.

On 17 April 1546, Paget, Lisle, Hertford and Dr Nicholas Wotton, ambassador in Flanders, were commissioned to meet French envoys to discuss peace terms, on neutral ground. The king's instructions did not waver from some of his old demands. They should 'require to have Boulogne and [its hinterland] for ever, or if that is refused, provoke [the French] to declare what part they would have restored'. Henry's annual pension and its arrears should be paid immediately, or 'at least one half and the residue to be paid at Michaelmas'. French payments for England's war costs and expense for holding Boulogne should total at least 8,000,000 crowns. The Scots should be included in the peace treaty 'upon condition that they shall also deliver presently into Our hands their young queen for the performance of the marriage with Our son Prince Edward'.[76]

Negotiations began a week later in a sometimes wet and uncomfortable tent outside Guisnes, with the French delegation led by Admiral Claud d'Annebaut, armed with powers granted him by Francis I.[77] It was never going to be easy and the sessions sometimes lasted seven hours without a break. The French were both amazed and aghast at the scale of English demands for war reparations: 'Eight millions, quoth they. You speak merrily! All Christendom has not so much money. We may as well offer you again 100 crowns! You speak of recompense; if any recompense should be made, we should have it, for you have made us spend twice as much as you.'[78]

Paget had vowed that he and his colleagues would 'show ourselves men of stomach' in seeking revenge 'upon this proud nation'. On 27 May, now totally exasperated by French intransigence, he told Sir William Petre: 'Send us fire and sword, for other things cannot bring these false dogs to reason. God give them pestilence, false traitors! The king... has been trifled [with] too long already and seeing these false, wicked men work after this fraudulent fashion, God shall revenge us upon their iniquity and falsehood.'

After threats by both parties to break off negotiations, the French seemed at last willing to come to terms. Inevitably, Henry thought this a good moment to intervene. At first, he demanded that the entire Boulonnais be held by the English, but later settled for an area adjacent to the Calais Pale, extending inland to the headwaters of the River Liane. But no accurate map delineated the upper reaches of this meandering river. To settle this, Paget was packed off with a French counterpart to splash through the swamps and marshes of the Liane. They became hopelessly lost in the fields and woods around its source at Quesques, twenty-two miles (35km) upstream from Boulogne. The king also claimed the town's harbour as his – right up to the high-water mark, which also had to be precisely established in case of future doubt. Helpfully, he urged Paget and his fellow negotiators to show some English grit – 'stoutness' – in their dealings with the French.[79]

A peace treaty, in nine pages of Latin, was finally signed late on 7 June 1546 within another tent, this time pitched at Campagne, or

'Campe', between Ardres and Guisnes.[80] A face-saving formula had been discovered that allowed each king to live comfortably with each other and stop the haemorrhage of war, both in lives and money. Henry did not give up Boulogne and remained its conqueror – but the town would be handed back to the French in eight years' time, after their payment of 2,000,000 crowns in a lump sum within fifteen days after Michaelmas (29 September) 1554, when the king and his imperious pride would be long-since mouldering into dust. The arrears of Henry's pension would be made good by annual payments of 94,736 crowns a year during his lifetime and 50,000 crowns 'in perpetuity' remitted to his successors following his death. On top of this, a further 10,000 crowns a year would be paid for the commuted tribute of black salt. England would not make war on France unless the peace was broken.

A week afterwards, the Spanish ambassador van der Delft was granted an audience with Henry. He observed that, after all the expense and diplomatc posturing, Boulogne still remained in his hands. The king said nothing but just smiled.[81]

Henry had another matter to grin broadly about: the brutal destruction of an old and implacable enemy – Cardinal David Beaton, archbishop of St Andrews, papal legate and Lord Chancellor of Scotland. It is always satisfying when a plan comes together and succeeds beyond your wildest dreams. Conspiracies to murder Beaton had been under way for two years and Henry had agreed to underwrite the costs of the assassination, provided he was not implicated publicly and could swear he knew nothing about the plot. This business, he stressed (with sublime hypocrisy), was 'not meet for a king'.[82] At daybreak on 29 May 1546, seventeen assassins, some wearing armour, led by Norman Leslie, master of Rothes, and William Kirkcaldy of Grange, broke into St Andrews Castle, stabbing and killing the porter at its gates and hurling his body into the castle ditch. The noise of the disturbance brought the cardinal out of his chamber, and he was promptly hacked to death.

The alarm was sounded in the town of St Andrews and a crowd of around 400 men gathered outside the castle gate. Leslie, now standing atop its walls, shouted to them, inquiring 'what they desired to see'. Immediately, Beaton's mutilated corpse was thrown out of a window and suspended in mid-air, his body tied by a pair of sheets by arm and foot. Leslie 'bade the people see there their god'[83] – the prelate who had defied Henry and was sustained by French gold and papal interdicts.[84]

They held the castle for a year until it fell to a seaborne assault from French galleys

When the news of Beaton's death reached Thomas Thirlby, bishop of Westminster and ambassador to the Imperial court, he expressed his delight to Paget and added: 'It is half a wonder here that you dare to be so bold to kill a cardinal.'

The king ratified the treaty of Ardres-Guisnes on 17 July 1546[85] and Francis I swore a solemn oath to fulfil its obligations in the royal chapel at Fontainebleau on 3 August.[86] In 'a loud voice' he gave Henry his style and title of 'Defender of the Faith and Supreme Head of the Church of England and Ireland', even though there were six cardinals listening in the chapel. Unsurprisingly, Francis pointedly omitted the phrase 'King of France'.[87]

Amid the splendours of the French court lurked an old acquaintance of Henry's, now tasked with an unlikely mission. An Italian called Guron Bertano had been his trusty agent during the divorce from Katherine of Aragon, and in 1530 had carried the address from the English nobility to Pope Clement VIII, praying him to consent to Henry's desires and avoid 'the evils which arose from delay'. He had returned to Italy after Henry's marriage to Anne Boleyn.

His new assignment was totally unexpected. Paul III, that same pope who had tried to forge a holy crusade against England in 1539, had suffered a dramatic conversion in his beliefs, if not policy. Following the Anglo-French peace treaty, Paul now considered it more politic to reconcile Henry to the Holy See and, on condition that the king recognised the papacy's supremacy in matters ecclesiastic, pledged that 'he shall be satisfied in all other matters'.[88] Bertano was an astute choice to carry that message to Henry.

He was granted permission to travel to England and on 3 August, met the king. The immediate issue was an English presence at the Church's Council of Trent and Henry unexpectedly said he was content 'to remit his affairs to the Council' provided such a meeting of 'learned men' was held in a more convenient place, like France, and was called 'by the authority of all the Christian princes'.[89] If any of Henry's subjects had engaged in such a conversation with a papal envoy it would have cost them their heads, and it is difficult to discern the king's motivation in even toying with the idea. Perhaps the notion of Christian princes taking control of Church negotiations appealed.[90] He might also have believed this could scupper the Council of Trent by rendering it meaningless.

The Vatican was always hopelessly tardy, if not incompetent, in dealing with the Tudors. This time, the Pope's failure to respond quickly fuelled Henry's suspicions that he was being mocked. After a fruitless two months, Bertano was told to pack his bags and depart 'because my presence begins to be known and he does not wish his people to take offence or fall into error about it'. The emissary was greatly disappointed: 'You may imagine ... how it displeased me, my labours thrown away by the slothfulness of those of Rome. I answered that the answer must come soon – it was a long journey to Rome ... but to no purpose, for they told me resolutely [that] I must depart'.[91] Even if a papal letter arrived it would be too late. Henry had decided the proposal was 'an assault on [his] whole state and policy'.[92]

Meanwhile, the French admiral d'Annebaut was in London, attended by 200 French nobles and their liveried followers to celebrate the Anglo-French peace treaty. He had arrived aboard the *Great Zachary* of Dieppe on 20 August, escorted by fourteen galleys and after several days of courtly entertainments at Greenwich, rode to Hampton Court.[93]

Preparations for this last glorious great state occasion of Henry's reign had been under way since 2 July. Two substantial banqueting houses were constructed in the great park of the riverside palace, with boarded walls and horn windows, lined with painted canvas.[94]

During February and March of 1546, Henry had been debilitated again by osteomyelitis and had been laid low by three weeks of fever. He remained infirm and the eight-year-old Prince Edward deputised for him, riding out on 23 August to greet formally the French entourage at Hounslow, Middlesex, with 1,000 nobles and gentlemen in attendance, escorted by eighty Yeomen of the Guard.

The admiral and his party rode down two lines of 500 mounted English yeomen, resplendent in new liveries, before halting in front of the young prince who impressed the French with his competent horsemanship and welcoming speech, delivered unfalteringly in fluent Latin.

Four days were spent hunting in pleasant pastime between the two former enemies. On the first evening after the feasting, Henry, leaning on Archbishop Cranmer for support, surprised d'Annebaut with far-reaching proposals for the 'establishment of sincere religion' in England and France.

Both nations, said Henry, should 'change the Mass into a [reformed] communion'. After Francis had publicly repudiated papal supremacy, Charles V should follow suit, or face a breach in relations with both England and France. Cranmer was asked to draw up detailed proposals to submit to the French king.[95] These radical ideas were the complete reverse of everything that had been so recently urged upon him by Pope Paul III, and of Henry's support and love of elements of the old liturgy. Was Henry merely being provocative, if not mischievous, or were these proposals a demonstration that he really was moving towards a more evangelical religious policy, akin to a vernacular Lutheran doctrine?

England's financial problems had not disappeared. On 7 September, Wriothesley reported that he had 'travailed' with Sir Edmund Peckham for £4,000 of profits from the York mint, but it would be 'the end of next week before we get the money due for corn from the City of London'. This would be used to pay the labourers on the Boulogne fortifications. He had received declarations by various treasurers 'showing what money they had on Sunday last'. Wymond Carew, treasurer of the First Fruits and Tenths, had 'made no declaration because he had nothing'.[96]

Of the £1 million the king borrowed from the Antwerp bankers, more than £75,000 remained unpaid at Henry's death in January 1547.

The economic crisis was now overshadowed by the conspiracies to seize power by those around the king, as he grew steadily more infirm. Factional fighting at court over religion became a major preoccupation of his government. Some of the greatest figures in the land, and those closest to Henry, were now in fear of their lives.

12

Mad, Bad and Dangerous to Know

We are all familiar with all those striking, stately portraits of the king, who, after a parliamentary Act of 1544, was styled 'Henry the Eighth, by the grace of God, King of England, France and Ireland, Defender of the Faith and of the Church of England and also of Ireland, on earth, the Supreme Head'.[1] The title rolls off the tongue in sonorous, majestic cadence and its message of power and authority had to be matched by his subjects' vision of their autocratic sovereign lord. An ink and watercolour preparatory sketch by the royal artist Hans Holbein the Younger played a major role in shaping that definitive, imperious image of Henry. It remains iconic to this day.

Prince Edward's birth in October 1537 inspired his commission to paint a dynastic mural covering one wall of the Presence Chamber of the Palace of Whitehall, depicting Henry, his parents and his beloved third queen Jane Seymour, mother of his precious heir. The intention was to remind everyone that the Tudor dynasty was here to stay. This painting is sadly lost[2] and only the left side of Holbein's working study survives in London's National Portrait Gallery.[3]

Henry is shown standing in an insufferably proud and arrogant pose, one hand grasping a pair of gloves, the other poised above his dagger. He stares commandingly out of the drawing, daring us, at our peril, not to fall down on our knees before him, awestruck by his commanding magnificence. His father, Henry VII, is seen behind him, as founder of the ruling House of Tudor, a regal ghost from a distant but not forgotten past. This is unsubtle, unashamed propaganda, even down to the size and prominence of the royal codpiece, jutting out stiffly from below the king's slashed doublet.

It is a very contrived image. Tiny holes pricked in the paper as part of the laborious process for creating the mural, are clues that Henry's face was originally shown in three-quarter profile. This was changed, probably at the sitter's insistence, to directly face and challenge the observer.[4] Holbein also lengthened the king's legs to make him look slimmer and more muscular. We know, from the measurements of his bespoke armours, that his legs were much shorter.

The sketch was copied in a number of portraits commissioned by the great and good to hang in their houses as loyal demonstrations of their allegiance to their despotic sovereign. Dendrochronological analysis[5] of the oak planks on which two were painted – one at Petworth House, West Sussex, and the other now in Liverpool's Walker Art Gallery[6] – indicate that they were completed in the 1540s.[7]

All these portraits are outright lies.

By this time, the king no longer resembled the haughty, domineering figure represented by Holbein. Henry had changed dramatically, both physically and mentally.

In the few years since Holbein's painting had been completed, the king had transformed into a geriatric monarch, the chronic osteo-myelitis of his legs forcing him to walk with a staff, his weight ever ballooning and his temper becoming more unpredictable and frightening than ever, as he struggled to cope with old age and infirmity.

Afflicted by 'the worst legs in the world', the stairs to his 16,000 square feet (1,486m²) of privy apartments on the first floor at Whitehall, were now an insurmountable obstacle. Norfolk confided to his mistress Bessie Holland that 'the king was much grown of his body and that he could not go up and down stairs, but was let up and down by a device'.[8]

This must have been a primitive lift, attached to ropes and pulleys, which, very gently, was raised and lowered, probably by sweating (and apprehensive) members of Henry's Yeomen of the Guard. The 'dumb waiter' used to carry food upstairs from the kitchens in restaurants seems an appropriate simile. An entry in the 1542 inventory of royal possessions in Whitehall Palace describes a chair, upholstered in purple velvet, comfortably quilted with silk of the same colour, and decorated with an embroidered 'rose of Venice gold'. It explained that this 'serving in the king's house, goes up and down', the royal feet supported on an attached footstool.[9] It had recently been purchased at the king's command and may have connected his 'secret study' with the ground floor.[10] Such visible evidence of advancing royal decrepitude was carefully concealed from public gaze.

The royal apartments were littered with footstools – many upholstered in cloth of gold – which, with a plethora of comfortable soft cushions perched on top, enabled the king to rest his ulcerated legs. Frequently sedentary, he felt the cold, so there were fourteen screens at Whitehall to protect him from chilling draughts, some made of wickerwork, covered with silk taffeta. Two were delivered in 1543 and another three years later.[11]

As well as being increasingly immobile, Henry also suffered from health problems that affected his personality. The old tyrant was not going quietly, sometimes being more 'furious than a chained lion'.[12] As early as January 1539, one Spanish diplomat commented that each day, Henry was 'growing more inhuman and cruel'.[13] From the end of 1543, he became paranoid, if not psychotic, deeply suspicious of those around him, even the people he loved or held in high esteem. He also was increasingly irrational, unexpectedly changing his mind on a decision made only hours before. One theory about Henry's psychosis and aggression suggests that he was suffering from schizophrenia.[14]

The royal court had long been dominated by conspiracy, double-dealing and distrust, as factions or indivduals battled over religious policy, jockeyed for political power or sought to acquire wealth and property for themselves. During Henry's declining years, this febrile and unstable atmosphere grew ever more threatening as time began to run out for those plotting in the shadows behind the throne to form the regency government of Prince Edward. All this was exacerbated by the king's irascible moods and irrational outbursts that threatened the lives or status of many. Everyone feared the risks and dangers that came with a glittering life at Henry's court; those who knew their Bibles could recognise the Psalm's warning: 'You place them on slippery ground; you cast them down to ruin.'[15] Some must have believed the king insane, but it was too dangerous to voice this opinion within others' hearing. Others cynically sought to exploit his unreasonable, sometimes illogical, behaviour for their own ends.

Henry's failing health ruled out the long and stately progresses through the Home Counties which had continued into the early 1540s. Instead, the court was confined to a handful of houses in and around London, the Palace of Whitehall becoming the most frequently used. Here, the king built a new riverside façade with opulent lodgings and the King Street Gate during the last five years of his reign.[16]

Despite all his mania and tantrums, it is difficult not to feel some compassion over his relentless pain and suffering. A once athletic and boisterous king had fallen prey to physical decay and poltroonery. Fear of disease had haunted him all his adult life but loss of mobility and failing strength, as well as the agony of his legs, made his final years a living nightmare. As a bitter reminder of his lost youth, Henry kept a painted terracotta bust of himself in his teenage years in a wooden box in his secret study at Whitehall.[17]

Three short entries in the 1542 Whitehall Inventory throw light upon Henry's anguish and his acute sense of vulnerability and isolation from the dazzling and strutting court around him.

The first two concern his staves, which he was forced to use by 1540 to assist his walking. Grim-faced, he is seen gripping a gold-topped stave in a half-length portrait of 1542 by Holbein, possibly once owned by Norfolk and later in Castle Howard, Yorkshire, before its sale in 2015. One entry describes two such sticks, 'one of them having a cross upon the upper end of black horn with a whistle at either end of the nose' and the other 'having a whistle of white bone at the upper end'. The third entry describes two 'trunks', one covered in black leather, the other 'painted green with metal gilt at both ends'.[18] These, we are informed, were for 'shouting'; today we would call them megaphones or loud hailers.

Except for those surprisingly infrequent periods when Henry was enjoying his conjugal rights in the royal marriage bed, the king was always closely attended by his Privy Chamber staff. A page slept on a straw-filled mattress at the foot of his great bed and the Gentleman of the Stool stood ready to attend to his most intimate requirements, as he was helped on and off the Close Stool.

While almost never alone, Henry now needed to summon help in an emergency, either by loud and repeated blasts on his whistle, or by bellowing through his speaking 'trunk'. As we have seen, one stave had two whistles, possibly in case he fumbled and lost one in his panic. The king must have dreaded falling down, and given his huge bulk, it would have been difficult to get him back up on his feet, requiring assistance by many anxious attendants. Such accidents would have punctured the royal dignity and ego by emphasising that he was a helpless old man, rather than an omnipotent sovereign. Does this not strongly suggest deep insecurity, vulnerability and ever-present anxiety in a sovereign who was losing his confidence?

Henry was the first English king to insist on 'your majesty' as a form of address. But majesty had faded away as the years took a heavy toll on his body. The word 'pathetic' springs to mind, as we compare and contrast the decrepit reality of Henry's last years with the untruthful and anachronistic propaganda portraits of a hale and hearty monarch, standing proud in all his Imperial splendour and might.

Henry's extensive staff of doctors, surgeons, apothecaries and barbers was probably the largest medical team to look after any European monarch in the mid-sixteenth-century.

Given just how challenging their quick-tempered royal patient must have been to treat, they were long-suffering but well-rewarded for all their trouble. Strict court protocol severely curbed their effectiveness. However ill the king might be, they could not treat him without him first seeking a consultation. Determining symptoms was also problematic as the royal physicians were not allowed to speak to the king, unless addressed first, or touch him without permission. Some examinations were conducted in complete silence, aside from the grunts, moans and winces from Henry as they ministered to his legs.[19]

These physicians and surgeons also laboured with the scant knowledge of medicine and anatomy available in Tudor times. Medical theory was rooted in the beliefs of the Greek doctor Aelius Galenus (129–*c.*200 AD). As well as the seasons of the year and the twelve astrological signs, one's health and method of treatment were influenced by the imbalance of the four bodily 'humours' – *blood, phlegm, black bile* (melancholy) and *yellow bile,* linked to the four supposed elements of air, earth, fire and water. Those with serene personalities were associated with air but others who were insolent, melancholic or stubborn were related to earth. Exuberance, temper and audaciousness were hallmarks of fire and the unflappable or unwise were associated with water.[20] Red-haired people – like Henry VIII and his children – revealed the predominance of yellow bile, providing them with fiery emotions.

Healthy balance was restored by manipulating the body's liquids, through sweating, urinating or blood-letting, either by scalpel – taking eight to ten fluid ounces (227–284ml) at a time – or by using leeches. These loathsome olive-green creatures were expensive to use, as they normally only fed once a year. Each one broke the skin with their three jaws, injected an anti-coagulant, and became engorged up to six times their length by sucking 0.6 fluid ounces (17ml) of the patient's blood. Up to sixteen were applied at one time.

Physicians also emphasised the importance of urine as a diagnostic tool and health was judged by its colour, smell and taste. Some doctors recommended 'lusty singing' to aid recovery.[21] The sick-room must have been a noisy place.

One of Henry's surgeons owned a fifteenth-century manuscript copy of *Chirugia Magna*, notes on surgery written by the French doctor Guy de Chauliac (1320–68), physician to Pope Clement VI.[22] As well as handy tips based on his experiences, de Chauliac had sound cautionary advice to those who might overrate their surgical skills. He emphasised: '*Si nasus ex toto cedederit amplius non potest reunire*' – 'It is not possible to reunite a nose that has been completely cut off'.

The Renaissance brought new ideas for the treatment of disease, many enthusiastically espoused by Henry. The Flemish physician Andreas Vesalius (1514–43) believed that surgery should be firmly grounded in anatomy – today, of course, a truism. His dissection of human bodies swept away many misconceptions held since the time of Galenus. The Swiss physician Theophrastus von Hohenheim (1494–1541) also rejected the old teachings of the four bodily humours and became the founder of modern pharmacology. His book *Die große Wundarzney* foreshadowed our knowledge of antisepsis, based on his personal experiences as a military surgeon during the Venetian wars.

The king began his reign with three doctors on the Royal Household payroll. The first was Thomas Linacre who became court physician to Henry VIII at his accession in 1509 on a salary of £50 a year (£42,000 today). Linacre persuaded him to found the Royal College of Physicians nine years later, with him as first president. In 1546, the College was granted its own very appropriate coat of arms: *an ermine cuff with a hand feeling the pulse of an arm*. Linacre retired in 1520 and became tutor to the six-year-old Princess Mary three years later. He died in 1524 from kidney stones, at the remarkable age (for the Tudor period) of sixty-four.[23]

John Chambre, or Chambers (1470–1549), graduated as a doctor

from the University of Padua in 1506 and was appointed physician to
Henry VII and later his son. Like Linacre, he combined medicine with
a career in the Church. After a plurality of lucrative clerical appointments, Chambre was rewarded for his loyalty to Henry over the divorce
to Katherine of Aragon by being made dean of the collegiate chapel
of St Stephen's at Westminster in 1536. He became chief physician to
Henry on Linacre's retirement and attended Anne Boleyn during the
birth of Princess Elizabeth.[24]

With two other royal doctors, William Butts and George Owen, he
probably performed a caesarean section on Queen Jane Seymour on
12 October 1537 after more than thirty hours of labour at Hampton
Court. Henry had joyfully received his longed-for son, but Jane died
twelve days later. Tellingly, Chambre hedged his bets by signing himself
as 'p'rst' (priest) on the letter announcing her rapidly declining condition: 'All this night, she has been very sick and rather [worsens] than
amends.'[25] Cromwell blamed the queen's death on 'the faults of them
that were about her' who had allowed her to eat the wrong kind of food
'as her fantasy in sickness called for'.[26] With Butts, Chambre signed the
certificate swearing to the king's non-consummation of his marriage
with Anne of Cleves in 1540.[27]

At his own cost of £7,300, Chambre built the cloisters of St Stephen's
Chapel at Westminster but saw the chapel dissolved in 1547 to become
the debating chamber of the House of Commons, with the Speaker's
chair on the altar steps and members on either side in the choirstalls
– the origin of the confrontational arrangement of seating in today's
Commons chamber.

The Spaniard Fernando de Victoria was the third doctor in Henry's
early medical team. He arrived in England in 1501 with his wife, an
attendant to Katherine of Aragon. He later fell from royal favour when
the queen sent him to Spain to inform her nephew Charles V about
Henry's plans to divorce her. He died in 1529, already succeeded by
Edward Wotton, physician to Norfolk and Margaret Pole, countess of
Salisbury. Wotton was president of the Royal College of Physicians in
1541–3. He died in 1555.

A Venetian doctor, Augustin de Augustinis – more simply 'Augustine'
– was appointed a physician to the royal household in October 1537,
receiving a gold brooch from Jane Seymour's jewellery[28] and, the following March, an annuity of £20.[29] His appointment was due to William

Sandys, first baron Sandys, Lord Chamberlain, who had been cured of Sweating Sickness by Augustine.

His presence in England dated from the arrival of his uncle, Girolamo Ghinucci, as papal legate and later bishop of Worcester.[30] Augustine was personal physician to Wolsey around 1523 and, after his disgrace, begged Cromwell to arrange the supply of leeches, ideally 'hungry ones', to counter the dropsy that was troubling the cardinal.[31] On 4 November 1530, Wolsey was arrested for treason. The physician was also detained as a traitor and taken to the Tower. After spending an anxious night there, Augustine was moved to Norfolk's London home and there gently interrogated while being 'treated as a prince'. He sang 'the tune as they wished him' – like a canary.

The doctor signed a recognizance pledging payment of £100 to the king to 'keep secret from any man all such matter as is mentioned in a book written with his own hand concerning the late cardinal of York and presented by him to my lord Norfolk'.[32]

He then spent some years fulfilling diplomatic duties in Europe, first for Norfolk and then Cromwell, even working as physician to Cardinal Lorenzo Campeggio who so vexed Henry at his legatine court hearing on the divorce at Blackfriars. This association may have proved dangerous as Augustine found himself back in the Tower in April 1533, at Norfolk's instigation. He appealed to Cromwell for help, bleating that 'I have been punished almost to death, but what advantage would the duke gain by my death'?[33]

After being released, he resumed private practice in London, which he maintained when in royal service. This included espionage for Henry. In October 1540, Chapuys told Charles V that 'An Italian physician attached to the king's household . . . came to dine at this embassy on four different days. He is the king's spy and has come . . . for no other purpose than to learn what I am about and to persuade me to intercede with your majesty for a closer and particular friendship and alliance and to procure also the princess's [Mary's] marriage'.[34]

Augustine decided to return to Venice in July 1546. The English ambassador there was instructed to seek the city state's licence for him and his servants to carry weapons to defend themselves.[35] Were Augustine's former clandestine activities catching up with him? His case for self-defence must have been compelling, as permission was granted

in December 1546. He died peacefully in bed in the Tuscan walled city
of Lucca on 20 September 1551.

William Butts (c.1485–1545) was Henry's favourite and most trusted
physician, being rewarded for his skills and loyalty by a knighthood
in 1544. He was one of the first doctors not to pursue a career in the
Church and joined the royal household in the early 1530s. He treated
Norfolk and his ill-fated niece and nephew, Anne Boleyn and her
brother George, and later Jane Seymour. He also attended Henry's
illegitimate son Henry Fitzroy, duke of Richmond, and took the leading
role in providing medical evidence about Henry's non-consummation
of his marriage with Anne of Cleves in 1540. Butts received a salary of
£125 a year as chief physician, plus another £20 for treating Richmond.
He was given a suit of blue and green damask for attending Princess
Mary, together with similar liveries for his two servants and cloth for
his apothecary, probably Philip Greenacre.[36]

Butts also attended the already articulate Prince Edward in 1542 when
he was aged almost six. In a rare surviving letter about medical matters,
he reported: 'Thanks to God, [he] proceeds in mending daily . . . taking
of meats and took yesterday broths, conveniently digesting the same
and exercises himself on foot in his accustomed pastimes. This night
he slept quietly from nine of the clock to this present hour [3 a.m.] and
now having drink, turns again to sleep. Yesterday, after his meat, [he]
had one siege of corrupt matter and no disposition to vomit.' Edward
was very much an embryo Tudor monarch, as Butts indicated, tongue
in cheek, in a postscript: 'He has prayed me to go away and has called
me a fool. If I tarry till he calls me "knave"; then I shall say "*Nunc
dimittis servum tuum Domine, secundum verbum patris tui*"' – 'Let now
thy servant depart, according to thy father's word.'[37]

The doctor was a fervent religious reformer and a staunch ally of
Queen Katherine Parr and Thomas Cranmer. He died of malaria in
November 1545 at Fulham Manor in Middlesex and was buried in the
local parish church of All Saints, beneath a monumental brass, now
sadly lost, which depicted him in full armour, as a demonstration of
his armigerous status. His death was a dire blow to the king as not only
did he lose a highly valued doctor, but also a close friend and confidant.
The Spanish ambassador van der Delft, reporting another of Henry's
afflictions in 1546, added: 'I do not know what will come of it, as his
principal medical man, Dr Butts, died last winter.'[38]

Thomas Wendy (1499–1560) succeeded as chief physician. He had studied medicine at Ferrara in north-east Italy and his Protestant sympathies lay behind his appointment as doctor to Queen Katherine Parr in 1546. Wendy treated Henry during his last hours and was one of the witnesses to the royal will, together with his fellow physicians George Owen and Robert Huicke who all received legacies of £100. He was appointed physician extraordinary to Edward VI in March 1547 and to his half-sister Mary and attended both at their deaths.

Henry's other royal physicians included Dr Walter Cromer, 'the Scot' who lived in Wood Street in the City of London and gave Henry that impromptu lesson on the geography of Scotland in 1542. He died in 1547. Owen (1499–1558) perished in 'an epidemic of intermittent fever' but Huicke (c.1515–81), who survived a very public and acrimonious divorce from his wife Elizabeth in 1546,[39] continued to enjoy royal patronage from Edward and Elizabeth. He was one of the witnesses to Katherine Parr's will.

This was a formidable array of medical talent but it did not preclude other doctors from being summoned to provide a second opinion on Henry's health. Thomas Bille, for example, a physician from St Bartholomew's Hospital, was paid £100 for treating Henry during the last year of his life.[40] The former monk Andrew Boorde (c.1490–1549) was also called in to examine the king on Norfolk's recommendation. He reported Henry as 'fleshy' with large arteries, ruddy cheeks and pale skin. His hair was 'plenty and red, pulse great and full, digestion perfect; anger short [and] sweat abundant'.[41] He was alarmed by the king's obesity.

Boorde may still have worn the Carthusian's hair shirt next to the skin but his interests extended far outside the moral confines of his old monastic cell. After moving to Winchester, he was accused of maintaining three prostitutes in his chamber and was imprisoned in London's Fleet Prison in 1547. He died there on 9 April 1549, sparking gossip that he had poisoned himself.[42]

Henry also employed surgeons, the most famous being Thomas Vicary (?1490–1562) who had been 'but a mean practiser in Maidstone [Kent] ... that had gained his knowledge by experience' until he cured the king's 'sore leg' during a royal progress at Canterbury in 1527–8.[43] He was appointed sergeant-surgeon to the king in 1536 with an annual salary of £26 13s 4d (£14,840 in today's money). It was Vicary who persuaded the king to agree to the amalgamation of the Barbers' Company with the Surgeons' in 1540. To improve surgical training, the new company was granted the corpses of four executed felons each year for dissection by students.[44]

Other surgeons employed by Henry included Sir John Ayliffe, paid £30 a year, who successfully treated the fistula on his leg in 1538 at Brinkworth, Wiltshire, 'for which the king bestowed on him a great estate in gratitude' and bequeathed him £100 in his will.[45] James Mumforde (or Motforde) was surgeon to the king at the end of his reign and Richard Ferris is believed to have attended Henry during his last illness in 1546–7. Also listed is William Bullein, a 'nurse-surgeon' who wrote a book on the Sweating Sickness and other works on herbal medicine and pleurisy.

Finally, there are the apothecaries and barbers. By 1540, the grocer[46] Thomas Alsop had become chief apothecary to Henry on a quarterly salary of £6 13s 4d. In addition to his pay, he was allowed a suit of livery and a cap of Minerva fur at Christmas from the Great Wardrobe. Alsop supplied various medicines to the royal family, including Lady Margaret Douglas, who was prescribed 'two glasses with *aqua lactis virginis*', a dilute benzole tincture for 'the morphew' – brown skin blemishes, a late symptom of scurvy. Due to Henry's poor health, the number of apothecaries was increased in 1540 and again six years later, with the employment of John Hemingway and Patrick Reynold. George Carlton was also appointed at Christmas 1546, possibly because of growing demands on the pharmacy imposed by the king's last illness or because of concerns over the health of Prince Edward.[47]

Their work was not only concerned with producing medicinal pills and potions. Alsop supplied liquorice and sugar for the king's hounds and rhubarb and sugar candy for his hawks.[48] The royal apothecary also provided small pottery urinals, costing three pennies each, for discreet and disposable use by Privy Councillors beneath their voluminous robes, so that important debate on the king's business would not be interrupted by pressing calls of nature.[49] Alsop retained his post as 'gentleman apothecary' throughout Edward's reign and most of Queen Mary's, before dying in 1557.

Henry employed three barbers during his reign: Edmund Harman, Nicholas Simpson and John Pen. This was a privileged position, as the barber was one of only fifteen attendants allowed to enter the king's

Privy Chamber and his tour of duty lasted one month at a time.[50] Wages were fifty shillings (£2.50) a quarter with a daily allowance of meat and drink for the barber and his attendant.

The king had grown a beard several times during his reign, but Katherine of Aragon disliked his facial hair and persuaded him to shave it off. His familiar close-trimmed red beard appeared after 1535 when he instructed his courtiers to grow whiskers – but to keep their hair cut short.

Like the physicians, strict rules governed their work. The barber should be ready for duty at Henry's rising, having 'in readiness his water, basins, knives [razors], combs, scissors ... for trimming and dressing of the king's head and beard'. He should pay 'special regard to the pure and clean keeping of his own person and apparel, using himself honestly in his conversation, without resorting to the company of vile persons or of misguided women, [to avoid] such danger as by that means he might do to the king's most royal person'. The slightest infringement would lose him his post and invoke 'further punishment at the king's pleasure'.[51]

Harman had entered royal service by 1535 and clearly pleased Henry as he was appointed to the sinecure post of 'common packer' for exports, collecting tariffs in the port of London as the king's revenue officer. He was also granted a manor in Middlesex in 1544 and monastic properties in Gloucestershire and Oxfordshire in 1545–6. The extra income was welcome as he had sixteen children. Harman was with the king at Boulogne in 1544, contributing four cavalrymen, six archers and six pikemen to the Army Royal. His Lutheran opinions got him into trouble with Henry's children when they ascended the throne, and his talents as a barber were not required. He died in 1577.[52]

Many barbers practised blood-letting, minor surgery and dentistry, as well as shaving and haircutting.[53]

It was the responsibility of surgeons to treat syphilis, and many children leave school today with the belief that Henry VIII was a victim of this scourge of the sixteenth century because of his shameless, immoral life with a succession of women, some of them regular mistresses. Moreover, they are taught that he died from its ravages in 1547.

This sexually transmitted disease was first recorded in the French army at the siege of Naples in 1495 and spread rapidly throughout Europe,[54] reaching the British Isles two years later.[55] Its various nicknames followed traditional nationalistic prejudices: the Russians called it 'the Polish disease', Poles branded it 'the German disease' and the English, of course, referred to it as 'the French Pox'. Physicians referred to syphilis as 'the Great Pox', to distinguish it from smallpox or chickenpox, and quickly learnt to recognise its symptoms.[56]

Traditionally, it was believed that it was imported into Europe by Christopher Columbus's sailors returning from the New World in the 1490s, while another theory postulated that the epidemic was the emergence of a virulent form of a disease that had been dormant for centuries, or had gone unrecognised by doctors. Recent research suggests the traditional view is probably true.[57]

Whatever its origins, its symptoms were horrible, beginning with a small painless genital ulcer, followed by a fever, rash and nocturnal muscle pains. Later, large, painful and foul-smelling abscesses appeared on the body – sores that could destroy the nose and lips.[58] Erasmus wrote in 1520 that this was the most 'destructive of all diseases... which for years has been raging with impunity... What contagion does thus invade the whole body, so much resist medical art, becomes inoculated so readily and so cruelly tortures the patient.'[59]

Henry's 'sore leg' was the genesis of the belief that he suffered from syphilis. This was not borne out of malevolent Catholic propaganda but was first proposed in 1888 by the Scottish obstetrician Andrew Currie, who maintained it was the cause of Katherine of Aragon's many miscarriages and stillbirths. The king's ruthless actions as an absolute monarch were later considered symptomatic of his fearless 'syphilitic psychasthenia, of [his] frightful moral and physical degeneration'. The general atmosphere in Henry's court of 'lust, obscenity, grandiose ideas... and violence combined with cowardice especially about disease, is all very typical of syphilis... almost... diagnostic.'[60]

It was claimed that the king could have contracted the disease during his youth or when he was campaigning in France in 1513. However, Henry was not the great libertine of folklore, or television dramas, although earlier, he was often promiscuous during the last stages of royal pregnancies. Aside from court dalliances and flirtations, such as with Anne Stafford, the newly-wed wife of George, Lord

Hastings, in 1510, he is known only to have had extramarital relations with just three women: Elizabeth Blount (mother of his illegitimate son Henry Fitzroy); Mary Boleyn and possibly Margaret Shelton. Before he became king in 1509, he was under virtual house arrest and afterwards, was under constant scrutiny by foreign ambassadors, eager to report scurrilous gossip from his court. Compared to Francis I with his seven mistresses, Henry was an also-ran in the European royal promiscuity stakes. A variant of the theory was that he was infected by Katherine of Aragon who, two years before their marriage in 1509, had an 'intimate and extremely scandalous' relationship with her young and domineering Castilian confessor, the friar Diego Fernandez.[61]

After Wolsey's downfall in 1529, the cardinal's Act of Attainder alleged that he tried to infect the king with 'the Great Pox, having broken out upon him in diverse places, came daily to your grace, rowning [whispering] in your ear and blowing upon your most noble grace with his most perilous and infective breath'.[62] Aside from the dubious medical grounds for infection, this is again pure propaganda, provided to Norfolk by Augustine, Wolsey's opportunist doctor. Henry's varicose ulcer, or deep vein thrombosis, on his thigh in 1527–8, say the theory's supporters, was in reality a broken-down gumma or swelling, a symptom of tertiary syphilis, although an unusual location for this.[63] Gummata are not normally painful, but the king suffered terrible agonies with his legs.

Several portraits of Henry after 1536, such as the full-face sketch in black, red and white chalk from Holbein's workshop in 1540,[64] show a very small deformity of the nose, a slight swelling about the size of an almond, reaching from the lower part of the nasal bone to the wing of the nose. This, it was believed, is characteristic of a syphilitic gumma. This swelling is missing from other portraits such as the painting of him granting the charter of the Barber-Surgeons of 1542, perhaps because Henry ordered the disfigurement not to be shown.[65]

During the late stages of the disease, speech is affected by indistinct articulation and difficulty in framing words and sentences. Facial tremors develop and writing becomes increasingly difficult. The victim becomes progressively demented, unaware of their surroundings and incapable of meaningful personal interaction.[66] In fact, everyone understood only too well what Henry was saying (or shouting) and while his face may have been often contorted by rage, there were never any reported signs of tremors. He was not suffering from dementia, as he plainly knew where he was and exactly what he was doing.

There is no sign of syphilis in the king's children, none of whom presented symptoms, like its visible stigmata of rashes or sores. None had subsequent histories of congenital syphilis.

Early treatment used the bark from *Guaiacum*, a genus of shrubs and trees brought back from the Caribbean and South America, probably based on indigenous reports of its efficacy. Unfortunately, this cure was not only expensive but also ineffective. Instead, the Swiss doctor and alchemist Theophrastus von Hohenheim advocated the use of an ointment made from metallic mercury, mixed with the saliva of a fasting man, to be rubbed into the skin, or inhaled as vapour. The treatment was administered several times a day in a hot, stuffy room, near a large fire to make the patient sweat. This regime was followed for up to six weeks and caused the wretched sufferer to produce copious flows of saliva and his gums to become red and sore.[67] He had to expel between two and three pints (1.1–1.7l) of saliva every day, measured in special jars, before the treatment stopped.[68] It could continue intermittently for years (spawning the hoary aphorism of 'one night with Venus and a lifetime with Mercury'), but there were unpleasant side-effects: damage to the nerves that control movement or bodily functions, kidney failure, severe mouth ulcers and loss of teeth. Mercury is also a deadly poison.

Henry never underwent such trials at the hands of his apprehensive physicians. Although Andrew Boorde reported Henry's 'abundant sweat', this was more likely to be caused by his obesity and heavy clothing than the mercury treatment. A drooling king did not shower saliva over his fawning courtiers, had no lengthy, unexplained absences from public view at court, and no purchases of mercury by his apothecaries appear in surviving accounts. Those prying ambassadors, eager for gossip from generously bribed sources at court, reported nothing that suggests he suffered from syphilis – unlike Francis I. Nor did they notice a lesion or swelling on his nose. Perhaps today's history teachers should amend their lessons accordingly.

So what was so grievously afflicting Henry in the evening years of his tempestuous life?

The king normally ate three meals a day, plus snacking in the evening, during his obsessive gambling at cards or dice or playing chess with his cronies. Breakfast was served in his bedchamber, around thirty minutes after a page lit the fires in his apartments sharp at seven. Henry then went to Mass and consumed his 'dinner' at around ten o'clock. Most of the day would be spent hunting or some other activity before supper was served at four in the afternoon.

Eating at the Tudor court was a case of feast or famine. There was fasting on Fridays and sometimes also on Saturdays, when no meat was eaten. During Lent, by law, no flesh was allowed, nor butter, eggs or other dairy products. On other days, the Tudors were enthusiastic carnivores, consuming large quantities of meat, hoofed or feathered. Up to 80 per cent of their daily intake of food was protein. The slaughter of birds was prodigious: larks, stork, gannets, heron, swan (and cygnets), snipe, bustard, bittern, quail, partridge, capons, teal, mallard, cranes, woodcock, pheasants, thrush and robins all appear on their menus. An especial court favourite was stewed sparrows. Ecology was plainly an alien concept.

The meat course would include beef, mutton, veal, lamb, kid, pork and brawn – a terrine made with flesh from the head of a calf or pig, set in gelatine. Venison was reserved as a kingly or noble dish. Henry's favourite dishes were galantines (mixed meats, pressed and preserved in aspic), game pies and haggis – today, a traditional Scottish recipe, consisting of a sheep's stomach stuffed with minced offal and oats.

The second course was fish – salted and smoked cod, ling, carp, herrings, salmon and eels (conger and sand), and sometimes the unlucky dolphins and porpoises that ventured upriver in the Thames; the latter being a firm favourite of Katherine of Aragon. Most meats and fish were flavoured by an abundance of spices to disguise their lack of freshness.

Little roughage was eaten, as fresh fruit was shunned because it was thought to cause diarrhoea and fever, although the king had a fondness for cherries, quince marmalade and orange pies. Desserts included junkets, comfits and syllabubs or roasted pears with custard. Similarly, green vegetables, as well as turnips, carrots and parsnips, were avoided as 'they engendered wind and melancholy'[69] although cucumbers, lettuces, chives, radishes and the succulent and nutritious herb purslane were eaten as healthy salads for the first course. One ingenious theory for some of Henry's ailments claimed that he suffered from scorbutic disease, or scurvy (like Lady Margaret Douglas), caused by a chronic lack of vitamins supplied in our modern diet by fresh vegetables and fruit.[70]

The king's food was prepared in his privy kitchen by his master cook John Bricket and generally eaten alone in his secret apartments. On the covered table before him were laid a silver trencher or plate, a knife and spoon and a manchet (a wheat bread roll), wrapped in a napkin. He graciously indicated his choice of food from a huge buffet laid out nearby. A courtier, known as the Sewer, on bended knee, would wash the royal hands in warmed, scented water before and after each course. Every dish and goblet of wine was tasted beforehand for poison. The king's plate would be served with the food already cut up into small pieces for him to elegantly toy with. Contrary to popular portrayals, Henry was a neat and dainty eater – half-gnawed chicken carcasses were never hurled over the royal shoulder to the floor – and gargantuan portions were not served him. On more formal occasions, after trumpets signalled his arrival, he dined in the Presence Chamber, seated beneath a gold canopy of state, watched by a crowd of courtiers.

The purpose-built Hampton Court kitchens – then the largest in Europe – catered for the 400 courtiers who were entitled to dine in 'messes' (or separate tables, each seating four), twice a day in the Great Hall.[71] This was an industrial-scale food production line; hot, dirty, noisy and heavy work.

The diners, armed with spoons and their personal knives, would eat off square wooden plates which were snatched away and wiped between courses. These trenchers originated the phrase, 'a square meal'. Hundreds of bun-shaped bread loaves were also baked, with the bottom half, soiled from the filthy oven floor, supplied to the more humble diners and the clean and crispy top portion reserved for the nobility, eating separately off more opulent menus in the adjacent Great Watching Chamber. This in turn gave rise to another English saying, 'the upper crust' – meaning the aristocracy.

All this was washed down with 600,000 gallons (2,727,654L) of low-alcohol 'small beer' each year, supplied by the royal brew houses and served in leather 'jacks' or jugs for each mess. The nobility and guests drank their way through 300 barrels of wine per annum. Henry liked gin 'marvellously well'.

Each dining session was governed by accepted etiquette: napkins were laid across the left shoulder and no elbows should rest upon the tables. Noses must be wiped politely on the sleeve, and head scratching was forbidden. In 1530, Erasmus recorded some other tips on good table manners in his book *De civilitate morum puerilium*: 'Sit not down until you have washed. Once you sit, place your hands neatly on the table; not on your trencher and not around your belly. Do not shift your buttocks left and right as if to let off some blast. Sit neatly and still'.[72]

That lack of roughage was probably the cause of Henry's regular and acute bouts of constipation. In September 1539, he was suffering from a particularly bad attack and his physicians resorted to the painful insertion of a greased copper tube, fitted with a pig's bladder, as an enema. Sir Thomas Heneage, then Groom of the Stool, reported progress to Cromwell: 'The king's majesty went [early] to bed [and] slept until two of the clock... Then his grace was to go to the stool which, by waking of the pills and glister [enema]... had a very fair siege as the physicians [have reported], not doubting but the worst is past, by their perseverance, to no great danger or any further grief to remain in him... His grace had very good rest and finds himself well, saving he has a little soreness in the body'.[73]

One year on and the king had grown into a veritable man mountain. As a young man in 1514, his armour, specially made for him, shows that he was 6ft 1in (1.85m) in height and had a trim waist measurement of 35in and a chest diameter of 42in (89, 107cm). Here was a fit athlete, the muscular embodiment of chivalry and sixteenth-century sporting prowess, with a svelte Body Mass Index (BMI) of 25.6 – 27kg/m². Jump forward to 1540 and another armour being made. The change is dramatic. Henry's waist had swelled to a massive 54in and his chest to 58in (137, 147cm). By the time he died just over six years later, he must have weighed at least twenty-eight stone (178kg) with a BMI of 51.9 kg/m². His weight is off the scale used in calculating BMI today.

Henry's super-obesity was not caused by overeating and the lack of exercise imposed by his difficulties in walking, although this would not have helped. The king was afflicted by something more insidious than syphilis and just as terrible in its effects on the human body. The condition was unrecognised and thus untreated by the scant medical science of his time.

After the passage of nearly five centuries, no diagnosis based on the purely anecdotal reports of his courtiers and inquisitive ambassadors can be anything like 100 per cent certain. Having said that, Henry's recurrent symptoms are strongly suggestive. That huge royal bulk was probably the unfortunate victim of an endocrine abnormality called Cushing's Syndrome,[74] a rare affliction that today affects ten to fifteen people per million of the population. The disease is caused by the secretion of excessive levels of the hormone cortisol, secreted by the adrenal glands (located above the kidneys) over long periods.

Most victims have gross obesity in the body's trunk with increased fat around their necks and sometimes a 'buffalo hump' on their back, caused by cortisol inducing the body to store huge amounts of fat. There is a loss of muscle bulk around the shoulders. The lower face is swollen with substantial fat deposits, creating the so-called 'moon face', characteristic of Cushing's Syndrome. The skin becomes fragile and thin, bruising easily, and wounds and lesions are slow to heal. The bones are weakened and any exercise – even as simple as rising from a sitting posture – can cause severe backache, even fractures of the ribs. The muscles around the hips are wasted. Blood pressure is increased, as are blood sugar levels. There may be mild diabetes as a side effect, causing frequent thirst – Henry sometimes drank ten pints of beer a day.

Irritability, depression or melancholia, anxiety, insomnia and sudden mood swings become commonplace in around 20 per cent of cases. In this group, the sufferer may also become psychotic, exhibiting a paranoia that spawns a deep suspicion of everything and everyone around them. Sometimes the victim becomes emotionally detached from their loved ones or those close to them. They have frequent headaches, chronic fatigue and can become quarrelsome and abnormally aggressive. All these symptoms match the contemporary descriptions of Henry's condition in the last five or six years of his life. He did have gross obesity in his upper trunk and lower face. He suffered periods of melancholy and severe headaches. He was psychotic, displaying irrational anger and aggression. He was sometimes detached from those he was fond of (demonstrated by the arrest warrants he signed for Cranmer and Katherine Parr, as we shall see in the next chapter) and displayed mood swings and sudden changes of mind (such as his later decisions to inform victims of the threat they faced). Look at the later portraits of the king, and we can see the moon face, together with the loss of muscle around the shoulders.

If Henry did have Cushing's Syndrome, how did he contract it? Recent research indicates that traumatic brain injuries – such as the one he suffered in January 1536 while jousting at Greenwich – can cause several neuro-endocrine effects. Symptoms in adults include increased fat mass with visceral obesity and reduced bone mass and muscle weakness.[75] This view of the potential cause has been hailed as 'one of the historically accurate and clinically compelling' explanations for the king's transformation.[76]

Other research confirms the importance of that traumatic brain injury to Henry's health. He may also have been suffering from a consequential deficiency in the male hormone testosterone, which can cause low libido, infertility, muscle wasting and other abnormalities. This is called post-traumatic hypogonadism.[77]

Alternatively, if Henry did indulge in excessive consumption of beer and wine – and a fondness for gin – he may have been suffering from a condition called 'alcoholic pseudo-Cushing's' which shares some of the features of the syndrome, mainly the moon face.

Cushing's Syndrome is today successfully treated by hormone-inhibiting drugs, or chemotherapy or radiation treatment. In some cases, surgery can remove associated tumours on the adrenal glands. None of these recourses was available to Henry's doctors, who lacked knowledge about the human body and relied mainly on herbs for prescriptions.

The only way to establish with certainty whether this theory is correct is to examine the king's body, buried in the 'royal peculiar' of St George's Chapel, Windsor. If the bone of the small cavity within his large skull where the pituitary gland is located has been enlarged by the presence of a tumour, then he certainly suffered from Cushing's Syndrome.

If the vertebrae in his back had collapsed, this would also be evidence of a Cushing-induced osteoporosis – fragility in the bones with increased susceptibility to fracture. However, it is extremely unlikely that permission would ever be granted for a pathologist to undertake a forensic examination.

One poignant image sums up Henry's terrible suffering in his last years, contained in the *King's Psalter*[78] of psalms, preserved in the British Library. The 176-page book, bound in red velvet, was written for the king on vellum by John Mallard around 1540. It includes a miniature of Henry seated, hunched up on a coffer, his legs crossed, playing a small harp. His wrinkled face has a wistful, if not melancholic expression, and although he wears a heavy furred robe, his back looks distinctly humped.

His faithful fool Will Somers stands on the right, obviously downcast. On another page, alongside verse twenty-five of Psalm 17 – 'I have been young and now are old' – Henry has noted, '*dolus dictum*': 'A painful saying'.

Even tyrants cannot escape the uncertainties and frailties of old age.

13

Religion and an Embattled Court

To the hour of his death, Henry VIII believed himself a better Catholic than the despised pope. He certainly was never a Protestant, despite the belief held by some in the Anglican Church today. The sometimes contradictory swerves in religious policy during his final years seem to stem from his being pushed and pulled in different directions by factions at court, struggling to protect traditional rites or establish reformed liturgy. In reality, Henry kept a strong grasp on religion and some of these apparent inconsistencies are more likely to be actions of astute political or diplomatic expediency, rather than planned doctrinal change. In religion, as in all other areas of government, little of importance could be enacted without royal approval. This monarch was his own theologian.

Moral order and religious unity became Henry's main objectives and the unyielding punishment of sin lay at the core of his faith.[1] He also fought the growth of dangerous radical religious dogma in England, primarily involving sacramentaries who denied Christ's presence in the communion wafer and Anabaptists who rejected infant baptism, advocated social and economic reforms and separation of Church and state. These zealots' creeds were abominations to Henry.

All births are painful and that of the Church of England particularly so.

Reform of his Church and its perceived abuses came high on Henry's agenda during his last decade. The 1543 *King's Book* contained Henry's claim that '[As] in the time of darkness and ignorance, finding Our people seduced from the truth by hypocrisy and superstition, We, by the help of God and His Word, have travailed to purge and cleanse Our realm from [their] ... enormities.'

On his deathbed, Henry VIII passes his realm to his nine-year-old son, Edward. The book that unkindly strikes the pope's head is inscribed with the reformer's mantra: 'The Word of the Lord endures for ever', while the motto on the papal robes proclaims 'All flesh is grass'. The Regency Council looks on, with Archbishop Cranmer clean shaven, although he swore an oath never to shave again after Henry's death.

These changes must have bewildered and mortified many of his subjects, who felt they were witnessing the body of their forefathers' faith being brutally dismembered before their very eyes. Cherished centuries-old beliefs became unexpectedly illegal and new, unfamiliar religious tenets introduced. Henry's spiritual policies caused uncertainty, unease and fear throughout his dominions and they often divided the generations in their opinions.

Henry had been particularly fond of venerating saints in the early years of his reign. He made pilgrimages to shrines, including one to that of the popular miracle worker John Schorne[2] at North Marston, Buckinghamshire, in May 1521 to give thanks for his recovery from a virulent fever. In May 1537 he authorised Sir Thomas Pope, then Treasurer of the Court of Augmentations, to deface all saints' relics among the possessions of the religious houses being suppressed.

The religious injunctions of 1538 ordered the removal of 'feigned' images and banned candles being placed before any statue, apart from the Holy Rood and the Easter Sepulchre. The king believed some statues were permissible, if used for 'remembrance', but others – those 'abused' by being venerated – should be swept away, like the shrines of saints.

In October 1541, Henry repeated his order that the shrines should be destroyed, after he discovered that some were still standing and being venerated. It was ordered that 'the images and bones that [pilgrims] resorted and [made] offerings to, with the ornaments of the same and all such writings and monuments [about] feigned miracles [at the shrines] be taken away'. No lights or candles would be suffered, except those placed before the Blessed Sacrament.[3]

The king did not accept the reformers' absolute condemnation of all religious images and especially venerated the crucifix. Bishop Gardiner recalled hearing him strongly refute Cranmer's argument that the Second Commandment forbade all such iconography, during discussions about the religious statues in the royal palace of New Hall at Boreham, Essex.[4]

The Church taught that only saints could go straight to heaven after death. Ordinary mortals, burdened down by their sins committed in life, must suffer the pains of purgatory before final redemption. It was therefore in the interests of the faithful that those left after them should offer up prayers to reduce their time in this terrible halfway house. From 1543, the concept of purgatory mysteriously disappeared and prayers for souls before images were 'utterly abolished and extinguished'. One could continue to pray for the dead in general, but not for individual souls of the departed.[5]

Unless they were royal. Throughout the 1540s, prayers for his dead queen Jane Seymour's soul were an important part of the duties laid down in the statutes of the new cathedrals as mother churches of dioceses.[6] During Henry's funeral rites in 1547, the sacred banners of the Holy Trinity, the Blessed Virgin Mary, St George and King Henry VI[7] were displayed on the corners of his hearse.[8]

During his last years, there were state assaults on many 'popular superstitious practices' that preserved the fabric of England's ancient faith. A royal proclamation of 22 July 1541 abolished the observance of the feast days of St Mark (25 April), St Helena (21 May, which celebrated her 'discovery of the True Cross') and St Laurence (10 August). It also decreed that the 'childish superstitions... still used in diverse places' on St Nicholas (6 December), St Catherine (25 November), St Clement (23 November) and Holy Innocents' days, should cease forthwith. On the last feast day, on 28 December, children traditionally dressed up like 'counterfeit priests, bishops and women' and collected money from bystanders. Boys also sang Mass and preached in the pulpit 'rather to the derision than any true glory of God'. Henceforth, 'such superstitions' were forbidden.[9]

Other religious changes, imposed by reformist clergy, caused further dismay. Hugh Latimer, bishop of Worcester, ordered all his priests in 1537 to buy the Bible in English – which had been legalised the previous year – and require their parishioners to learn by rote the Creed, Lord's Prayer and the Ten Commandments in English. They knew them well enough in Latin but those who could not recite the vernacular versions were barred from taking communion.[10]

Rancour and protest were sure to follow. In 1539, Gardiner had warned the king of 'civil tumults and commotions within this realm' sparked by religious innovation.[11] William Hoo, suffragan bishop of Chichester, claimed that radical preachers might call themselves 'Children of Christ' but were, in truth, Satan's offspring. He scoffed that a befuddled monarch only allowed them to preach because those 'that rule about [him] make great banquets and give him sweet wines and then they bring Bills and he puts his sign to them'.[12] Thomas Cowley, vicar of Ticehurst, Sussex, continued to extol miracles and images, despite their prohibition. During a sermon in June 1538, he had held up a coin bearing Henry's head and demanded of his congregation: 'Dare you spit on his face? You dare not do it. But will you spit upon the [religious] image [and so] spit upon God? Within four years, we shall have it as it was again. Therefore, do as you have done. Offer up a candle to St Eloi for your horse and to St Anthony for your cattle.'[13] Conversely, one religious reformer declared in 1543 that he cared not 'a fart' for the king's injunctions and reverenced the gallows more than the cross.[14]

Other legislation was born out of Henry's own personal aversions, rather than indicating a tectonic shift in religious policy. An example came in May 1543, with the 'Act for the Advancement of True Religion' that restricted the reading of English Bibles to clerics, the nobility, gentry and the wealthier merchants. 'Gentle' women were allowed to read them alone and in private. Lower classes were forbidden access to the Scriptures in their own language. The Act claimed that '[M]alicious minds, intending to subvert the true exposition of scripture, have taken upon them, [with] printed ballads [and] rhymes, subtly and craftily to instruct people, and especially the youth of this realm, untruly.' Henry believed it was 'most requisite to purge ... all such books, ballads, rhymes, and songs, as being pestiferous and noisome'[15] and possession of these, or their printing, was now a criminal offence. Someone very close to the king blithely ignored this injunction.

Henry was also determined to stamp out heresy. In November 1538, he presided over a show trial in the Palace of Whitehall of the sacramentary John Lambert, once chaplain to the English community in Antwerp. Henry, who piously removed his cap at every mention of his Saviour's name, bullied the terrified prisoner over his beliefs about the consecrated wafer. The king impatiently insisted: 'Tell me plainly, whether you say it is the body of Christ or no.' Lambert answered: 'It was not his body. I deny it,' and the king told him: 'Now you shall be condemned even by Christ's own words: "This is my body" ... You must die, for I will not be a patron to heretics.'[16] Six days later, Lambert suffered a markedly cruel death at the stake at Smithfield. After his legs and thighs had been burnt to the stumps, the blaze sank lower, so to finish him off, two officers stepped forward, and with their halberds, lifted his still living body and dropped it back into the flames. He cried out: 'None but Christ, none but Christ!' as he finally expired.[17]

Lambert's death failed to stem the rising tide of heterodoxy, particularly in the cities. In July 1540, twenty heresy indictments were lodged as 'true bills' in London, with the accused representing a wide spectrum of occupations and income. They included a barber surgeon, a minstrel, tailors, carpenters, a brewer, a bricklayer, a plumber, several masons, a shoemaker and a grocer.[18] One Coventry tradesman thought so little of the sacrament of the altar that he would rather 'turn his arse to it as his face'. In Essex, John Ellis fed his dog consecrated bread and others believed ditch water was as miraculous as that held in a font.[19]

A thin streak of anti-clericalism sometimes stirred Henry's own heart, perhaps triggered by his own experiences with the unbending Catholic Church. However, when it came to the question of priests being allowed to marry, he was determined to maintain traditional custom and practice.

The Six Articles Act, which reasserted clerical celibacy (much to Cranmer's discomfort), stipulated that this was not just a matter of Church discipline, but was forbidden 'by the law of God', according to Henry's own annotation of the preamble to the legislation.[20] In April 1541, the king harangued the French and Spanish ambassadors about the perils of priests marrying. If allowed, 'they would tyrannise princes and make benefices hereditary' to their sons. They could 'domineer over kings and make themselves lords of the world, spiritual and temporal'. With the 'look of an angry man afraid of consequences... [he said] he would die sooner than consent' to this.[21] Henry was not blessed wth a sense of irony. With his record of marriages, he would not have tolerated this discipline himself, but he was adamant it should be imposed on others.[22]

Because state and Church were now inextricably entwined, the impact of religious belief on the morals and work ethics of Henry's subjects became his concern as a matter of theology. The royal vision for his kingdom was one populated by sober, industrious, obedient and devout Christians. He possessed a rigid and austere opinion of beggars and the lazy, undeserving poor. There was no place in his heart for compassion towards such uncouth and unworthy subjects.

The king was enraged over suggestions that references to 'our daily bread' in the Lord's Prayer, should refer to the fruits of God's good grace, rather than rewards for honest labour at the loom or in the fields. 'The true labouring man, doing truly the office [whence] he is called, shall attain salvation as surely as any other creature,' he told his bishops. 'They that do contrary, shall be in jeopardy of damnation.'[23] His subjects must not be led into indolence, nor their souls endangered by living as worthless vagabonds. Many would rather live 'by the craft of begging slothfully than either work or labour for their living' and anyone who gave charitable alms to such miscreants 'would gain no virtue', he thundered.

A surprising legacy from the Vatican's old authority was the last official preaching of a crusade against the Turks in 1543. During that summer, Henry had promised £10,000 to Ferdinand, King of the Romans and of Hungary, to help his brother Charles V in his defence of Christendom against the Ottoman Empire.[24] The Turks had invaded Hungary in 1526 and now only the north-west region (present-day Slovakia, western Croatia and parts of north-east Hungary) remained under Imperial rule. Ferdinand had tried to recover the twin cities of Buda and Pest in 1542, but was repulsed by the Ottomans. They had launched a fresh offensive 'not only to devastate, spoil and destroy the country with most miserable slaughter of the Christian people ... men, women and children, but to subvert and extinguish the true religion of Christ'.

Superficially, the offer looks a generous act of Christian piety on Henry's part but beware, his motives were always opaque. Could this donation be possibly linked with Frances I's decision to allow the wintering of the Ottoman fleet in Toulon in 1543, or to send French artillery to aid the Turks in Hungary that same year?[25] Just who was a traitor to the Christian faith now? Francis, the fawning ally of the rampaging infidel Turks, or the schismatic Henry?

The money was released in two tranches in August and September. Naturally, Henry had no intention of providing the money himself and issued an appeal to every English diocese for voluntary contributions to recover his cash, needed for the invasion of France. Archbishop Cranmer issued an exhortation, instructing priests to request a 'benevolence' to be sought every Sunday and Holy Day up to Michaelmas (29 September) that year.

Unfortunately, the plight of Hungarian Christians proved unappealing and the English were unwilling to dig deep into their purses. Hungary was a long way away and its towns and villages had unpronounceable names. On top of this xenophobia, parishioners were already struggling

under the burden of Henry's taxation, so money was tight. The collections raised just under £2,000, or less than 20 per cent of what the
king had paid out, and the parishes were forced to reimburse the crown
again in late 1543 and early 1544.[26]

Bishop Gardiner, you will recall, was a leader of the religiously conservative party at court. In 1535, he wrote the *De Vera Obedientia Oratio*,
in defence of the royal supremacy and was consequently lambasted by
Catholic Europe as a 'great poltroon', and an 'unabashed rascal'. Even
the pope called him 'a scoundrel'. Yet, Gardiner maintained allegiance
to an enduring 'crypto-papism'. Rudolfo Pio da Carpi, papal nuncio
to France, believed he was 'most desirous of his king's returning to
the right road and wrote his book under compulsion, not having the
strength to suffer death patiently'.[27] In the years that followed, Gardiner
became a remorseless hunter of heretics during his campaign to preserve the traditional liturgy in England.

No one was safe from his intrigues. Archbishop Cranmer had naively
appointed six preachers at Canterbury Cathedral, three evangelical
and three conservative, so 'that they might between them try out the
truth of doctrine', despite the prebendaries' protests that dissension
would follow. Gardiner, journeying home from an overseas diplomatic
mission, heard Mass at Canterbury and afterwards asked one of them
'how they did in Canterbury, meaning as to the quietness of Christ's
religion'. The bishop was told of disagreements in doctrine and sermons
advocating radical reform. 'This is not well', said Gardiner. 'My Lord
of Canterbury will look upon this, I doubt not, or else such preaching
will grow into an evil inconvenience.'[28]

Encouraged by Gardiner and Sir John Baker, his ally on the Privy
Council, seven of the traditionalist canons accused Cranmer in April
1543 of sanctioning heretical sermons within the diocese of Canterbury.
Their accusations were sent to Henry.

As the king was rowed upriver on his barge one evening, he spotted
Cranmer outside the gates of Lambeth Palace. The boat came alongside the jetty and the archbishop, clambering aboard, was stunned
by Henry's hearty greeting: 'Ah, my chaplain! I have news for you. I
know now who is the greatest heretic in Kent!'[29] His joviality quickly

disappeared as he produced a document listing the allegations and showed it to Cranmer. The king trusted the archbishop and was fond of him. With a neat sleight of hand, he appointed him to head the inquiry examining the accusations against himself.

Gardiner was outraged and disgusted at how cravenly the accusers backed down during Cranmer's investigation. He told one of their servants: 'Your master seems like a child. Bid him not weep for shame but answer like a man.' When he heard how 'men were handled for setting forth of the truth', the thwarted bishop exclaimed: 'My Lord of Canterbury cannot kill them. Let them suffer for it.'[30] But after six weeks of deliberations, a general pardon was issued to all concerned.

Even so, Cranmer did not feel secure.

That Easter, Gardiner seized his opportunity to 'bend his bow against the head deer', as he graphically described it, and arrested the former diplomat Sir Philip Hoby, a Gentleman of Henry's Privy Chamber, who was involved in the king's persecution of the Jews. Hoby was accused of employing a clerk well known 'to be a man of evil opinions touching the sacrament of the altar' and was held in the Fleet Prison. Edmund Harman, the king's Barber Surgeon, a courtier called Thomas Carwarden[31] and Thomas Sternhold, a Groom of the Robes, were also caught up in Gardiner's sweep for heretics but were pardoned, possibly because they were close to the king.[32]

In July, Gardiner summoned Richard Turner, a preacher from Chartham, Kent, in Cranmer's diocese, to appear before the Privy Council. He was accused of falling foul of the Act of Six Articles by preaching that Christ was the only true priest who had said Mass 'on the altar of the Cross, sacrificing for the sins of the world for ever and that all other Masses were but remembrances and thanksgivings for that one sacrifice'. Turner was interrogated and committed to prison while inquiries continued.[33]

Cranmer's secretary Ralph Morice wrote to two religious reformers at court to ask for help: Henry's chief physician William Butts, and Anthony Denny, another Gentleman of his Privy Chamber. 'My Lord of Canterbury dare do nothing for the poor man's delivery; he has done so much already. His grace has told me plainly that it is put into the king's head that he is the maintainer and supporter of all the heretics in the realm,' Morice warned.[34] Butts duly tackled Henry about the issue early one morning, as the king was having his ginger beard washed and trimmed. After speaking 'some pleasant conceits to refresh and solace the king's mind', the doctor produced Morice's letter, which Henry told him to read. After briefly considering the matter, the king 'so altered' his mind that 'whereas before he commanded Turner to be whipped out of the country, he now commanded him to be retained as a faithful subject'.[35]

During the last week of November 1543, Cranmer's conservative enemies on the Privy Council struck again. Henry was once more told of his archbishop's blatant heresy and was urged to send him to the Tower. The king agreed to Cranmer's arrest, planned for the next day at a Privy Council meeting at Whitehall.

But that night, around eleven o'clock, Henry sent Denny to Lambeth to summon the prelate to his presence. After being roused from his bed, he was rowed across the Thames and met the king in a darkened gallery at the palace. Given the hour, Henry was short and to the point, warning Cranmer of his planned arrest at nine o'clock the next morning. He told him: 'I have granted their requests, but whether I have done well or not, what say you, my lord?'

Cranmer said he was happy to be committed to the Tower, as he knew the king would not allow him an unfair hearing about his doctrine. Henry grew impatient at his unworldliness: 'Lord God! What fond simplicity you have! Do you not consider ... how many great enemies you have? Do you not think that once they have you in prison, three or four false knaves will be procured to [stand] witness against you and to condemn you? Think you have better luck that way than your master Christ had? Whilst at liberty, [no one] dares to open their lips or appear before your face. I see you will run headlong into your own undoing.' The king added: 'No, not so, my lord. I have better regard towards you, than permit your enemies to overthrow you'.

He pulled a ring off his finger and passed it to Cranmer. 'They well know I use [it] for no other purpose but to call matters from the Council into my own hands to be ordered and determined.' When they make their accusations and arrest you, show them the ring and you will be safe, he promised. Cranmer was close to tears of gratitude, but Henry sent him home to Lambeth with the sharp valediction: 'Go your ways, my lord, and do as I have bidden you.'

At eight o'clock the next morning, the Privy Council sent for the archbishop, but deliberately kept him waiting outside their chamber. He stood among a throng of 'serving men and lackeys above three-quarters of an hour, many councillors and other men now and then going in and out'. Along came Dr Butts and chatted to the apprehensive Cranmer before he entered the presence chamber and told Henry: 'I have seen a strange sight... My lord of Canterbury has become a lackey or serving man, for he has been standing among them for almost an hour... so that I was ashamed to keep him company there any longer.' Henry was enraged at Cranmer's humiliation and exclaimed: 'Have they served me so? It is well enough; I shall talk with them bye and bye.'

The archbishop was finally summoned before the Privy Council and was told that 'a great complaint' had been made to both king and councillors. He and others 'by his permission, had infected the whole realm with heresy. Therefore it was the king's pleasure that they should commit him to the Tower... [to] be examined for his trial.'

Pale-faced but calm, Cranmer told his enemies: 'I am sorry, my lords, that you drive me to the exigency [of] appeal[ing] from you to the king's majesty who, by this token, has taken this matter into his own hands and discharges you thereof.' He held aloft Henry's ring for all to see – and to fear its symbolic power.

There was an astonished silence, broken by John, Lord Russell, Lord Privy Seal, who burst out: 'Did I not tell you, my lords, that the king would never permit my lord of Canterbury to have such a blemish as to be imprisoned, unless it were for high treason? Do you think the king will suffer this man's finger to ache? Much more, I warrant you, will he defend his life against babbling varlets!'

The would-be prisoner and his frustrated accusers were then ushered into the royal presence. Their mutterings were silenced by the sight of Henry lumbering painfully to his feet. He told his mortified advisers: 'Ah! My lords, I thought that I had a discreet and wise council. But now I perceive I am deceived. How have you handled my lord of Canterbury here? What makes you [treat him like] a slave, shutting him out of the council chamber amongst serving men? Would you be so handled yourselves?'

His tone grew serious and sombre. 'I would you well understand that I believe Canterbury as faithful a man towards me as ever was prelate in this realm and one to whom I [am in] many ways beholden.' He laid his hand on his heart. 'By the faith I owe to God... therefore, who so loves me will regard him [so] thereafter.'

Norfolk sought to belittle the seriousness of the conspiracy against Cranmer. 'We meant no manner of hurt to my lord of Canterbury in that we requested to have him in durance [imprisonment]. We only did [so] because he might, after his trial, be set at liberty to his more glory.'

His oily explanation did not fool Henry: 'Well, I pray you not use my friends so. I perceive now well enough how the world goes among you. There remains malice among you, one to another. Let it be avoided out of hand, I would advise you. Well, well my lords, take him and well use him as he is worthy to be and make no more ado.'[36]

Public humiliation was one of Henry's favourite weapons with which to cut his ministers and courtiers down to size, and he deployed it adeptly as ever during this drama. But his approval of the arrest warrant and sudden decision to warn Cranmer about his impending doom, are also symptomatic of Cushing's Syndrome.

At a later stage, in the presence of Wriothesley (then Gardiner's ally), Henry asked the bishop point-blank whether he felt 'any embittered feelings' against Cranmer. 'How coldly I answered the king', the bishop later recalled, 'lest he smell any dissension.'[37]

Gardiner himself had a narrow escape in the early spring of 1544 when his secretary and nephew Germain was indicted for denying the royal supremacy and communicating with Cardinal Pole. He had also been intimately concerned in the earlier 'Prebendaries' Plot' against Cranmer. Suffolk, in league with Hertford and Lisle, believed that Germain had been protected by his uncle. After all, he could 'never stand so stiff in defence of the bishop of Rome's usurped power and authority, without his master's advice, knowledge and persuasion'. He demanded the bishop be sent to the Tower for investigation 'about such things as may be objected against him'.

However, Norfolk warned Gardiner and he hastened to Whitehall to head off his arrest. Henry told the bishop that it was 'thought you are not at all clear in this offence, but that you are of the same opinion with him [Germain Gardiner]. Therefore, my lord, be plain with me. Let me know if you be in that way infected or no. If you tell me the truth, I will... pardon the fault, but if you halt or dissemble with me, look for no favour at my hands.' Gardiner did not hesitate.

Down on his knees, he admitted that he has formerly held some of his nephew's views, but promised 'from that day forward to reform his opinions and become a new man'. A full pardon was granted to him immediately.

The following morning, Suffolk was astonished to hear that Gardiner had escaped scot-free. He complained to Henry about him preventing 'our commission which I and others had from your grace, concerning my lord of Winchester's committal to the Tower'. The king cut him short: 'You know what my nature and custom has been in such matters, evermore to pardon them that will not dissemble but confess their faults.'[38] Another case of inconsistency caused by Cushing's Syndrome? Perhaps, but if Henry could not afford to abandon Cranmer, he also could not lose Gardiner's expertise in European diplomacy, particularly as he was to embark on his invasion of France.

Germain Gardiner was executed at Tyburn on 7 March 1544. (He was beatified in 1886 as a Catholic martyr.) Four others were convicted with him for treason, most of whom had been connected with the family of Sir Thomas More: John Ireland, vicar of Eltham, Kent, who had once been More's chaplain; John Larke, vicar of Chelsea; Robert Singleton, a Lancashire gentleman, and Thomas Hayward who recanted as he was being tied to the hurdle and was pardoned. The others were executed.

Henry's final words at the dénouement of the plot against Cranmer – 'There remains malice among you, one to another. Let it be avoided out of hand, I would advise you' – were spoken straight from the heart. One of the main objectives of his religious policy was to achieve unity in his own Church. Accordingly, he planned a stern appeal to Parliament, urging 'charity and concord' to cure the bitter 'dissension and discord' over religion that infected the Privy Council, court and indeed his realm.

On the morning of Christmas Eve, 24 December 1545, Henry made what was to be his farewell speech to Parliament. This was to mark its prorogation until 4 November the following year and the ceremony was normally the task of Lord Chancellor Wriothesley. Such routine protocol was put aside and the king made an unexpected and dramatic appearance in his crimson velvet and ermine-trimmed parliamentary robes and cap.

Standing up painfully, Henry delivered an emotional and compelling speech, spoken fluently and without reference to notes. It has since been called the 'pioneer royal Christmas broadcast'.[39]

He began by thanking his 'well-loved Commons' for their generosity in meeting 'his great charges in their defence' and for passing the Bill sequestering the assets of the chantry chapels, colleges and fraternities[40] even though the measure had narrowly escaped defeat only at the eleventh hour.[41] Polite niceties dealt with, he moved on to the main thrust of his speech:

> My loving subjects, study and take pains to amend one thing which surely is amiss and far out of order, to which I most heartily require you... Charity and concord is not amongst you, but discord and dissension bears rule in every place. What love and charity is amongst you when one calls the other heretic and Anabaptist and he calls him again papist, hypocrite and Pharisee? Are these tokens of charity amongst you? Are these signs of fraternal love between you?[42]

The king then turned to the bishops and clergy:

> I see and hear daily of you of the clergy who preach one against another; teach contrary to [one] another; inveigh one against other, without charity or discretion...

Henry, half-jokingly, used a curious contemporary metaphor for the religious dissent rivening his kingdom: 'Some [are] too stiff in their old Mumpsimus, others too busy and curious in their new Sumpsimus.'[43] He went on:

> All men almost be in variety and discord and few or none preach truly and sincerely the word of God, according as they ought to. Alas! How can the poor souls live in concord when you preachers sow amongst them in your sermons debate and discord? To you, they look for light and you bring them darkness. Amend these crimes, I exhort you, and set forth God's word both by true teaching and good example giving.

It was time to remind them that he was God's own deputy on earth:

> I, whom God has appointed his vicar and high minister here, will
> see these extinct and these enormities corrected, according to my
> very duty, or else I shall be accounted an unprofitable servant and
> untrue officer.

The secular MPs and lords and his subjects outside the confines of
Westminster next came in for severe royal censure:

> You of the temporality be not clean and unspotted of malice and
> envy, for you rail on bishops, speak slanderously of priests and rebuke
> and taunt preachers, both contrary to good order and Christian fra-
> ternity... Although you are permitted to read Holy Scripture and to
> have the Word of God in your mother tongue, you must understand
> that you have this licence only to inform your own conscience and to
> instruct your children and family, not to dispute and make Scripture
> a railing and a taunting stock against priests and preachers as many
> light persons do.

Pious Henry was deeply shocked at how the Word of God was being
mistreated by his lewd subjects:

> I am very sorry to know and hear how irreverently that most precious
> jewel, the Word of God is disputed, rhymed, sung and jangled in
> every alehouse and tavern, contrary to the true meaning and doctrine
> of the same.

This was the final chance for Parliament and people to forget their
religious differences and unite behind the teachings of his Church:

> For this I am sure, that charity was never so faint amongst you and
> virtuous and giddy living was never less used, nor God himself
> amongst Christians never less reverenced, honoured or served.
> Therefore... be in charity one with another, like brother and brother.
> Love, dread and serve God (to which I, as your supreme head and
> sovereign lord exhort and require you) and then I doubt not the love
> and league... shall never be dissolved or broken between us.[44]

The king's ministers were startled by Henry's eloquence, sincerity and passion; some were even moved to tears. But these royal appeals for moderation and an end to dissension fell on barren ground. The conservative faction had its eyes set on an even bigger target than the archbishop of Canterbury.

Gardiner was out of the country in January 1546 on diplomatic duties at the court of Charles V. After some discussions with Henry, Cranmer decided to take advantage of his absence to sweep away more of the vestiges of ritual surviving from the unreformed religion. These included the giant veil that shrouded church chancels during Lent; congregations creeping to the Cross on Good Friday and the pealing of muffled bells during the nocturnal vigil of All Hallows, when the dead were remembered.

Cranmer drafted a letter describing the new policy for the king to send Gardiner in Utrecht. Sir Anthony Denny read it to Henry late one afternoon in his Privy Chamber but was abruptly stopped by the king snapping: 'I am otherwise resolved!' Brusquely, he instructed Denny to tell the archbishop 'that since I spoke to him about these matters, I have received letters from my lord of Winchester . . . and he writes plainly to Us that the league [with Charles V] will not prosper or go forward if We make any other innovation, change or alteration either in religion or ceremonies.'[45]

The king's mercurial decision heralded a period of almost six months when Gardiner and Norfolk's party held almost total sway in the desperate infighting for supremacy at court.

Queen Katherine was regarded as 'quieter than any of the young wives the king had. As she knew more of the world, she always got on pleasantly with the king and had no caprices.'[46] Tradition maintains that she spent hours with one of the king's stinking bandaged legs on her lap, while she distracted him from his pain and the trying affairs of religion and state by her ready wit and cultured conversation.

Katherine held decided evangelical opinions. In many respects, she has a strong claim to the title of the first Protestant queen of England.[47] Her Privy Chamber was full of ladies with similar religious allegiances, who had long been thorns in the sides of the conservatives. Such ideas, volubly expressed, were dangerous. Katherine, twenty-five-year-old duchess of Suffolk, was wholly irrepressible. One contemporary remarked drily of her: 'It is a pity that so godly a wit waits upon so forward a will.' Her pet dog was mischievously named 'Gardiner' and was frequently teased and playfully taunted in the sight of those at court.

It had been Katherine's habit to hold daily scripture classes for her ladies and, accompanied by them, to listen to lengthy (and to our ears, wearisome) sermons preached by her chaplain John Parkhurst, especially during Lent. Since 1544, her liturgy had been Cranmer's authorised vernacular litany with its minimal emphasis on the traditional invocation of the saints, although she also continued to hear Latin Masses as well.[48] She held many conversations with her ailing husband on religious questions, urging him 'that as he had ... to the glory of God and his eternal fame, begun a good and godly work in banishing that monstrous idol of Rome, so he would thoroughly perfect and finish the same, cleansing and purging his Church of England clean from the dregs thereof, wherein as yet remains great suspicion'. These talks, however, became more infrequent as the pain of his legs stopped him visiting her and his temper became more unpredictable.[49]

After his narrow escape, Gardiner was wise to inveigle Wriothesley to be the main protagonist in a plot to destroy the queen. Others involved probably included Norfolk, Paget and Sir Richard Rich. Katherine's unquestionable propriety ruled out sexual misconduct as a means of entrapment. Heresy seemed the best weapon against her but they also pondered whether Norfolk's daughter, the duchess of Richmond, could become another femme fatale to lure Henry's affections away from his sixth wife – despite the previous fate of two Howard women.

The plot against the queen began as a widespread whispering campaign against her. On 27 February 1546, van der Delft wrote to the emperor: 'I hesitate to report that here there are rumours of a new queen. Some attribute it to the sterility of the present queen, while others say there will be no change during the present war with [France] ... The king shows no alteration in his demeanour of the queen, although she is said to be annoyed at the rumours.'[50]

A week later, Stephen Vaughan in Antwerp told Wriothesley and Paget that a Dutch merchant had mentioned talk of the king taking 'another wife' and these reports were rife in the city. Gardiner was in

Antwerp, on the way back from his diplomatic mission. Like ripples on a pond, the poison spread to England. Cornelius Sceppurus, a member of the emperor's council, heard the same whispers in London the following month and coyly reported: 'I dare not write [about] the rumours current here with regard to the feminine sex. Some change is suspected to be pending.'[51]

Katherine felt both increasingly threatened and vulnerable as the king's health was visibly deteriorating. In March 1546 he was ill for three weeks with a fever caused by his legs and he passed his time in ill-tempered games of cards with unlucky opponents. He probably played pique, or *saunt*, alone with Lisle and primero (a forerunner of poker), with three other players, when substantial bets were regularly staked.[52]

Towards the end of the month, Henry told visiting diplomats that although his leg still troubled him, his robust constitution had helped him through. His face betrayed that this was patently a lie. The queen meanwhile ordered lockable iron-bound coffers and boxes for her privy apartments to prevent unauthorised prying into her papers and correspondence.[53] Some of her prohibited evangelical books were hidden in her garderobe, or lavatory, and others were sent into the safekeeping of her uncle, her chamberlain, at his house in Horton, Northamptonshire.[54]

Gardiner and Wriothesley targeted supposed heretics close to the queen. One of the first to be ensnared was Norfolk's second son, Lord Thomas Howard. On 2 May, he was up before the Privy Council, charged with 'disputing indiscreetly of scripture with other young gentlemen of the court'.[55] Five days later, he was offered clemency 'if he would confess what he said in disproof of sermons preached at court last Lent and his other talk in the queen's chamber and elsewhere concerning scripture'. Howard refused to disclose 'those particulars which the Privy Council would have him confess'[56] and escaped with a stern adjuration to mend his ways, as did another of the queen's supporters, Sir Edward Warner.

The witch hunt continued apace, partly overseen by Henry himself. At least twenty people were investigated and another sixty fled England to save themselves.

The fashionable reformist preacher Dr Edward Crome was also questioned by the Privy Council about his sermon at St Thomas Acre, London, on 11 April. He had been in trouble with the ecclesiastical authorities four times since 1529 and on one occasion was rescued by the king himself.[57] Crome was ordered to recant in a sermon at St Paul's Cross on 9 May,[58] but defiantly declared: 'I have come not hither to recant, nor God willing, I will not recant.' That refusal did not go down well with Gardiner and his allies and Crome faced agonies of indecision while committed into Wriothesley's custody at Greenwich. Should he save his skin, or allow his supporters to capitalise upon his martyrdom in the evangelical cause? In the end, he meekly opted for life.

The London merchant Otwell Johnson, who had listened approvingly to Crome setting forth 'the glory of the eternal living God' in a sermon two years before, now heard him urge his listeners on Trinity Sunday (27 June) to 'embrace the ancientness of Catholic doctrine and forsake new fangleness'. Johnson sarcastically told his brother: 'Our news here [is] of Dr Crome's canting, recanting, decanting, or rather double canting.'[59] Afterwards, Crome was discharged and it is ironic that a few weeks later, in that extraordinary conversation about reforming the Mass with the French admiral at Hampton Court, Henry was eager to deny what Crome had denied and assert what Crome had recanted.[60]

His freedom came at a terrible price to others.

While in Wriothesley's charge, he 'accused diverse persons of the court and the city with other persons of the country, which put many persons to great trouble and some suffered death after'.[61] Under interrogation, he exposed a number of evangelicals at court, or others having connections to the royal household. The first was John Lassells, a Sewer of the king's Privy Chamber, who had provided that damning information about Katherine Howard to Cranmer. As well as being a 'leading spirit' of the evangelicals, he was denounced as a patron of the London 'prophet' Richard Laynam, who had rashly predicted Henry's imminent overthrow.[62] Another was William Morice, a Gentleman Usher and the brother of Cranmer's secretary Ralph. He had earlier fallen out with Sir Richard Rich over the ownership of a manor in Essex. He was thus a marked man, and was alleged to have breached the Six Articles Act. But the evidence against him was thin and he escaped retribution by paying a recognizance of £33 to appear again before the Council.

Finally, Crome named Anne Askew, a Lincolnshire woman who had been in trouble in London the previous year after preaching against the 'Real Presence' of Christ in the communion wafer. Then, she had been set free after an investigation by the Lord Mayor, Sir Martin Bowes.

Anne, aged twenty-five and described as an 'elegant beauty and rare wit', had been thrown out of her home by her husband Thomas Kyme because of her unorthodox religious views.

After her latest arrest, she was questioned by the Privy Council for five hours at Greenwich. Gardiner angrily demanded that she gave direct answers, rather than speaking in parables, telling her she was merely a 'parrot'. Anne insisted: 'I was ready to suffer all things at his hands, not only his rebuke, but all that should follow besides, yes and that gladly.' The bishop said he would speak 'with me familiarly. I said: "So did Judas when he unfriendly betrayed Christ."'[63] Gardiner warned that she was in danger of being burnt at the stake, but she retorted: 'God will laugh your threatenings to scorn.'[64] She was determinedly donning the mantle of a martyr and was returned to Newgate Prison, where she lay in her cell in 'extremity of sickness'.

Another questioned was a page of the Pallet Chamber named Richard Worley, who was imprisoned for uttering heretical statements at court, although in his case, his inquisitors were more interested in whether he had brought evangelical books, smuggled from Europe, into the palace for the queen.[65] Dr William Huicke, probably a relation of Henry's physician Robert, was arrested for supporting Crome and committed under the Six Articles Act for 'erroneous opinions' but escaped unscathed after a personal appeal to Henry. John Bette, probably a relation of two members of Katherine's household, was condemned to death on 16 May for offences under the same Act.

Anne was arraigned at the Guildhall Court on 18 June for heresy concerning the sacrament of communion. Her fellow defendants were John Hadlam (or Adams), an Essex tailor, Nicholas White, a gentleman from London and Dr Nicholas Shaxton, who had resigned his bishopric of Salisbury in protest at the passing of the Six Articles Act in 1539 and was imprisoned. He was married but separated from his wife Cicely and crassly exhorted her (in verse!) to live a chaste life and remain single thereafter. Norfolk was among the judges and without trial by jury, the accused were found guilty and sentenced to be burnt.

The next day, Henry sent Edmund Bonner, bishop of London, and Nicholas Heath (who had replaced John Bell as bishop of Worcester in 1543), together with two royal chaplains, Nicholas Ridley and Richard Coxe, to interview Shaxton in Newgate. After their 'good exhortation and doctrine' and more pertinently, dire warnings not to defy Henry's will, these earnest episcopal visitors convinced Shaxton and Nicholas White to repudiate their heresy. However, Anne Askew was taken off to the Tower for further questioning about her relationship with the queen's ladies-in-waiting.

Wriothesley, Rich and Sir John Baker, now Chancellor of the Exchequer, were her interrogators. Baker had earned the unenviable cognomen of 'Bloody Baker' by his brutal persecution of reformers and their handling of their young prisoner certainly matched this nickname.

In papers reputedly smuggled out of prison, Anne described her horrific treatment at the hands of Henry's councillors. 'They asked me [about] my lady of Suffolk, my lady of Sussex,[66] my lady of Hertford,[67] my lady Denny and my lady Fitzwilliam.'[68] She told them that some ladies at court had sent her money while she was imprisoned and admitted 'there was a man in a blue cloak who delivered me ten shillings (50p) and said that... Lady Hertford sent it me, and another in a violet coat gave me eight shillings (40p) and said Lady Denny sent it me... Then they asked: "Were there any of the [Privy] Council that maintained me" and I said "No".'[69]

She remained obdurate in refusing to answer their questions. Sir Anthony Knyvett, former governor of Portsmouth and now Lieutenant of the Tower, was ordered to strap her to the rack for torture. Knyvett was horrified but reluctantly complied, instructing his men just to 'pinch her', as a warning to reveal all, before worse torments followed. Their questions remained unanswered and he was told to rack her body still further. Knyvett refused, pointing out that to rack a woman was illegal, even under Henry's harsh penal laws.

Angrily, Wriothesley and Rich cast off their bonnets, stripped off their gowns and turned the windlasses controlling the rack, tearing her muscles and sinews. Anne later described her ordeal: 'Because I confessed no ladies nor gentlewomen [of the court] to be of my opinion, they kept me [on the rack] for a long time. And because I lay still and did not cry, my Lord Chancellor and Master Rich took pains to rack me [with] their own hands till I was nigh dead.'

Knyvett demanded that the torture be stopped and that she should be removed from the rack. Hard words among the inquisitors followed. 'I immediately swooned and then they recovered me again. After that, I sat two long hours reasoning with my Lord Chancellor upon the bare floor where he, with many flattering words, persuaded me to leave my opinion. But my Lord God gave me grace to persevere and will do (I hope) to the very end.'

The Lieutenant, disgusted at her treatment (and no doubt fearing punishment for his role if the torture became public), took a boat to Westminster to inform Henry of Anne's suffering. 'When the king had understood, he seemed not very well to like their extreme handling of the woman,' and pardoned Knyvett.[70]

On 8 July, a proclamation banning heretical books was issued in London, requiring that 'from henceforth, no man, woman or other person of what estate... shall after the last day of August have, take, or keep in their possession the text of the *New Testament* of [William] Tyndale or [Miles] Coverdale.'[71] Such books should be delivered to the Lord Mayor or Bishop Bonner to be publicly burnt by the hangman. The queen almost certainly had a copy of Coverdale's translation in her library of evangelical books. She must have feared that Gardiner's net was drawing ever closer around her.

The king was meanwhile suffering from one of his regular bouts of profound depression. The Imperial ambassador van der Delft reported that a 'secret source' had told him that Henry was experiencing 'continued melancholy. Certainly, although dressed for Mass, he did not go that day, nor did he go into his gardens, as his habit is in summer.'[72] He had also suffered from colic on the night of 6 July and took medicine to ease it.

The court had emptied, with some of the evangelical party out of the country; Hertford was on a military mission to Boulogne and Lisle on a diplomatic mission to France. With his enemies absent, the time was perfect for Gardiner to strike at Queen Katherine.

Her forceful discussions about religion had become tedious and irksome to her husband. After one such session at Greenwich, Henry wished her a half-hearted 'Good night, sweetheart'. He turned to Gardiner, who was conveniently present, and snapped crossly: 'A good hearing it is when women become such clerks [scholars] and a thing much to my comfort to come in my old age to be taught by a woman.'

Here was the bishop's golden opportunity. He murmured in the king's ear that Katherine's opinions about religion were heretical under Henry's own laws. Gardiner pledged that 'he, with others of his faithful councillors, could, within a short time, disclose such treasons cloaked with ... heresy, that his majesty could easily perceive how perilous a matter it is, to cherish a serpent within his own bosom.'[73]

Hearing these malicious words, the king must have recalled a similar conversation about the morals of another of his queens, Katherine Howard, five years earlier. As then, Henry allowed an investigation to proceed.

Gardiner must have been planning such an inquiry for some weeks. The private closets of three women close to the queen – her sister Anne Herbert, Maud Lane and Elizabeth Tyrwhitt – would be searched for the proof provided by possession of heretical books. However, they were warned and removed the damning tomes before the bishop's searchers could lay hands on them.[74] Some credible evidence must have been gathered, because Henry signed the warrant for Katherine's arrest, possibly on 4 July.

A few days before her planned seizure – and being carried off to the Tower by night – the king confided in Dr Thomas Wendy about the dangers facing the queen. The physician was sworn to secrecy.

Shortly afterwards, a copy of the arrest warrant was opportunely dropped by night in one of the corridors of the queen's apartments in Greenwich Palace.

It was quickly delivered to Katherine and she became both terrified and hysterical, taking to her bed and pleading ill-health. Henry dutifully sent his doctors to her and later visited her bedside himself. 'She uttered her grief, fearing lest his majesty had taken displeasure with her and had utterly forsaken her. He, like a loving husband, with sweet and comfortable words, so refreshed and appeased her careful mind that she began to recover.'[75]

Despite these soothing assurances, the queen knew she was not safe. It was unwise to throw herself on Henry's mercy. Abject apologies or appeals for clemency from an erring wife could become fatal admissions of guilt. The key to her salvation was Henry's psychology. He was not being cuckolded, as with her predecessor, but he could not tolerate being made to look a fool.

That evening, Katherine went to the king's bedchamber, accompanied by her sister Anne Herbert and the nine-year-old Lady Jane Grey, carrying a candle.

Tradition maintains that she sat uncomfortably on his lap, although this seems unlikely, given the agonising osteomyelitis of his legs. There was an unwritten script for this dramatic nocturnal meeting. Henry deliberately raised the issue of religion. It was an obvious test and one the queen had to pass to prove her innocence. Katherine told him she was 'but a poor silly woman, accompanied by all the imperfections natural to the weakness of her sex'. She promised to defer her judgement in religious matters 'in this, [as] in all other cases, to your majesty's wisdom, as my only anchor, Supreme Head and Governor here on earth, next to God, to lean unto'.

The king was not completely placated and maliciously toyed with her. 'Not so, by St Mary,' he said. 'You are become a doctor, Kate, to instruct us (as we take it) and not to be instructed or directed by us.' The queen flattered him and humbled herself: 'If your majesty take it so, then your majesty very much mistakes me, for I have always held it preposterous for a woman to instruct her lord. If I have presumed to differ from your highness on religion, it was partly to obtain information for my own comfort regarding nice points on which I stood in doubt.'[76] Katherine had discussed these matters 'not only [that] your majesty might with less grief pass over this painful time of your infirmity, being attentive to our talk and hoping that your majesty should reap some ease thereby. Also that I, hearing your majesty's learned discourse, might receive to myself some profit thereby.'

A grimace, masquerading as a smile, spread slowly across Henry's bloated features. His piggy eyes glinted in the candlelight. 'And is it even [so] sweetheart? And tended your arguments to no worse end? Then perfect friends are we now, as ever any time heretofore.'[77] With those words, he pulled her into his arms and tenderly kissed her.

Late the next afternoon, possibly 14 July, Henry and Katherine were sitting in the sunshine of the Greenwich privy gardens with three of the queen's ladies – Anne Herbert, Lady Tyrwhitt and little Jane Grey. The king seemed 'as pleasant as ever he was in all his life before' and was talking 'merrily'. His face darkened as he saw Wriothesley with an escort of forty halberdiers marching up the pathway between the low parterre hedges.

The Lord Chancellor had come at the appointed hour to arrest the Queen of England and her ladies.

Henry pulled him roughly aside. Falling to his knees, Wriothesley reminded the king of arrangements to take Katherine to the Tower that night. Angrily, the king shouted: 'Arrant knave! Beast and fool!' and, according to some later reports, cuffed him hard about the head. With an imperious sweep of his hand, he ordered Wriothesley to 'avaunt [leave] my sight!' and turned on his heel, leaving a thoroughly confused Lord Chancellor. He was forced to make an embarrassed retreat, accompanied by the steady tread of his equally confused guards behind him.

Katherine tried to soothe away the king's anger. 'Ah, my poor soul,' said Henry, 'you little know how evil he deserves this grace at your hands. Oh, my word sweetheart. He has been towards thee, an arrant knave, so let him go'. [78]

Was this inconsistent behaviour another manifestation of the paranoid king's medical condition? After a rare experience of royal guilt, Henry tried to make amends to Katherine. Between 25 July and the end of November, he issued licences for French, Flemish and Florentine jewellers to import gemstones and furs into England as costly presents for her. The Parisian jeweller John Lange and his son Gilles could 'bring or send into the king's dominions all manner of jewels, pearls, precious stones, as well as set in gold... skins and furs of sable... clothes [and] new gentleness of what fashion or value the same be... for the pleasure of Us [and] Our dearest wife the queen'.[79] Henry also took her on a restricted progress to Otelands, Guildford and Chobham in Surrey, ending up at Windsor Castle. There was much hunting and Katherine sent thoughtful presents of venison to Anne of Cleves and Viscount Lisle.[80]

Katherine's fire of reformist zeal had been extinguished. She spent more time studying Spanish.

The fall-out from Gardiner and Wriothesley's purge of reformers meanwhile continued. During the night of 12 July, one of the king's Gentlemen of the Privy Chamber was suddenly arrested on Wriothesley's orders. George Blagge had been involved in attempting to free the Protestant agitator John Porter from prison in 1542 and now he was thrown into Newgate. The next morning, he appeared at the Guildhall, accused of heresy. Two witnesses, Sir Hugh Calveley and

Edward Littleton, swore they had heard him denouncing the Mass.
Blagge was condemned to death.

That night, Anne Askew was brought by boat from the Tower to
Blackfriars, and carried to Newgate, as she could not walk after being
racked.

Four days later, there was another execution of heretics at Smithfield.
Anne was brought there sitting in a chair, mounted on a dung cart,
escorted by two sergeants. She was tied to the stake, still slumped in
her chair. Norfolk was watching eagerly, sitting on a scaffold especially
erected for spectators. By Henry's commandment, Shaxton had to
deliver a sermon before the prisoners were burnt. A small gunpowder
charge, hidden amid the wooden faggots surrounding Anne's stake,
exploded, bringing her sufferings quickly to an end.

With her were Blagge, John Hemley (formerly an Observant friar),
the tailor John Hadlam and John Lassells.[81] The king issued a last-
minute pardon to Blagge and he was released immediately. The others
were burnt as heretics, and as they died piteously, there was a huge
thunderclap, inevitably interpreted by evangelicals as a mark of divine
displeasure at their deaths.

Henry had remonstrated with Wriothesley over Blagge's arrest – 'for
coming so near to him, even to his Privy Chamber'. The courtier was
one of his favourites at court and wearily bore the burden of the king's
nickname of 'my pig'. When he next saw him, he called out 'Ah, my pig!
Are you safe again?' Blagge, bowing low, replied: 'Yes, sire. And if your
majesty had not been better to me than your bishops, your pig would
have been roasted ere this time.'[82]

The king did not easily forgive the conservative faction for the conspiracy against the queen. By August, Hertford and Lisle had returned
to court and Henry began to spend more time with them. Persecution
of reformers immediately stopped. Paget, for so long Gardiner's right-
hand man, deserted him after the debacle over the queen's arrest, and
actively supported Hertford in the Privy Council.

14

Last Days of the Tyrant

Bishop Stephen Gardiner escaped punishment for his part in the failed conspiracy to burn the queen just as he had when his nephew was executed for denying the royal supremacy. Did this bombastic bishop enjoy a charmed life? Religious reformers called him 'Wily Winchester'[1] and he claimed complacently that as long as Henry lived, 'no man could do me hurt'.[2]

He survived because the king was enjoying his accustomed game of playing one faction off against another, like a malevolent puppet-master, jerking the strings to determine the fate of those around him. Henry sometimes voiced doubts over Gardiner's support for him as Supreme Governor of the Church and believed the bishop 'too wilful in his opinions and much bent to the popish party'. In later years, Paget disclosed that the king 'misliked the . . . bishop ever the worse' and 'abhorred' him 'more than any man in his realm'. The haughty prelate was blissfully unaware of this royal antipathy.

Henry could destroy the bishop at a whim. He kept a dossier on Gardiner with evidence that would commit him to the miseries of the Tower. Gloatingly, he sometimes asked Paget to produce this 'writing touching the bishop, commanding him to keep it, that he might have it when he called for it' again.[3] These documents may have concerned his treasonous negotiations with a papal legate while ambassador in Germany in 1541.[4] Henry could have 'used extremity against him' but he still prized Gardiner's experience and diplomatic skills in promoting his cause overseas.[5] The same practical considerations safeguarded Lord Chancellor Wriothesley, who suffered only the pain and indignity of having his ears boxed when he arrived in the Privy Council garden to arrest the queen.

Meanwhile, Gardiner had published the book *A Detection of the*

Devil's Sophistry that railed against the sacramentaries and Anabaptists that Henry reviled so much. The devil, wrote the bishop, tried to persuade men that death for such a cause was proof of its righteousness. Such 'stubbornness, mixed with vainglory' had brought many to a fiery death at Smithfield. 'The Anabaptists and sacramentaries have, with devilish pertinacity, manifested their heresies, whose wilful death in obstinacy... [would bring] the truth of God's scriptures... into much perplexity.'[6]

Less welcome to the king was the bishop's nostalgia for those halcyon days when England lived in 'faith, charity and devotion, when God's Word dwelt in men's hearts and never... in men's tongues' – a slighting reference to the evangelical reformers. The piety of the old religion had been swept away by 'jesters, railers, rhymers, players, jugglers, prattlers and simpering parrots [who] take upon them[selves] to be... officers to set forth God's Word' instead of ordained priests. The *Devil's Sophistry* was widely read and 'received in many places more reverently than the blessed Bible' among the king's religiously conservative subjects.

Henry's health was in rapid decline. He had celebrated his fifty-fifth birthday on 28 June 1546 – a good age for a man in Tudor times and a tribute to the increasingly desperate ministrations of the royal doctors. From the late spring, he had to be carried about in one of the 'king's trams' – an old English word for a two-shafted cart. Three were purchased, luxuriously quilted with tawny or russet silk with a Tudor double rose embroidered on the back.[7] Four beefy attendants lugged the king about and one hopes the trams had small wheels to ease their dreadful burden. The Spanish ambassador van der Delft saw Henry 'passing in his chair' at Windsor on 7 October.[8] No doubt the king gave him a cheery wave.

Henry's eyesight was also failing and from 1544, wire-framed spectacles, ten pairs at a time, were bought in Germany.[9] These would be clipped onto the nose; the repeated orders suggest the king's proclivity for losing them. His poor sight, coupled with a distaste for paperwork, created the need for a new method of approving government business.

The solution was the 'dry-stamp', employed instead of the royal autograph on state papers from September 1545. This was a wooden block with a raised royal signature that was impressed on every document. The outline would afterwards be inked in by William Clerk of the Lord Privy Seal's department. Sir Anthony Denny and John Gates were designated witnesses to the process. Because of the system's vulner-ability to abuse, these transactions were recorded by Clerk in a special ledger, examined by the king each month.[10]

Initially, the signature block, kept in a locked black leather casket, was retained by Henry himself. After his melancholy increased and attention waned, he handed its custody to Gates.

The king had meekly yielded his authority for the daily governance of his realms to his closest advisers. Forging the royal signature was high treason so, with typical Tudor assiduity, those involved were routinely retrospectively pardoned.

In September 1546, 141 documents were signed with the dry-stamp; eighty-six in October, 121 in November and sixty-four in December. Most concerned humdrum affairs of state – but some were diplomatic letters, or repayments of debts to German and Italian bankers.

Others throw light on the arcane life of Henry's court. In November, there were warrants for the Great Wardrobe to buy new dresses for Christmas for the princesses Mary and Elizabeth, and a doubling of pay for 'Richard Woodward, bagpipe player' whose music clearly delighted his monarch. Edmond Moody, the vigilant footman who had saved the king's life in 1525 when he fell headfirst into a ditch, received an annuity of £20 on 17 October, probably on retirement. George Blagge, who barely escaped execution for heresy, was appointed as Comptroller of Petty Customs in the port of London as consolation for his tribula-tions.[11]

Two entries reveal the aftermath of the king's vainglorious campaign in France. On 4 October, John Cotton, gentleman, 'maimed at the assault of Hardelot Castle', was granted an annuity for his remaining life[12] and the same month, 4d a day was granted to William Edwards, a Yeoman of the Privy Chamber, 'who has served your majesty long in the wars'.[13] These are unexpected examples of royal munificence, as the Tudor monarchy generally ignored their soldiers' and sailors' sufferings once the guns had fallen silent.

We have to scour the archives to discover the fate of relatives of those who died during Henry's last war in France. The short answer seems to be impoverishment. The London tailor David Lewes petitioned the Court of Chancery for an annual licence to beg in the streets for the family of the Welsh soldier William Dowding, killed at Boulogne.[14] William Bateman, a Herefordshire 'petty captain', who also probably died in the siege, prudently left means to support his wife, son and daughter and two illegitimate offspring, Richard and Isabel.[15] He was wise to ensure his affairs were in order, as there were court actions over property wrongfully denied dependants of soldiers who served in the Army Royal in 1544.

Hugh Mathos was forced to go to law on behalf of his grand-daughters, Joan and Alice, daughters of Richard Smythe, killed at Boulogne, to reclaim the deeds of his property at Bodenham, Herefordshire.[16] Elizabeth, daughter and heir of Thomas Briggs of London, who was pressed into service with the king's guard, also sought legal redress to regain a house and land in Cradley, Worcestershire, in 1544.[17] The following year, Anne Whitney sued in the Court of Requests to recover the goods of her late husband, a victualler to Henry's Yeomen of the Guard at the siege.[18] No doubt there were many other cases, now lost to us. The king's brothers-in-arms were never more than so much cannon fodder. Those who had died for him, or were left destitute by their menfolk's death in action, were forgotten.

While Henry remained as vexed as ever about the devious Scots and French, it became obvious to many at court that Death was casting his shadow inexorably over him.

Although treasonous, there were many predictions of his imminent death in his last years. One of the most widespread prophesies was that Henry was the 'Mouldwarp' king, 'cursed with God's own mouth'. Each of six English kings who had followed King John in 1216 was represented by an animal displaying its own characteristics. In Henry's case it was the Mouldwarp, or mole, and it was predicted that he would be driven out of England by a dragon, wolf and lion (symbolic of foreign monarchs) to live on 'an island in the sea' before finally drowning.[19]

Back in 1533, Elizabeth Amadas, estranged wife of the master of the royal jewel house, had warned that Henry was the Mouldwarp, who would be banished like the Welsh king Cadwaladr, hidden in the mists of time.[20] Her utterances were given some credence by Henry's inclusion of this dim and distant monarch's red-dragon badge into his royal heraldry. Her 'painted' book of prophecies, all of them incoherent and discordant, indicated that she was barking mad. Elizabeth also alleged that the king had tried to meet her for trysts at a courtier's home and sent her 'offerings and gifts' as love tokens.[21] Predictably, she was arrested, but her insane ramblings were recognised as more troublesome than treacherous and she was released.

The prophecy lingered on and cost another his life. Two years later, John Hale, vicar of Isleworth, Middlesex, also claimed Henry was the Mouldwarp, 'accursed of God's own mouth'. Until 'the rulers of this realm be plucked . . . we shall never live merrily in England'. These injudicious statements followed a fall off his horse and 'I was troubled in my wits, as also by age and lack of memory'.[22] A bang on the head was not enough to save him from being hanged, drawn and quartered at Tyburn on 4 May 1535. In June 1546, Robert Barker, one of the earl of Surrey's servants, was accused of listening to prophesies of the exile of the Mouldwarp.[23]

State business meanwhile continued in desultory fashion. Henry was incensed that the French were building fortifications that threatened Boulogne's harbour and ordered their destruction. These, he said, breached the Anglo-French peace treaty and such was his fury that the French ambassador feared he would 're-enter war without regard to the welfare of his realm'. Francis I immediately backed down and demolished what remained standing. The king's pleasure at his dealings with the French was greatly magnified by the arrival of 52,358 crowns and 'odd sous' (£13,100) on 2 November as the first instalment of his pension arrears.[24] There were rumours of a new war with Scotland, with warships mobilised, and Henry gave another set of visiting ambassadors from Edinburgh short shrift.

Then comes one of those madcap issues that rub shoulders with great matters of state in the Tudor period. Henry Lord Neville had been appointed a carver to the king in 1545 and had fought in Hertford's attack on Edinburgh. But the twenty-one-year-old son and heir of Ralph, fourth earl of Westmorland, was heavily in debt from gambling. Despite the penalties of the Witchcraft Act of 1542, he hired a sorcerer to change his luck. Gregory Wisdom practised medicine as an 'empiric', outside the regulatory confines of the Royal College of Physicians, and supplemented his income by wizardry. Neville was reassured by his appearance, which was 'both wise and wealthy, not in a threadbare coat . . . but well apparelled like a cunning man in his craft'.

Wisdom suggested the foolproof use of a magic ring, worked 'by the holy angels'. Neville could expect £3,000 in winnings and, in return, he demanded £20 a year for life. The nobleman offered him £10 annually after his father's death and payment by results beforehand. This was accepted and the sorcerer worked his magic with the ring in the early hours and again between five and six in the afternoon, as 'the angels could not be spared from their divine service all the day long. Therefore they must be taken before matins and after their evensong'.

Neville's first card game using the ring's magic resulted in winnings of £30. Wisdom was paid £2 and offered, in return for another £4, to 'make him play as well on the lute and virginals as any man in England'. There was no limit to this wizard's skills.

A few days later, Neville lost heavily at dice and demanded his money back. As a distraction, Wisdom reported that £2,000 was buried under a stone cross outside one of his father's towns in the north of England, as revealed by a spirit trapped within a crystal. Neville gave him £7 to find the cache, but the sorcerer returned empty-handed.

Neville was playing tennis at Whitehall when he next met Wisdom, who offered to use his magic to murder his wife Anne[25] and also announced he had 'practised the death' of his father and mother.

The young nobleman was arrested on 1 October and thrown into the Fleet on witchcraft charges. He bombarded Paget with pleas to spare his life. The sorcerer had induced him to agree to his wife's murder because 'he did not love her and was ruining his body and soul with harlots'. When she was dead, 'her soul would be saved and he could be free to marry a wife whom he loved'.[26]

Neville remained in prison and was freed only after Henry's death and the repeal of the Witchcraft Act early in Edward VI's reign. His father was ordered to pay his debts. Neville's wife died of natural causes in 1549 and he married twice again.[27] Wisdom continued his profitable business as a quack and was admitted to the Royal College of Physicians, despite opposition to his candidature.[28]

In mid-September 1546, Henry departed London for the joys of hunting near Guildford, Surrey. He could no longer pursue his quarry on horse-back. The unfortunate stag was now brought into a fenced enclosure for

Henry to kill at short range with his crossbow, as he stood unsteadily, supported by attendants.

A new French ambassador, Odet de Selve, heard that 'the king was ill', but Wriothesley insisted 'it was only a cold and [was] now cured'.[29] Two days later, the Spanish envoy was told secretly 'that the king was very ill and the physicians [had] little hope of his recovery'. But Henry was now convalescing and van der Delft[30] saw him at Windsor in early October. Paget was deputed to see de Selve on 28 October, because Henry was again indisposed.[31]

That rascal Ludovico da l'Armi wrote to the king from Venice after hearing that he 'was so ill that the doctors had no hope of his living many weeks'. His 'sorrow was turned to joy' to hear 'that the rumour was quite false'. Harvel, Henry's ambassador in Venice, had grown suspicious about da l'Armi's sinister activities. Three weeks before, Harvel had sent a messenger to London to deliver, by word of mouth, warnings about da l'Armi's 'proceedings, which the king should know'. He begged Paget to 'keep such things secret; for all that I have written of him has been disclosed to him and [he] has moved against me extremely'.[32]

After almost two months away from London, Henry returned to Whitehall in early November for medication and 'certain baths which he usually has at this season'.[33] He then moved to Otelands, Surrey, leaving behind acrimony within the Privy Council. Lisle had been banished for a month after striking Gardiner in the face during an acrimonious debate and Seymour had used 'violent and injurious words' against Wriothesley.[34] Both were rehabilitated and 'well received' by the king.

A key player in court machinations was Anthony Denny, keeper of the dry-stamp. Sir John Cheke, tutor to Prince Edward, thought Denny was 'able to mould Henry's mind, now mixing the useful with the sweet, now weaving the serious things with the light ones, great with small'.[35] His influence over the king was feared. When Sir Thomas Cheney, Treasurer of the Household, broke off his son's engagement with Denny's niece, he was warned that Henry's favourite was a man 'near about the king and one unmeet to be trifled or mocked with. Your slipping away may not only lose you friendship but cause displeasure'.[36]

Denny supported the religious radicals and was close to Cranmer, although he concealed his allegiances. The conservative Sir Thomas Heneage, the sometimes impecunious Chief Gentleman of the Privy Chamber and Groom of the Stool, was suddenly dismissed in October

1546 after a decade's service in the post and twenty years as a courtier. Denny succeeded him and William Herbert, brother-in-law to the queen, became his deputy.

Denny was keeper of the Privy Purse, which involved handling large sums of money for the king's private requirements. During the last five years of the reign, he received £243,387 1s 6d (£105 million at today's prices) for personal use by the king. This 'slush fund' was kept in locked coffers in the 'withdrawing chamber' at Whitehall and regularly topped up by revenue departments. Expenditure ranged from settlement of his gambling debts to paying for building works at Dover Castle. Henry also could not resist a little retail therapy for the beautiful things he liked to see around him. Thirteen items of gold and silver-gilt – bowls, flagons and heavy wine cups – were ordered from the royal goldsmith Morgan Wolf in March 1546 alone.[37]

The king was determined to bequeath settled dominions to his nine-year-old son, free from dangers of religious and political strife. The shape and complexion of the young king's regency government needed to be established. The first victim in the struggle for power in the aftermath of Henry's death was Bishop Gardiner.

His downfall followed his arrogant misjudgement about an exchange of land. Henry sought a parcel of Winchester's diocesan property to tidy the boundaries of a royal estate. Such exchanges were common. Cranmer surrendered thirty-six manors to the king in 1533–47 and successive archbishops of York had swapped more than twice that number. Gardiner had given up just one in thirteen years.[38]

His watching enemies may well have joyfully pounced on this crass decision, but more likely, Henry seized the opportunity to cut the bishop down to size. Either way, Gardiner paid dearly for his temerity and truculence.

A probably apocryphal story relates how the king spotted the bishop lurking awkwardly among his fellow councillors at Windsor. 'Henry turned to Wriothesley [and said:] "Did I not command you that he should come no more among you?" [Wriothesley replied:] "My lord of Winchester has come . . . with the offer of a benevolence [a voluntary tax] for the clergy."' Mollified by the prospect of revenues,

Henry accepted the offer but excluded him from council deliberations thereafter.[39] Privy Council registers indicate that Gardiner did
not attend meetings after 14 November. He might have been occupied
by Church or state business, but he was absent for the remainder of
the year.[40]

On 2 December he wrote cringingly to the king in an attempt to
heal the rift. He begged: 'Pleased [be] your most excellent majesty to
pardon me, that having no opportunity to make humble suit [in] your
presence ... I am bold to molest your majesty with this letter. [I] only
desire [your] accustomed goodness and clemency to be my good and
gracious lord.'

He would not willingly offend Henry 'for no worldly thing' and 'if
my doings or sayings to be otherwise taken in this matter of land ... I
will lament my infelicity and most humbly, on my knees, desire your
majesty to pardon it.' Gardiner insisted: 'I never said "nay" to any
request, to resist your highness' pleasure ... Because I have no access
to your majesty, I cannot forebear to open truly my heart ...'[41]

Gardiner also wrote to Paget, his erstwhile protégé in royal service,
asking him to deliver his letter personally to Henry, as he feared its
interception by his enemies. 'I hear no [details] of the king's majesty's
disappointment in this matter of lands, but that my doings are not well
taken ... I pray you send me some word.'[42]

Unknown to him, Paget, guardian of the king's secret file of papers
that hung, like the Sword of Damocles, over Gardiner's fate, had
deserted the bishop. Not for nothing was he reputed to be the 'master
of [secret] practices'.

Henry fired off a brutal response on 4 December. His letter is terse,
angry and unforgiving. 'Had your doings ... been [matched by] such
fair words as you have written, you should neither [have] had cause to
write this excuse, nor We to answer it. But We marvel at your writing
that you never said "nay" to any request for those lands, considering
that to our Chancellor [Wriothesley], Secretary [Paget] and Chancellor
of Our Court of Augmentations [Sir Edward North], [claim] you utterly
refused any conformity, saying that you would make your answer to
Our own person.'

Henry ended with a scorching phrase that bore the ring of finality.
Being 'not yet disposed to show that conformity of which you write,

We see no cause why you should molest Us further.'[43] The letter was signed with the dry-stamp.[44]

The leader of the religious conservatives at court had been neutralised but there were others who, in the eyes of Hertford, Lisle and their allies, must be destroyed by fair means or foul.

Norfolk and his son, Henry Howard, earl of Surrey, arrogantly disdained the upstart nouveau riche that thronged Henry's court – the families who, in the cutting words of that twentieth-century political jibe, were forced to buy their furniture, rather than inheriting it from their forebears.

The Howards were openly contemptuous of these 'newly arrived' men of low birth who had supplanted old noble families in the corridors of power. Up to the 1570s, the dukes of Norfolk styled themselves 'right high and mighty princes' in official documents and lived in palaces in East Anglia. The Howards were among the last to cling onto the hated medieval feudal system and their stewards regularly charged their servile bondsmen – Norfolk cosily referred to them as 'my own folk' – for his ducal permission to move home, or for their daughters to marry.

Surrey seems a thoroughly objectionable figure to modern eyes, as he was to many contemporaries. He was vain, conceited and quick to anger over suspected slights to his status or honour. The earl was an extraordinary paradox: a sensitive, eloquent and moving poet one moment, the next, transformed into a rowdy hooligan and proud coxcomb, whose bumptious behaviour affronted those unfortunate to be near him. The king had loved 'this most foolish proud boy [in all] England',[45] because in his youth, Surrey had spent two happy years at Windsor Castle sharing his schooling with the king's bastard, Henry Fitzroy, who later married his sister Mary.

That uncontrollable temper landed Surrey in trouble with the authorities, particularly for any fracas within the court precincts or its verge – a zone twelve miles (19km) around wherever the king was staying, regulated by its own laws, enforced by its own court. Aged nineteen, the earl was imprisoned at Windsor for two weeks in March 1536 for striking Seymour in the face after he alleged that Surrey sympathised with the Pilgrimage of Grace rebels. That row probably was sparked by his unwanted flirtations with Seymour's wife. Then in July 1542, the earl challenged Sir John Leigh, another member of the royal household, to a duel. He was again jailed, this time in the Fleet Prison, for a few weeks and was only freed after paying the huge sum of £6,666 as a surety for his good behaviour, or (in his words) to 'bridle my heady will'.[46]

Seven months later, Surrey and a party of young bucks staged a minor riot in the City of London. After a night's heavy drinking, they armed themselves with hunting crossbows (which fired stones) and smashed the windows of houses and nearby churches. Taking to a rowing boat on the Thames, they had huge fun firing potshots at the prostitutes plying their trade outside the brothels or 'stews' on Bankside in Southwark. Complaints from the Lord Mayor of London about these jolly japes reached the Privy Council and their investigations rooted out a Mistress Millicent Arundell of Cheapside, at whose house Surrey and his debauched friends had spent the night of the riot.

She swore that the earl 'and other young noblemen frequented her house, eating meat in Lent and committing other improprieties. At Candlemas, they went out with stone bows at nine o'clock at night and did not come back till past midnight. The next day there was great clamour [about] the breaking of many glass windows ... and shooting at men that night in the street. The [word] was these hurts were done by my lord and his company ...'[47]

Surrey was up before the Privy Council again, this time charged with eating forbidden flesh in Lent and on Fridays and behaving in the London streets 'in a lewd and unseemly manner'. He enjoyed a special licence to eat meat during religious fasts but pleaded guilty to the second charge, claiming he only broke the windows of papists' houses. He was back in the Fleet but was freed the following month.

To avoid further trouble, Norfolk packed him off to the wars in Europe and we have already learnt of his martial exploits at Montreuil and Boulogne and his subsequent fury at being displaced from his command by Hertford.

The earl returned home in June 1546, full of angry spleen, but still encumbered by debts. He was also 'scarce reconciled' with his father over the duke's manoeuvres over his letters to Henry. That October, Surrey wrote to Paget about the former Benedictine priory of Christchurch, Norwich, which could 'discharge me out of the misery of debt'. If Henry 'were to give it me, I will faithfully promise never to trouble his majesty with any suit of profit hereafter'.[48]

He came to court to press his case for the priory, but at the beginning of December, the Privy Council heard incriminating information about him from the courtier Sir Richard Southwell, Surrey's old comrade-in-arms at Boulogne.[49] His accuser was no paragon of virtue; he had paid out £1,000 for a pardon for his involvement in the murder of a Norfolk magistrate in 1531. Southwell now had damning evidence about 'the earl that touched his fidelity to the king'.[50] Surrey had also written 'a letter, full of threats to a gentleman'. Southwell was held for questioning and Sir Anthony Wingfield, Captain of the King's Guard, was ordered to arrest the earl.

The next day, Thursday, 2 December, Wingfield was in the great hall at Whitehall. 'He had a dozen halberdiers waiting in an adjoining corridor and approaching [Surrey], said: "I wish to ask you to intercede for me with the duke, your father, in a matter in which I need his favour, if you would deign to listen to me." So he led him to the corridor and the halberdiers took him... without attracting notice.'[51]

Surrey was taken, not to the Tower, but to Wriothesley's home in Ely Place. He 'vehemently affirmed himself a true man, desired to be tried by justice, or else, fight in his shirt' with Southwell. Such bluster was wasted breath. His interrogators knew that the king had not only withdrawn 'much of his wonted favour' from the Howards, 'but promised immunity to [any who] could discover' anything damaging to them.[52] There was talk of a conspiracy against the crown, revealed by two gentlemen in exchange for this indemnity from prosecution. After cutting down Gardiner, Henry had become the instrument of destruction for the Howards, father and son.

Norfolk had been at Kenninghall since early November and news of his son's arrest reached him by special messenger. The duke wrote urgently to friends at court for information but his letters were intercepted. Norfolk was summoned to London.

He arrived on Sunday, 12 December, and was arrested at Whitehall. In a humiliating reprise of Cromwell's downfall six years before, Norfolk was degraded as Lord High Treasurer and stripped of his white wand of office and his Garter insignia. He was taken by boat to the Tower and 'both in the barge and on entering' the fortress, loudly declared 'that no person had been carried thither before who was a more loyal servant [of the king] than he was and always had been'. His protests were studiously ignored.

At the same time, Surrey was marched through the London streets to the same forbidding destination, his humiliating progress marked by his anger and 'great lamentation'.[53]

Between three and four o'clock that Sunday afternoon, a party of horsemen left London post-haste for Norfolk's palace in Norfolk. They were led by John Gates, his brother-in-law Sir Wymond Carew and Southwell, freed from custody. They arrived at Thetford on Monday night and were outside the porter's lodge at Kenninghall, seven miles (11km) away, by dawn the following morning.

News of Norfolk's and Surrey's arrests had not yet penetrated the bucolic calm of Norfolk. Like a secret police raid, they hammered on the doors of the silent palace and were admitted by a sleepy Henry Symonds, the duke's almoner. The entrances were secured and Mary, duchess of Richmond, and Norfolk's mistress Bessie Holland, who had only just risen, were ordered to the dining room for interrogation.

After Fitzroy's death, Mary had suffered penury through Henry's meanness over her marriage jointure, only relieved by grudging grants made after 1540. Now twenty-seven, she possessed radical religious beliefs and had 'grown [into] an extreme enemy of her brother'.[54] Shocked and dishevelled, she was 'sore perplexed, trembling and like to fall down' but recovered enough to sink to her knees.

Gates and his colleagues that night reported her little speech to Henry. 'Although nature constrained her sore to love her father, whom she had ever thought a true and faithful subject and also to desire the well-[being] of his son, yet she would not hide or conceal any[thing] from your majesty's knowledge.' They searched her apartments but discovered 'no writing worth sending'. The duchess's possessions were also not worth much to write home about. 'Her chambers and coffers [were] so bare, as your majesty would hardly think. Her jewels, such as she had, [all] sold or [pawned] to pay her debts...'

Then the investigators turned their attentions to blousy Bessie Holland, who, because of the duke's doting largesse, possessed a wealth of pretty trinkets and baubles, including gold brooches bearing Our Lord in Pity, the Holy Trinity and more romantically, Cupid. 'We have found girdles, beads, buttons of gold, pearl and rings set with stones, whereof, with all other things, we [will] make a book to be sent to your highness.' Trusted servants were sent to the other Howard properties in East Anglia 'to prevent embezzlement', including Bessie's new-built

house in Suffolk 'which is thought to be well furnished with stuff'.
Norfolk's letters and documents were 'diligently perused'.

Both women were told to travel to London for further questioning 'in
the morning or the next day at the latest'. There remained Surrey's wife
Frances, pregnant with their fifth child, who was 'looking to her time
to lie in at this next Candlemas' (2 February). She lived at Kenninghall
with her children and 'the women in the nursery attending upon them'.
What should Gates do with them?[55]

Henry's investigators methodically inventoried all the duke's possessions at Kenninghall and at Castle Rising, another ducal seat in Norfolk,
down to the horses in the stable (including an old nag called 'Button')
and the stocks of salted fish in his larder. The same process continued
at Surrey's mansion at St Leonard's, outside Norwich.[56] Eventually, the
pregnant Frances Howard was sent away, one of Norfolk's worthless
old nightgowns 'much worn and furred with coney and lamb' wrapped
around her legs against the winter chill.[57]

The duke's income from his official appointments was also totted up.
This amounted to more than £700 a year (£301,400 in today's money),
the most lucrative being the fees of £365 as Lord High Treasurer and
£20 as Earl Marshal.[58]

Henry was still at Otelands but had fallen ill again about 10 December.
An audience with de Selve was delayed because he had such a bad cold
'that he could not speak' but was well enough to go 'daily to the fields'
for hunting.[59] The king later told van der Delft that he had suffered a
'sharp attack of the fever which lasted in the burning stage for thirty
hours, but now he was quite restored'. The ambassador did not believe
him: 'His colour does not bear out [this] statement and he looks to me
greatly fallen away.'[60]

Back in London, Surrey had been told of his father's arrest and wrote
a one-page letter to the Privy Council with an impudent request. 'Since
the beginning of my [imprisonment], the displeasure of my master . . .
with my sorrow to see the long approved truth of my old father brought
into question by any stir between Southwell and me, has sore enfeebled
me.' He recalled his appearance before the Council over his nocturnal hi-jinks in London and sought the same sympathetic quartet of

councillors (Wriothesley, John, Lord Russell, Bishop Gardiner and Sir Anthony Browne), to investigate these latest accusations. 'My desire is you four, and only you, may be sent to me, for so it [should be best for his] majesty's service, to whom I intend to discharge [my conscience]...'[61]

Prisoners in the Tower were in no position to make such demands and Surrey had not heard of Gardiner's downfall. Neither did he realise that Wriothesley, following Paget's example, had also changed sides, recognising that his future now lay with the Seymours.

Probably on the same day, a bewildered Norfolk, lodged in two rooms of the Constable's apartments in the Tower, wrote to Henry, begging for mercy, once again 'prostrate' at his feet. The duke believed himself the victim of some wicked plot. 'I am sure some great enemy of mine has informed your majesty of some untrue matter against me. God knows, in all my life, I never thought one untrue thought against you, or your succession, nor can no more judge... what should be laid to my charge, than the [innocent] child that was born this night.'

Norfolk bullishly wanted to confront his accusers and face down their allegations. 'Then, if I shall not make it apparent that I am wrong... let me have punishment according to my deserts... Most merciful prince... let me not be cast away by false enemies' information.'

If not a conspiracy against him, Norfolk feared he was imprisoned because of his conservative religious beliefs. 'I know not that I have offended any man... unless it were [those who] are angry with me for being quick against... sacramentaries. And as for all causes of religion... I know you to be a prince of such virtue and knowledge that whatever laws you have in times past made... I shall to the extremity of my power stick to them as long as my life shall last...' The seventy-three-year-old duke, alone and frightened, begged for Henry's pity, the return of his 'gracious favour' and the charges against him to be revealed.

He also asked the Council to send books from his house at Lambeth for him to read 'ere I fall to sleep and after I wake again, [for] I cannot sleep, nor did not this dozen years.' Could he walk in his rooms' ante-chamber for exercise, while 'in the night to be locked in?' Finally, there was a mundane request for clean sheets for his bed.[62]

In the black night of his despair, Norfolk jotted down his rambling thoughts in a pathetic letter to the Privy Council. He was no closet papist, since the pope was 'the king's enemy'. The duke was haunted by the grinning spectres of his old enemies. 'My lords, I trust you think Cromwell's service and mine are not [too] like... He was a false man, and surely, I am a true, poor gentleman'. There was his old adversary Cardinal Wolsey who 'for fourteen years [sought] to destroy me'. Buckingham, his father-in-law, 'of all men living... hated me the most, thinking I was the man that hurt him the most to the king's majesty' and his brother-in-law, Thomas Boleyn, father of Anne, 'who confessed the same and wished he [could] thrust his dagger in me'. There was the 'malice borne me by both my nieces whom it pleased the king to marry'.

So much loathing, so much malignancy; no wonder the dark corners of his remembrance provoked night terrors. 'I have always shown myself a true man to my sovereign and have received more profits of his highness than before. Who could think that I should now be false? Poor man as I am yet, I am his near kinsman. For whose sake should I be untrue'? he asked wretchedly.[63]

Wriothesley told the ambassadors that Norfolk and his son planned by 'sinister means' to 'obtain the government of the king, who was too old to be governed, by murdering all the council and taking control of the prince by them alone'.[64]

His investigation gathered pace with depositions taken from the Howards' enemies. One of their kith and kin, Sir Edmund Knyvett, who had fallen out with Norfolk, was suspicious about the Italians in Surrey's household. He believed his cousin's conversations with them included 'some ill device' and one servant, possibly Thomas Fryer,[65] 'had been with Cardinal Pole in Italy' and 'was received again on his return'. The earl also employed an Italian jester named 'Pasquil' who 'was more likely a spy and so reputed'.[66]

You will recall from Chapter 7 that Norfolk had sought a marriage alliance with the Seymours: his daughter Mary would wed Sir Thomas Seymour. Surrey's children and those of his second son Lord Thomas Howard could marry Hertford's offspring. But Surrey's plans were more ambitious. His sister told Sir Gawain Carew of 'as strange a practice of her brother's as ever he heard of'. Surrey had suggested that she should prevaricate over the match with Sir Thomas Seymour to allow time for the king 'to cast some love unto her, whereby... she should bear as great [influence] about him as Madame d'Étampes does about the

French king.'[67] The Howard penchant for offering their young women as royal mistresses was as strong as ever, despite their lamentable record of failures. The duchess was incensed and told Surrey that 'they should perish and she would cut her own throat, rather than consent to such a villainy'.[68]

Surrey had other aspirations for family power. George Blagge quarrelled with him over his claim that Norfolk was 'the meetest' for the regency after Edward came to the throne, 'both for good services done and for estate'. Blagge 'trusted never to see that day' and should it happen 'then the prince [would be] evil taught ... Rather than it should come to pass that the prince should be under the government of your father or you, I would ... thrust this dagger in you.'[69]

Mary, duchess of Richmond, may have become 'bitter, eager to do anything to harm her brother'.[70] She confirmed her father's plan to marry her off to Sir Thomas Seymour, but the match was unwelcome to her brother who had snapped: 'These new men loved no nobility and if God called away the king, they should smart for it.'[71] Norfolk's mistress Bessie Holland repeated her lover's belief that 'none of the Council loved him because they were no noblemen themselves [and] because he believed too truly in the Sacrament of the Altar [the Eucharist].' Norfolk told her that Henry 'was much grown of his body and that he could not go up and down stairs, but was let up and down by a device. His majesty was sickly and could not long endure and that the realm [is] like to be in an ill case through diversity of opinions.'[72]

All this was hearsay, gossip, even pillow talk and, aside from the treason of predicting the king's death, was only testimony to just how insufferably snobbish the Howards were. It did not amount to hard evidence to put before even a rigged jury. Something more damning was required to seal the fates of Norfolk and Surrey.

The duchess of Richmond probably disclosed the obscure heraldic issue that was to prove her brother's downfall. She blurted out a description of her brother's new coat of arms. 'Instead of the duke's coronet was put ... a Cap of Maintenance[73] [in] purple, with powdered fur, and with a crown ... Underneath the arms was a cipher which she took to be the king's cipher "HR" [*Henricus Rex*].'[74] Surrey had reassumed the arms of their grandfather, Edward Stafford, third duke of Buckingham, attainted and executed for treason by Henry twenty-five years before. (These were the royal arms inherited from Thomas of Woodstock,

The portrait of Henry Howard, earl of Surrey, painted in 1546 by an unknown Italian artist, which was used as evidence to convict him of treason – his claim to bear royal arms. His arrogance and self-esteem cost him his head, the last man to be executed in Henry VIII's reign.

first duke of Gloucester, the youngest surviving son of Edward III who was murdered in 1397). Surrey had therefore implicitly repudiated Buckingham's attainder and reinstated a latent claim to the crown of England.[75] Moreover, he included the arms of the Saxon king St Edward the Confessor which had been granted to Thomas Mowbray, first duke of Norfolk, by Richard II, of whom the Howards were successors.

One piece of physical evidence against Surrey was his new portrait, depicting him in a gorgeous doublet, leaning nonchalantly against a broken pillar inscribed with the words *sat super*, 'enough remains'.[76] He is flanked by two *arabesques*, holding shields, one of which bears the arms of Thomas Woodstock. Although the earl was entitled to this heraldry, the portrait appears to be an allegory representing his royal descent from Edward the Confessor and Edward III.[77] Surrey's pride and egomania proved his undoing.

On 23 December, Henry returned to Whitehall via his huge new palace at Nonsuch, near Ewell, Surrey, still suffering from 'some grief of his leg' and a fever. The Spanish ambassador reported that the king is 'so unwell that, considering his age and corpulence, he may not survive another attack, such as he recently had at Windsor'.

The accounts of Thomas Alsop, chief apothecary, had grown steadily larger over the previous five months as potions and medicines were more frequently prescribed. These totalled £5 (£2,153 in today's values) in August, rising to £25 in December. These included fomentations, glisters, plasters and sponges for the stomach and anus and eyebright water for bathing the eyes. This bewildering array of concoctions, listed in dog Latin, yield few clues about what was being used to ease the king's sufferings, aside from the increasing use of the phrase *ut patet* – 'to be clear' – which implies the prescription was a new one and that it had been copied for inspection.[78] There is a whiff of desperation in the doctors' efforts to keep Henry alive, mingled with the foul stench of his legs.

The king was now 'secluded at court, all but his councillors and three or four gentlemen of the chamber being denied entrance'. Unusually, the queen and the court were packed off to Greenwich for Christmas so that Henry could supervise Norfolk and Surrey's prosecution without

distraction. Van der Delft was told that the investigations would preclude any audience, so to discover whether this was a pretext to hide
his poor health, the envoy sent a servant to court. He had 'learnt from
a friend that the king was not at all well, although he had seen him
dressed the previous day'.

The ambassador recognised the ascendancy of the Seymours and
Lisle at court and heard rumours 'that the custody of the prince and
the government of the realm will be entrusted to them. The misfortunes
of the house of Norfolk may come from that quarter.' Their supporters
also 'do not conceal their wish to see the bishop of Winchester and
other adherents of the ancient faith sent to the Tower to keep company
with the duke of Norfolk'.[79]

Wriothesley drew up a list of questions to be put to Surrey: If 'the
king should die in my lord prince's tender age, whether you have
devised who should govern him and the realm?' 'Whether you procured any person to [deceive] . . . the king's majesty [with] the intent
that the same might grow in his favour?' This last question had been
amended as Wriothesley's draft had read: '. . . procured your sister or
any other woman to be the king's concubine or not?'[80]

Sitting in his study within the dark and silent palace, spectacles
perched on his nose, Henry carefully annotated the questions in bold
capitals: 'If a man [craftily planning] TO GOVERN THE REALM, DO
ACTUALLY GO ABOUT TO RULE THE KING and should, for that
purpose, advise his daughter, or sister, to become his harlot, THINK-
ING THEREBY TO BRING IT TO PASS AND SO WOULD RULE BOTH
FATHER AND SON.'[81]

With daily interrogations, Surrey's frustration must have driven him
to desperation. Within his accommodation in St Thomas's Tower was
a vertical shaft, built as a garderobe, or lavatory, that emptied into the
tidal moat below.[82] One contemporary report claimed the earl asked his
servant to smuggle a dagger into his room, hidden in his breeches, for
use in an escape. Surrey would clamber down the lavatory shaft, cross
the moat at low tide, and get away by a boat in St Katherine's Dock on
the Thames. At midnight, he began his descent down the shaft but was
caught by the arm by a guard. The alarm was raised and shackles placed
on Surrey's legs. 'The servant who had taken the boat went away with
[the earl's] money and nothing more was heard of him.'[83]

There is evidence that provides some corroboration. The accounts of Sir Walter Stonor, newly appointed Lieutenant of the Tower, list an 'allowance for the earl's irons – £13 6s 8d' – probably the shackles mentioned in this report. They also include payments for a new black satin coat, trimmed with rabbit fur, bought 'against [Surrey's] arraignment'.[84]

On 12 January 1547, his father scuppered any lingering hopes of survival that Surrey might have retained. Norfolk abjectly admitted that his son had adopted the arms of St Edward the Confessor and that he had wilfully concealed his treason. The confession, made 'without compulsion, without force, without advice or counsel',[85] would have been dictated to him. In the faint hope of saving his own head, all he had to do was to sign it. The duke, whose loyalties to his nearest and dearest always vanished when he was endangered, willingly put pen to paper.

As well as the heraldic offences and misprision, Norfolk confessed to 'disclosing and opening of [the king's] private and most secret counsel at sundry times, to the great peril of his royal highness'. This crime of revealing state secrets probably emanates from the testimony of a spy called John Torre, who alleged that Norfolk and his half-brother William paid night-time visits to the former French ambassador Charles de Marillac between May 1541 and late 1542.[86] While Norfolk was notoriously pro-French in his political beliefs – he received an annuity from France for years – these visits were made on the king's orders. The charge was included as a makeweight, and any allegations of treachery involving the French would blacken his name.

The next day Surrey was arraigned at the Guildhall. He was preceded by the black-coated executioner, carrying his axe with the sharp blade turned away from the prisoner. The judges included his enemies Hertford, Wriothesley and Paget, sitting as commissioners. The earl pleaded not guilty to treason charges of usurping and displaying the arms of Edward the Confessor, former king of England.

The trial continued into the late gloom of a January afternoon, with the jury retiring at five to consider their verdict after eight hours of evidence and petulant cross-examination. Paget scurried away to report events to the king at Whitehall and returned an hour later, possibly with a royal message for the jurymen. They returned soon afterwards and declared a 'guilty' verdict, with the chilling rider 'and he should die'.[87] The court erupted and it was some time before order could be restored.

The headsman now turned his axe blade to face Surrey, who shouted defiantly at the jury: 'Of what have you found me guilty? Surely you find no law that justifies you! But I know the king wants to get rid of the noble blood around him and employ none but low people.'[88] Wriothesley then pronounced sentence: death by hanging, drawing and quartering at Tyburn.

On 19 January 1547, Surrey was executed at Tower Hill, the sentence again being commuted to beheading. He was buried in the church of All Hallows, close by in Upper Thames Street.[89]

Henry turned to pressing personal matters. On the evening of 26 December, he decided to revise the will he had made before invading France in 1544. Paget was told to draft a new version, inserting the names, as executors, of 'some that were not named before and to put out the bishop of Winchester's name ... a wilful man, not meet to be about his son, nor trouble his Council any more'.[90] Thomas Thirlby, bishop of Westminster, was also deleted because 'he was schooled' by Gardiner. The executors, who would become his son Edward's councillors, included Cranmer, Wriothesley, William Paulet, Lord St John, Russell, Hertford, Lisle, Cuthbert Tunstall, bishop of Durham, Sir Anthony Browne and Paget.

Browne, an ally of Gardiner's, tried to restore him in Henry's favour. He went to the king's bedchamber, which measured forty feet by twenty (12 x 6m) and was hung with scarlet wool hangings and furnished with red footstools. The king's great bed, with red silk hangings and curtains embroidered with gold thread, pearls and blue gemstones, had been enlarged in March 1543 because of his increased bulk.[91]

The courtier, kneeling by the bed, cautiously suggested that Gardiner's name had been mistakenly omitted from the will. Without the bishop, he added, 'the rest shall not be able to [decide] your great and weighty affairs committed to them'. Henry's faculties were as sharp as ever and he was not going to be dragooned. 'Hold your peace!' he snapped. 'I remember him well enough and, of good purpose, have left him out. Surely, if he were in my testament and one of you, he would encumber you all and you would never rule him, he is so troublesome a nature. I could use him and rule him [in] all manner of purposes, as it seemed good to me – but so shall you never do.'

When Browne tried to raise the issue again, the king angrily told him: 'Have you not yet done . . . to molest me in this matter? If you will not cease to trouble me, by the faith of God, I will surely dispatch you out of my will also. Therefore, let Us hear no more.'[92]

Paget had completed writing the twenty-eight pages of the new will by 30 December. Henry hoped that his final testament would be acceptable to 'Almighty God, Our only Saviour Jesus Christ and the whole company of Heaven and the due satisfaction of all godly brethren on earth.'[93] He bequeathed his soul to 'Almighty God, who in the person of the Son, redeemed the same with His most precious Body and Blood in [the] time of his passion. And for Our better remembrance, have left here with Us in his church militant, the consecration and administration of His precious Body and Blood to Our no little consolation.' With total self-confidence, he 'instantly require[d] and desire[d] the Blessed Virgin Mary, His mother, with all the company of heaven continually to pray for Us and with Us, while We live in this world and in the time of pass[ing] out of the same.'[94]

The vital issue of the succession was carefully spelt out. The Imperial crown and the realms of England, Ireland and the title of France, followed the terms of the Act of Succession of 1544. These would pass directly to Edward and then to any lawful heirs of his body and, in default, to Henry's daughter Mary and her heirs, 'upon condition that she will not marry without the written permission and sealed consent of a majority' of Edward's surviving Privy Council. In the event of her death without children, the crown would pass to Elizabeth, with similar conditions placed on her marriage. If none of this was applicable, the succession would be settled on the heirs of Lady Frances, eldest daughter of Henry's late sister Mary, or to the fifth in line, Lady Frances' sister, Lady Eleanor.[95]

Together with the crown, Edward was left all Henry's plate and 'household stuff', artillery and other ordnance, warships, money and jewels – valued at an estimated £1,200,000[96] or £517 million at 2019 prices.[97] Debts – and Henry, in a remarkable lapse of memory, knew of none – were his executors' first duty to settle after his burial.

He bequeathed £10,000 in money, jewels and plate to each of his daughters for their marriage and both would have £3,000 a year from the hour of his death. The queen was to have £3,000 in plate, jewels and household goods and to take what she liked of what she already possessed. She would further receive £1,000 in cash in addition to the enjoyment of her marriage jointure – the estate settled on her during her lifetime after the king's death.[98]

The will was signed with the dry-stamp and its eleven witnesses included his doctors – Wendy, Owen and Huicke – presumably enabling them to testify that the king was of sound mind. Another signature – 'Patrec' – was probably that of Patrick Reynolds, an additional apothecary appointed at Michaelmas 1546.[99] Others included the ubiquitous John Gates and William Clerk, keeper of the dry-stamp.

Predictably, the use of the stamp has raised questions about the timing of Henry's validation of the will, or, indeed, if new clauses or content were inserted after his approval. What has reinforced this conjecture was the fact that the will appears as the penultimate item in Clerk's register of stamped documents for January 1547, a month late. He must have already prepared the schedule for that month when it was realised that both the will and the royal assent to Surrey's and Norfolk's attainder had been forgotten. An extra piece of parchment, 100mm in depth, was stuck onto the last page containing these two entries, plus Clerk's own signature. The conspiracy theorist would point out that the king was in no fit state to inspect this register in late January. Was this merely forgetfulness, which seems unlikely, or incompetence, which again seems improbable? Conspiracy or cock-up? The resolution of this mystery seems unlikely ever to emerge.

For Henry, after all those years of brutality and tyranny, it was now time to meet his Maker.

15

Ashes to Ashes

Henry had demonstrated his habitual ruthlessness in neutralising the threat to his son apparently posed by Surrey and Norfolk. Although falling ill again at the end of December, he was still well enough to handle the daily business of the Tudor state. Later, as he took to his bed and began to lapse in and out of consciousness, there were some at court who spotted a final opportunity for personal enrichment during the last days of the old despot.

At the Privy Council meeting on 27 December, there were hard words about the failure of the laggard English administration in Boulogne to supply information about the garrison's strength, its stock of rations and how much money was available for pay and other expenses. The king had 'marvelled not a little that they had been remiss in neglecting so special a point, [as] these four months, they had reported nothing touching these matters ... of such importance'. Sharp reprimands were sent to Boulogne. Two days later, the President and Council of the North of England were informed of a rare royal pardon of two convicted sacramentaries. These heretics should now recant publicly 'and forsake their former opinions'.[1] Two government agencies, the Court of Augmentations and the Court of General Surveyors of the King's Lands, 'in which there has been great disorder', were merged on 1 January 1547. Sir Edward North was appointed Chancellor, together with a string of officials to administer the new court.[2]

Royal properties and sequestered monastic land continued to be sold off to offset the considerable remaining royal debts. Four properties were disposed of that December, realising £1,410, and a further six in January, contributing £4,511.[3]

On 23 January, Paget announced that the king, remembering the 'good service of Sir Thomas Seymour and minding to have him trained in the knowledge of his majesty's council', had appointed him a member. He was immediately sworn in by Lord Chancellor Wriothesley. Lisle had a different recollection of Henry's opinion about his former rival for Katherine Parr's affections. He told how the king, on his 'deathbed, and hearing [Seymour's] name amongst those elected to the council, cried out "No, no!" though his breath was failing him'. Silver-tongued Hertford had changed Henry's mind.[4]

Trepidation gripped those courtiers who attended the king in Whitehall's empty galleries and chambers. Sick as he was, Henry remained implacable in his long-held principle that 'fear begets obedience'. Following Gardiner's banishment and Surrey and Norfolk's downfalls, most lived in mortal dread that even in his last hours, Henry would punish any hint of disloyalty or treason among those around him.

As always, at least his malevolence was equitable in his manipulation of the factions at court, even though the reformists had finally gained the upper hand. Paget still kept Gardiner's dossier close to hand, but he also had another file secreted away with the names of 'many men . . . in a catalogue, accused to the king by the bishop of Winchester and other prelates'.[5] Such was the anxiety about Henry's final reckoning that no councillor dared advise the king honestly or 'tell him his mind', for fear that a 'snare had been laid for him'.[6]

Perhaps with an old man's forlorn optimism, Henry was still buying items for future enjoyment, such as the thirty-four pieces of glassware, bought on 24 December, which included a silver and gilt pot and sets of gilt wine cups.[7] On 20 January, Denny, Herbert and Gates delivered 'gold, rings and precious stones' from the secret jewel house at Whitehall to the goldsmith Everard Everdayce for 'garnishing a porcelain cup and a gripe's egg'[8] for the king.[9]

There was a £20 order for 'apple trees and setts [cuttings or bedding plants]' from France for his privy gardens.[10] A passport was issued for John de Leu, a priest who was also royal gardener at Hampton Court, to collect them.[11] On 14 January, £60 was paid to Nicholas Dowsing, keeper of Greenwich manor, for new gardens and orchards to be laid out there for the king.[12]

More prosaically, William Green presented a £4 bill for making and delivering a new close stool, covered in black velvet, with a silk fringe and ribbons. Three pounds (1.4kg) of (?duck) down was used for stuffing its seat and armrests for royal comfort.[13]

On 27 December, the Imperial ambassador van der Delft reported the king in better health and anticipating a meeting with his French counterpart. Then Henry suffered a severe relapse.[14]

At the turn of the year, de Selve, the French ambassador, had been 'waiting from day to day to speak with the king' but his audiences had been postponed repeatedly by Paget because Henry was suffering from yet another 'indisposition of the legs'.[15] A week later, de Selve noted that he 'has been so ill for the past fifteen days that he was reported dead. Many people here still believe him so . . . seeing that . . . few persons have access to his lodging and chamber'. He thought the king 'has been very ill and is scarcely well yet'.[16]

However, well-bribed sources told him on 9 January that Henry had rallied after surviving 'great danger owing to his legs'. The royal physicians had cauterised them with sizzling hot irons to burn away infected tissue. In his great agony, the king had 'let himself be seen by very few persons. Neither the queen nor the Lady Mary could see him, nor do we know that they will now do so.' De Selve had 'great reason to conjecture that, whatever his health, it can only be bad and will not last long,' he warned Francis I.[17] The same day, van der Delft promised Mary, regent of the Netherlands: 'When I have an opportunity of access to the king, I will not fail to fulfil your majesty's orders. There is no [immediate] possibility of my obtaining an audience, owing to his indisposition.'[18]

Queen Katherine apparently returned to Whitehall from Greenwich around this time, as she wrote a letter from the palace in reply to one from Prince Edward at Hertford, congratulating him on the elegance of his prose and his diligence in his Latin studies.[19]

On 17 January, both the French and Spanish ambassadors were finally allowed meetings with Henry; van der Delft the first to enter the king's chamber. His interview was brief, and according to Wriothesley, he emerged a disappointed man, having failed to achieve any diplomatic objective. De Selve followed him and thought the king 'fairly well', although Henry needed Paget's prompting to remind him of details. But the old fox had not lost his skills in double-dealing. Henry refused to disclose his terms for an agreement on new French fortifications near Boulogne, until Francis had shown his hand first. Discussion then turned to measures to reduce Anglo-French tensions, and the king declared that he had 'approved of none', but always favoured 'a closer amity – such as a defensive league'.²⁰ These two diplomatic meetings were the last time the king was seen by anyone from outside the court.

Two days later, Henry was overseeing plans for the investiture of Edward as Prince of Wales.

As the shadows gathered around Henry, his closest advisers' fears were eased by expectations of new riches and status, after he had told Paget that the huge Howard estates would be 'liberally dispersed and given to noblemen and others [who were] his good servants'. The king also believed that England's nobility 'was greatly decayed, some by attainders, some by their own misgovernance and riotous wasting, [and] some by sickness'. (Was this some kind of macabre joke? After all, Henry was responsible for a good number of the aristocracy losing their heads.) Anyway, he 'devised the advancement of some to higher places of honour' to mark his gratitude for their loyalty.

The names of those who would receive such bountiful generosity were jotted down by Paget in a small notebook after consulting his sovereign. Hertford would be a duke; Lisle, Wriothesley, Lord St John and Lord Russell created earls and Sir Thomas Seymour and Sir Richard Rich would become barons, all receiving additional income from grants of land. However, the Chief Secretary considered the suggested amounts too miserly and also pointed out that the king had forgotten the faithful Anthony Denny, despite his daily 'painful [assiduous] service' to him. Paget suggested that Henry should grant him the Benedictine priory of Bungay in Suffolk.

Henry had not lost his mordant sense of humour, nor his delight in toying with his advisers, like a cat with a trapped mouse.

He suggested that Paget should ask his colleagues to determine what they believed would be suitable revenues, commensurate with their new status in Tudor society. This task completed, he discovered to his horror that the king had changed his mind overnight. Henry would not give away any of the Howard estates 'except certain [lands] in Sussex and Kent, but would keep them all to himself'. Alternative distributions of titles and lands were considered and ultimately, a final list was drawn up which Paget read out to Henry. Afterwards, the king took the sheet and tucked it into the 'pooke', or pocket, of his voluminous white nightshirt.

With Henry's permission, the secretary scurried off to tell the happy recipients that their hopes of reward had been realised.

The list was never seen again. Henry had enjoyed his last laugh.

After the king's death, Paget had to reconstruct the contents of that list. He was blessed with an excellent memory and those who survived the reign boldly rewarded themselves with lands worth a total of £108,000 in annual income, or £59 million at present-day prices.[21] These included £200 income from lands and the priory at Bungay for Denny; £260 a year to William Herbert (which the king had 'promised him to help him out of debt') and £66 to John Gates.

Three witnesses who testified against Surrey were also abundantly rewarded. Sir Richard Southwell was created Keeper of Kenninghall and its estate and steward of all Norfolk's lands in the county, for his loyalty in bringing down the Howards. Sir Edmund Knyvett was granted the lordship of Wymondham and Sir Edward Warner that of Castle Acre, both in Norfolk.

An undignified scramble to acquire appointments or sinecures from the dying old ogre followed.

Paget was allowed a parliamentary Bill, passed in the dying days of the session, for 'the better assurance' of the king's grant to him of lordships, manors and parks. Sir William Herbert was given manors in Wiltshire, once owned by the Benedictine abbey at Wilton, with an annual income of £120.[22] Sir Anthony Browne was appointed Standard-bearer of England on 1 January with an annual fee of £100, together with properties and lands in Cambridgeshire, Essex, Kent and Sussex. Henry's doctor, Walter Cromer, received a chantry and lands in South Mimms, Hertfordshire, 'for his services' to the king.[23] His goldsmith, Morgan Wolfe, who became rich by fulfilling the king's passion for buying expensive baubles, was given Chepstow priory and various manors in Monmouthshire.[24]

John Gates did particularly well. He was appointed Keeper of the Southwark mansion and park formerly owned by Charles Brandon, duke of Suffolk, and became Bailiff of the Liberty of Southwark and Chief Steward of the lands of St Mary Overie, formerly an Augustinian priory near London Bridge. The same day he was granted the site of

Thomas Becket's hospital in Southwark and its ancillary properties in Surrey and Essex. On 27 January, Gates was also made Under-steward, Clerk of the Forest and Clerk of the Swainmote Court[25] of Waltham Forest in Essex.

More junior figures at court felt emboldened enough to dip their own questing fingers into the royal honeypot of fortune. Agnes Harrison, the king's laundress, received the Vine Garden and lands called Millbank within Westminster Abbey's precincts. John Jocelyn, Serjeant of the Pantry, was delighted to acquire Chacombe Manor and its water mill in Northamptonshire and Richard Audley, Equerry of the Stables, was granted a lease of a mill and lands in East Retford, Nottinghamshire.[26] Philip Bale, one of Henry's chaplains, was given the parsonage of Pyworthy, Devon, 'at the Queen's suit, preferred by Mr Herbert'.[27] So this catalogue of avarice continued, with footmen, yeomen of the chamber and other royal servants taking advantage of their master's pain-racked and hazy last days to line their pockets.

William Clerk, who had so diligently inked in Henry's signature over the previous months, managed to secure a lucrative wardship and custody of the manors in Huntingdon and Hertfordshire 'in the king's hands by the minority of John Sewster'. Both were sanctioned on 27 January, only hours before the king's death, by wielding the dry-stamp.[28]

Meantime in Venice, Ludovico da l'Armi was up to his old murderous tricks. In early November, the Venetians issued a warrant for the arrest of the merchant banker Mafio Bernardo, accused of divulging state secrets and involvement in secret treasonous negotiations with the French. On 16 November, Bernardo was killed brutally in a pine forest near Ravenna in northern Italy, after being stabbed eighteen times. A letter was found in the sleeve of his bloodstained doublet which had been given by da l'Armi to the cut-throats, his 'intimate comrades'. The motives for this frenzied murder remain unclear. Was this another of da l'Armi's private feuds – or was he involved in his own secret dealings with France and, fearing that Bernardo knew too much, had to silence him before he could blab?

Da l'Armi wrote to Paget on 11 December from Venice and included a casual reference to his latest escapade: '[If] perchance you hear anything of the death of Mafio Bernardo, which seems to touch my honour, either privately or as the king's servant . . . tell them who malign me that I have always proved myself studious of my master's honour and my own', he insisted.[29]

Five days later, the city's Council of Ten had established that da l'Armi had ordered Bernardo's death. Again, fear of Henry's displeasure stayed their hand in wreaking justice upon a man they regarded 'as odious to the state as words can express'. If the king opposed his execution for this fresh outrage, then he should recall da l'Armi from Venice 'so that all cause of scandal and disturbance may be removed'. They anxiously awaited his decision.[30]

But with what strength he had remaining, Henry was more concerned with imposing his own justice. A special mandate was given to Wriothesley, Lord St John, Russell and Hertford to deliver the royal assent to Surrey and Norfolk's Act of Attainder.[31] It was dated January 1547, but the day of the month left blank.[32] In the event, assent was given by commission on Thursday, 27 January, as Wriothesley explained that the king was too ill to be present.[33] Henry wanted it enacted without delay 'in order that certain offices held by Norfolk could be given to others' because of the approaching investiture of Edward as Prince of Wales.[34]

At mid-morning on 27 January, possibly after the stamping of Clerk's windfall wardship and manors, the king received communion from his confessor, perhaps John Boole. Afterwards, he was conscious enough to discuss state business with a few advisers, probably Paget and Hertford.[35] As the cold day wore on towards a murky twilight, all who saw him knew that Henry was rapidly losing his last battle to cheat Death.

Those in the Palace of Whitehall were well aware that it was high treason to predict or 'imagine' the king's demise. Throughout Henry's reign, many had died on the scaffold for doing just that. The king still had the power to kill as he had just given royal assent to Norfolk's execution for treason. His nervous doctors also knew of the king's absolute repugnance to any talk of his mortality. After a whispered conference, they decided the risk of a final tantrum was too perilous for them to take. They would not tell their patient that he was dying.

Yet, surely it would be common humanity to warn the king that
his time was running out to make his peace with his Maker. After
much equivocation among the fearful courtiers, that dangerous duty
fell inevitably to Sir Anthony Denny, who, as Groom of the Stool, had
looked after the king's most intimate bodily needs in life and now had
the unenviable task of warning him of his approaching death.

He entered Henry's silent blood-red bedchamber that evening and
knelt beside the great nine foot (2.7m) square bed, with its four pillars
and crimson hangings. The king's huge torso was propped up on fine
holland[36] pillows piled up against the carved walnut headboard. A
scarlet nightcap was perched upon his head and he lay supine beneath
sheets of lawn,[37] narrowly fringed with Venice gold fabric or silk.[38] He
was conscious and may have found it difficult to breathe evenly. In the
flickering and scented light of beeswax candles, Henry stared down at
the kneeling Denny in ominous silence, as the courtier summoned up
courage to utter the hitherto unspeakable.

He warned his master that in 'man's judgement you are not like to
live' and hurrying on, exhorted him to prepare for death. There was
another hush, then Denny urged the king to remember his sins 'as
becomes every good Christian man to do'.

Henry said he believed 'the mercy of God is able to pardon me all
my sins, yes, [even if] they were greater than they be'. Wisely, Denny
skirted around the delicate question of a priest to administer the last
rites. Instead, he asked if the king wanted to 'see any learned man to
confer with and open his mind to'. The king nodded, saying, 'If I had
any, it should be Dr Cranmer, but I will first take a little sleep. And
then, as I feel myself, I will advise upon the matter.'

These were the king's last known words. Shortly afterwards he lost
the power of speech and sank into unconsciousness.

The transfer of power in any totalitarian state is always the most
hazardous time for any regime and its supporters. Outside the royal
bedchamber, there were now scattered knots of Privy Councillors
whispering and plotting in any dark and lonely corner of the palace.
During these muttered meetings, alliances were forged, deals done,
promises made and strategies and policies defined.

We can discern a flavour of those furtive nocturnal negotiations
from testimony provided by one such conspirator. Two years later,
Paget, still in royal service, reminded Hertford pointedly about these

secret deliberations: 'Remember when you promised me in the gallery at Westminster before the breath was out of the body of the king ... Remember what you promised immediately after; devising with me concerning the place you now occupy ... And that was, to follow my advice in all your proceedings, more than any other man's. Which promise I wish your grace had kept.'[39]

As this power-broking continued in the shadows, Archbishop Cranmer was summoned from his palace in Croydon, Surrey, eleven miles (18km) south of Westminster. It was very cold that January night and the frozen unmade roads slowed his ride to London. He arrived at Whitehall some time after midnight, chilled and shivering after the short ferry trip from Lambeth.

Henry was probably still insensible, faithfully watched in silent vigil by Denny and other Gentlemen of his Privy Chamber. Had he been conscious and able to speak, the archbishop would have heard his confession and given him the *Viaticum*,[40] the Eucharist administered to a person near death.

His old friend scrambled up awkwardly on to the great bed, bending his head to whisper into the king's ear. Cranmer 'comfortably' urged him to give some sign or token, no matter how slight, to demonstrate that he still put his trust in God, through the mercy of Jesus Christ. The merest nod, a flicker of the eyelids, or a tiny gesture with a hand was all that was required. There was no response in that silent room, apart from the laboured breathing of the dying man. Cranmer grasped the king's hand and then, suddenly, Henry 'did wring his hand as hard as he could'.[41] Those present took this as a conclusive sign that the king still dwelt firmly in the faith of Christ.

Henry died shortly afterwards, probably around two o'clock in the morning of Friday, 28 January 1547. He was aged fifty-five years and seven months and had ruled England, Wales and Ireland with a mailed fist for thirty-seven years and 281 days.

For someone so much larger than life, with so much blood staining his hands, the king's passing was undramatic. Tyrants are rarely blessed with such serene deaths. In his passing, Henry unwittingly confirmed a Tudor tradition that the true villains died peacefully in their beds, while many decent men suffered violent ends. Melodramatic reports such as the last-gasp demand for a cup of white wine to quench his thirst, or the despairing cry of 'All is lost!' are pure fiction.[42]

The king died content in the knowledge that the Tudor dynasty would continue with his nine-year-old son Edward. True, the precious succession was fragile, without the insurance of a spare heir, and the new king would reign until the age of eighteen supported by a fractious regency government. But after a turbulent life with two wives divorced, two more executed, another dying following childbirth, and a terrible litany of stillbirths, miscarriages and post-natal deaths of his progeny, it was something of a minor miracle that the Tudor line would live on.

His sixth wife Katherine Parr probably did not see Henry before his death and had now become a widow for the third time. All her jewellery was collected up and sent to the jewel house in the Tower. She changed into her widow's weeds again, and would acquire mourning jewels, including a gold ring, mounted with a grinning death's head, for her finger.

After the lengthy catalogue of medical conditions that had tortured him for so long, what finally killed Henry Tudor? There rarely is just one affliction that finally causes us to shuffle off this mortal coil. The final *coup de grâce* can be administered, for example, by broncho-pneumonia, heart or kidney failure. The king could have died from a combination of oedema (or dropsy), inflammation, pyogenic suppuration and chronic osteomyelitis. As he was speechless and probably helpless in the last hours before his death, Henry may have suffered a stroke that was ultimately fatal. Alternatively, his stupor could have been caused by kidney failure against a background of chronic nephritis (inflammation of the kidneys).[43]

As dawn broke that morning, Norfolk, anxiously pacing up and down in the Tower, must have wondered what was going on. His execution was scheduled for early that morning. There was no dreaded knock on the door to call him to the scaffold. Had he cheated the headsman's axe, or was there a cruel delay in delivering Henry's bloody vengeance on the Howards?

Henry's Privy Councillors acted speedily to secure the realm. Military roadblocks were thrown up around London and the ports along the south coast were closed. Shortly after the king died, Hertford and Paget had another private conversation as they walked along the darkened gallery at Whitehall[44] and it is possible that the letters patent conferring the office of Lord Protector on Hertford were drawn up immediately afterwards.[45]

As the king's bloated and stinking corpse grew cold, the earl hurriedly departed the palace with Sir Anthony Browne. Accompanied by 300 cavalry, they galloped the twenty-five miles (40km) to Hertford Castle to secure his nephew and new king, Edward. Hertford did not tell him of his father's death but escorted him to Elsyng Palace[46] in Enfield, Middlesex, where thirteen-year-old Princess Elizabeth was living. Bringing the children together on the evening of Saturday, 29 January, the earl told them, as kindly as he could, of the king's death. They 'both broke forth into such unforced and unfeigned passions... Never was sorrow more sweetly set forth.'[47]

After retiring to bed, the earl was woken some hours after midnight by a messenger with an urgent letter from Paget at Whitehall. In his haste, Hertford had left without giving him the key to the wooden casket containing Henry's will. Paget now requested it and sought the earl's opinion on whether the testament's contents should be made public.

Hertford replied, agreeing that 'it might be well considered how much ought to be published'. On balance, 'I think it not convenient to satisfy the world. In the meantime, I think it sufficient, when you [announce] the king's death... to have the will with you... and [name] the executors and councillors.' Its contents could be announced in Parliament the following Wednesday morning. Hertford's letter was endorsed with stern instructions to his messenger: 'Post-haste, with all your diligence, for your life.'[48] He remembered to enclose the key to the will's box.

Late on Sunday night, Hertford and Browne, still at Enfield, wrote to the Privy Council after receiving their note about a general royal pardon being proclaimed, as was customary at the start of a new reign. Norfolk, still awaiting his fate in the Tower, must have loomed large in the earl's mind. As far as Hertford was concerned, more time was needed to decide whether the duke should live or die and he warned that any general pardon should be delayed until Edward's coronation, so the boy monarch could benefit from his subjects' gratitude. If it was proclaimed now, 'his father, whom we doubt not to be in heaven, would take the credit from him, who has more need of it'.

The earl promised that Edward 'the king shall be in the saddle by eleven tomorrow morning and so at the Tower by three'. As an afterthought, he also suggested that Anne of Cleves should be told of the king's death.[49]

For three days, Henry's death remained a close secret, known only to a handful of people at Whitehall. A few hours after his passing, members of the Privy Council, led by Cranmer, entered the bedchamber and formally took their leave of their dead master. They paid their humble respects to a king they had feared, maybe even loathed, but to whom they all owed their status. As they left that darkened room, there must have been a sudden flash of relief for some that they had survived the terrors of his reign.

Those formalities over, the first macabre priority was to stabilise the twenty-eight stone (178kg) corpse, already corrupted by the blood and pus of his ulcerated legs, by 'splurging, cleansing, bowelling, cereing, embalming and dressing with spices'.[50] The royal apothecary Thomas Alsop supplied perfumed unguent oils – including cloves, myrrh and sweet-smelling nigella and musk – for the surgeons to use and to be placed into the coffin, at a total cost of £26 12s 2d, or £15,000 in today's money.[51]

Alsop and his yeoman apothecaries assisted the surgeons and wax-chandlers in the unpleasant task of embalming Henry's stiffening body. Manhandling such a bulk must have been exhausting. The royal bowels were removed and the body wrapped in multiple layers of waxed cere-cloth, before being swathed with lengths of the finest velvet, bound with silken cords. A small label, cast in lead, was secured to the breast with 'writing in great and small letters . . . containing his name and style [and] the day and year of his death'.

The king's Serjeant Plumber and carpenters from the royal household then sealed the corpse inside an anthropoidal lead shell and made the 6ft 10ins (2.1m) long coffin's outer casing in solid elm.[52]

This weighty casket was covered with a pall of cloth of gold, a large cross placed on top and then set on trestles in the Presence Chamber. It was watched over by the king's chaplains and his Gentlemen of the Privy Chamber, who took their turn during a twenty-four hour vigil for five days. Henry's entrails and bowels were buried in the palace chapel.

The secret was bound to leak out, although a frustrated Giacomo Zambon, the Venetian Secretary in London, complained on 30 January that, daily, he had requested an audience with Henry to decide Ludovico da l'Armi's fate, but was repeatedly told 'that his majesty cannot see him by reason of indispositions and business'. He had been promised an interview 'as soon as possible, nor will I fail to urge it', he told the impatient Council of Ten in Venice.[53] He was not alone; de Selve's audience, arranged for the morning of Saturday, 29 January, was also postponed for two days.[54]

One of their fellow diplomats was better informed. By 31 January, van der Delft had 'learnt from a very confidential source that the king (whom may God receive in His Grace) had departed this life, although not the slightest signs of such a thing were seen at court. Even the usual ceremony of bearing in the royal dishes to the sound of trumpets was continued without interruption. I should like to have conveyed this intelligence... before this, but all the roads have been, and still are, closed, so that in order to send [this] letter, a passport has been necessary.'[55] That same day, Henry Radcliff, earl of Sussex, wrote to his wife from Ely Place, with news of Henry's death.[56]

De Selve finally heard the news from 'five or six quarters, although the thing is kept so secret that no man dare mention it'. He reported that the new king 'is to be in this town today with the earl of Hertford... and he will lodge in the Tower for greater security against any insurrection'.[57]

Edward arrived at the fortress under heavy guard and was publicly proclaimed king by the heralds,[58] amid the celebratory roar of crashing cannonades from the guns on its battlements, echoed by ships on the Thames. Norfolk must have been startled by the salvoes, but with his knowledge of state ceremonial as Earl Marshal, probably guessed that the king had died. Hopes that he would survive blossomed in his heart.[59]

Upriver at Westminster, Lord Chancellor Wriothesley, his voice choking with emotion and tears rolling down his cheeks, that morning announced Henry's death to a grieving Lords and Commons. Paget then read out extracts from the royal will relating to the succession and Parliament was dissolved.

That afternoon the Regency Council held its first meeting and noted that Henry's will had granted them 'full power and authority... to do any act... that may tend to the honour and surety of our sovereign lord's person or the advancement of his affairs'.[60] On 4 February, they appointed Hertford 'Protector of all the realms and dominions of the king's majesty' but with a 'special and express condition' that 'he shall not do any act but with the advice and consent' of the other executors of the will.[61]

Within Whitehall, officials were scuttling about arranging the king's funeral. The ceremony was made more complicated by Henry's requirement that he should be buried in St George's Chapel, Windsor, alongside the body of his third wife, Jane Seymour, the mother of his heir. These obsequies were regulated by the Westminster *ordo*,[62] under rules formulated both by the College of Arms and Henry's feisty grandmother Margaret Beaufort, long before he came to the throne.

Elaborate hearses were constructed for the chapel at Whitehall, another for the former Bridgettine convent church at Syon, the overnight stop midway on Henry's last journey, and a third at Windsor. These were not vehicles in the modern sense, but large gilded wooden structures, adorned with a myriad of candles and colourful heraldry. The coffin would rest on a catafalque beneath the hearse while Masses and *diriges* were said or sung – the latter derived from the first antiphon in the Matins of the Dead: *Dirige, domine, Deus meus, in conspectu tuo vitam meam* – 'Direct my way in your sight O Lord my God.'[63] There was also the *placebo*, from the Vespers of the Dead, named from the opening antiphon, based on Psalm 116, verse 9: *Placebo Domino in regione vivorum* – 'I will walk before the Lord in the land of the living.'

To emphasise the solemnity of the occasion, black sombre hangings were hung around the walls of each of these resting places and fabric was also acquired to make the clothes for the official mourners. The Lord Mayor of London, for example, was allowed nine yards (8.2m) for apparel; Will Somers, the king's fool and the Keeper of the Royal Spaniels, four yards (3.7m) apiece.[64] Almost 33,000 yards (27,432m) of black cloth, 8,085 yards (7,393m) of black cotton and ninety-nine yards (91m) of black kersey[65] was purchased from eighty London merchants. Because of the urgency of the order, an inflated price of £12,000, or almost £6.5 million, was charged.

On the evening of 2 February, Henry's coffin was moved to the palace chapel and placed beneath the six-pillared hearse, lit by eighty-two square wax tapers.[66] At each corner stood banners depicting saints, woven in gold thread on damask. Above the hearse hung a canopy of rich cloth of gold. At the east end was an altar 'covered with black velvet, adorned with all manner of [gold] plate and jewels upon which ... there was said Mass continually during the time the corpse was there remaining.'[67]

The next morning, between nine and ten, Gilbert Dethicke, Norroy King of Arms, stood at the choir door, resplendent in his richly embroidered tabard. He cried out in a loud voice: 'You shall of your charity, pray for the soul of the most famous Prince, King Henry VIII, our late most gracious King and Master.'[68]

Gardiner, as prelate of the Order of the Garter, had come in from the cold to take the lead in many of the Requiem Masses held night and day at Whitehall. After the Mass on 3 February, the mourners moved to the Presence Chamber 'where was prepared for them a sumptuous dinner with service, saving [without] the state, as if the king's majesty personally present.'[69]

The bishop's notorious temper had not deserted him. He found time to write to Paget on 5 February, complaining vociferously about plans to stage a comedy by actors in Southwark, just before Henry's funeral. 'It seems a marvellous contention that some should profess mirth and some sorrow at one time. I follow the common determination in sorrow till our late master be buried. And what these lewd fellows should mean in the contrary, I cannot tell or cannot reform and therefore write to you ... If you will not meddle, send word and I will myself [ask] the Protector.'[70] The play was cancelled.

For all Henry's horror of beggars, on 7 February, 21,000 poor people received alms at Leadenhall and at St Michael's in Cornhill, in the City of London 'to the great relief and comfort of the people'. With such numbers, there was no chance to separate the deserving poor from the king's despised feckless ne'er-do-wells. Every man received a groat (4d) in the heaving press that began at noon and continued noisily for six hours. In return, they were expected to pray for their departed king's soul, but one strongly suspects the alms bought celebratory drinks. The next day, they had their chance to offer up their prayers as every parish church in the capital and throughout England held a requiem Mass for Henry, their bells summoning the faithful.[71]

As well as arranging the funeral, the royal household also had simultaneously to plan Edward's coronation, set for Sunday, 20 February, at Westminster. It was decided to redraft its order of service 'lest the tedious length should weary the king, being yet of a tender age'.[72] On 8 and 12 February, Hertford removed old broken gold items and girdles, together with rubies, emeralds and diamonds, from Henry's jewel house at Whitehall, to be made into a new, smaller and lighter crown for the boy king.[73]

Work was meanwhile continuing on constructing the massive and 'stately' gilded chariot that was to convey Henry's body from Westminster to Windsor and on the life-size effigy of the king that was to lie atop the coffin during the cortège's twenty-four-mile (38.6km) journey. The head and face were fashioned in wax as a likeness, but the torso was stuffed like a common tailor's dummy beneath its sumptuous robes.

The ever-painstaking Tudor administration ordered the 'clearing and mending of all the highways between Westminster and Windsor where the corpse should pass and the noisome boughs cut down [on] every side [of] the way [to prevent] prejudicing the standards and banners. And where the ways are narrow, there were hedges [cut down] on either side so the footmen might have free passage.'[74] Bridges were also inspected in case they needed repair. Lord Worcester, the king's almoner, arranged for two carts to deliver boards painted with heraldic arms for display in the forty-one parishes in Middlesex, Buckinghamshire and Berkshire through which the funeral procession would pass. His deputies also distributed dole money and torches to the priests at each church.

On Sunday, 13 February, three final solemn Masses were said over the old king's coffin in the chapel at Whitehall. At their conclusion, the bishops, led by Gardiner, vested in black, liberally blessed the corpse with incense and holy water before withdrawing into the vestry, the choir singing *Libera me, Domine* – 'Deliver me, Lord.'

Monday, 14 February, was the day appointed for the first stage of the funeral. Those wearing official black livery were instructed to muster at Charing Cross, just up from Whitehall, by seven o'clock in the morning for the first stage to Syon, twelve miles (19km) away, broadly following the route of today's A4, west of London. Instructions were contained in a document running to twenty-nine folios.[75]

Because of its scale, the cortège became a nightmare to organise. Once on the move, it would stretch four miles (6.4km) in length and include more than 1,000 horsemen, as well as many hundreds on foot, all carrying torches, regularly replenished along the way from carts already stationed en route. These were to be lit only when passing through towns and villages.

At its head, rode John Herd and Thomas Martin, two porters from the royal household, carrying black staves and acting as stewards, or 'conductors', to clear the way so that 'neither cart, horse nor man, should trouble... them in this passage'. Immediately behind was a tall, jewelled ceremonial cross, carried by a crucifer, who was followed by forty-six priests and choirboys from the Chapel Royal, lustily singing doleful hymns and psalms, as befitted the occasion. They were flanked by 250 'bedesmen' – poor men in 'long mourning gowns and hoods with badges on their left shoulders, the red and white cross in a sun shining [with] a crown imperial'. These were professional mourners; it was ordered that they should be 'numbered and billed', as they were paid a pittance for their trudging services that day.

After this section came Thomas Bridges, carrying a banner bearing the dragon, the badge of Owen Tudor; Sir Nicholas Sturley, with one blazoned with the Lancastrian emblem of a greyhound, escorted by twelve London aldermen; and Lord Windsor with the lion, a standard that Henry had adopted for his own use. They were followed by lords, barons, viscounts, earls and bishops, riding two by two in order of precedence. Then came the foreign ambassadors 'accompanied by such lords as best could entertain and understand their language'. Francis van der Delft, as the diplomatic representative of an emperor, was accorded special status, riding beside the archbishop of Canterbury. Cranmer was unshaven, in fulfilment of the vow to evermore grow a beard in memory of his dead sovereign and friend.

Lord Talbot, bearing a banner with the king's arms, was followed by heralds carrying Henry's helmet, his shield, and mighty war sword. Sir Christopher Barker, Garter Principal King of Arms, had the dead sovereign's 'rich coat of arms, curiously embroidered' mounted on a staff. Behind him were twelve gentlemen and knights carrying 'banners of descent', that colourfully displayed the arms of the king's favoured marriages and ancestors, led by those with Jane Seymour and Katherine Parr.

The centrepiece of the procession was, of course, the gilded chariot, drawn by eight great horses draped in black velvet, six being ridden by 'a child of honour' bearing bannerols of the king's dominions and the ancient arms of England. Knights who rode alongside carried banners of the Blessed Virgin Mary, the Holy Trinity, St George, Henry VI 'of blessed memory' and the arms of Henry, his wife and his father and mother, Henry VII and Elizabeth of York.

The great coffin was covered with cloth of gold and blue velvet and upon it lay the lifelike funeral effigy 'wonderfully richly apparelled with velvet, gold, and precious stones of all sorts',[76] secured to the chariot's pillars by silken ribbons. It wore a 'crown imperial of inestimable value' over a black satin bonnet; around the neck was a collar of the Order of the Garter, and a Garter of gold worn on one leg.[77] On the feet were crimson velvet slippers, scarlet hose on the legs and two gold bracelets were on the effigy's wrists. A 'fair arming sword' laid by its side and a gold sceptre was placed in the right hand, a gold orb in the left. John Bruges, now the king's tailor, had been paid 13s 4d (67p) for making its robe of estate in blue velvet and John Benyns received four shillings (20p) for making its doublet of blue satin, edged with velvet.[78] The waxen head was probably modelled by Nicholas Bellin of Modena, who had been working on Henry's still uncompleted tomb. His skill was so impressive, as a Spanish eye-witness thought 'the figure looked exactly like that of the king himself and he seemed just as if he were alive'.[79]

Denny and Herbert clambered up on to the chariot and took their seats at the head and foot of the coffin.

Immediately after the chariot came six mounted and hooded henchmen, carrying heraldic escutcheons bearing the arms of pre-conquest England and those reputed to have been held by the ancient (and mainly legendary) English kings: Brutus, Belin, Athelstan, Arthur, Edmund and St Edward.[80]

Behind rode the chief mourner, Henry Grey, third marquess of Dorset, and Henry FitzAlan, earl of Arundel, the Lord Chamberlain, whose department had organised the funeral. He must have been a nervous man that morning. Sir Edward Dymock, the king's hereditary champion, followed and behind came a bare-headed Sir Anthony Browne, leading Henry's great courser, trapped 'in cloth of gold down to the ground'. Sir Anthony Wingfield, Captain of the King's Guard, led his men, three abreast and dressed all in black, with their halberds resting on their shoulders, points down. Bringing up the rear were the servants of those nobility taking part.

Other places were filled by the legion that formed Henry's household. Among their serried ranks were Henry's extensive medical team:

the four physicians, Doctors Chambre, Owen, Cromer and Wendy; his five surgeons, led by John Ayliffe, and two apothecaries, Alsop and Reynolds.

Listed among the contingent forming the queen's household, was Henry's faithful jester and long-time companion, Will Somers, listed as 'the fool'.[81]

The weather was fair but cold. It must have been tiresome to wait for about three hours while the heralds rode up and down the column, trying to ensure that everyone was in their correct position, according to the strict rules of precedence.

At last, at about ten o'clock, the nobles mounted their horses and the procession moved off 'in goodly order'. It soon passed out into the open fields and proceeded at about three miles an hour, via the parishes of Knightsbridge, Chelsea, Kensington, Fulham, Hammersmith, Acton, Ealing, Chiswick, and Brentford to Syon. At each village, bells tolled out muffled funeral knells in greeting. Priests, wearing their best vestments, emerged from their churches to offer up prayers for Henry and censed and sprinkled the chariot with holy water as it trundled by. The cortège was watched silently by 'innumerable people' who had come to pay their last respects to their monarch, or perhaps to convince themselves that he was finally dead.

The head of the procession reached Syon, on the Thames riverbank, at about two o'clock. The Bridgettine house had surrendered to the crown in 1539 and apart from Henry sending an adulterous wife and recalcitrant niece there, it had lain forlorn until the king converted some of its buildings into a factory to manufacture munitions for his wars against France and Scotland. Edward IV's coffin had rested at Syon overnight en route to Windsor in 1483, and the funeral rites for Henry followed suit. The great convent church 260 feet (79m) long with its twin naves remained. The chariot was brought to the west door and was carried in by sixteen yeomen of the guard, to be reverently placed within another gilded hearse before the high altar. The effigy was removed to the vestry.

Further requiem Masses were said by the bishops of London, Bristol and Gloucester before Paulet, Lord Steward of the Household, set an overnight watch over the coffin. Everyone else retired gratefully for much-needed sustenance after that long, cold ride (or walk) from London.

Now comes a horribly intriguing but possibly apocryphal story.

During the night (it was reported later), putrid matter leaked from Henry's great elm coffin and stray curs wandered into the church and licked it up.

You will recall that grim prediction by the Franciscan friar William Peto in 1532 that if Henry continued to behave like the Biblical king Ahab, dogs would lick his blood just as they had Ahab's. Had this prophecy now come true?

A nineteenth-century account, quoting an uncited 'contemporary document', tells of the coffin 'being cleft by the shaking of the carriage [and] the pavement of the church was wetted with Henry's blood. In the morning came plumbers to solder the coffin [the anthropoidal shell] under whose feet was suddenly seen a dog creeping and licking up the king's blood. If you ask me how I know this, I answer William Greville (who could scarcely drive away the dog) told me, so did the plumber also.'[82] It is possible that a soldered joint of the inner lead shell containing the king's body may have sprung open and that after all that jolting on the way from Charing Cross, the elm coffin was cracked. Certainly, more than two weeks after his death, the king's body would have been in an advanced state of putrefaction.

Bishop Gilbert Burnet, in the next century, pointed out that as Syon had been a house of religious women, this was seen to be 'a signal mark of the displeasure of heaven, that some of his blood had dropped through the lead at night'.[83]

This grisly story must have gained widespread currency, as Peto's reputation thereafter flourished in the Catholic Church and among those of Henry's subjects who cherished the old religion. He was still living in Rome and later that year was appointed bishop of Salisbury by Pope Paul III, a post he could not possibly take up.[84]

If hasty repairs to Henry's coffin were necessary, they would have been hidden from public gaze by its pall. Between six and seven o'clock the next morning, after three warning blasts on trumpets, the procession formed up and resumed its progress, reaching Windsor at about one o'clock. It was greeted by a group of Eton scholars, kneeling bare-headed in white surplices, holding tapers and singing psalms. At the foot of the bridge over the Thames 'the mayor and most substantial men stood on one side and on the other priests and clerks and by them, the corpse passed through the castle gate'.[85]

Another painted and gilded hearse had been built in St George's Chapel inside Windsor Castle, this one of two storeys, thirty-five feet (11m) in height, fringed with black and gold silk and with thirteen pillars with branches holding candles made from 4,000lb (1,814kg) of the finest beeswax. Those sixteen tall yeomen laboured to slide the coffin onto trestles inside the hearse and the effigy was laid on top of a black velvet pall. Watching from a closet above was Queen Katherine, wearing blue velvet robes and a purple bodice specially made for the occasion. Another Mass and *dirige* were said and sung before the mourners dispersed for the night.

The next morning, Wednesday, 16 February 1547, the funeral was held, led by Gardiner, assisted by Edmund Bonner, bishop of London and Thomas Goodrich, bishop of Ely. Henry's coat of arms, his shield, sword and helmet were laid upon the altar. Chidock Paulet, a 'man of arms', rode his horse into the chapel's choir. He was wearing armour, 'save his headpiece' (helmet) and carried a 'pole-axe in his hand, with the point downward'.[86] This was also placed upon the altar.

The bishop of Winchester climbed up into the pulpit for the sermon, taken from the text 'Blessed are the dead which die in the Lord', from Revelation, chapter 14, verse 13. There must have been a late change of plan because Henry Holbech, bishop of Rochester, was originally scheduled to preach.[87]

He was present as prelate of the Order of the Garter, although some who heard him considered him a closet papist and a persecutor of religious reformers All must have known that he had been banished from government by the king's pique. Gardiner, who must have relished the occasion for a variety of reasons (none particularly Christian), spoke of the frailty of man and the 'community of death to the high and to the low'. He provided words of comfort – the prospect of 'the resurrection in the life to come' – and exhorted the congregation 'to rejoice and give thanks to Almighty God, having sent so virtuous a prince to reign over us'.[88] Six knights finally removed the effigy to the vestry, as the bishops processed to the hearse, singing *Circumdederunt me* – 'Surround me with Your protection.'

The entrance to the vault in the choir where Henry was to be buried was then uncovered. The sixteen yeomen, using 'five strong linen towels', then slowly lowered the coffin into the grave, with Gardiner standing at its head, reciting the burial service, with the officers of the household crowding around him in the flickering candlelight.

The bishop threw handfuls of earth down on to the coffin, reciting *Pulverem, pulveri et cinerem cineri* – 'Dust to dust, ashes to ashes'. Paget and his fellow household officers stepped forward, snapped their white wands of office and threw them into the grave, 'not without grievous signs and tears'. Their power and authority had ceased with Henry's death.

The vault was closed off with wooden planks and Sir Christopher Barker, Garter, moved to the centre of the choir. In a loud, clear voice, he declaimed: 'Almighty God of his infinite goodness, give good life and long to the most mighty Prince, our sovereign lord King Edward VI, by the grace of God, King of England, France and Ireland, Defender of the Faith and on earth, under God, of the Church of England and Ireland, the Supreme Head and Sovereign of the Most Noble Order of the Garter.'[89]

Then he shouted '*Vive le noble Roy Edward!*' – the cry echoed three times in unison by the officers of arms about him. Above them, in the rood loft, the trumpets rang out 'with great melody and courage to the comfort of all that were there present'.[90]

Items used in the funeral rites were later handed over to officials as gifts or in lieu of fees.[91] St George's Chapel received the hearse cloth[92] and eight banners. Three still hung there in the early seventeenth century.[93]

After dinner, the Privy Council rode to London in some haste. The old king was dead. Another, a young, impressionable boy, was on the throne and his ceremonial entry into his capital was planned for Saturday, 19 February, twenty-four hours before the coronation at Westminster.

A new reign had begun. What was different? The Tudor line continued, with the same figures, with a few notable absences, wielding power on behalf of the crown. The implacable and imperious Henry had departed, succeeded by a nine-year-old boy, with his uncle governing as Lord Protector.

Some time that February, Cardinal Reginald Pole wrote to Pope Paul III, pointing out that Henry's death provided a unique opportunity for the Catholic Church to 'regain England'. He urged that the Vatican should send an ambassador to Charles V as soon as possible, as it was 'above all necessary to have the support of the Emperor' to achieve this glorious end.[94]

The pope had already heard the news from France and had insisted 'that this opportunity must not be allowed to slip of endeavouring to bring the country to submission again'.[95]

16

Epilogue

A week after ascending the throne, Edward wrote a dutiful but stilted letter to his stepmother Queen Katherine, offering belated condolences on Henry's death. He acknowledged that as it 'seemed good to God' to call 'my father, your spouse, the most famous king... the two of us share one common grief'. His 'most noble sire' had promoted all 'religion and driven forth all superstition' and so would enjoy 'a most sure way into Heaven'. Though 'nature bids me weep and shed much tears for the loss... nevertheless, scripture and wisdom bids me restrain these sentiments, lest we seem void of all hope in the resurrection of the dead and life eternal'.[1]

Hertford, his uncle, was created duke of Somerset, with the style and title of 'Governor and Protector of the king, Lieutenant General of his majesty's land and sea armies, Treasurer [of the Exchequer] and Earl Marshal of England, Governor of Jersey and Guernsey'.[2] Lisle was made earl of Warwick and appointed Great Chamberlain.

The 'rough wooing' of Scotland was far from over. In 1547, Somerset led another land and sea invasion, designed to establish English garrisons in the Scottish lowlands as a military buffer zone to protect the border. His army inflicted a crushing defeat on the Scots at the Battle of Pinkie, close to Musselburgh, East Lothian, on 10 September.

William Patten, serving with the English expedition, was a horrified eyewitness. His graphic description of the slaughter of the Scottish troops and the terrible effects of Tudor weaponry makes uncomfortable reading. The bodies of the fallen piled in heaps on the battlefield were a pitiful sight. 'Some with their legs off; some but [hamstrung] and left lying half-dead. Others with their arms cut off; [many] with their necks asunder; many their heads cloven off, the brains [bashed] out... with a thousand other kinds of killing.' In the ensuing rout, most Scots were killed by wounds 'either in the head or neck, for our horsemen could not well reach them lower with their weapons'.[3] Estimates of 15,000 Scots killed in action were exaggerated, as the true figure was probably about 6,000, with between 500 and 600 English dead.[4]

Despite this triumph, the campaign's outcome was less than satisfactory as far as Somerset was concerned. The Scots government dispatched Mary Queen of Scots to France, beyond English reach and rendering impossible Henry's old plan for her to marry Edward. Furthermore, a 10,000-strong French force was sent to Scotland to harass the new English strongholds. Somerset was forced to withdraw his troops from Scotland after a French attack on Boulogne in August 1549 and also to suppress a threatening rebellion against the imposition of Cranmer's new prayer book in English.

With further debasement of the coinage and rampant inflation, the cost of war had become impossible for England to sustain. Boulogne, Henry's much-vaunted prize of war, was meekly returned to France in March 1550, four years ahead of the agreed time.

After reigning six years, Edward died on 6 July 1553 at Greenwich Palace.

After contracting measles, he fell victim to tuberculosis. His doctors were packed off and a 'wise woman' brought in to give him noxious stimulants to keep him alive while the succession was settled. The king had lost much of his hair and fingernails and his toes were gangrenous. He could not breathe easily, suffered from a violent cough, his legs swelled, his pulse began to fail and his skin changed colour. His death, at the age of fifteen, was said to have been caused by putrefaction, although there were rumours of poison.[5] The surgeon who cut open Edward's chest in a primitive post-mortem pronounced that 'the disease whereof his majesty died was ... of the lungs'.[6] His symptoms were typical of acute broncho-pneumonia, leading to a 'suppurating pulmonary infection' or lung abscess, septicaemia and kidney failure.[7]

He was buried in his grandfather Henry VII's chapel in Westminster Abbey on 8 August.[8] The rites of the new *Book of Common Prayer* were used for his funeral, although his Catholic half-sister Mary also arranged a requiem Mass for him in one of the Tower's chapels royal.

Francis I, known to his subjects (but not to his face) as *François du Grand Nez* – 'Francis the Long Nose' – did not last much longer than Henry VIII. After news arrived of the English king's demise, the decrepit monarch had arranged elaborate symbolic obsequies for him on 21 March in Notre Dame Cathedral.[9] A maledictory farewell letter from Henry, written on his deathbed, counselled his old enemy to 'bear in mind that you too are mortal'. Francis believed this was a chilling message from the grave, warning him of his own imminent death. St Mauris, the Imperial ambassador in Paris, believed 'this admonition amazed and distressed the king to the extent that he fell ill from that moment' with bouts of fever.[10]

Francis heard rumours of his son's drunken parties and his cronies' avaricious speculation about who would acquire the lucrative great offices of state after his succession. The monarch was enraged and, with members of his loyal Scottish Guard, stormed off to his son's apartments. He found them empty, apart from the messy detritus of debauched revelry and cowering servants. A heady cocktail of adrenaline and anger gave Francis unexpected strength. He hurled chairs, bedding, mirrors and even lackeys out of the windows in a terrifying display of an old man's embittered frustration at his heir's insensitive temerity and manifest youth.[11]

The French king died at the Château de Rambouillet in the Île-de-France, thirty-one miles (50km) south-west of Paris on 31 March – a long-awaited present on the twenty-eighth birthday of his successor, Henry II. Francis was fifty-two and may have died from syphilis, or a disease of the urinary tract. Seven weeks of funeral ceremonies followed, attended (as befitting 'The Most Christian King') led by a red-robed radiance of eleven cardinals. Francis was buried with his first wife, Claude, duchess of Brittany, in the basilica at Saint-Denis, now in the northern suburbs of Paris. Their tomb, together with the other monuments in this royal necropolis, was desecrated and their bodies rudely exhumed during the French Revolution.

Charles V abdicated as king of Spain in favour of his son Philip in January 1556 and as Holy Roman Emperor the following September, his brother Ferdinand succeeding him. He retired to the monastery of San

Jerónimo de Yuste in Spain's Cáceres province to spend his last days in pious contemplation of his life and his approaching time in purgatory.[12]

His spartan accommodation abutted the choir of the church, to enable him to watch the services from his bed, where he was marooned by his chronic gout. The walls of one of his four rooms were lined with clocks, as a noisy reminder of the short time still allowed him.

The former emperor was troubled by his conscience and the need to suffer penance for his sins grew into a morbid obsession. He wept uncontrollably, sang hymns, recited psalms incessantly and regularly scourged himself with a whip until his upper body bled freely. The Jeromite monks were sometimes noisily awakened by Charles, worried they would be late for their midnight prayers for his soul.[13]

He even rehearsed his own funeral rites before his death. Wearing his shroud, he lay supine in his coffin, and was reverently carried up the nave of the church to the high altar, where he enthusiastically recited the prayers for the dead. Then he received the last blessing and clambered awkwardly out of his coffin to limp back painfully 'to his apartments, full of awful sentiments'.[14]

In the early hours of 21 September 1558, he died, aged fifty-eight, grasping the crucifix which his wife Isabella had held at her demise nineteen years earlier, together with a consecrated candle from the Virgin's shrine at Monserrat. Just as his clocks struck two, Charles cried out loudly 'Ay Jesus!' and the former emperor was gone.[15] His funeral was repeated, this time with him taking a more passive role.[16]

In England, Henry's sixth wife was now the dowager queen. The king repaid her devoted care for him and her love for his children with substantial legacies, granted for her virtues of 'great love, obedience, chastity of life and wisdom'. Katherine's income and matronly good looks made her an attractive catch to any gallant, bold or impertinent enough to woo her.

And just who might that gallant be? Within a month after Henry's death, she had again become smitten by her old sweetheart, the un-scrupulous Thomas Seymour, now Admiral of England, and created first baron Seymour of Sudeley in that grand bazaar of honours shared out so liberally after Henry's death. By March 1547, Katherine had probably accepted his proposal and the couple may have exchanged rings only thirty-four days after Henry's death. They probably were not wed until late May or early June that year.

News of the marriage sullied Katherine's prized reputation as a chaste, unblemished widow. Suggestions of improper haste and secrecy were followed by lewd jokes in London's raucous taverns. Katherine, duchess of Suffolk, that spirited mistress of satire (remember her dog 'Gardiner'?) mischievously named a black stallion in her stables 'Seymour' and her ambling bay mare 'Parr'.[17] Enraged by the widespread gossip, Seymour demanded a special parliamentary Act to prohibit such profane ribaldry about his bride and warned that '[W]hosoever should go about to speak evil of the queen, he would take his fist [to] their ears from the highest to the lowest.'[18]

Another issue rankled. The Lord Protector had disputed the owner-ship of the jewellery given to Katherine by Henry, including her wed-ding ring. The jewels removed from the queen included the gold cross and pearl pendants left to Katherine by her mother. Finally, they were returned.

After her three previous marriages, the dowager queen discovered that she was pregnant, at the age of around thirty-five.

Attended by Henry's former physician Dr Robert Huicke, she gave birth to a healthy daughter on 30 August 1548 at Sudeley Castle, Gloucestershire. She was named Mary, after her elder stepdaughter.

But all was not well; Katherine contracted an infection after child-birth. She died from puerperal fever early on Wednesday, 5 September and was buried that evening in the castle chapel. Her baby was sent to live with her mother's old friend and lady-in-waiting, Katherine, duch-ess of Suffolk, at Grimsthorpe Castle, Lincolnshire. The infant probably died at or before she had reached the age of two.

The Lord Admiral was seemingly devastated by his wife's death, but his grief soon withered on the vine. By January 1549, he was talking of wearing mourning black only 'for one year and would then know where to have a wife'.[19] He had his eye on Princess Elizabeth as a replacement bedfellow.

Seymour badly overreached himself. He was arrested that month to face thirty-three charges of treason. Van der Delft reported that 'the Admiral, with the help of some people about the court, attempted to outrage the person of the young king and has been taken to the Tower.

The alarm was given by the gentleman who sleeps in the king's chamber who, awakened by the barking of the dog that lies before the king's door, cried out "Help! Murder!" Everybody rushed in but the only thing they found was the lifeless corpse of the dog. Suspicion points to the Admiral because he had scattered the watch that night on several errands and because it has been noticed that he has some secret plot on hand, hoping to marry... the lady Elizabeth...'[20]

His brother Somerset signed his death warrant and the Lord Admiral was beheaded on Tower Hill on 20 March 1549 and buried in St Peter ad Vincula within the fortress. He was probably aged forty-one.

Somerset's authority was damaged by his brother's disgrace and he was toppled from power after openly quarrelling with his old ally, John Dudley, earl of Warwick. The Protector confessed to twenty-nine charges, summarised by Edward himself as: 'ambition, vainglory, entering into rash wars in my youth... enriching himself of my treasure, following his own opinion, and doing all by his own authority.'[21] However, he was released in February 1550, pardoned and restored to the Council the following April. But his scheming continued and he was arrested again on trumped-up charges of treason in October 1551 and when these failed to stick, was convicted of conspiring to overthrow the government.

Seven weeks after his trial, he was executed. Edward, always something of a cold fish, recorded his uncle's death in his personal journal: 'the duke of Somerset had his head cut off upon Tower Hill on 22 January 1552, between eight and nine o'clock in the morning.'[22] John Dudley, earl of Warwick, created duke of Northumberland in October 1551, became Lord President of the Council and quickly secured peace with France and Scotland.

There remained the familiar thorny question of the succession to the throne. When Edward fell ill, Princess Mary visited him at his sickbed, the Council offering 'duty and obeisance to her as if she had been Queen of England'. Two months later, Northumberland restored her full title and arms, denied her since the 1530s.[23] On 21 May 1553, Guildford Dudley, his younger son, married Lady Jane Grey, the Protestant daughter of Henry Grey, third marquess of Dorset, who had been made duke of Suffolk when Dudley was created duke of Northumberland. Through her mother, Frances Brandon, Jane was a grand-niece of Henry VIII.

The prospect of the staunchly Catholic Mary succeeding to the crown had horrified Edward. He changed his will to make his cousin Jane his successor, ignoring Henry's will, or the Succession Act of 1544, that gave precedency to Mary and then Elizabeth. Three days after the king's death, Northumberland, Suffolk and other members of the Privy Council named Lady Jane Grey queen. Her rule was to last just nine days as, confronted by large forces rallying to Mary in East Anglia, the Council staged a sudden volte-face and proclaimed Henry's eldest daughter as the first Tudor queen on 19 July.

Mary rode triumphantly into London on 3 August 1553, amid a wave of popular support, accompanied by her half-sister Elizabeth and more than 800 noblemen.

Of Henry's former advisers, Denny died in September 1549. His sister Joyce married the London lawyer William Walsingham and their only son was Francis, who later became Elizabeth I's secretary of state and spymaster.

Paget was arrested in 1551 on suspicion of plotting against Warwick. The following year, he was fined £6,000 after allegations that he had used his position for personal gain. After Edward's death, he was a member of Lady Jane's council but again adroitly changed sides. He was appointed one of Mary's Privy Councillors and became Lord Privy Seal in 1556. On Elizabeth's succession, he quit all offices and died in 1563.

That master of intrigue Wriothesley was created earl of Southampton in the distribution of titles after Henry's death, but on 6 March 1547, the Lord Chancellor's Great Seal was taken from him after he was accused of abusing his authority and forced to pay a £4,000 recognizance.[24] Wriothesley still held conservative beliefs and he was put under house arrest in January 1550. He died on 30 July, possibly from tuberculosis.

We left Norfolk locked up in the Tower, having escaped the axe by the opportune death of Henry VIII. Throughout Edward's reign he remained incarcerated, although in the more comfortable Beauchamp Tower, with £5 a week allowed for food and drink and £75 a year for clothing. Eighty pounds a year was for 'spending money'.[25] In March 1549, the Privy Council agreed that his daughter and wife could visit him.[26] This ostensibly kind decision was a double-edged gesture. During the last fourteen years, Norfolk had been separated from his vituperative wife Elizabeth, ever since he kicked her out in favour of his mistress Bess Holland. Now he had to suffer her undiminished spleen, with no escape from her tirades.

Henry Howard, earl of Surrey, had left two sons and two daughters and his widow Frances bore a third daughter, Margaret, three weeks after his beheading. Mary, duchess of Richmond, had custody of her nephews and nieces and was allowed £100 a year for their upkeep. She probably died in 1555 and was later buried beside her husband, Henry Fitzroy, in his tomb in St Michael's Church, Framlingham, Suffolk.

Bess Holland had her jewellery, baubles and her new house restored to her as reward for her co-operation in Surrey's prosecution. She married the magistrate Henry Reppes, but died shortly after giving birth before April 1548.

Given the Protestant complexion of Edward's government, it was inevitable that Bishop Gardiner would join Norfolk in prison. Thomas Watson, his chaplain, had warned of rumours of his arrest, but arrogant as ever, Gardiner dismissed these as mere 'tales, for he thought that he never pleased the council better in all his life'. Sir Anthony Wingfield detained him at his palace in Southwark after dinner on 30 June 1548. Gardiner told his servants: 'There is no cause why you should so lament. I shall do well enough.'[27] His confidence was built on shifting sands and he spent Edward's reign behind the Tower's walls.

The ordeal of Norfolk and Gardiner ended when Mary, as the new queen, arrived at the fortress. Amid salvoes of celebratory cannon fire, the new queen greeted them as they knelt on Tower Green, traditionally reserved for executions. She kissed both, declaring 'these be my prisoners' and raised them to their feet. The next day they were freed with Edward Courtenay, heir to the marquess of Exeter, the last survivor of the 'White Rose' faction, who had been locked up for fifteen years. He was created earl of Devon and what remained of his family's estates restored to him.[28]

Revenge was swift and merciless. On 18 August, as High Steward of England, Norfolk sat in judgement on Northumberland on charges of treason. After being condemned, the prisoner asked to 'confess to a learned divine' and was visited by Gardiner, now Mary's Lord Chancellor. He took communion during a Catholic Mass and asserted that '[T]he plague that is upon the realm . . . is that we have erred from the faith these sixteen years.'[29] Sir John Gates was tried the following day by Norfolk. Like Northumberland, he recanted his Protestant faith and died on the Tower Hill scaffold on 22 August. Three axe-blows were needed to sever his head.

Norfolk recovered his gold ducal crown, the collar and badge of the Garter and his jewels and plate from Northumberland's estate. His attainder was reversed that October and his grandson Thomas, now earl of Surrey, restored in blood. Eventually, two-thirds of his property was recovered.

His last military campaign was against Kentish rebels in January 1554 when his ill-luck as a general continued. A significant section of his force defected to the insurgents, turning their cannon on the duke's loyal troops. Norfolk fled the field, leaving behind his artillery and his honour.

He died in his bed on 25 August 1554 at Kenninghall, aged eighty-one. For all his conspiracies, intrigue and the tumult of his life, he was the great survivor. The same could not be said for some others in the Howard dynasty. Thomas, who succeeded him as fourth duke of Norfolk, was executed at Tower Hill in 1572 for treason – his plan to marry Mary Queen of Scots.

Gardiner also died peacefully in the Palace of Whitehall on 12 November 1555, between noon and one o'clock. His body was taken to Winchester Cathedral, where a funeral service was held on 28 February 1556. His elaborate chantry chapel was completed later that year in the south presbytery aisle, with his effigy, grimly portrayed as a grinning, emaciated cadaver, placed in a niche behind a metal grille. The head was later joyfully hacked off by Protestant iconoclasts. A requiem Mass was said for Gardiner in the cathedral in 1989, followed by an interdenominational service of reconciliation.

Cranmer's Protestant beliefs, and his signature on the document naming Lady Jane Grey queen, brought his arrest and imprisonment in the Tower, accused of treason and sedition. He was later taken to Oxford, accused of heresy. Confronting death, the former archbishop's resolve weakened and he signed papers acknowledging papal supremacy and the truth of Catholic doctrine. In the end, he withdrew his recantations and was burnt at the stake on 21 March 1556.

After becoming queen, Mary tried to wind the clock back and return her dominions to Catholicism. Cardinal Pole arrived as papal legate to receive her realms back into the Vatican's fold. On 22 March 1556, he became the last Catholic archbishop of Canterbury and acted as the queen's *de facto* chief minister.

Those who still practised the reformed religion risked death as heretics. A total of 284 Protestants perished in the flames and more than 800 others fled England for the safety of the Lutheran states in Europe. In comparison, sixty-three religious reformers were judicially killed during her father's reign and forty-two abbots, monks, friars and priests executed for denying the royal supremacy in 1537–44.

Mary was aged thirty-seven on her accession and her major priority was to find a husband and produce an heir to prevent her Protestant half-sister Elizabeth following her on to the throne. Her cousin Charles V suggested she marry his only son Philip and she agreed. Under the terms of her Marriage Act, he was styled 'King of England', but only during Mary's lifetime.

Lady Jane Grey, her husband Guildford Dudley and her father the duke of Suffolk were executed in February 1554, following a dangerous rebellion in Kent over Mary's marriage plans. Elizabeth was imprisoned in the Tower for two months and then lived under arrest at various royal houses for the remainder of Mary's reign.

The queen was denied her Catholic heir. Her husband persuaded her to support Spain in another war against France. In January 1558, the French captured Calais. Her reaction to its surrender was the possibly apocryphal comment 'When I am dead and opened, you shall find "Calais" lying in my heart.'

She died on 17 November 1558, aged forty-two, at St James's Palace, probably from ovarian cysts or uterine cancer. Her death occurred during a virulent influenza epidemic that claimed Pole's life twelve hours later. Philip, who was in Brussels, only acknowledged: 'I felt a reasonable regret for her death.'

Meanwhile Anne of Cleves was growing old comfortably and after Mary's accession, wisely converted to Catholicism. After her health declined, she was allowed to live at Chelsea Old Manor and she died there on 16 July 1557, just before her forty-second birthday. After a lavish funeral,[30] she was buried in Westminster Abbey on 3 August 1557, near the high altar in a low tomb decorated with her initials 'A.C', a crown, lions' masks and crossed bones, the symbols of mortality. Although the monument was probably unfinished and today scarcely receives any attention from tourists, she is the only one of Henry's wives to be buried in the 'House of Kings'.

Elizabeth succeeded Mary and returned England to the Protestant faith. In 1569, there was a major Catholic rebellion in northern England. Elizabeth was truly her father's daughter; more than 450 rebels were executed and yet she demanded still more vengeance. Pope Pius V issued a Bull the following year that declared 'Elizabeth, the pretended Queen of England and the servant of crime', to be a heretic. She was excommunicated and her subjects released from allegiance to her. Those who obeyed her laws faced their own excommunication.

Catholic Mary Queen of Scots went to France at the age of five as the future wife of the Dauphin and in April 1558 married him. Her father-in-law Henry II died in July the following year and her husband succeeded as Francis II. His reign was short; an infection of the middle ear led to a brain abscess and his death in December 1560.

She returned to Scotland in 1561 but was deposed and, seven years later, fled across the border, only to face imprisonment by Elizabeth because of her threat to the throne of England. Eventually, she was entrapped by a conspiracy to murder Elizabeth, linked with a harebrained plan for a Spanish invasion of England. Mary was put on trial and a death warrant signed (despite Elizabeth's misgivings about executing an anointed monarch) and she was beheaded in February 1587.

One last character in the drama of the last years of Henry's reign needs to be revisited: his 'gangster', Ludovico da l'Armi, whom we left, still deep in trouble, in Venice after the brutal murder of another victim. In London, Paget told Giacomo Zambon, the Venetian representative, three days before Henry died, that da l'Armi was 'no longer in favour and he was certain that his iniquities, which caused him to be in disgrace with the entire court, would greatly displease the king'.[31] The following month, Paget confirmed that da l'Armi's commission was cancelled by the king's death and would not be renewed.

The assassin fled Venice in January 1547 and headed for the Duchy of Milan, without servants and riding hired horses. Seeking the protection of large crowds, he attended a glittering entertainment, but strangely made no effort to look inconspicuous, other than wearing a mask.

Ever the showy dandy, da l'Armi wore a crimson velvet cloak and a flamboyant cap of red *ormesin*[32] with a gold band, 'which costume, coupled with his handsome figure, made everyone stare at him'. He was swiftly recognised and Don Ferrante, Governor of Milan, imprisoned him in his castle.[33]

The Venetians were determined to repatriate da l'Armi to face justice and such was his reputation, that they sent 200 cavalry as an escort to prevent his rescue. By the end of April, the troops and their prisoner were in Padua. 'Twenty-five good infantry' from the city's garrison, under a lieutenant, guarded him for the final phase of the journey by barge on the Brenta Canal.

Da l'Armi was always handcuffed and 'should he refuse to eat, the food should be forced down his throat', after first testing it for poison to prevent suicide. He arrived in Venice on 29 April and that evening, a Council committee interrogated him in the torture chamber of the Doge's prison. On Sunday, 11 May 1547, da l'Armi was condemned and the Council ordered that on 'Saturday next, he shall be taken between the Two Pillars, where on a lofty scaffold, his head shall be severed from his shoulders so that he dies'.[34]

In fact, they did not wait that long to exercise long-delayed Venetian justice. The following day, the *piovani* or rector of the nearby Chiesa San Luca Evangelista was told 'that should he choose to go and confess' da l'Armi, 'and remain with him until he is taken to execution, leave will be given him to go'.[35]

Early the next morning, da l'Armi was brought out of his cell in the ducal prison and under heavy guard, walked the short distance along the broad waterfront to the place of execution in the Piazza San Marco, between two tall granite columns bearing the winged lion of St Mark and the statue of San Todaro (St Theodore) standing atop a crocodile. The last things he would have seen were the blue waters of the Basin of San Marco and the island and monastery of San Giorgio Maggiore, before the world was finally rid of a ruthless, yet elegant assassin.

The status-conscious City of Venice noted briefly his passing in their official *Fliza Necrologia*, the obituary roll of noblemen who had died: '12 May 1547. Ludovico da l'Armi, beheaded by order of the most illustrious Council of Ten.'[36]

Finally, the question remains of how Henry VIII wanted to be remembered. Propaganda portraits had projected his imperiousness and kingly might. But a magnificent royal tomb would embody his immortality and boast of his prowess and achievements for centuries to come, with no one left to gainsay them. Henry began planning his grandiose monument nine years after his accession. The tomb's splendour would know no bounds, nor its expense any limit.

In this project, the king was thwarted, just as he was thwarted in his choice of wives; thwarted in neutralising the threat of Scotland; thwarted in his ambitions to win back the crown of France and thwarted in his quest for glory in a decisive battlefield victory.

During those twilight days in late December 1546, the king left instructions for his burial in St George's Chapel, Windsor, beneath 'an honourable tomb for Our bones to rest [in] which is well onward and almost made already, with a fair grate [grating] about it, in which We will also that the bones and body of Our true and loving wife Queen Jane be put'. A 'convenient altar' should be 'honourably prepared and apparelled with . . . things requisite and necessary for daily masses there to be said perpetually while the world shall endure'.[37] This chantry chapel would be endowed with lands worth £600 a year to pay for two priests to say Masses for the king and Jane Seymour and to keep four solemn Masses every year, when £10 should be distributed only, of course, to the deserving poor.[38]

The first contract for the design of a monument to Henry and his first wife Katherine of Aragon was awarded in 1518 to the Florentine sculptor Pietro Torrigiano, who, three years earlier, had completed the splendid Renaissance tomb to the king's father and mother in Westminster Abbey for £1,500, or just over £1 million in 2019 values. The new tomb was to be of white marble and black touchstone, 25 per cent bigger than Henry VII's, and to cost no more than £2,000.[39] But Torrigiano quibbled over the payment terms and departed England in high dudgeon the following year.

Undaunted, Henry cast around for another sculptor and another design. In 1527, the Venetian Jacopo Sansovino considered undertaking an ambitious project at a cost of £18,750, or an eye-watering £12.2 million in today's money. It has been argued[40] that this was the Renaissance tomb described a century later by John Speed in his *Historie of Great Britaine*.[41] This was of truly megalomaniac proportions, twenty-eight feet (8.5m) in height and fifteen feet (4.6m) wide, topped by an effigy of the king on horseback. Beneath this high canopy would be figures of the king and Queen Jane Seymour. Again, this design was never carried out.

During the same period, Cardinal Wolsey, who also never had a modest opinion of himself or his rightful place in history, commissioned other Italian sculptors, Benedetto da Rovezzano and Giovanni da Maiano, to build him a monument, not at Windsor, as was believed until recently, but probably at York Minster or Canterbury. It included a black marble sarcophagus seven feet (2.1m) tall and four feet (1.5m) wide, with a bronze effigy of the prelate, with two griffins at its feet. This tomb-chest, complete with a marble cardinal's hat, would rest on a black marble platform with four bronze pillars, topped by figures of angels, at the corners. Work began in 1524 at a workshop within the precincts of Westminster Abbey, but was incomplete at the Cardinal's downfall five years later.[42]

Henry not only took over Wolsey's palaces at York Place and Hampton Court, but he also commandeered his tomb. The gilt effigy was melted down, the cardinal's hat and papal symbols discarded, but the king reused the sarcophagus and the angels in a revised design. By December 1530, Benedetto and Giovanni were working on a monument with a gilded bronze life-size figure of Henry lying on top of Wolsey's tomb-chest, with bronze friezes inserted into its walls. Pillars surrounded the sarcophagus, capped by figures of the four evangelists, Matthew, Mark, Luke and John, the Apostles, St George and the prophets. Between them were bronze candlesticks some nine feet (2.7m) tall[43] and Wolsey's four angels.

To the east of the tomb would be an altar, surmounted by a canopy. At its base were sixteen effigies of children, holding candlesticks.[44] Both monument and altar would be surrounded by a four-foot-high (1.2m) bronze and marble enclosure (Henry's 'grate') to form a separate chantry in St George's Chapel, where priests would pray for the royal souls (even though 'purgatory' had disappeared from the liturgy).

Work continued on Henry's monument during his final decade, hindered by sporadic delays, caused by the cost of the wars in Scotland

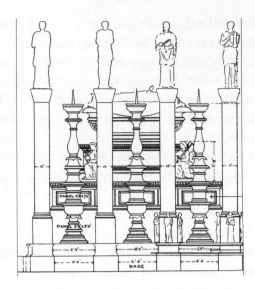

*Vanity of Vanities! Henry VIII's ambitious plans for his tomb in
St George's Chapel, Windsor, came to naught. This conjectural drawing
of 1894 suggested what the finished monument could have looked like.*

and France. That Jack of all trades, Giovanni Portinari, responsible for
blowing up the huge priory church at Lewes, Sussex, for Cromwell during
the Dissolution and later supervising the construction of Sandown Castle
on the Isle of Wight, was paid £37 in December 1543 for copper work and
other charges incurred in working on the tomb that month.[45] Another
Italian, Nicholas Bellin of Modena, took over responsibility for completing the monument in the Westminster workshop, possibly in 1544.

At Henry's death, the monument had not been erected at Windsor
and its components remained at Westminster. With the accession of
Edward VI, his father's plans turned to ashes. His chantry and masses
were forgotten by his own executors; indeed, the money given to the
dean and chapter at Windsor for the Masses ended up in Somerset's
own purse.[46] The monument was still unassembled at Edward's death in
1553. In minutes drafted for his will, the young king could only plead:
'The king, my father's tomb to be made up.'

His successor Mary also nurtured pious hopes of completing the
monument, but may have decided against this in case she was seen
to be endorsing the memory and conduct of a schismatic from the
Church of Rome.

Eight years into Elizabeth's reign, her pangs of conscience about Henry's monument may have become irresistible. A survey of the components at Westminster showed that the principal elements survived, but the smaller items – 'small dragons and lions and other small beasts' – were missing, probably filched. The great gilded effigy of Henry remained, weighing eight hundredweight (406kg) out of the twenty hundredweight (1,016kg) of metalwork in the tomb.[47] Two years later, a new design and a model was completed by Richard Rowlands at a cost of £13 16s 8d and the components transported to Windsor and erected.

Henry had wanted it built between the chapel's choirstalls and the high altar, but this would have been an inconvenient obstacle for the clergy during divine service. So it was erected twelve yards (11m) away to the east in the disused Lady Chapel. The king's remains were not reburied beneath the monument, but remained in the vault where he was deposited in 1547.

The huge structure of bronze, white marble and black touchstone became a visitor attraction, but it endured for less than eighty years. With the usurpation of power by the Republican Commonwealth in the seventeenth century, its days were numbered. Parliamentary soldiers had already damaged it, before an order to remove all 'scandalous monuments and pictures' from churches was promulgated in December 1643. In April 1646, Henry's effigy and 'the images there defaced' were ordered to be sold off to 'the best advantage of the state'. Of the proceeds, £400 was paid 'to Colonel [Christopher] Whichcot, Governor of Windsor Castle', for him to disburse to meet the pay arrears of the garrison.[48]

Four giant bronze candlesticks from the tomb, bearing Henry's arms, supported by dragons and greyhounds, ended up in the cathedral of St Bravo in Ghent, Belgium, apparently presented by Anthony Triest, bishop of Ghent 1622–57.[49] They are still there today.

The four angels from Wolsey's tomb were incongruously placed on top of gateposts at Harrowden Hall, Northamptonshire. At some stage they disappeared, but many years later appeared on the art market, to be bought by the Victoria & Albert Museum in 2015 for £5 million.

The final indignity came in the nineteenth century. In 1804, plans were announced for a new royal mausoleum beneath 'Henry VIII's tomb house'. During its construction, the last remnants of Henry's monument were swept away. The black sarcophagus and its base were sent to London by a parsimonious government in 1808 for reuse in the monument to Admiral Lord Nelson in the crypt of St Paul's, where it rests today – commemorating its third person after Wolsey and Henry VIII.

Henry and Queen Jane Seymour were not allowed to rest in peace.

Their burial vault was opened in February 1649 for the burial of Charles I after his execution by Parliament. A slab was levered up and in the gloom below, the velvet palls still covering the royal coffins could be seen. While the grave was being readied, 'a foot soldier hid himself... and being greedy, crept into the vault and cut so much away of the... pall that covered [Henry's] great body... and wimbled a hole through the coffin... probably fancying that there was something well worth his adventure. The sexton... espied the sacrilegious person, who being searched, a bone was found about him with which he said he would haft a knife.'[50]

The vault was also examined when the pavement was relaid with black and white marble slabs in February 1686: 'The vault... is about eight or nine feet (2.4–2.7m) wide, encompassed on all sides with brick and a brick arch... over the top of it. It is about seven or eight feet deep, neither is there any passage by steps or otherwise. On the north side lies the body of the Lady Jane Seymour and next to her the body of [Henry], both of them lying in coffins of lead... upon wooden trestles. On the south side... lyeth the body of King Charles... in a coffin of lead.'[51]

Another opening was made on 1 April 1813, in the presence of the Prince Regent, later George IV. Henry's coffin was made of lead, enclosed in an elm shell one or two inches thick, then decayed and in fragments. 'The leaden coffin appeared to have been beaten in by violence about the middle and a considerable opening of it expose[d]... the skeleton of the king. Some beard remained on the chin...'[52]

In 1888, when the then Prince of Wales, deposited some relics of Charles I in the vault through a hole in the floor, the dilapidation of Henry's coffin was confirmed. 'The king's skull, with its very broad frontal, his thigh bones, ribs and other portions of the skeleton are exposed to view as the lead has been extensively ripped open, apparently to judge by the fractured edges, owing to the action of internal forces outward.'[53] It seems highly unlikely that Henry's coffin 'had been split open by the fumes of decomposition', after many centuries, as one later report suggested.[54]

A watercolour by W. J. Nutt of the royal vault in St George's Chapel, looking west in 1888. Left to right are the coffins of Charles I, Henry VIII and his third queen, Jane Seymour.

After the destruction of the king's monument, there was nothing to mark his passing. In 1818, the dean and chapter agreed to insert an inscription in the floor of the chapel[55] although the work was not undertaken until 1837 'by command of King William IV'. The black marble slab records the burials of Henry, Charles and an infant child of Queen Anne at the end of the seventeenth century.

The slab is incorrectly positioned. The royal vault lies thirteen feet (4m) to the east, in the middle of the next bay of the chapel, exactly where Henry directed his monument should stand in his will.[56]

For all his power and might, all his grandiose plans for an imposing Renaissance monument, this greatest of all English kings is commemorated only by a handful of brass letters set in a humble marble slab – in the wrong place. So much for his overdeveloped ego.

Henry laid the foundations of today's medical care and science; oversaw the birth of the modern administration and governance of Britain; manipulated public opinion adroitly through compelling propaganda; laid the foundations of the Anglican Church; created the Royal Navy and, above all, made his realm a major player in European politics, rather than merely a remote island on the edge of the old world.

He ruled ruthlessly, equipped with all the totalitarian machinery of a police state. Retribution and vengeance were bywords in his creed. Even in religion, after promising to lead the English Church out of Rome's bondage, his actions as Supreme Head were more remorseless than any pope. His crimes, in peace and war, may make him an ideal candidate for history's hall of infamy, alongside recent despots, but one cannot help feeling a shred of sympathy for all his terrible sufferings in his last years.

Most of Henry VIII's dreams went unfulfilled. His precious Tudor dynasty was snuffed out just fifty-six years later by the death of his daughter Elizabeth. So many people had died needlessly to keep it alive.

FINIS

Acknowledgements

This book could not have been written without the constant enthusiastic and very willing help and valuable support of my dear wife Sally who, like me, has come to lead almost a double existence, immersed in the labyrinthine conspiracies and complexities of Tudor life. This included field work scrambling around French landing places on the Isle of Wight and, much more enjoyably, research in Venice.

Like my other books, most of the material for this work has been drawn from contemporary documents and other sources, where possible employing the written or spoken words used by the protagonists living in those dangerous times.

I am very grateful for the generous help provided by the staffs of the National Archives at Kew, the British Library at Euston, the Wellcome Library, Hatfield House library and archives, St George's Chapel Archives, Windsor, and the State Archives in Venice. My thanks also go to Heather Rowlands, Head of Library and Collections and her staff at the Society of Antiquaries of London, and Kay Walters and her team at the incomparable library of the Athenaeum in Pall Mall.

A great number of friends and colleagues have kindly given invaluable assistance on a bewildering variety of facets of Tudor life and useful research directions, including Dr Adrian Ailes, Dr Jeremy Ashbee, the late Claude Blair, Edward Copisarow, Robin Harcourt Williams, Dr Julian Hoad, Dr Clare Rider, formerly Archivist and Chapter Librarian at St George's, Dr Richard Robinson (for invaluable assistance on forensic medicine), my fellow author Chris Skidmore MP, and Tim Tatton-Brown OBE, for our enjoyable discussions and his helpful information on Henry's monument. My thanks are also due to Marcel Hoad for his very kind logistical support.

I am also grateful, as always, for the loyal support and patient encouragement of Alan Samson and Simon Wright at Weidenfeld & Nicolson. My gratitude is also due to John English, my diligent copy-editor, David Atkinson, who compiled the index, and to Natalie Dawkins for her work on the illustrations. Finally, my thanks go to my agent Andrew Lownie.

Any errors or omissions are entirely my responsibility.

Robert Hutchinson
West Sussex, 2019

List of Abbreviations

Add. MS(S).	Additional Manuscript(s)	*HJ*	*Historical Journal*
APC	Acts of Privy Council	*HLQ*	*Huntington Library Quarterly*
Arch.	Archaeology/Archaeological	HMC	Historical Manuscripts Commission
Ass.	Association	HMSO	Her (His) Majesty's Stationery Office
Biog.	Biography		
BL	British Library	*HR*	*Historical Research*
BMJ	*British Medical Journal*	Int.	International
Bod. Lib.	Bodleian Library	Jnl.	Journal
Bull.	Bulletin	*Jnl. Eccl. Hist.*	*Journal of Ecclesiastical History*
c.	*circa*		
Coll.	College/Collection	*LP*	*Letters & Papers, Foreign & Domestic Henry VIII*
CP	Cecil Papers		
CSP	*Calendar State Papers*	Med.	Medical/Medicine
d.	died.	*Met. Mus. Jnl*	*Metropolitan Museum Journal*, New York
ed.	edited	MS(S)	Manuscript(s)
edn	edition	n.d.	no date
Econ. Hist. Rev.	*Economic History Review*	no.	number
EHR	*English Historical Review*	*ODNB*	*Oxford Dictionary of National Biography*
f, ff	folio(s)	p(p)	page(s)
fn.	footnote	Proc.	Proceedings
Hist.	History/Historical	pt.	part

r	recto	SP	State Papers (TNA)
RCHM	Royal Commission on Historical Manuscripts	St. P.	State Papers
		TNA	The National Archives, Kew
rep.	reprinted		
rev.	revised	*Trans.*	*Transactions*
Rev.	Review	transl.	translated
s.	series	*TRHS*	*Transactions Royal Historical Society*
SAL	Society of Antiquaries of London	v	verso/versus
Soc.	Society	*VCH*	*Victoria County History*
SGC	St George's Chapel, Windsor	vol.	volume
		VSA	Venice State Archives

Notes

Chapter 1 – Royal Obsessions

1   Shakespeare, *King Henry IV, Part 2*, Act III, Scene 1.

2   *Parliamentary Rolls of Medieval England*, vol. 15, p.93; Hutchinson, *Young Henry*, p.1.

3   Two of Henry's sisters died young: Elizabeth, aged three in 1495 and Katherine, soon after her birth in 1503. Margaret married James IV of Scotland and died in October 1541. Mary was married to Louis XII of France, thirty years her senior, in 1514 but he died three months later, supposedly from over-exertion in the marriage bed. She secretly married Charles Brandon, first duke of Suffolk, in 1515.

4   There have been suggestions that Henry VII and his wife Elizabeth of York had four sons rather than three, with another child, Edward, born around 1498 but dying the following year.

5   See Flugel, *Men and Their Motives*, p.277; 'On the Character and Married Life of Henry VIII', in *Psychoanalysis & History*, p.124ff.

6   *Correspondencia de Gutierre Gomez de Fuensalida, embajador en Alemania, Flandes é Inglaterra*, ed. Jacopo Stuart Fitz-James, duque de Alba, (Madrid, 1907), p.449.

7   Starkey, *Henry: Virtuous Prince*, pp.230–2.

8   Hutchinson, *Young Henry*, pp.95–6.

9   *LP*, vol. 10, pt. ii, p.117.

10   *LP*, vol. 14, pt. i, p.53.

11   J.S. Brewer, *Reign of Henry VIII*, vol. 1, p.97.

12   See Theodore Millon, *Disorders of Personality: DSM-IV-*[TM] *and Beyond* (New York: John Wiley, 1996), p.393.

13   22 Henry VIII, *cap.* 10. *Statutes of the Realm*, vol. 3, p.327.

14   David Mayall, *English Gypsies and State Policies* (Hatfield: University of Hertfordshire Press, 1995), p.20.

15   *APC*, vol. 1, p.304. Jews were formally allowed to return to England in 1655.

16   *LP*, vol. 17, p.26.

17   32 Henry VIII, *cap.* 16. *Statutes of the Realm*, vol. 3, p.765.

18 *CSP Spain*, vol. 5, pt. ii, p.28.

19 33 Henry VIII, *cap.* 8. *Statutes of the Realm*, vol. 3, p.837.

20 C.S.L. Davis & John Edwards, 'Katherine of Aragon', *ODNB*, vol. 30, p.895; MacNalty, *Henry VIII: A Difficult Patient*, p.162, who dates the birth in November 1513.

21 Dewhurst, 'The Alleged Miscarriages of Catherine of Aragon and Anne Boleyn', pp.49–56.

22 MacLennan, 'A Gynaecologist Looks at the Tudors', p.69, based on reports that the queen 'was feigned to be ripped'. Another writer believes it could have been a tear in the area of the body between the anus and vulva, or an episiotomy, an operation to enlarge the vulval orifice by cutting into the perineum to facilitate childbirth. Devonald, 'Henry VIII', p.20.

23 Anthony Hoskins, 'Mary Boleyn's Children – Offspring of Henry VIII?', *Genealogists' Magazine*, vol. 25 (1997), pp.347–8; Hetherington, 'Health of Henry VIII', p.956.

24 Hutchinson, *Young Henry*, p.223.

25 MacLennan, op. cit., p.68.

26 Whitley & Kramer, 'A New Explanation for the Reproductive Woes and Midlife Decline of Henry VIII', pp.827–48; Stride & Lopes Floro, 'Henry VIII, McLeod's Syndrome and Jacquetta's Curse', p.359.

27 Barrett, 'King Henry the Eighth', p.219.

28 George C. Kohn, *Encyclopaedia of Plague and Pestilence from Ancient Times to the Present*, 3rd edn (New York: InfoBase Publishing, 2011), p.228.

29 Dyer, 'Influence of Bubonic Plague in England 1500–1667', p.309.

30 On 8 October 1540, the Privy Council ordered the dean of Windsor and the town's mayor 'to cause the inhabitants of the infected houses with their families and household stuff to void the town to some good distance and from such other places as where the king's highness resorts, signifying unto them that the king would bear the charge of their removing'. Nicholas, *Proceedings . . .*, pp.56–7.

31 *LP*, vol. 18, pt. i, p.488.

32 MacNalty, op. cit., p.61.

33 Von Arni, 'The Treatment of Injury and Disease' in Rimer et al., *Henry VIII: Arms and the Man*, p.68.

34 Taviner, Thwaites & Gant, 'The English Sweating Sickness 1485–1551: A Viral Pulmonary Disease?', pp.96–8.

35 Caius, *A boke or counseill against the disease commonly called the sweate or sweatyng sicknesse*, f.9.

36 Hutchinson, *Thomas Cromwell*, p.23.

37 MacNalty, op. cit., p.57.

38 The leper Naaman bathed in the River Jordan seven times to cleanse himself of the disease (Second Book of Kings, chapter 5, v. 10) and Joshua was commanded to march around Jericho for seven days, with seven priests blowing seven trumpets outside the city's wall (Joshua, chapter 6, vv. 3–4).

39 BL, Add. MS 6,716, f.98*v*.

40 Hutchinson, *House of Treason*, p.79.

41 Peter Razell & Christine Spence, 'Social Capital and the History of Mortality in Britain', *International Jnl. of Epidemiology*, vol. 34 (2005), p.477. About 5 per cent died from smallpox in the mid-sixteenth century, with mortality rising to 30 per cent for those with the more virulent *variola major*.

42 Typhus was caused by the bite of the body louse, *pediculus humanus humanus*. It was brought to Europe in 1489 from Cyprus. During the 'Black Assizes' in Cambridge in 1522, the judges died from this disease.

43 MacNalty, op. cit., p.55.

44 The 1510 epidemic was proportionately as devastating as that of 1918–19, when a quarter of the British population was infected and 228,000 died.

45 Stow, *Annals*, p.995. Foxley lived for another forty-one years.

46 BL, Sloane MS 1,017, f.30*v*.

47 BL, Sloane MS 1,047. Other cures are by his royal doctors, Walter Crome, John Chambre, Sir William Butts and the Italian Dr Augustine.

48 Bloom & James, *Medical Practitioners...*, p.1.

49 Hutchinson, *Young Henry*, p.187.

50 In 1540, the king was reported 'somewhat troubled by a tertian [fever]. The extremity is past and his highness [is] clean rid... and out of all danger'. BL, Harleian MS 6,989, f.45.

51 Hall, *Chronicle*, p.674; Keynes, 'Personality and Health of Henry VIII', p.176.

52 MacNalty, op. cit., p.90.

53 Hall, *Chronicle*, p.697.

54 Kybett, 'Henry VIII – A Malnourished King?', p.22.

55 Barrett, op. cit., p.231.

56 Park, *Ailing, Aging, Addicted...*, p.44.

57 *LP*, vol. 12, pt. i, p.486.

58 Hutchinson, *Last Days of Henry VIII*, p.129.

59 Chalmers & Chaloner, '500 Years Later...', p.516.

60 *LP*, vol. 13, pt. i, p.368. Another cause could be deep vein thrombosis which may have caused veinous hypertension, although ulcers are surprisingly painless unless complicated by cellulitis. See Perkins, 'Henry VIII's Leg Ulcers', p.81.

61 'Lisle Letters', vol. 5, p.1415. This demonstrates Henry's then adherence to the Catholic liturgy.

62 *St. P.*, vol. 8, pt. v, p.500: Wallop to Henry VIII; Mellune, 28 December 1540.

Chapter 2 – Safeguarding the Realm

1   TNA, SP 1/116/92.
2   *LP*, vol. 14, pt. 1, p.14.
3   Wilkins, *Concilia...*, vol. 3, p.840. The Bull could not be published in England, so was read out as close as papal authority could reach: at Coldstream, across the border in Scotland and in France, at the Channel ports of Boulogne and Dieppe.
4   The full title of the book, first published in Rome in 1539, was *Pro ecclesiasticæ unitatis defensione* – 'Defence of the Unity of the Church'. Pole insisted it was originally for Henry's eyes only. For an analysis of its contents, see Mayer, *Reginald Pole, Prince & Prophe*t, pp.13–30.
5   BL, Add. MS 25,114, f.262.
6   Margaret was the daughter of George Plantagenet, first duke of Clarence, younger brother of Edward IV, who was allegedly drowned in a butt of malmsey wine in the Tower of London on 18 February 1478, but more probably was beheaded secretly.
7   *LP*, vol. 14, pt. 1, p.57.
8   *St. P.*, vol. 8, pt. 5, p.166.
9   *LP*, vol. 14, pt. 1, pp.165, 169.
10 Hutchinson, *Thomas Cromwell*, p.188.

11 Robinson, *Original Letters...*, p.624.
12 These rumours stemmed from Cromwell's order that parishes should keep their own registers of births, deaths and marriages.
13 Colvin et al., *History of the King's Works 1485–1660*, vol. 4, pt. 2, p.369. Seventy-four Martello towers were built along England's coasts in 1804–12. Later in the nineteenth century, formidable defences were erected to protect Portsmouth naval base after fears of invasion by Napoleon III; the so-called 'Palmerston Follies'.
14 Ibid., p.330.
15 Ibid., p.339.
16 Ibid., p.224.
17 Morison, *An Exhortation...*, signatures Diii^r–Diiii^r. During the Parliament that met from April, Morison also urged the granting of a generous sum to Henry to enable him to save England from the enemies of God and the crown, in a speech corrected by Cromwell. See BL, Cotton MS, Titus B, i, ff.103. Two weeks before Parliament sat, he was appointed a Gentleman of the Privy Chamber.
18 Ibid., signatures Biii–Biv, Bv^v, Bvi, Cii^v, Ciii^v. See also Sharpe, *Selling the Tudor Monarchy*, pp.123–5.
19 *LP*, vol. 14, pt. 2, p.340.
20 'Morris pikes' were long polearms, fifteen to eighteen feet (4.6–5.5m) in height, carried

by massed infantry. The name derived from 'Moorish pikes' in the belief that they were used by the Moors. Sir Charles Oman, *A History of War in the Sixteenth Century* (London: Methuen & Co., 1937), p.291.

21 Bills or pole weapons included halberds (with combined axe and spear point), partisans (spear point) and glaives, a long edged weapon with protruding hooks for attacking horsemen. Many bill weapons were derived from agricultural implements.

22 Wriothesley, *Chronicle*, vol. 1, pp.95–7.

23 *LP*, vol. 14, pt. 1, p.440.

24 Thomas Lott, 'Muster of the Citizens of London in the 31st year of the reign of Henry VIII, Communicated from the Records of the Corporation of London', *Archaeologia*, vol. 32 (1847), pp.30–7.

25 Wriothesley, *Chronicle*, vol. 1, pp.99–100. See also Anglo, *Spectacle, Pageantry and Early Tudor Policy*, pp.269–70.

26 Mayer, op. cit., pp.95–6.

27 *LP*, vol. 14, pt. 1, p.209: Pole to the Constable of France; Girona, 16 March 1539.

28 Ibid., p.235: Pole to Cardinal Farnese; Carpentras, 25 March 1539.

29 Kaulek, *Correspondence politique...*, p.95: Marillac to Francis I; London, 1 May 1539.

30 Scarisbrick, *Henry VIII*, pp.365–6.

31 Kaulek, op. cit., p.436.

32 BL, Add. MS 8,716, f.67r.

33 TNA, SP 1/219/51.

34 A museum devoted to the Spanish Inquisition is located in the remains of the Castillo de San Jorge, headquarters of the *Tribuno del Santo Oficio de la Santa Inquisicion* in 1481–1785

35 Ellis, *Original Letters...*, 2nd s., vol. 2, p.151; BL, Harleian MS 295, ff.146.

36 *LP*, vol. 15, p.428: William Ostrych to Roger Basing; Sanlúcar, 8 July 1540.

37 *St. P.*, vol. 8, pt. 5, p.426: Roger Basing to earl of Southampton; Seville, 15 August 1540.

38 *LP*, vol. 16, pp.123, 163–3.

39 Nicholas, *Proceedings...*, vol. 7, p.131.

40 *APC*, vol. 1, p.60.

41 *CSP Spain*, vol. 8, p.173.

42 Mary and Elizabeth were declared illegitimate under the Second Succession Act of 1536. However, the Third Succession Act of 1543 (35 Henry VIII, *cap.* 1) reinstated Mary and Elizabeth to the succession, after their half-brother Edward.

43 *Cal. Patent Rolls Edward VI*, vol. 1, 1547–8, ed. Sir Maxwell Lyte (London: HMSO, 1924), pp.66–8.

44 'The Act for the Subsidy', 32 Henry VIII, *cap.* 49, 50.

45 Now Guînes.

46 *LP*, vol. 14, pt.1, p.502: Sir Edward Ringley to Cromwell; The Downs, 11 June 1539: 'This

week we had business with the King's labourers, saying they would have six pence a day but after I had spoken to them I caused them to return to work.'

47 'Oyer and Terminer' is a partial translation of the Anglo-French phrase *oyer et terminer*, which means literally 'to hear and determine'.

48 *LP*, vol. 16, p.445: Sir John Wallop to the Privy Council; Guisnes, 22 June 1541.

49 Colvin et al., op. cit., p.371.

50 Colvin et al., op. cit., p.377.

51 The base of the bastion at Yarmouth now forms, incongruously, one wall of the corridor to the ground-floor toilets of the George Hotel as, over the centuries, buildings have been constructed abutting the castle walls.

52 Now in the eastern part of the Czech Republic.

53 O'Neil, 'Stefan von Haschenperg...', p.145.

54 Hutchinson, *Thomas Cromwell*, pp.228, 171–2, 226, 313.

55 *LP*, vol. 20, pt. 1, pp.634, 653.

56 TNA, SP 1/166/183.

57 *LP*, vol. 16, p.260. Earl of Hertford and Richard Lee to Henry VIII; Calais, 19 February 1540; Colvin et al., vol. 3, pt. 1, p.355.

58 BL, Cotton MS, Augustus I. i, f.49.

59 *St. P.*, vol. 9, p.527.

60 A 'hackbut' is an early form of musket.

61 *LP*, vol. 18, pt. 2, p.175. Wallop to Sir William Paget; the camp before Landrecy, 26 October 1543.

62 *St. P.*, vol. 9, p.543. Wallop to Sir William Paget; 'our camp two leagues from Cambrai called Lyney', 7 November 1543.

63 The earliest known working refracting telescopes appeared in 1608 in the Netherlands and are credited to the German spectacle-maker Hans Lippershey (1570–1619).

64 Kaulek, op. cit., p.289: Marillac to Anne de Montmorency, Constable of France; London, 10 April 1541.

65 Scarisbrick, op. cit., p.500.

66 Rodger, *The Safeguard of the Sea*, vol. 1, p.210.

67 David Loades, 'Henry's Army and Navy' in Rimer et al., *Henry VIII: Arms and the Man*, pp.52–3.

68 Gonson 'feloniously killed himself' (*LP*, vol. 20, pt. 1, p.56) and a suicide's body was not normally buried in consecrated ground. However, Gonson was buried in his parish church of St Dunstan's in the East, London, which suggests the circumstances of his death were concealed.

Chapter 3 – Death of a 'Most False and Corrupt Traitor'

1 Cromwell was probably held in the lodgings of the Lieutenant of the Tower, on the east side

of the inner ward. Borman, *Thomas Cromwell...*, p.384.

2   *Spanish Chronicle*, p.103.

3   Bird was executed for treason in August 1540. He claimed that if the king went to fight the rebellion himself 'he will never come home again...' and declared: 'O good Lord, I [think] all the world will be heretics in a little time.' T.B. & T.J. Howell, *Complete Collection of State Trials*, vol. 1, p.483.

4   'Act of Attainder', 32 Henry VIII, *cap*. 61.

5   Evidence supporting the charge of sodomy came from 'an old woman called Mother Huntley', as suggested by the Privy Council instruction to interrogate her about 'certain grave misdemeanours'. *LP*, vol. 15, p.369.

6   Mary, born in 1529, was Hungerford's daughter by his second wife, Alice, daughter of William Lord Sandys. (Bernard Burke, *A Genealogical History of the Dormant, Abeyant and Extinct Peerages of the British Empire*, London: Harrison, 1866, p.292.) Mary went on to marry Thomas Baker and after his death, Thomas Shaa, and died in 1613. (Ibid.) The eldest daughter Eleanor, mentioned only in an indenture of 14 April 1528, was reportedly the wife of William Maister, named in the sodomy charge. (*Antiquary*, vol. 4 (1881), pp.50, 114.) The rape allegation was made by the French ambassador on 29 July 1540. (Kaulek, *Correspondence politique...*, p.207.)

7   The Buggery Act (25 Henry VIII, *cap*. 6) was the first penal law against homosexuals. Those found guilty were hanged and their property forfeited to the crown. Nicholas Udall (1504–56), cleric, Provost of Eton College and playwright of the early English stage comedy *Ralph Roister Doister*, was the first to be charged solely under this Act in 1541 for offences against his pupils. His death sentence was commuted to life imprisonment, but he was released from the Marshalsea Prison, Southwark, before a year was out, thanks to friends at court. Buggery remained a capital offence in England and Wales until the Offences against the Person Act was passed in 1861.

8   *Spanish Chronicle*, p.98.

9   A wherry was a passenger boat, rowed by two men. They were clinker-built, with long overhanging bows so that passengers could step ashore dry-shod. Kaulek, op. cit., p.193: Marillac to Anne de Montmorency, Constable of France; London, 23 June 1540; *Spanish Chronicle*, p.99.

10 Kaulek, op. cit., p.189: Marillac to Frances I; London, 10 June 1540.

11 The Drapers' Company hall now

occupies the site of Cromwell's house.

12 Kaulek, op. cit., pp.193–4: Marillac to Anne de Montmorency; London, 23 June 1540.

13 Ibid., p.193.

14 Starkey, *The Inventory of King Henry VIII*, items 904, 1094, 12101.

15 Jenkyns, *Remains of Thomas Cranmer*, vol.1, pp.298–9.

16 Hall, *Chronicle . . .*, p.839.

17 Kaulek, op. cit., pp.193–4: Marillac to Anne de Montmorency; London, 23 June 1540.

18 Ibid., p.191: Francis I to Marillac; Fontainebleau, 15 June 1540.

19 Scarisbrick, *Henry VIII*, p.368.

20 Düren is today in North-Rhine-Westphalia in Germany.

21 Hatfield House, CP 1/27.

22 Wriothesley, *Chronicle*, vol. 1, p.109.

23 *Eccles. Mems.*, vol. 1, pt. 2, pp.456–7.

24 Wriothesley, op. cit., vol. 1, p.110.

25 *Eccles. Mems.*, vol. 1, pt. 2, p.455.

26 A partlet was worn around the neck and the upper part of the chest.

27 *Eccles. Mems.*, vol. 1, pt. 2, p.457. This description of events differs from those published by chroniclers. Wriothesley has the king departing to cast off his disguise and returning to Anne's room when everyone 'did him reverence'. Anne herself 'humbled [herself] lowly to the king's grace . . . and so talked together lovingly and afterwards [Henry] took her by the hand and led her into another chamber where they solaced [provided pleasure] that night and till Friday afternoon'. (*Chronicle*, vol. 1, p.110.) Raphael Holinshed provides a similar account: The king came 'suddenly to her presence, whereof she at the first was somewhat astonished, but after he had spoken to her and welcomed her, she with loving countenance and gracious behaviour, welcomed him on her knees, whom he gently took up and kissed and all that afternoon communed and devised with [and] supped that night with her'. (Holinshed, *Chronicles*, vol. 3, p.811.)

28 Her nickname was first used by Bishop Gilbert Burnet in the late seventeenth century.

29 Hatfield House, CP 1/27.

30 *LP*, vol. 15, p.388.

31 Hatfield House, CP 1/27.

32 Holinshed, *Chronicles*, vol. 3, p.814.

33 BL, Cotton MS, Titus B, i, ff.409–11; Hatfield House, CP1/27.

34 *Eccles. Mems.*, vol. 1, pt. 2, p.460.

35 Ibid., pp.458–9.

36 TNA, E 101/422/15.

37 Hatfield House, CP 1/27.

38 *Eccles. Mems.*, vol. 1, pt. 2, pp.462–3.

39 Hatfield House, CP 1/22.

40 *LP*, vol. 15, p.206. Marillac to Anne de Montmorency; London, 10 April 1540.

41 BL, Harleian MS 6,074, f.57r.

42 Ponet, *A Short Treatise of Political Power*, book XLVI, p.78.

43 Fuller, *History of the Worthies of England*, vol. 3, p.169.

44 See, for example, Glyn Redworth, *In Defence of the Church Catholic; The Life of Stephen Gardiner* (Oxford: Blackwell, 1990).

45 Riordan & Ryrie, 'Stephen Gardiner and the Making of a Protestant Villain', pp.1040, 1046.

46 'An Act for abolishing of Diversity of Opinions of certain Articles concerning Christian Religion', 31 Henry VIII, *cap*. 14.

47 Wriothesley, *Chronicle*, vol. 1, p.103.

48 Nichols, *Narratives*, p.258.

49 The British Library has a copy of the proposals, copiously corrected by the king, which indicates his personal involvement in drafting the legislation. (Cotton MS, Cleopatra E, v, ff.313–20.) Unsurprisingly, all his amendments were included in the final text.

50 MacCulloch, *Thomas Cranmer, A Life*, p.254.

51 Nichols, *Narratives*, p.294.

52 Williams, *Henry VIII and his Court*, p.193.

53 TNA, SP 1/158/124.

54 *Eccles. Mems.*, vol. 1, pt. 2, pp.459–60.

55 32 Henry VIII, *cap*. 24; *Statutes of the Realm*, vol. 3, p.778.

56 Hall, *Chronicle*, p.838.

57 Lisle had complained to Sir Anthony Browne, Master of the Horse, that Cromwell's inaction against religious reformers in Calais had made his task of enforcing the Six Articles impossible. He ended: 'I beseech you, keep this matter close, for if it should come to my Lord Privy Seal's knowledge or ear, I [would be] half undone.' '*Lisle Letters*', vol. 5, no. 1415.

58 Kaulek, op. cit., p.187: Marillac to Anne de Montmorency; London, 1 June 1540.

59 *St. P.*, vol. 8, p.362: Henry VIII to Sir John Wallop; 22 June 1540.

60 'Attainder of Thomas Cromwell, earl of Essex', 32 Henry VIII, *cap*. 62; BL, Cotton MS, Titus B, i, f.503; Scarisbrick, op. cit., pp.378–9.

61 McLaren, 'Queenship in Early Modern England & Scotland', p.943.

62 Ellis, *Original Letters*, 2nd s., vol. 2, p.162. Gregory's wife Elizabeth afterwards wrote to Henry thanking him for the mercy 'shown her poor husband' and herself which had relieved the 'extreme indigence' brought them by the 'heinous offences' of her father-in-law. BL, Cotton MS, Vespasian F, xiii, f.157.

63 Carlton: 'Thomas Cromwell: A Study in Interrogation', pp.118, 120.

64 BL, Cotton MS, Otho C, x, ff.242–5. For reconstruction of damaged portion, see Scarisbrick, op. cit., fn. pp.379–80.

65 Hatfield House, CP 1/27.

66 Hatfield House, CP 1/23.

67 BL, Cotton MS, Otho C, x, f.232.

68 TNA, E 30/1470.

69 32 Henry VIII, *cap.* 25.

70 TNA, 30/1472/4.

71 Hatfield House, CP 1/28.

72 Hatfield House, CP 1/29.

73 Foxe, *Acts & Monuments*, vol. 5, p.438; Bell, *Notices of the Historic Persons . . .*, p.113.

74 Hall, *Chronicle*, p.839.

75 Stow's *Annals*, p.976; Hall, *Chronicle*, p.837; BL, Harleian MS 3,362, f.17. It may have taken three blows of the axe to finally decapitate Cromwell. See Borman, *Thomas Cromwell*, p.385.

76 *LP*, vol. 21, pt. ii, p.284.

77 The Oatlands Park Hotel (Oatlands Drive, Weybridge KT13 9HB) now occupies the site of the palace (Ordnance Survey National Grid reference TQ 078 651). It was acquired by Henry in December 1537 and new royal apartments created. The structure was extended to include a turreted gateway and polygonal lantern tower at a total cost of £17,000. See Colvin et al., *History of the King's Works*, vol. 4, pt. ii, pp.183, 205–17.

78 Hall, *Chronicle*, p.840.

79 'Greyfriars Chronicle', p.44.

80 Hall, *Chronicle*, p.840.

81 *LP*, vol. 15, pp.492, 493.

Chapter 4 – A King Besotted

1 The date of Katherine's birth is uncertain, but family records suggest she was born between 1518 and 1524 – probably nearer the later date. Her age of nineteen at her marriage seems the most plausible estimate.

2 Clark, *Dynastic Politics . . .* (unpublished thesis), pp.241, 243.

3 Strickland, *Lives of the Queens of England . . .*, vol. 2, p.337. In 1535, Sir Richard Page asked Viscount Lisle for help in recovering Howard's debt of £60 which he had 'forborne him this fifteen years': '*Lisle Letters*', vol. 2, p.507.

4 Ibid., pp.499–500.

5 Bindoff, *House of Commons 1509–58*, vol. 2, p.564.

6 Warnicke, 'Katherine Howard', *ODNB*, vol. 30, p.906.

7 Clark, op. cit., p.243.

8 *LP*, vol. 16, p.270. Richard Hilles to Henry Bullinger; London, February 1541.

9 TNA, SP 1/167/160.

10 Lacey Baldwin Smith, *Tudor Tragedy*, p.103.

11 Nichols, *Narratives*, p.259.

12 *CSP Spain*, vol. 6, pt. i, p.37.

13 William Leadbetter, yeoman, and his son, also called William, husbandman, of Washington were indicted for the murder of Richard Bollockherd. They fled

justice, probably overseas. See *LP*, vol. 15, p.295.

14 BL, Royal MS 7 C. XVI, f.60.

15 Warnicke, 'Katherine Howard', p.907.

16 Hall, *Chronicle*, p.839; *LP*, vol.15, p.419: Marillac to Montmorency; London, 6 July 1540.

17 Kaulek, *Correspondence politique*..., p.201: Marillac to Francis I; London, 21 July 1540.

18 Ibid., p.203. The gossip about Katherine being pregnant was widespread in diplomatic circles. A report to King John III of Portugal on 26 July said she 'is already with child': *LP*, vol. 15, pp.453–4.

19 *LP*, vol. 15, p.438.

20 BL, Cotton MS, Otho C, x, f.250.

21 Smith, *Tudor Tragedy*, p.123.

22 Wriothesley, *Chronicle*, vol. 1, pp.121–2.

23 *LP*, vol. 15, p.490.

24 Ibid.: Marillac to Montmorency; London, 15 August 1540 and *LP*, vol. 16, p.4: Marillac to Francis I; London, 3 September 1540.

25 Kaulek, op. cit., p.217: Marillac to Montmorency; 3 September 1540.

26 *Spanish Chronicle*, p.77.

27 BL, Stowe MS 559, ff.55–69r.

28 *LP*, vol. 15, p.498: Marillac to Montmorency; London, 24 August 1541.

29 Mary Howard had married Henry's bastard son Henry Fitzroy in November 1533 but he died in June 1536. Their marriage was never consummated. Four

years later, Mary was granted thirteen manors and lands formerly owned by religious houses in East Anglia: *LP*, vol. 15, p.205.

30 Wriothesley, *Chronicle*, vol. 1, p.123.

31 *LP*, vol. 16, p.148.

32 Grafton Manor was acquired by Henry in 1526. The two-storey building on the site is a seven-teenth- and nineteenth-century house.

33 Nicholas, *Proceedings*..., vol. 7, pp.16–17, 21; Tighe & Davis, *Annals of Windsor*, p.566.

34 *LP*, vol. 16, p.19. Cranmer to Wriothesley; Lambeth, St Matthew's Day (21 September) 1540.

35 Hutchinson, *House of Treason*, pp.77–9.

36 TNA, SP 1/167/127.

37 TNA, SP 1/163/46r.

38 Wriothesley, *Chronicle*, vol. 1, p.119.

39 *LP*, vol. 16, p.270: Richard Hilles to Henry Bullinger; London, February 1541.

40 Stow, *Annals*, p.977; Hall, *Chronicle*, p.840.

41 Mary I refounded a small number of religious houses in 1555–7, including that at Westminster.

42 *CSP Spain*, vol. 6, pt. i, pp.294, 308.

43 Reported by Marillac on 1 October 1540. He doubted the rumour's veracity: Kaulek, op. cit., p.228.

44 Warnicke, 'Katherine Howard', p.907; BL, Sloane MS 3,837.

45 Kaulek, op. cit., p.274: Marillac to Montmorency; London, 3 March 1541.

46 Ibid., p.273: Marillac to Francis I; London, 3 March 1541.

47 Lacey Baldwin Smith, *Henry VIII: The Mask of Royalty*, p.169.

48 *LP*, vol. 16, p.328.

49 Henry had two royal barges, *Lyon* and the *Greyhound*, moored at Lambeth, although a new dock was built at Whitehall in 1540.

50 Sowerby, 'Richard Pate...', pp.265–6.

51 *LP*, vol. 16, p.220.

52 This bishopric was vacant because of the death in Rome of Geronimo de Ghinucci who had been deprived of the see by Henry in 1535 and replaced by Hugh Latimer.

53 *LP*, vol. 16, p.318: Privy Council to Lord William Howard; London, 26 March 1541.

54 Muir, *Life and Letters of Sir Thomas Wyatt*, p.67.

55 BL, Harleian MS 78, f.5.

56 Nicola Shulman, *Graven with Diamonds: The Many Lives of Thomas Wyatt, Courtier, Poet, Assassin, Spy* (London: Short Books, 2011), pp.227–9.

57 *LP*, vol. 16, pp.319–20: Eustace Chapuys to Charles V; London, 27 March 1541; *CSP Spain*, vol. 6, pt. i, p.315: Chapuys to Queen of Hungary; 27 March 1541.

58 Warnicke, 'Katherine Howard', op. cit., p.907.

59 Wriothesley, *Chronicle*, vol. 1, p.73.

60 *LP*, vol. 16, p.239.

61 The claim was made by Richard Hilles in May 1542. See Robinson, *Original Letters*, pp.226–7.

62 Wriothesley, *Chronicle*, vol. 1, p.118.

63 Nicholas, op. cit., pp.155–6; *LP*, vol. 16, p.298.

64 Kaulek, op. cit., p.289: Marillac to Montmorency; London, 10 April 1541.

65 Russell, *Young and Damned and Fair...*, p.192.

66 Warnicke, 'Katherine Howard', op. cit., p.908.

67 Robert Holgate was Lord President of the Council of the North from 1538. Once master of the Gilbertine religious order, he was a protégé of Cromwell. He was archbishop of York from 1545.

68 Pontefract Castle, in West Yorkshire, was built in 1070 to the east of All Saints' Church. It now lies in ruins.

69 *CSP Spain*, vol. 6, pt. i, p.319: Chapuys to Charles V; London, Easter Day [17 April], 1541.

70 Kaulek, op. cit., p.294: Marillac to Montmorency, London, 27 April 1541.

71 *CSP Spain*, vol. 6, pt. i, p.321: Chapuys to Charles V; London, 1 May 1541.

72 Tudor bureaucracy recorded the eight shillings charged for the prisoners' manacles,

and the three shillings paid to Thomas Robinson, smith, for fitting the prisoners' fetters in York. The sheriff's officers were recompensed for hanging up the quartered bodies and they also petitioned to receive the prisoners' clothing as has been 'evermore accustomed': *LP*, vol. 16, pp.413–15.

73 Sansom, 'The Wakefield Conspiracy of 1541...', pp.222–3.

74 Dickens, 'Yorkshire Submissions...', p.267.

75 TNA, C 65/147/22.

76 *LP*, vol. 15, p.217.

77 Pierce, *Margaret Pole...*, p.172.

78 *LP*, vol. 14, pt. ii, p.64. Pole to Cardinal Contarini; Carpentras, 22 September 1539.

79 Nicholas, op. cit., p.147.

80 BL, Arundel MS, 97, f.186.

81 *LP*, vol. 16, p.205; Cardinal Pole to the bishop of Lavour, undated but probably late 1540.

82 Pierce, op. cit., p.176.

83 *LP*, vol. 16, p.436: Chapuys to the Queen of Hungary: London, 10 June 1541.

84 [L. Beccadelli], *Life of Cardinal Reginald Pole by Ludovico Beccadelli* (London: C. Bathurst, 1766), pp.155–6.

85 Kaulek, op. cit., p.320: Marillac to Francis I; London, 18 July 1541.

86 Wriothesley, *Chronicle*, vol. 1, p.124.

87 *LP*, vol. 15, pp.397–9.

88 Kaulek, op. cit., p.309: Marillac to Francis I; London, 29 May 1541.

89 Kaulek, op. cit., p.309.

90 Sansom, op. cit., p.233.

91 Thornton, 'Henry VIII's Progress through Yorkshire...', p.238.

92 Hall, *Chronicle*, p.842.

93 Thornton, op. cit., pp.239–40.

94 At his accession in 1509, Henry had issued a charter confirming all St Mary's liberties and possessions. With fifty choir monks and fifty stewards, it was one of the richest abbeys in England with a net annual value of £1,650, or more than £1 million at today's prices. See *The Noble City of York*, ed. Alberic Stacpoole (York: Cerialis Press, 1972), pp.665 and 671.

95 Scarisbrick, *Henry VIII*, p.428.

96 'Hamilton Papers', vol. 1, p.98.

97 Kaulek, op. cit., p.350: Marillac to Francis I; London, 29 October 1541.

Chapter 5 – Deadheading the 'Blushing Rose'

1 An early keyboard spinet, popular in the sixteenth century.

2 BL, Cotton MS, Otho C, x, f.250; Nicholas, *Proceedings...*, vol. 7, pp.354–5.

3 Kaulek, *Correspondence politique...*, p.363: Marillac to Francis I; London, 22 November 1541.

4 Nicholas, op. cit., p.353.

5 Dereham was notorious in Ireland for committing acts of piracy.

6   BL, Cotton MS, Otho C, x, f.250; Nicholas, op. cit., p.355.
7   *LP*, vol. 16, p.635.
8   Ibid., p.622.
9   TNA, SP 1/167/117-29.
10 TNA, SP 1/167/100.
11 Kaulek, op. cit., p.352: Marillac to Francis I; London, 12 November 1541.
12 Jenkyns, *Remains of Thomas Cranmer*, p.308.
13 TNA, SP 1/167/121.
14 'Bath MSS', vol. 2, pp.8–9.
15 Davenport later testified that 'Mr Johns, the queen's gentleman usher had fallen out with Dereham for sitting at dinner or supper with the queen's council.' He sent a message tartly inquiring whether Dereham was a councillor and he replied: 'Go to Mr Johns and tell him I was on the queen's council before he knew her and shall be when she has forgotten him.' *LP*, vol. 16, p.619.
16 Ibid., p.650.
17 Kaulek, op. cit., p.370: Marillac to Frances I; London, 7 December 1541; Smith, *A Tudor Tragedy*, pp.178ff.
18 BL, Cotton MS, Otho C, x, f.250; Nicholas, op. cit., p.355.
19 *LP*, vol. 16, p.611: Chapuys to the Queen of Hungary, London, 10 November 1541.
20 TNA, SP 1/167/123.
21 Ironically, Baynton was also vice-chamberlain to Anne Boleyn at the time of her disgrace.
22 Joyce Culpeper's first marriage was to Ralph Leigh, who died in 1509.
23 TNA, SP 1/167/123.
24 TNA, SP 1/167/161.
25 BL, Cotton MS, Otho C, x, f.250; Nicholas, op. cit., p.355.
26 Kaulek, op. cit., p.352: Marillac to Francis I; London, 14 November 1541.
27 TNA, SP 1/167/159.
28 Kaulek, op. cit., p.363: Marillac to Francis I; London, 22 November 1541.
29 A kirtle was a type of gown or outer petticoat.
30 'Bath MSS', vol. 2, pp.9–10.
31 Wriothesley, *Chronicle*, vol. 1, pp.130–1.
32 TNA, SP 1/167/123.
33 The deposition by Katherine Tylney is in two distinct hands.
34 TNA, SP 1/167/131-4.
35 Hoyle & Ramsdale, 'The Royal Progress of 1541 . . ., p.264.
36 TNA, SP 1/167/133-4.
37 TNA, SP 1/167/159.
38 TNA, SP 1/167/14.
39 Smith, *Mask of Royalty*, p.174.
40 *CSP Spain*, vol. 6, pt. i, pp.410–11: Chapuys to Nicholas Perrenot, sieur de Granvelle; London, 3 December 1541.
41 *LP*, vol. 16, p.655.
42 *St. P.*, vol. 1, p.706: Privy Council to Sir Anthony Browne and Sir Ralph Sadler; 6 December 1541.
43 *St. P.*, vol. 1, p.698. The four Clerks of the Signet were officials who attached seals to letters patent.

44 Ibid., p.701: Council with the King to the Privy Council in London.

45 Nicholas, op. cit., p.279.

46 *CSP Spain*, vol. 6, pt. i, p.410: Chapuys to Charles V; London, 11 December 1541.

47 *St. P.*, vol. 1, pp.716–17: Cranmer to Henry VIII; Lambeth, 13 January 1542.

48 Kaulek, op. cit., p.373: Marillac to Francis I; London, 16 December 1541.

49 *LP*, vol. 16, p.619.

50 Ibid., p.652: Chapuys to Charles V; London, 3 December 1541.

51 Ibid., p.628.

52 Kaulek, op. cit., p.369.

53 Wriothesley, *Chronicle*, vol. 1, pp.130–1.

54 *LP*, vol. 16, pp.645–6.

55 Kaulek, op. cit., p.370: Marillac to Francis I; London, 7 December 1541.

56 The place of execution at Tyburn is modern-day Marble Arch.

57 *St. P.*, vol. 1, p.707.

58 Wriothesley, *Chronicle*, vol. 1, pp.131–2.

59 Smith, *Mask of Royalty*, p.174.

60 Bellamy, *Tudor Law of Treason*, p.41.

61 Kaulek, op. cit., p.363: Marillac to Francis I; London, 22 November 1541.

62 *St. P.*, vol. 1, p.710.

63 Ibid., p.708. The Privy Council was told that all Lord William Howard's gold plate was lost during the crossing of the English Channel. The captains of the fortresses on the Kent coast were ordered to discover whether this was true 'or only a device to conceal' his wealth. His valuables eventually turned up safely 'except the horses and mules'.

64 *CSP Spain*, vol. 6, pt i, p.409: Chapuys to Charles V; London, 11 December 1541.

65 Kaulek, op. cit., p.373: Marillac to Francis I; London, 16 December 1541.

66 *St. P.*, vol. 1, p.721: Norfolk to Henry VIII; Kenninghall Lodge, [Norfolk], 15 December 1541.

67 *LP*, vol. 16, p.685: Chapuys to sieur de Granvelle; London, 30 December 1541.

68 Head, *Ebbs and Flows of Fortune...*, p.189.

69 Kaulek, op. cit., p.388. Marillac to Francis I, London, 13 February 1542. The dowager's fortune of 400,000 or 500,000 crowns (i.e. £100,000 or £125,000), equates to £58–£73 million in today's money.

70 The queen's name may also have been expunged from reports of parliamentary proceedings.

71 33 Henry VIII, *cap.* 21.

72 Lehmberg, 'Parliamentary Attainder in the Reign of Henry VIII', pp.695–7.

73 33 Henry VIII, *cap.* 21; *Statutes of the Realm*, vol. 3, p.857.

74 The last British monarch to grant royal assent in person was Queen Victoria in 1854.

75 Hall, *Chronicles*, p.843.

76 33 Henry VIII, *cap.* 20. *Statutes of the Realm*, vol. 3, pp.855–7.

77   *CSP Spain*, vol 6, pt i, p.465:
     Chapuys to Charles V; London,
     29 January 1542.
78   Ibid., p.472: Chapuys to Charles
     V; London, 25 February
     1542. Henry's hypochondria
     demanded the curative powers
     of the ring.
79   Ibid., p.472: Chapuys to Charles
     V; 25 February 1542.
80   Kaulek, op. cit., p.388: Marillac
     to Francis I; London, 13
     February 1542.
81   In 1876, the chapel was repaved.
     Many of those buried there
     were found barely two feet
     (0·6m) below the floor. Traces
     of a large amount of quicklime
     were discovered in the earth,
     used to destroy the corpses.
     Little was left of the bones
     of Katherine Howard. See *St.
     Paul's Ecclesiological Soc.*, vol. 2
     (1886–90), p.352.
82   Ellis, *Original Letters...*, 1st s.,
     2nd edn, vol. 2, pp.128–9.
83   Stow's *Annals*, p.981.
84   *CSP Spain*, vol 6, pt i, p.473.

**Chapter 6 – The 'Rough Wooing'
of Scotland**

1   BL, Cotton MS, Titus B, i, f.551.
2   'An Act that the King of
     England, his Heirs and
     Successors be Kings of Ireland';
     33 Henry VIII, *cap.* 1. This Act
     was repealed in 1962 by the
     'Statute Law Revision (Pre-
     Union Irish Statutes) Act.
3   Lambeth Palace Library, Carew
     MS 621, f.14. Although given the
     date of 1541, the document was
     probably written earlier.
4   'An Act for Laws and Justice to
     be ministered in Wales in like
     form as it is in this Realm'; 27
     Henry VIII, *cap.* 26. See *Statutes
     of the Realm*, vol. 3, pp.563–9.
5   'An Act for Certain Ordinances
     in Wales': 34 & 35 Henry VIII,
     cap. 26.
6   'Act of Union (Ireland) 1800'; 40
     George III, *cap.* 3.
7   Head, 'Henry VIII's Scottish
     Policy: A Reassessment', p.3.
8   Merriman, *Life and Letters of
     Thomas Cromwell*, vol. 1, p.34;
     Elton, *Reform & Reformation*, p.90.
9   See Donaldson, *James VI –
     James VII*, pp.26–30; Mackie,
     'Henry VIII and Scotland',
     p.113; Slavin, *Politics and Profit:
     A Study of Sir Ralph Sadler
     1507–47* (New York: Cambridge
     University Press, 1966), p.95.
10   Margaret had married James IV
     in a proxy wedding in January
     1502 but her health was con-
     sidered too delicate to journey
     north. She crossed the border in
     July 1503 to meet her husband,
     aged just over thirteen.
11   Eaves, *Henry VIII's Scottish
     Diplomacy...*, p.11.
12   Head, op. cit., p.8.
13   Andrea Thompson, 'Women at
     the Court of James V 1513–42',
     p.80, in Elizabeth Ewan &
     Maureen M. Meikle (eds.),
     Women in Scotland c.1100–c.1750
     (East Linton: Tuckwell Press,
     1999).

14 James V and Mary married at St Andrews on 17 June 1538.

15 *LP*, vol. 12, pt. ii, p.449.

16 Head, op. cit, pp.8, 16.

17 *St. P.*, vol. 5, p.190.

18 Donaldson, op. cit., p.59.

19 Bonner, 'Genesis of Henry VIII's "Rough Wooing" . . .', p.46.

20 'Hamilton Papers', vol. 1, p.103.

21 *St. P.*, vol. 5, pp.192–3.

22 'Hamilton Papers', vol. 1, p.104.

23 Ibid., p.113: James V to Henry VIII; Edinburgh, 22 October 1541.

24 *CSP Spain*, vol. 6, pt. i, p.463. Chapuys to Charles V; London, 29 January 1542.

25 Savoy was the feudal territory of the House of Savoy during the eleventh to fourteenth centuries and included the Western Alps from Lake Geneva to Dauphiné. The area is now part of France, Italy and Switzerland.

26 Charolais is a historic region of France, now in the Saône-et-Loire département.

27 *LP*, vol. 17, p.67: Marillac to Francis I; London, 4 March 1542.

28 Kaulek, *Correspondence politique . . .*, p.394: Francis I to Marillac; 12 March 1542.

29 Ibid., p.422. Marillac to Francis I; London, 3 June 1542.

30 *CSP Spain*, vol. 6, pt. i, p.481: Charles V to Chapuys; Valladolid, 14 March 1542.

31 Ibid., p.483. Charles V to Chapuys; Valladolid, 14 March 1542.

32 Kaulek, op. cit., p.426: Marillac to Francis I; London, 20 June 1542.

33 Westminster was one of six new dioceses founded by Henry in 1539–40, the others being Bristol, Chester, Gloucester, Oxford and Peterborough. Thirlby was the sole bishop of Westminster: the see was reunited with London in 1550. The Catholic diocese of Westminster was founded in 1850.

34 *St. P.*, vol. 9, 68ff.

35 Smith, *Mask of Royalty*, p.181.

36 'Hamilton Papers', vol. 1, pp.153–4.

37 A hackbut was the English name for a matchlock musket, derived from the Dutch *hakebus* from its hook-like projection. Its fire was deadly, up to 400 yards (366m) and could penetrate armour, but it took between thirty and sixty seconds to reload.

38 *APC*, vol. 1, p.22.

39 'Hamilton Papers', vol. 1, pp.155–6.

40 Ibid., p.156.

41 Ibid., pp.156–7. The battlefield site is at Ordnance Survey National Grid reference NT 778 341.

42 *SP*, vol. 5, p.250.

43 Ibid., pp.229–30.

44 Kaulek, op. cit., p.461: Marillac to Francis I; London, 11 September 1542.

45 *LP*, vol. 17, pp.4, 70–1.

46 A tun contained about 216 Imperial gallons (982 litres).

47 'Hamilton Papers', vol. 1, p.189:

Norfolk to the Privy Council;
Kenninghall, Norfolk, 11
September 1542.

48 Ibid., p.214.

49 Ibid., p.213: Norfolk and Browne
to Privy Council; York, 20
September 1542.

50 *LP*, vol. 17, p.514: Commissioners
at York to the Privy Council;
York, 2 October 1542.
The Pentland Firth, 'the
most dangerous place in
Christendom', separates Scotland
and the Orkneys and is subject
to strong tides with overfalls.
At the north end of Stroma lies
the 'Swilkie' (from the old Norse
svelgr meaning 'swallower'), a
whirlpool created at ebb and
flood tides.

51 Ibid., p.658.

52 *St. P.*, vol. 5, p.198; *LP*, vol. 17,
p.520.

53 'Hamilton Papers', vol. 1, p.262:
Privy Council to Commissioners
in York; Greenwich, 8 October
1542.

54 *St. P.*, vol. 5, p.212; BL, Caligula
B, vii, f.289 and f.322.

55 *LP*, vol. 17, pp.514–15: Norfolk to
Gardiner and Wriothesley; York,
2 October 1542.

56 'Hamilton Papers', vol. 1,
pp.264–5.

57 Ibid., pp.273, 282. Lord Lisle
was subsequently appointed
Lord Warden of the Marches in
November 1542.

58 *Chronicle of John Hardyng*,
ed. and published by Richard

Grafton in London in January
1543.

59 'Hamilton Papers', vol. 1, p.277.

60 Ibid., p.284.

61 *LP*, vol. 17, p.551.

62 'Hamilton Papers', vol. 1,
pp.291–4.

63 Bath Place was next to
Furnivall's Inn, on the west
side of the City of London. See
London Topographical Record,
vol. 10 (1916), pp.133–4.

64 'Hamilton Papers', vol. 1,
pp.294–5.

65 Ibid., p.295.

66 Ibid., pp.297–300.

67 *LP*, vol. 17, pp.585–6.

68 'Hamilton Papers', vol. 1, p.304.

69 Hatfield House, CP 231/15:
Sir Thomas Wriothesley to
Hertford; Westminster, 25
November 1542.

70 *LP*, vol. 17, p.596: James V to
Pope Paul III; Edinburgh, 9
November 1542.

71 The battlefield is at Ordnance
Survey National Grid reference
NY 383 677. The landscape has
changed dramatically since 1542,
due to agricultural enclosure
and the draining of the River
Esk flood plain.

72 *CSP Spain*, vol. 6, pt. ii,
pp.233–4.

73 'Hamilton Papers', vol. 1, p.312.

74 Ibid., p.313.

75 Ibid., pp.339–40.

76 *LP*, vol. 18, pt. i, p.20.

77 Head, op. cit., p.19.

78 Scarisbrick, *Henry VIII*, p.436.

Chapter 7 – The Sixth Wife

1 Lesley Smith, 'King Henry VIII's Other Great Matter', p.201.

2 James, *Kateryn Parr: The Making of a Queen*, p.112.

3 *CSP Spain*, vol. 6, pt. i, p.409.

4 *LP*, vol. 18, pt. i, p.28.

5 *LP*, vol. 17, pp.668–9: Chapuys to the Queen of Hungary; London, 21 December 1542.

6 *LP*, vol. 18, pt. i, pp.28–9: Chapuys to Charles V; London, 15 January 1543.

7 James, 'Katherine Parr', *ODNB*, vol. 30, p.901.

8 Porter, *Katherine the Queen*, p.37.

9 For Maud Parr's tenacious negotiations over the marriage agreement, see Barbara Harris, 'Women & Politics in early Tudor England', *HJ*, vol. 33 (1990), pp.262, 268.

10 TNA, PROB 11/24/153.

11 Elizabeth wrote to Cromwell in November 1537, complaining of 'the trouble I am put to by Lord Borough who always lies in wait to put me to shame'. Her husband 'dared do nothing but as his father will have him do'. *LP*, vol. 12, pt. ii, p.378.

12 34 Henry VIII, *cap*.40: 'Elizabeth Borough's Children, deeming them Illegitimate'.

13 Mueller, *Katherine Parr, Complete Works...*, p.8.

14 TNA, PROB 11/24/153.

15 *LP*, vol. 12 pt. ii, p.35.

16 John Weever, *Ancient Funerall Monuments* (London, 1631), p.371. Sir William Dugdale, in his *History of St Paul's Cathedral*, 2nd edn (London, 1716), p.48, records Latimer's tomb being destroyed during the reigns of Edward VI and Elizabeth I. It probably included a monumental brass, ripped up for the value of the metal.

17 34 & 35 Henry VIII, *cap*. 43. Anne spent the next few years living in exile at the manor of Little Wakering, in Essex. She was reduced to poverty after giving birth to at least another child by Lyngfield.

18 James, *Catherine Parr: Henry VIII's Last Love*, pp.82–4.

19 Katherine, as queen, prudently retained a copy of his will in her papers, together with 'a kerchief' on which was written details of her marriage jointure of Latimer's lands. See Starkey, *The Inventory of King Henry VIII*, items 17754 and 17759, p.437.

20 Her height is estimated from the length of her coffin discovered in the ruins of the chapel of Sudeley Castle, Gloucestershire, in 1782. See Nash, 'Observations of the Time of Death... of Queen Katherine Parr', *Archaeologia*, vol. 9 (1789), p.2.

21 James, 'Katherine Parr', *ODNB*, p.903.

22 Scarisbrick, *Henry VIII*, p.456.

23 Lesley Smith, op. cit., p.201.

24 *Spanish Chronicle*, p.107.

25 *St. P.*, vol. 1, pp.576–8: Sadler to

Cromwell; Chobham, Surrey, 14 July 1538.

26 Flugel, *Men and their Motives*, p.277.

27 James, *Catherine Parr: Henry VIII's Last Love*, p.96.

28 *LP*, vol. 17, p.51.

29 Parr was one of twelve knights granted exemption from attending the feast of the Order at Windsor Castle on 6 May as they were engaged in 'certain causes to be executed and done' by the king's command – in this case, military service in the north. See BL, Harleian MS 304 f.136r.

30 Arthur Plantagenet, Viscount Lisle, died in the Tower on 3 March 1542 and Dudley was created Viscount Lisle nine days later 'in right of his mother'.

31 Hutchinson, *Last Days of Henry VIII*, p.58.

32 *Spanish Chronicle*, p.107.

33 TNA, E 30/1472/6.

34 'Bonair' means yielding, polite and gentle.

35 TNA, E 30/1472/5.

36 Strickland, *Lives of the Queens of England...*, vol. 2, p.409.

37 James, *Kateryn Parr*, p.24.

38 LP, vol. 18, pt. i, p.498.

39 *St. P.*, vol. 5, p.321: Wriothesley to Parr; Otelands, 20 July 1543.

40 Starkey, op. cit., items 2643, 2648, 2661, p.78. These jewels were included in the inventory of Henry VIII's possessions completed in 1548.

41 *LP*, vol. 18, pt. ii, p.18.

42 *CSP Spain*, vol. 6, pt. ii, p.436: Chapuys to Philip, crown prince and regent of Spain; London, 12 July 1543.

43 *LP*, vol. 18, pt. i, p.490.

44 *CSP Spain*, vol. 6, pt. ii, p.447: Chapuys to Charles V; London, 27 July 1543.

45 *LP*, vol. 18, pt. i, p.513: Chapuys to Charles V; London, 27 July 1543.

46 *Spanish Chronicle*, p.108.

47 *CSP Spain*, vol. 6, pt. ii, p.447: Chapuys to Charles V; London, 27 July 1543.

48 The outbreak of the plague was so bad in London, causing 'great death', that the law courts were moved to St Albans, Hertfordshire, for the Michaelmas term. See Hall's *Chronicle*, p.859.

49 *LP*, vol. 18, pt. i, p.493.

50 *LP*, vol. 18, pt. ii, p.32. Widespread flooding that wet summer meant that timber could not be transported to rivers for onward carriage to London, causing a great shortage. See Wriothesley, *Chronicle*, vol. 1, p.141.

51 *LP*, vol. 18, pt. ii, p.184.

52 Hall, *Chronicle*, pp.858–9; Foxe, *Acts & Monuments*, vol. 5, pp.486–92.

53 *LP*, vol. 18, pt. ii, p.115.

54 Haugaard, 'Katherine Parr: The Religious Convictions of a Renaissance Queen', p.350.

55 See John Charles Brooke, 'Description of the Great Seal

of Catherine Parr', *Archaeologia*, vol. 5 (1779), pp.232–4.

56 James, *Catherine Parr*, p.102.

57 Two dog collars of crimson velvet appear in the queen's possessions in the 1547 Inventory of Henry's possessions. See Starkey, op. cit., item 3530, p.95.

58 TNA, E 101/423/12 f.4.

59 For more on the unsavoury Udall, see notes to Chapter 3, note 7.

60 James, 'Katherine Parr', *ODNB*, p.904.

61 *LP*, vol. 21, pt. i, p.321.

62 Southworth, *Fools and Jesters at the English Court*, p.103.

63 Strickland, op cit., vol. 2, p.412.

64 *St. P.*, vol. 10, p.569.

65 *LP*, vol. 18, pt. ii, p.272.

Chapter 8 – Fie on You, Traitor!

1 Those recently expelled from the Order of the Garter for treason were Thomas, first lord Darcy, who had joined the Pilgrimage of Grace rebellion (1537); Henry Courtenay, marquess of Exeter (1537), and Sir Nicholas Carew (1539).

2 The Latin register, called the *Liber Niger*, or 'Black Book' (after the colour of its velvet binding), was richly illuminated by the Fleming, Lucas Horenbout, royal painter from 1525. Its contents include the Order's statutes, ceremonies and details of the elections of knights.

3 SGC. G.1, *Liber Niger*, f.283; *LP*, vol. 15, p.312.

4 *Liber Niger*, f.275. Cromwell was elected to the Order in August 1537. Another hand, perhaps that of a supporter of Cromwell, has tried to erase four insertions of the word '*proditor*' over his name on f.276.

5 Dawson, *Memoirs...*, p.321. Aside from foreign rulers, later at war with Britain, the last knight to be degraded by this ceremony was James Butler, second duke of Ormond, in 1716.

6 Tanner, *Tudor Constitutional Documents*, p.379. See also Thornley, 'The Treason Legislation of Henry VIII', pp.87–123.

7 'An Act that Proclamations made by the King's Highness with the Advice of his Honourable Council shall be obeyed and kept as though they were made by Act of Parliament'. 31 Henry VIII, *cap.* 8, section VI. See *Statutes of the Realm*, vol. 3, p.726.

8 Lord Judge, Lord Chief Justice 2008–13, has criticised the use of Henry VIII clauses: 'You can be sure that when [these] clauses are introduced, they will always be said to be necessary. William Pitt [Prime Minister 1783–1801 and 1804–6] warned us how to treat such pleas with disdain. "Necessity is the justification for every infringement of human liberty. It is the argument of tyrants, the creed of slaves."'

(Lord Mayor's dinner for the judiciary, 13 July 2010.)

9   26 Henry VIII, *cap.* 13. See *Statutes of the Realm,* vol. 3, p.508.

10 Bellamy, *Tudor Law of Treason,* pp.27, 92–3; Thornley, op. cit., p.107.

11 Scarisbrick, *Henry VIII,* p.332.

12 Pope Paul established the 'Supreme Sacred Congregation of the Roman and Universal Inquisition' in 1542 as a permanent part of the Roman *Curia* or the Holy See's bureaucracy, tasked with maintaining and defending the integrity of the faith and investigating and prosecuting those guilty of error and heresies.

13 BL, Cotton MS, Galba B, x, ff.21–25*r.*

14 Robinson, *Original Letters . . . ,* p.211.

15 Cited by Smith, *Mask of Royalty,* p.239.

16 Stow, *Annals,* p.980.

17 Elton, *Policy and Police,* p.387.

18 Bellamy, op. cit., p.45.

19 35 Henry VIII, *cap.* 1. See *Statutes of the Realm,* vol. 3, p.955.

20 35 Henry VIII, *cap.* 2. See *Statutes of the Realm,* vol. 3, p.958.

21 35 Henry VIII, *cap.* 3. See *Statutes of the Realm,* vol. 3, p.958.

22 Dillon, 'The Rack', p.49.

23 TNA, SP 1/176/137; Bellamy, op. cit., p.111.

24 Dillon, 'The Rack', p.51.

25 Ibid., p.51.

26 Sir Edward Walsingham was Lieutenant 1521–43, followed by Sir William Sidney and Sir Anthony Knyvett (1543–6).

27 BL, Add. MS 32,621, f.93. Sir Thomas More, when Lord Chancellor, may have devised this means of torture against poachers. A Lutheran report from Germany in 1536 suggested that 'he made them put on new shoes and tied them to posts, then exposed the soles of their feet to hot fire, the pain used to make them confess'. See Bellamy, op. cit, p.262.

28 Bellamy, op. cit., p.97.

29 Dillon, op. cit., p.56. The Jesuit priest Edmund Campion spent four days in the Tower's 'Little Ease' in 1581. This may, however, have been a reused fireplace, walled up to create a tiny cell, possibly in the Beauchamp Tower. My thanks to Dr Jeremy Ashbee for this information.

30 Tanner, op. cit., p.421.

31 35 Henry VIII, *cap.* 23, removed this right. See *Statutes of the Realm,* vol. 3, p.863.

32 Harris, 'Law & Economics of High Treason . . .', p.100.

33 Wriothesley, *Chronicle,* vol. 1, p.115.

34 Harris, op. cit., p.97.

35 Numbers extrapolated from estimates given in Elton, op. cit., pp.388–9, 395–6.

36 Elton, op. cit., pp.395–6.

37 31 Henry VIII, *cap.* 15: 'Attainder for Marquess of Exeter and Others'.

38 Sowerby, *Renaissance and Reformation in Tudor England*, p.139.

39 Ahab was king of Israel in 871–852 BC.

40 Lehmberg, 'Parliamentary Attainder in the Reign of Henry VIII', p.686.

41 *LP*, vol. 15, p.163.

42 Ibid., p.241.

43 *St. P.*, vol. 8, p.316: Henry VIII to Commissioners at Calais; 17 April 1540.

44 Ibid., pp.343, 367.

45 *LP*, vol. 15, p.502: Cardinal Marcellus Cervinus to bishop of Liège; 29 August 1540.

46 32 Henry VIII, *cap.* 60.

47 Smith, *Treason in Tudor England*, p.8.

48 Wriothesley, *Chronicle*, vol. 1, p.121.

49 *LP*, vol. 14, pt. ii, p.256: Wyatt to Henry VIII; Blays, 16 December 1539.

50 Cloth made waterproof by impregnating it with wax.

51 *St. P.*, vol. 8, pp.220–9: Wyatt to Henry VIII; Paris, 7 January 1540.

52 Kaulek, *Correspondence politique...*, p.153: Francis I to Henry VIII; Le Fère sur Oyse, Hauts-de-France, 27 January 1540.

53 Ibid., p.56: Marillac to Francis I; London, 2 February 1540.

54 Smith, *Mask of Royalty*, p.153.

55 *LP*, vol. 15, p.69.

56 Ibid., p.123: Cardinal Farnese to Pope Paul III; Ghent, 5 March 1540.

57 *LP*, vol. 18, pt. i, p.77: Paget to Henry VIII; Paris, 4 February 1543.

58 *St. P.*, vol. 8, p.298: Paget to Henry VIII; Paris, 6 February 1543.

59 *LP*, vol. 18, pt. i, p.98: Paget to Henry VIII; Paris, 15 February 1543.

60 Ibid., p.301: Raleigh and Brant to the Privy Council; Milan, 5 May 1543.

61 *St. P.*, vol. 8, p.436.

62 *LP*, vol. 15, p.453.

63 *St. P.*, vol. 8, p.428.

64 Ibid., pp.437–9: Wallop to Henry VIII; Mantes, 27 September 1540.

65 *St. P.*, vol. 1, p.652.

66 Bod. Lib., Ashmole MS 1729, ff.3–4r.

67 *St. P.*, vol. 8, pp.512–13.

68 *St. P.*, vol. 9, p.388.

69 Only one clerical exile returned to England voluntarily: the Dominican William Perryn, who fled to Louvain in 1534, returned nine years later and supplicated for a Bachelor of Divinity degree at Oxford. See Revd. C.W. Boase (ed.), *Register of the University of Oxford*, vol. 1 (Oxford: Oxford Historical Soc.), p.205.

70 *LP*, vol. 19, pt. i, p.442.

71 Gout-ridden Cardinal Campeggio was joint papal legate with Cardinal Wolsey

in the abortive hearing at Blackfriars into Henry's divorce with Katherine of Aragon in 1529. Campeggio died in 1539, aged sixty-four.

72 *LP*, vol. 19, pt. ii, p.36.

73 Ibid., p.53. Russell to Paget; Camp before Montreuil, 20 August 1544.

74 Harrison, 'Henry VIII's Gangster', p.265.

75 *LP*, vol. 20, pt. i, p.38: Harvel to Henry VIII; Venice, 25 January 1545.

76 Nereo Vianello, *Venice and its Lagoon* (Padua: Edizioni Erredici), rep. 2007, p.469.

77 Sydney Freedberg, *Painting in Italy 1500–1600* (New Haven & London: Yale University Press, 1993), p.535.

78 *CSP Venice*, vol. 5, pp.217–18 and fn.

79 *LP*, vol. 20, pt. i, p.85.

80 Ibid., p.132: Harvel to Henry VIII; Venice, 1 March 1545.

81 *LP*, vol. 20, pt. i, p.199.

82 *CSP, Venice*, vol. 5, pp.134–5: Venier to the Council of Ten; Rome, 5 May 1545.

83 Ibid., pp.135–6; Venier to the Council of Ten; Rome, 8 May 1545.

84 Ibid., pp.142–3.

85 *St. P.*, vol. 10, pp.563–5: Harvel to Henry VIII; Venice, 13 August 1545.

86 *LP*, vol. 20, pt. ii, p.203.

87 Ibid., p.481.

88 *CSP Venice*, vol. 5, pp.151–3.

Chapter 9 – The Last Chance of Military Glory

1 Wriothesley, *Chronicle*, vol. 1, p.143; SAL Proclamations, vol. 1, no. 128.

2 Pierre Terrail, seigneur de Bayard (1473–1524), was a French knight, famed for being 'without fear and beyond reproach'. During the Battle of the Spurs, he rallied his men but found his escape cut off and was forced to surrender. Henry was so struck by his gallantry that he released him without ransom.

3 Flemish school, *c*.1513. Royal Collection RCIN 406784. Now on public display in the Wolsey Room in Hampton Court Palace.

4 The site is now known as Enguinegatte, from the nearby village, ten miles (16km) from Saint-Omer in north-east France.

5 Hutchinson, *Young Henry*, pp.178–9.

6 Royal Collection RCIN 72834. Now in the Lantern Lobby of Windsor Castle.

7 'Hamilton Papers', vol. 1, pp.499–501.

8 BL, Royal MS 18 B VI, ff.153*v*–154.

9 *LP*, vol. 18, pt. i, p.271: Henry VIII to Sadler; 25 April 1543.

10 *St. P.*, vol. 5, p.280: Privy Council to Sadler; [1 May] 1543. Beaton was consecrated bishop of Mirepoix, Languedoc, in

December 1537 on Francis I's recommendation. The see had an annual income of £750.

11 *LP*, vol. 18, pt. i, pp.454–5.

12 Scarisbrick, *Henry VIII*, p.439.

13 Hatfield House, CP 232/103.

14 Scarisbrick, op. cit., p.440.

15 *LP*, vol. 17, pp.573, 575: Chapuys to Charles V; London, 2 November 1542.

16 TNA, E 30/1031. Pope Paul III rescinded the title of Defender of the Faith in 1538, but it is still used by English monarchs.

17 *LP*, vol. 18, pt. ii, p.277.

18 Ibid., p.108.

19 'Calais Chronicle,' p.213.

20 Now called Landrecies. The town is in Hauts-de-France, 80 miles (128km) from Brussels, Belgium.

21 TNA, SP 1/182/39.

22 'Hamilton Papers', vol. 2, p.4: Sadler to Henry VIII; Edinburgh, 1 September 1543.

23 Ibid., p.20: Sadler to Suffolk and Bishop Tunstall; Edinburgh, 5 September 1543.

24 Ibid., p.24: Sadler to Suffolk and Bishop Tunstall; Edinburgh, 11 September 1543 'at midnight'.

25 Ibid., p.43: Henry VIII to Suffolk; 14 September 1543.

26 Sadler, 'State Papers', vol. 1, p.324.

27 *LP*, vol. 18, pt. ii, p.168.

28 Ibid., p.207.

29 *St. P.*, vol. 5, p.350.

30 Sadler, op. cit., vol. 1, p.348.

31 BL, Sloane MS 2,442, f.34.

32 *St. P.*, vol. 5, p.351.

33 TNA, E 30/1032.

34 *CSP Spain*, vol. 6, pt. ii, p.541: Charles V to Férrante Gonzaga; Brussels, 13 December 1543.

35 Smith, *Mask of Royalty*, p.201.

36 *CSP Spain*, vol. 6, pt. ii, pp.531–4.

37 *St. P.*, vol. 1, pp.761–2.

38 *LP*, vol. 19, pt. i, p.235: Chapuys to the Queen of Hungary; London, 21 April 1544.

39 One last of gunpowder was the equivalent of twenty-four barrels, totalling 2,400lbs (1,089kg) of explosive.

40 After 200 arrows had been loosed, the bowstring lost its spring and was discarded. Archers carried their bowstrings under their helmets to keep them dry – the origin of the phrase 'keeping it under your hat'.

41 TNA, SP 1/184/288ff.

42 *LP*, vol. 19, pt. i, pp.149–57.

43 TNA, SP 1/184/24.

44 *LP*, vol. 19, pt. i, pp.120–1. One gun-shield survives in London's Victoria and Albert Museum (British galleries, Room 586, case 3; accession no. M507-1927). A smaller version is in the Walters Art Museum, Baltimore, Maryland, USA (accession no. 81.1414).

45 'Haynes' State Papers', p.12: Paget to Hertford; Westminster, 11 March 'at night' 1544.

46 'Hamilton Papers', vol. 2, pp.325–7: Privy Council to Hertford; Westminster, 10 April 1544.

47 *LP*, vol. 19, pt. i, p.256.

48 Smith, *Mask of Royalty,* p.165.

49 Hatfield House, CP 231/108.

50 *LP*, vol. 19, pt. i, p.230.

51 Hatfield House, CP 231/2.

52 Hatfield House, CP 231/53.

53 *LP*, vol. 19, pt. i, p.127.

54 Ibid., pp.305–6.

55 Hall, *Chronicles*, p.860.

56 Inchgarvie (Ordnance Survey National Grid reference NT 138 795) has four caissons support-ing the foundations of the Forth Bridge built on the rocks around it.

57 'Hamilton Papers', vol. 2, pp.361–3.

58 Stow, *Annals*, pp.986–7.

59 'Hamilton Papers', vol. 2, p.367; *CSP Spain*, vol. 7, pp.150–1.

60 'Hamilton Papers', vol. 2, p.369.

61 *LP*, vol. 19, pt. i, pp.332–3.

62 Hall, *Chronicles*, p.861.

63 BL, Harleian MS 442, f.197.

64 Hatfield House, CP 231/98.

65 Hatfield House, CP 231/110.

66 *LP*, vol. 19, pt. i, p.212: Chapuys to Charles V; London, 13 April 1544.

67 *CSP Spain*, vol. 7, p.164: Chapuys to Charles V; London, 18 May 1544.

68 *LP*, vol. 19, pt. i, p.326: Chapuys to Charles V; London, 18 May 1544.

69 Smith, op. cit., p.192.

70 *CSP Spain*, vol. 8, pp.76, 219–20.

71 *St. P.*, vol. 9, p.715. Norfolk to the Privy Council; the camp at Beaulieu, 22 June 1544.

72 *LP*, vol. 19, pt. i, p.411.

73 Ibid., p.433.

74 Ibid., p.435.

75 BL, Harleian MS 6,989, f.121.

76 Montreuil, in the Pas de Calais, was a prosperous port in the fifteenth century until the River Canche silted up. It was the headquarters of the British Army in France during the First World War.

77 *St. P.*, vol. 9, pp.727–8.

78 *LP*, vol. 19, pt. i, p.543.

79 Ibid., p.484.

80 BL, Harleian MS 6,989, f.127.

81 *LP*, vol. 19, pt. i, pp.548–9.

82 *CSP Spain*, vol. 7, p.138.

83 *LP*, vol. 19, pt. i, pp.553–4.

84 Ibid., p.537.

85 TNA, SP 1/190/23-5.

86 *LP*, vol. 19, pt. i, p.564.

87 Dillon, 'The Tudor Battle Flag of England', p.233.

88 Information kindly supplied by the late Claude Blair. On depart-ure from Calais, Somerset had been made a Gentleman of the Privy Chamber and principal esquire to the king.

89 Hewerdine, *Yeomen of the King's Guard . . .*, unpublished thesis, p.93.

90 'Calais Chronicle', pp.xxix–xxx.

91 A three-quarter armour lacks plates to protect the lower legs and feet.

92 Blair & Pyhrr, 'The Wilton "Montmorency" Armor', pp.95–143. The armour remains in the collection of the Metropolitan Museum, New York. A torn account for work done in the

king's armoury at Greenwich includes 'filing of the king's majesty's harness [armour] and other necessaries'. BL, Cotton MS, Appendix 28, f.69.

Chapter 10 – Fortunes of War

1 TNA, SP 1/190/76.
2 TNA, SP 190/78-9*v*.
3 Scarisbrick, *Henry VIII*, p.447.
4 *LP*, vol. 19, pt. i, p.582: Chapuys to Charles V; Calais, 21 July 1544.
5 TNA, SP 1/190/85-85*v*.
6 Possibly the sixteenth-century sketch of Boulogne in BL, Cotton MS, Caligula E, i, ff.63–6.
7 TNA, SP 1/190/91-91*v*.
8 TNA, SP 1/190/96-96*v*.
9 TNA, SP 1/190/103.
10 Murphy, 'Violence, Colonization and Henry VIII's Conquest of France', p.21.
11 Ibid., p.36.
12 W.A.J. Archbold (ed.), 'A Diary of the Expedition of 1544', *EHR*, vol. 16 (1901), p.504; Murphy, op. cit., pp.30–7.
13 Murphy, op. cit., p.43.
14 'Hamilton Papers', vol. 2, p.429.
15 TNA, SP 1/190/155.
16 TNA, SP 1/190/220.
17 James, 'Katherine Parr', *ODNB*, vol. 30, p.903.
18 *SP*, vol. 10, p.28: Queen Katherine to the Council with the King; Hampton Court, 6 August 1544.
19 White, 'The Psalms, War and Royal Iconography', pp.554–6.

20 James, 'The Devotional Writings of Queen Katherine Parr', p.137. A copy of the same prayers, translated into Latin, French and Italian by Princess Elizabeth with a dedicatory letter to her father, formed her New Year gift to him in December 1545. See BL, Royal MS 7D.X. This is the only surviving letter from Elizabeth to Henry VIII.
21 BL, Lansdowne MS 1,236, f.9.
22 Potter, *Henry VIII and Francis I: The Final Conflict*, p.187.
23 During sieges, mining involved tunnelling beneath the walls of a town or castle and supporting the roof of the mine with wooden pit-props. Wooden faggots were piled into the tunnel and set alight. When the props collapsed in the flames, the walls above tumbled down to create a breach. Alternatively, gunpowder charges were exploded.
24 *LP*, vol. 19, pt. ii, p.614.
25 TNA, SP 1/190/165.
26 *LP*, vol. 19, pt. ii, p.63.
27 Ibid., p.65.
28 Ibid., p.101.
29 TNA, SP 1/190/240.
30 *LP*, vol. 19, pt. i, pp.612–13.
31 TNA, SP 1/190/112.
32 TNA, SP 1/190/126.
33 TNA, SP 1/190/128.
34 TNA, SP 1/190/167.
35 *LP*, vol. 19, pt. ii, p.4: Norfolk and others to the Council; Montreuil, 2 August 1544.
36 Ibid., p.17: Norfolk to Suffolk; Montreuil, 5 August 1544.

37 *SP*, vol. 10, p.19.

38 Ibid., p.21: the Council (with the King) to the Queen; Boulogne, 5 August 1544.

39 BL, Add. MS 5,733, f.31.

40 LP, vol. 19, pt. ii, p.101.

41 Ibid., p.59.

42 Ibid., p.66.

43 These thermal weapons may have been tight balls of rags, soaked in pitch, tar and resin which were lit before being hurled into Boulogne. Alternatively, the 'wildfire' may have been made from the ancient formula of sulphur, tallow, resin, saltpetre and crude antimony.

44 Ellis, *Original Letters*, 1st s., vol. 2, p.130.

45 TNA, E 30/1480.

46 TNA, E 30/1481.

47 Wriothesley, *Chronicle*, vol.1, p.149.

48 Murphy, op cit., pp.24, 27.

49 LP, vol. 19, pt. ii, p.140. Norfolk claimed that many wagons 'were robbed by Frenchmen'.

50 *Elis Gruffydd and the 1544 'Enterprises of Paris and Boulogne'*, ed. Jonathan Davies (Farnham: Pike & Shot Society, 2003), p.67.

51 Hall, *Chronicle*, p.862.

52 Smith, *Mask of Royalty*, p.210.

53 BL, Egerton MS 990, ff.414–16.

54 *LP*, vol. 19, pt. ii, pp.129–30.

55 *SP*, vol. 10, p.69: Montreuil, 14 September 1544.

56 Nott, *Works of Henry Howard...*, vol. 1, p.lxviii.

57 BL, Cotton MS, Augustus I. ii, f.53. A map of Boulogne, by John Rogers in 1546, shows the English defences with new French fortifications on the opposite side of the River Liane, Fort d'Outreau and Fort de Chatillon.

58 *LP*, vol. 19, pt. ii, p.139.

59 Murphy, op. cit., p.46.

60 SP, vol. 10, p.75. Beer, wine 'and other necessaries' were to be 'laid with all diligence at such places thought meet for his majesty to rest and lodge at by the way': *LP*, vol. 19, pt. ii, p.141.

61 *SP*, vol. 10, p.82.

62 *LP*, vol. 19, pt. ii, p.167.

63 Ibid., p.161.

64 *SP*, vol. 10, p.104.

65 Smith, *Mask of Royalty*, p.213; Nott, op. cit., vol. 1, appendix 7, p.xvii; TNA, SP 1/193/92: Norfolk to the Council; Calais, 9 October 1544; *LP*, vol. 19, pt. ii, p.242; *Spanish Chronicle*, p.119.

66 TNA, SP 1/193/154.

67 The sword has a portrayal of the siege etched on the blade, with the city on the right and on the left, the mound with English artillery. A Latin inscription is translated as 'Rejoice Boulogne in the rule of the eighth Henry! Thy towers are now adorned by crimson [Tudor] roses; now are the scented lilies [of France] unrooted and prostrate, the [French] cock expelled and the lion reigns in the invincible

citadel. Thus, neither valour nor grace... will fail thee, since the lion is thy protection and the rose thy ornament.' It is now in the Royal Collection (RCIN 61316). See Blair, 'A Royal Swordsmith and Damascener: Diego de Çaias'.

68 Muller, *Letters of Stephen Gardiner*, pp.185–6.

69 *CSP Spain*, vol. 8, p.2: Chapuys to Charles V; London, 2 January 1545.

70 Brooks, *Cassell's Battlefields of Britain and Ireland*, p.291.

71 The site is at Ordnance Survey National Grid reference NT 617 271. The Scottish forces were commanded by Archibald Douglas, sixth earl of Angus, Henry's brother-in-law and erstwhile ally, who had switched allegiance. In early 1545, English troops had desecrated the Angus family monuments in Melrose Abbey.

72 'Hamilton Papers', vol. 2, p.565.

73 *SP*, vol. 5, p.432.

74 Wriothesley, *Chronicle*, vol. 1, p.157.

75 *APC*, vol. 1, pp.190, 192.

76 *LP*, vol. 20, pt. i, p.203.

77 Smith, op. cit., p.216; *CSP Spain*, vol. 8, p.198.

78 *LP*, vol. 20, pt. i, p.444.

79 Dominic Fontana, www.myold map.com/dominic/maryrose. Retrieved 16 March 2018.

80 Peter Marsden, *Sealed by Time: the Loss and Recovery of the Mary Rose* (Portsmouth: Mary Rose Trust, 2003), pp.181–2.

81 Christopher Dobbs, 'The Galley', in Peter Marsden (ed.), *Your Noblest Shippe: Anatomy of a Tudor Warship* (Portsmouth: Mary Rose Trust, 2009), p.133.

82 Mary was Carew's second wife, marrying him in 1540. After the loss of the *Mary Rose*, she was appointed lady-in-waiting to Princesses Mary and Elizabeth. She later married Sir Arthur Champernowne and died in 1570.

83 Fontana, www.myoldmap.com/ dominic/maryrose. Retrieved 16 March 2018.

84 Investigations in 2003–5, before dredging a new channel into Portsmouth harbour for the Royal Navy's *Queen Elizabeth* class aircraft carriers, recovered *Mary Rose*'s wooden figurehead badge. The new *Queen Elizabeth*'s ship's badge includes the Tudor Rose. See Pulvertaft, 'The Figurehead/Badge of the *Mary Rose*', pp.333–4.

85 *SP*, vol. 1, p.794.

86 A Frenchman rescued from the sea after his ship was sunk by *Blake of Rye* was sent for questioning by Lisle. See *APC*, vol. 1, p.213. William Blake was master of the *Magdalen of Rye*. The position of the sunken French galley is at Ordnance Survey National Grid reference SZ 6426 9402.

87   Wriothesley, *Chronicle*, vol.1, p.158.

88   Charles Dickens erected a shower bath here in 1849, illustrated by a drawing in *Punch* (8 September 1849).

89   Hall, *Chronicles*, p.863.

90   Peter Brett, *Bonchurch* (Bonchurch: Bonchurch Parochial Church Council, n.d.), p.1.

Chapter 11 – 'Old Copper Nose'

1   Nicholas Mayhew, *Sterling: The History of a Currency* (New York: Wiley, 1999), p.46.

2   William Camden, *Remains Concerning Britain* (London: Charles Harper, 1674), p.208.

3   Stow's *Annals*, p.988. For more information, see Challis & Harrison, 'A Contemporary Estimate of the Production of Gold and Silver Coinage 1542–56'.

4   *LP*, vol. 19, pt. i, p.318.

5   Ibid., p.319.

6   Challis, 'The Debasement of the Coinage 1542–51', pp.443, 454.

7   Evans, 'On a Counterfeit Groat of Henry VIII', pp.250–1.

8   Wriothesley, *Chronicle*, vol.1, p.176.

9   Bishop, 'Currency, Conversation and Control...', p.781.

10   Wriothesley, op. cit., vol.1, p.162.

11   Ibid., p.163.

12   Hoskins, 'Harvest Fluctuations and English Economic History 1480–1619', pp.28, 35.

13   Bod. Lib., Add. MS. 43.

14   A bond for repayment of a loan by Anthony Fugger in 1546 survives at TNA, E 101/601/16. This may be the 152,000 Flemish pounds which was repaid on 24 September 1546, the receipt for which is in BL, Cotton MS, Galba B, x, f.336. A bond for repayment of a loan to the Florentine banker Thomas Cavalcanti in London in 1544/5, is in TNA, E 101/601/14.

15   Outhwaite, 'The Trials of Foreign Borrowing...', pp.289–90. The Welsers were originally a patrician family from Augsburg who became financiers to Charles V. He granted them rights to govern part of modern-day Venezuela in 1528 as security for a loan.

16   *LP*, vol. 21, pt. i, pp.155–6.

17   Ibid., p.174.

18   Ibid., p.115.

19   Outhwaite, op. cit., pp.292, 295.

20   TNA, E 370/2/23.

21   Ives, 'Henry VIII', *ODNB*, vol. 26, p.549.

22   *LP*, vol. 20, pt. i, pp.44–5.

23   Read represented the ward of Farringdon Without in 1544–6. He died in 1550.

24   Dietz, *English Public Finance 1485–1558*, p.149; Doran (ed.), *King Henry VIII: Man & Monarch*, p.210.

25   Richardson, 'Some Financial Expedients of Henry VIII', pp.44–7; Dietz, op. cit., pp.172–4.

26   Potter, *Henry VIII and Francis I: The Final Conflict*, p.250.

27 Cited by Lehmberg, 'Parliamentary Attainder in the Reign of Henry VIII', p.232.
28 Richardson, op. cit., p.34.
29 *LP*, vol. 20, pt. ii, p.93.
30 *St. P.*, vol. 1, pp.830–1. Ely Place, 14 September 1545.
31 *LP*, vol. 20, pt. ii, pp.354–5.
32 37 Henry VIII, *cap.* 4.
33 Kenneth Pickholm, *Early Tudor Government* (Cambridge: Cambridge University Press, 2015), p.384.
34 Dietz, op. cit., p.159.
35 Scarisbrick, *Henry VIII*, p.454.
36 *LP*, vol. 20, pt. i, p.568.
37 *CSP Spain*, vol. 8, p.251.
38 *APC*, vol. 1, p.238.
39 Dietz, op. cit., p.155.
40 Hatfield House, CP 36/21.
41 Lambeth Palace Lib., MS 306, f.56r.
42 *St. P.*, vol. 1, p.835: Ely Place, 5 November 1545.
43 Ibid., pp.839–40: Ely Place, 11 November 1545.
44 *LP*, vol. 19, pt. ii, p.197.
45 TNA, SP 1/210/30.
46 *LP*, vol. 20, pt. ii, pp.465–6: Surrey to Henry VIII; Boulogne, 4 December 1545.
47 Davies, 'Surrey at Boulogne', p.345.
48 TNA, SP 1/213/47.
49 BL, Cotton MS, Titus B, ii, f.58.
50 TNA, SP 1/182/40.
51 *LP*, vol. 20, pt. ii, pp.304–5.
52 Potter, 'The International Mercenary Market...', p.27.
53 *LP*, vol. 20, pt. i, p.372.
54 TNA, SP 1/202/15-18.
55 TNA, SP 1/202/66-7.
56 *LP*, vol. 21, pt. ii, pp.243, 253.
57 TNA, SP 1/209/209-12; SP 1/210/67-70; Potter, opt. cit., p.43.
58 TNA, SP 1/209/215.
59 *LP*, vol. 21, pt. ii, p.374.
60 *LP*, vol. 20, pt. ii, p.489: Philip, Landgrave of Hesse, to Henry VIII; Spangenberg, 16 December 1545.
61 Accounts for mercenaries in 'the late wars' and for Scottish war are in TNA, E 351/43.
62 Potter, op. cit., p.29.
63 Cited by Jasper Ridley, *Henry VIII* (Harmondsworth Penguin, 2002), p.388.
64 TNA, E 315/254.
65 Nonsuch Palace was built on the site of Cuddington church and manor. Charles II gave it to Barbara, countess of Castlemaine, in 1671 but she sold its materials and gardens to George Berkeley, first earl of Berkeley, in 1682 to pay off gambling debts. Demolition of the inner court began in 1683 and the site was levelled in the eighteenth century.
66 Hayward (ed.), *The 1542 Inventory of Whitehall*, vol. 2, p.297.
67 Thurley, *Hampton Court*, p.73.
68 Scarisbrick, op. cit., p.458.
69 Smith, *Mask of Royalty*, p.219.
70 *CSP Spain*, vol. 8, p.143.
71 *LP*, vol. 20, pt. ii, p.307.
72 *CSP Spain*, vol. 8, p.219.
73 Smith, *Mask of Royalty*, p.219; Scarisbrick, op. cit., p.461.

74 *CSP Spain*, vol. 8, pp.241–2.

75 Ibid., pp.67–8.

76 *St. P.*, vol. 11, p.102.

77 TNA, E 30/1315.

78 *LP*, vol. 21, pt. i, p.374.

79 Smith, *Mask of Royalty*, pp.222–3; *St. P.*, vol. 11, p.173.

80 Hatfield House, CP 232/97. Another copy is in TNA, E 30/1318.

81 *LP*, vol. 21, pt. i, p.527.

82 *St. P.*, vol. 5, p.449ff.; *LP*, vol. 20, p.411.

83 *LP*, vol. 21, pt. i, pp.464–5.

84 Smith, *Mask of Royalty*, p.261.

85 Hatfield House, CP 232/17.

86 Francis I's oath to observe the terms of the treaty, dated 1 August 1546, is in TNA, E 30/1041.

87 *St. P.*, vol. 11, p.261.

88 *LP*, vol. 21, pt. i, p.603.

89 Ibid., p.709.

90 Marshall, *Heretics & Believers*, pp.298–9.

91 *LP*, vol. 21, pt. ii, p.81.

92 Ibid., p.101.

93 Wriothesley, op. cit., vol. 1, pp.171–2.

94 Thurley, op. cit., p.75. After the visit, the banqueting houses were dismantled and taken to the royal house at Chobham, Surrey, where Henry intended to re-erect them. This never happened and they were eventually sold for £26 3s 6d.

95 Foxe, *Acts & Monuments*, vol. 5, p.568.

96 *St. P.*, vol. 1, p.861.

Chapter 12 – Mad, Bad and Dangerous to Know

1 'An Act of the Ratification of the King's Majesty's Style', 35 Henry VIII, *cap.* 3.

2 The mural was destroyed on 4 January 1698 when the residential apartments caught fire. It was copied for Charles II by the Flemish artist Remigius van Leemput before he died in 1675 and this smaller painting remains in the Royal Collection (RCIN 405750) on display in the 'Haunted Gallery' of Hampton Court Palace.

3 The cartoon fragment (NPG 4027) measures 101 x 54 inches (257 x 137cm). The same image was reproduced as a woodcut on the title page of a play about Henry's reign entitled *When You See Me, You Know Me* by Samuel Rowley, first performed in 1604.

4 Bolland & Cooper, *The Real Tudors*, p.52.

5 Dendrochronology is a method of dating wooden artefacts using annual growth rings in timber.

6 The Petworth House portrait measures 93 x 47 inches (236 x 119cm). (NT 486186.) The Walker Art Gallery purchased the portrait in 1945. It measures 94 x 53 inches (238 x 135cm). (WAG inventory 1350.)

7 Bolland & Cooper, op. cit., p.55.

8 Herbert, *Life and Raigne of King Henry the Eight*, p.471.

9 Hayward, *The 1542 Inventory of*

Whitehall..., vol. 2, item 3,680, p.221.

10 Ibid., item 3,680, p.221. The 1547 inventory mentions 'the king's secret study, called the chair house' at Whitehall: Hayward, vol. 1, p.9.

11 Hayward, op. cit., vol. 1, p.37.

12 Barrett, 'King Henry the Eighth', p.232.

13 *CSP Spain*, vol. 6, pt. i., p.99.

14 See Bark, 'Did Schizophrenia Change the Course of English History?'

15 Psalm 73, verse 18.

16 Hayward, op. cit., vol. 1, pp.48–9.

17 Ibid., p.28. This was 'the square box with the image of King Henry wrought in earth' recorded in the 1547 Inventory of Whitehall and is probably the bust by the Florentine sculptor Petro Torrigiano, now in the Metropolitan Museum, New York.

18 Hayward, op. cit., vol. 2, items 1,214, 1,232–3, pp.119–20.

19 Barrett, op. cit., p.221.

20 Von Arni, 'The Treatment of Injury and Disease', p.60.

21 Copeman, *Doctors and Diseases in Tudor Times*, p.131.

22 BL, Sloane MS 1.

23 Furdell, *The Royal Doctors 1485–1714*, pp.23–4.

24 Ibid., p.24.

25 BL, Cotton MS, Nero C, x, f.3.

26 *LP*, vol. 12, pt. ii, p.348.

27 Hatfield House, CP 1/22.

28 *LP*, vol. 12, pt. ii, p.340.

29 *LP*, vol. 15, p.539.

30 Ghinucci was deprived of the bishopric by Henry in 1535 after the break with Rome.

31 BL, Cotton MS, Titus B, i, f.365; Hammond, 'Dr Augustine, Physician to Cardinal Wolsey and King Henry VIII', p.217.

32 Hammond, op.cit., p.224.

33 Ibid., p.234.

34 *CSP Spain*, vol. 6, pt. i, p.285: Chapuys to Charles V; London, 31 October 1540.

35 *CSP Venice*, vol. 5, p.182.

36 Furdell, *The Royal Doctors*, pp.26–7.

37 *LP, Addenda*, vol.1, pt. ii, p.523.

38 MacNalty, *Henry VIII: A Difficult Patient*, p.146.

39 The Privy Council heard his divorce case at Greenwich on 11–12 May and declared: 'We never in all our lives heard matter that more pitied us; so much cruelty and circumvention appeared in the man, so little cause ministered by the woman.' MacNalty, ibid., p.148.

40 Furdell, *The Royal Doctors*, p.28.

41 Ibid., p.28.

42 Copeman, op.cit., p.80; Furdell, *The Royal Doctors*, p.28; Furdell, 'Andrew Boorde', *ODNB*, vol. 6, pp.591–2; Fletcher, 'The Life of Andrew Boorde c.1490–1549', pp.243–52.

43 Thomas, 'Thomas Vicary and the Anatomie of Man's Body', p.235.

44 Furdell, *The Royal Doctors*, p.33.

45 MacNalty, op. cit., pp.69–70.

46 Most London apothecaries

were members of the Grocers'
Company in this period, only
forming their own Society of
Apothecaries in 1617.

47 Matthews, 'Royal Apothecaries
of the Tudor Period', pp.172–3.

48 Bayles, 'Notes on Accounts
Paid to the Royal Apothecaries',
p.796.

49 Matthews, op. cit., p.174.

50 Power, 'Some Notes on Edmund
Harman', p.70.

51 TNA, SP 2B/232.

52 Furdell, *The Royal Doctors*, p.35.

53 The red-, white- and blue-
striped pole hanging outside
barber's shops is a reminder of
these lost responsibilities.

54 Harper et al., 'The Origin
and Antiquity of Syphilis
Revisited ...', p.99.

55 Frith, 'Syphilis: Its Early History
and Treatment ...', p.50.

56 The name syphilis was applied
to the disease in 1530 by
the Italian doctor Girolamo
Fracastoro, who wrote an
epic poem called *Syphilis sive
morbus gallicus* ('Syphilis or
the French Disease'), about a
shepherd boy named Syphilus
who insulted the god Apollo and
was punished with a horrible
disease. The name was first used
by the medical profession in the
nineteenth century. See Crosby,
'The Early History of Syphilis',
p.219.

57 Harper et al., op. cit., p.126.

58 Frith, op cit., pp.49–50.

59 J.D. Rolleston, 'Venereal Disease

in Literature', *British Jnl.
Venereal Disease*, vol. 10 (1934),
p.147.

60 MacLaurin, 'Mere Mortals', p.68.

61 Brinch, 'The Medical Problems
of Henry VIII', p.352.

62 MacNalty, op. cit., p.161.

63 Park, *Ailing, Aging, Addicted*,
p.36.

64 Now in the State Graphics
Collection, Munich.

65 Brinch, op. cit., p.356.

66 Park, op. cit., p.42.

67 MacNalty, op. cit., p.161.

68 Barrett, op. cit., p.225.

69 Copeman, op. cit., pp.156–7.
Potatoes were brought to
England by Sir Francis Drake
after his circumnavigation in
1577–80. Another candidate
as first importer is Sir Thomas
Harriot, who brought back
potatoes from Raleigh's colony
at Roanoke Island, on the outer
banks of North Carolina, in
1586.

70 Kybett, 'Henry VIII – A
Malnourished King?', pp.19–25.

71 Another 250 servants were
entitled to meals as part of their
terms and conditions of employment but were not allowed to
dine in the Great Hall.

72 The first English version was
published in 1532, as *A Little
Book of Good Manners for
Children*.

73 *LP*, vol. 14, pt. ii, p.45:
12 September 1539 'between
10 and 11 a.m'.

74 First suggested by Clifford

Brewer, *The Death of Kings*, pp.123–4.

75 Ashrafian, 'Henry VIII's Obesity Following Traumatic Brain Injury', p.218.

76 Galassi, Habicht & Rühli, 'Henry VIII's Head Trauma', p.552.

77 Ikram, Sajjad & Salardini, 'The Head that Wears the Crown', pp.16–19.

78 BL, Royal MS 2A.XVI, f.63*v*.

Chapter 13 – Religion and an Embattled Court

1 Ryrie, 'Divine Kingship and Royal Theology . . .', p.49.

2 Schorne was rector at North Marston and died in 1313. He was said to have cast the devil into a boot, perhaps the origin of the jack-in-the-box toy. His remains were exhumed and reburied in St George's Chapel, Windsor.

3 *LP*, vol. 16, pp.588–9.

4 Muller, *Letters of Stephen Gardiner*, p.290; Rex, 'The Religion of Henry VIII', p.19.

5 Ryrie, *The Gospel of Henry VIII*, p.50.

6 Rex, op. cit., p.25.

7 Henry's father, Henry VII, had promoted the canonisation of Henry VI in Rome but progress was slow and it was hoped to accelerate matters in the late 1520s, when large fees associated with creating a saint were offered to expedite divorce proceedings against Katherine of Aragon. A shrine to Henry VI was erected in St George's Chapel, Windsor. See Rex, op. cit., p.14.

8 Loach, 'The Function of Ceremonial in the Reign of Henry VIII', p.63.

9 *LP*, vol. 16, p.487.

10 Ryrie, 'England's Last Medieval Heresy Hunt', p.39.

11 Foxe, *Acts & Monuments*, vol. 5, p.261.

12 *LP*, vol. 16, vol. 11, p.126.

13 TNA, SP 1/133/51-3.

14 *LP*, vol. 18, pt. ii, p.307.

15 34 & 35 Henry VIII, *cap.* 1. See *Statutes of the Realm*, vol. 3, pp.894–7.

16 See Foxe, op. cit., vol. 5, pp.181–234, for a full account of Lambert's case. Cromwell wrote after the trial of this 'miserable heretic sacramentary' that it was 'a wonder to see how fiercely, with how [much] gravity and inescapable majesty his highness exercised the very office of a supreme head of his Church of England; how benignly his grace assayed to convert the miserable man.' Cited in Hutchinson, *Last Days of Henry VIII*, p.88.

17 Wriothesley, *Chronicle*, vol. 1, p.80; Foxe, op. cit., vol. 5, p.236.

18 TNA, SP 1/161/61ff.

19 Smith, *Mask of Royalty*, pp.131–2.

20 BL, Cotton MS, Cleopatra, E, v, f.327*v*.

21 *LP*, vol. 16, pp.345, 347.

22 Scarisbrick, *Henry VIII*, p.418.

23 Cited by Smith, op. cit., p.128.

24 Ayris, 'Preaching the Last Crusade', p.683.

25 Daniel Goffman, *The Ottoman Empire and Early Modern Europe*, (Cambridge: Cambridge University Press, 2002), p.111.

26 Christopher Kitching, 'Broken Angels: The Response of English Parishes to the Turkish Threat to Christendom 1543-4' in W.J. Sheils & D. Wood (eds.), *The Church and Wealth* (Cambridge: Cambridge University Press, *Studies in Church History*, vol. 24, 1987), pp.209–17.

27 Muller, *Stephen Gardiner and the Tudor Reaction*, p.65.

28 Ibid., p.110.

29 Nichols, *Narratives*, p.252.

30 *LP*, vol 18, pt. ii, pp.328–9.

31 Carwarden received a patent as Master of Revels and Tents in 1544, and had been knighted at Boulogne in September of that year.

32 Brigden, *Letters of Richard Scudamore...*, p.78.

33 *APC*, vol. 1, p.156.

34 *LP*, vol 18, pt. ii, pp.l–lii.

35 Smith, op. cit., p.88.

36 Nichols, *Narratives*, pp.255–8; MacCulloch, *Thomas Cranmer, A Life*, pp.320–1.

37 Muller, *Letters of Stephen Gardiner*, p.326.

38 Smith, op. cit., pp.31–3.

39 MacCulloch, op. cit., p.348.

40 'An Act that all Chantries, Colleges etc. should be in the King's Disposition'; 37 Henry VIII, *cap.* 4.

41 *LP*, vol. 20, pt. ii, p.513.

42 The epithet 'Pharisee' is Henry's jibe based on the ancient Jewish sect that adhered strictly to traditional laws and enjoyed pretensions to superior sanctity.

43 'Mumpsimus' referred to someone obstinately adhering to old ways and was humanist ridicule, because of its suggestion of mummering, or play-acting. 'Sumpsimus' described opponents of classical learning and refers to the correct expression of something taking the place of an incorrect but popular belief. See Marshall, 'Mumpsimus and Sumpsimus...' pp.513–15.

44 Hall, 'Chronicle', pp.864–6. The chronicler wrote it down 'word for word as near as I was able to report it'.

45 Foxe, op. cit, vol. 5, p.562.

46 *Spanish Chronicle*, p.108.

47 Strickland, *Lives of the Queens of England...*, vol. 2, p.390.

48 Haugaard, 'Katherine Parr: the Religious Convictions...', p.353.

49 Foxe, op. cit., vol. 5, p.554; Scarisbrick, op. cit., p.479.

50 *LP*, vol. 21, pt. i, p.135.

51 Ibid., p.271.

52 My thanks to Edward Copisarow for information on early card games. Piquet, in which each player receives twelve cards from a thirty-two-card pack, is first mentioned in 1532. In December 1545, Thomas Hussey, Norfolk's treasurer, and another of his gentlemen, quarrelled violently over a game of primero, played for high

stakes, at 'Domingo's' house in Tothill Street, near Westminster Abbey. It was investigated by the Privy Council and the offenders committed to the Fleet Prison 'to await the king's pleasure'. *APC*, vol. 1, p.289.

53 TNA, E 314/22, f.44.

54 James, *Kateryn Parr*, p.268. After Henry's death, the now dowager queen sent a servant from St James's Palace to Greenwich to collect 'books of the garderobe [and sent] to the Lord Chamberlain'. TNA, E 101/423/12, f.124.

55 *APC*, vol. 1, p.399.

56 Ibid. p.408.

57 Scarisbrick, op. cit., pp.473–4.

58 St Paul's Cross was a preaching cross and open-air pulpit in the precinct of St Paul's Cathedral, in London.

59 Ellis, *Original Letters*, vol. 2, p.176; Laura Branch, *Faith & Fraternity: London Livery Companies at the Reformation 1510–1603* (Leiden: Brill, 2017), p.201.

60 Scarisbrick, op. cit., p.474.

61 Wriothesley, *Chronicle*, vol. 1, p.167.

62 Laynam, a 'mad prophesier', was comitted to the Tower on 7 June 1546 by the Privy Council (*LP*, vol. 21, pt. i, p.507). His fate is unknown.

63 *LP*, vol. 21, pt. i, pp.587–8.

64 Muller, *Stephen Gardiner and the Tudor Reaction*, p.137.

65 James, *Catherine Parr*, p.240.

66 Lady Sussex was Anne, the second wife of Henry Radcliffe, second earl of Sussex. She later separated from her husband and was accused of wanting to marry Sir Edmund Knyvett. She was imprisoned in the Tower in 1552 on charges of sorcery.

67 Anne Stanhope, wife of Hertford, afterwards duchess of Somerset.

68 Jane Fitzwilliam, the third wife of the London alderman Sir William Fitzwilliam.

69 Nichols, *Narratives*, p.311.

70 Ibid., p.304, fn.

71 SAL Proclamations, vol. 2, f.171.

72 *LP*, vol. 21, pt. i, p.607.

73 Foxe, op. cit., vol. 5, p.553ff.

74 James, *Catherine Parr*, p.246.

75 Martienssen, *Queen Katherine Parr*, p.218; Herbert, *The Life and Raigne of King Henry the Eight*, p.560.

76 Strickland, op. cit., vol. 3, p.246.

77 Foxe, op. cit., vol. 5, pp.559–60.

78 Martienssen, op. cit., p.220; Herbert, op. cit., p.561.

79 *LP*, vol. 21, pt. i, p.1383; *LP*, vol. 21, pt. ii, pp.236, 241.

80 TNA, E 101/423/12, ff.98, 170, 181–2.

81 Wriothesley, *Chronicle*, vol. 1, p.169.

82 Nichols, *Narratives*, p.42, fn.

Chapter 14 – The Last Days of the Tyrant

1 This was the nickname given to Gardiner by the Protestant

polemicist John Foxe. See *Acts & Monuments*, vol. 5, p.261.

2   Ibid., vol. 6, p.37.

3   Ibid., vol. 6, p.689.

4   Lipscomb, *The King is Dead*, p.71.

5   Foxe, op. cit., vol. 6, pp.162–4; Scarisbrick, *Henry VIII*, pp.489–90.

6   Muller, *Stephen Gardiner and the Tudor Reaction*, p.133.

7   TNA, E 315/160, f.133v.

8   *LP*, vol. 21, pt. ii, p.110.

9   Ibid., p.400. 'Ten pair of spectacles, 4d the pair, 3s 4d' (16 pence).

10 TNA, SP 4/1. The dry-stamp system was revived in the final months of Mary I's reign in 1558 when she became too ill to cope with signing state papers 'without distress and peril of her body'.

11 *LP*, vol. 21, pt. ii, pp.154, 226–7, 288.

12 John Cotton may be the same man as the 'Captain Cotton' who was singled out as 'meet to be remembered for [his] good service, now having double pay' in March 1546. *LP*, vol. 21, pt. i, p.235.

13 *LP*, vol. 21, pt. ii, pp.87, 153.

14 TNA, C 1/1244/32.

15 TNA, PROB 11/30/180.

16 TNA, C 1/1246/24.

17 TNA, C 1/1106/65-8.

18 TNA, REQ 2/6/181.

19 Tim Harris, *Politics of the Excluded c.1500–1850* (Basingstoke: Palgrave Macmillan, 2001), p.41.

20 In the Middle Ages, it was believed that Cadwaladr renounced the Welsh throne in 688 to become a pilgrim.

21 BL, Cotton MS, Cotton E, iv, f.84.

22 *LP*, vol. 8, pt. i, pp.214, 230.

23 TNA, SP 1/220/60-9.

24 *LP*, vol. 21, pt. ii, p.170.

25 Anne Neville was the daughter of Thomas Manners, first earl of Rutland. Neville had married her in July 1536 when she was aged twelve.

26 *LP*, vol. 21, pt. ii, pp.198–200.

27 After becoming fifth earl of Westmorland in 1550, he was in trouble again two years later when he faced charges of plotting to seize some treasure and to rob his mother. He died in 1563.

28 For more on Wisdom and related fraud in sixteenth-century England, see Alec Ryrie's *The Sorcerer's Tale: Faith and Fraud in Tudor England* (Oxford: Oxford University Press, 2008).

29 *LP*, vol. 21, pt. ii, p.52.

30 Ibid., p.56.

31 Ibid., p.145.

32 Ibid., p.128.

33 Ibid., p.185.

34 Ibid., p.173; *CSP Spain*, vol. 8, p.555.

35 Strype, *Life of the Learned John Cheke*, p.168.

36 *LP Addenda*, vol. 1, pt. ii, p.593.

37 TNA, E 315/160, f.361.

38 Lipscomb, op. cit., p.71.

39 Strickland, *Lives of the Queens of England...*, vol. 3, p.247.

40 *APC*, vol. 1, pp.536–57.

41 *SP*, vol 1, pp.883–4: Gardiner to Henry VIII; London, 2 December 1546.

42 Ibid., pp.884–5: Gardiner to Paget; Southwark, 2 December 1546.

43 Foxe, op. cit., vol. 6, p.138.

44 TNA, SP4/1.f.165.

45 Surrey was called this by Constantine Barlow, dean of Westbury, in 1539. See *Archaeologia*, vol. 23 (1831), p.62.

46 BL, Harleian MS 78, f.24.

47 Hutchinson, *Last Days of Henry VIII*, p.184.

48 *LP*, vol. 21, pt. ii, p.136.

49 Southwell (1504–56) was a commissioner for the suppression of monastic houses in Norfolk. The scars on his face and neck, shown in his portrait by Holbein, were not caused by wounds but probably by cutaneous tuberculosis.

50 Herbert, *The Life and Raigne of King Henry the Eight*, p.562.

51 *Spanish Chronicle*, p.144.

52 Herbert, op. cit., p.562.

53 'Greyfriars Chronicle', p.52.

54 Herbert, op. cit., p.562.

55 TNA, SP 1/227/84.

56 TNA, LR 2/115/1-81.

57 TNA, LR 2/115/18.

58 *LP*, vol. 21, pt. ii, p.289. The dukes of Norfolk remain hereditary Earl Marshals to this day.

59 *LP*, vol. 21, pt. ii, p.265.

60 *CSP Spain*, vol. 8, p.533.

61 TNA, SP 1/227/76.

62 Herbert, op. cit., pp.566–7.

63 BL, Cotton MS, Titus B, i, ff.94–96r.

64 *LP*, vol. 21, pt. ii, pp.294, 307.

65 Fryer studied medicine at Padua and had been associated with Pole there before 1536. See Brigden, 'Henry Howard, earl of Surrey and the Conjured League', p.535.

66 TNA, SP 1/227/f.97. 'Paskell' was arrested in January 1542 for uttering 'lewd words touching the king' and ordered to quit England. Nichols, *Proceedings*, vol. 7, pp.288, 291, 303, 319.

67 Anne Pisseleu d'Heilly, duchess of Étampes (1508–80), was Francis I's chief mistress and wielded considerable political influence at the French court, as well as enriching and elevating the fortunes of her own family.

68 TNA, SP 1/227/ff.104–5.

69 TNA, SP 1/227/103.

70 Edwin Casady, *Henry Howard, Earl of Surrey* (New York: Modern Language Association of America, 1938), p.199.

71 Herbert, op. cit., pp.563–4.

72 Ibid., p.563.

73 A cap of crimson velvet, lined with black and white ermine fur, which is carried before the sovereign on state occasions, but is also displayed on crests.

74 Herbert, op. cit., p.564.

75 Moore, 'The Heraldic Charge...', p.252.

76 National Portrait Gallery NPG 5291.

77 Brigden, op. cit., p.530; 'Henry Howard, earl of Surrey', *ODNB*, vol. 28, p.365.

78 Bayles, 'Notes on Accounts Paid to the Royal Apothecaries', p.796.

79 *CSP Spanish*, vol. 8, p.533.

80 TNA, SP 1/227/114.

81 *SP*, vol 1, p.891.

82 Childs, *Henry VIII's Last Victim*, p.299.

83 *Spanish Chronicle*, pp.145–6.

84 TNA, E 101/60/22.

85 BL, Harleian MS 297, f.256.

86 TNA, SP 1/227/106.

87 BL, Stowe MS, 396, ff.8–9.

88 *Spanish Chronicle*, p.148.

89 Surrey's body was removed to the Howard family's chapel in the church at Framlingham, Suffolk, in 1614. On the tomb, his earl's coronet is not worn by his effigy, but laid on a cushion by the legs.

90 Foxe, op. cit., vol. 6, p.163.

91 Hayward, *The 1542 Inventory of Whitehall...*, vol. 1, pp.32–3.

92 Foxe, op. cit., vol. 5, pp.691–2; vol. 6, pp.163, 170.

93 TNA, E/23/4, f.2.

94 TNA, E/23/4, f.3.

95 TNA, E/23/4, ff.9–15.

96 Starkey, *The Inventory of King Henry VIII*, p.xi.

97 TNA, E/23/4, f.19.

98 TNA, E/23/4, ff.24–5.

99 Lipscomb, op. cit., p.92.

Chapter 15 – Ashes to Ashes

1 *APC*, vol. 1, pp.559, 562.

2 *LP*, vol. 21, pt. ii, pp.408–9.

3 Ibid., p.373.

4 *CSP*, vol. 9, pp.340–1.

5 Foxe, *Acts & Monuments*, vol. 6, pp.138–9.

6 Ibid., vol. 5, p.695.

7 *LP*, vol. 21, pt. ii, p.348.

8 An egg supposedly of the mythical griffin.

9 TNA, SP 10/3/7.

10 *LP*, vol. 21, pt. ii, p.378.

11 TNA, SP4/1/166.

12 *LP*, vol. 21, pt. ii, p.376. The grounds at Greenwich were described as 'the apple orchard with the little garden and pond and the cocks and hens called "turkey cocks" with their chicks'. See *LP*, vol. 21, pt. ii, p.418.

13 TNA, SP 1/228/4.

14 *CSP*, vol. 8, p.537.

15 *LP*, vol. 21, pt. ii, p.348.

16 Ibid., p.356.

17 Ibid., p.360.

18 *CSP*, vol. 8, p.542.

19 BL, Cotton MS, Nero C, x, f.6.

20 *LP*, vol. 21, pt. ii, p.373.

21 *APC*, vol. 2, pp.16–20.

22 TNA, SP4/1/166.

23 *LP*, vol. 21, pt. ii, pp.409–10.

24 Ibid., p.441.

25 Swainmote courts dealt with minor offences such as poaching and illegal felling of timber in royal forests.

26 *LP*, vol. 21, pt. ii, p.436.

27 TNA, SP4/1/166.

28 TNA, SP4/1/166; *LP*, vol. 21, pt. ii, pp.419, 441.

29 *LP*, vol. 21, pt. ii, p.270.

30 *CSP Venice*, vol. 5, pp.182–3.

31 The Bill for the Attainder had been brought into Parliament on 18 January and passed six days later.

32 *LP*, vol. 21, pt. ii, p.420.

33 *House of Lords Jnl*, vol. 1 (1515–77) (London: HMSO, 1767–1830), p.289.

34 *LP*, vol. 21, pt. ii, p.389.

35 *Eccles. Mems.*, vol. 2, pt. i, p.17, records that Hertford and Paget were 'much about his person' while Henry lay on his deathbed.

36 A plain white linen, originally woven in Holland.

37 Lawn cloth is a plain-weave textile, originally of linen but now chiefly cotton.

38 Hayward, *The 1542 Inventory of Whitehall...*, vol. 1, pp.31–2. The bed was later moved to Windsor Castle; ibid., p.37.

39 *Eccles. Mems.*, vol.2, pt. ii, p.430.

40 Scarisbrick, *Henry VIII*, p.496.

41 Foxe, op. cit., vol. 5, p.689.

42 Smith, *Henry VIII: Mask of Royalty*, p.273.

43 Samuels, 'What was the Medical Cause of Death of Henry VIII?', pp.140–1.

44 *Eccles. Mems.*, vol. 2, pt. i, p.17.

45 Scarisbrick, op. cit., p.496.

46 Elsyng Palace was known as Little Park after 1539, when it came into Henry VIII's ownership. Forty Hall, a house built in the 1620s, occupies the site.

47 Cited by Lipscomb, *The King is Dead*, p.130.

48 TNA, SP 10/1/1.

49 TNA, SP 10/1/2.

50 *Eccles. Mems.*, vol. 2, pt. ii, p.289. 'Cereing' is a process of smearing the body with preservatives.

51 Bayles, 'Notes on the Accounts', p.795.

52 *Eccles. Mems.*, vol. 2, pt. ii, p.290.

53 *CSP Venice*, vol. 5, p.189. Da l'Armi's name alone is in cipher.

54 *LP*, vol. 21, pt. ii, p.389.

55 *CSP Spain*, vol. 9, p.4. The ports were reopened on 2 February. See *APC*, vol. 2, p.11.

56 BL, Cotton MS, Titus B, ii, f.51.

57 *LP*, vol. 21, pt. ii, p.389.

58 BL, Harleian MS 353, f.1.

59 De Selve wrongly reported on 31 January that Norfolk had been secretly beheaded the previous day.

60 *APC*, vol. 2, pp.3–4.

61 Ibid., p.5.

62 'Ordo de exequis regalibus' in *Missale ad usuum ecclesie Westmastereriensis*, ed. J. Wickham Legg, 3 vols. (London: Henry Bradshaw Society, 1891–7), vol. 2, p.416.

63 The modern word 'dirge' is derived from 'dirige'.

64 TNA, LC 2/2 f.84v, ff.83, 77.

65 TNA, LC 2/2 f.176.

66 A total of 1,800lbs (817kg) of wax was used for the candles on the Whitehall hearse.

67 *Eccles. Mems.*, vol. 2, pt. ii, p.290.

68 Francis Sandford, *Genealogical History of the Kings and Queens of England 1066–1707*, 2nd edn (London: John Nicholson & Robert Knaplock, 1707), p.493.

69 *Eccles. Mems.*, vol. 2, pt. ii, p.293.

70 TNA, SP 10/1/5.

71 Wriothesley, *Chronicle*, vol. 1, p.181.

72 TNA, SP 10/3/9.

73 TNA, SP 10/3/7.

74 *Eccles. Mems.*, vol. 2, pt. ii, p.296.

75 TNA, 10/1/17.

76 *Eccles. Mems.*, vol.2, pt. ii, p.277.

77 Ibid., pp.304–5.

78 TNA, LC 2/2, f.3.

79 *Spanish Chronicle*, p.154.

80 Loach, 'The Function of Ceremonial in the Reign of Henry VIII', fn. p.62.

81 TNA, LC 2/2, f.45.

82 Strickland, *Lives of the Queens of England . . .*, vol. 3, p.255.

83 Burnet, *History of the Reformation*, vol. 1, p.298.

84 Peto resigned the see of Salisbury on the accession of Mary I in 1553 and was created cardinal and papal legate to England in place of Pole. He declined the post because of his failing powers but was appointed Cardinal in 1557. Mary prevented his cardinal's hat being delivered from Rome and Peto died the following year.

85 *Eccles. Mems.*, vol.2, pt. ii, p.304.

86 Ibid., p.308.

87 TNA, 10/1/17.

88 Muller, *Stephen Gardiner and the Tudor Reaction*, p.143.

89 *Eccles. Mems.*, vol. 2, pt. ii, p.310.

90 Ibid., p.310.

91 Henry's funeral was the first time that the heralds were paid an attendance fee, totalling £40.

92 Maurice Bond, *Inventories of St George's Chapel, Windsor Castle 1384–1667* (Windsor: St George's, 1947), p.185.

93 Drawings of the banners *in situ* are in BL, Lansdowne MS 874, f.49.

94 *CSP Venice*, vol. 5, p.189.

95 *CSP Spain*, vol. 9, p.36.

Chapter 16 – Epilogue

1 BL, Harleian MS 5,087, no.35.

2 TNA, SP 10/1/12 and 14.

3 Thomas Seccombe (ed.), *Tudor Tracts 1532–88* (Westminster: Archibald Constable, 1903), p.125.

4 The battlefield site is at Ordnance Survey National Grid reference NG 357 712. This was the last battle between England and an independent Scotland.

5 Clifford Brewer, *The Death of Kings*, pp.129–30.

6 Skidmore, *Edward VI: The Lost King of England*, p.260.

7 Loach, *Edward VI*, pp.159–62.

8 Edward's grave was unmarked until 1966, when a stone was laid by Christ's Hospital School to commemorate its founder.

9 A later account of these obsequies is in BL, Add. MS 30,536, f.194v.

10 *CSP Spain*, vol. 9, p.62.

11 Smith, *Mask of Royalty*, p.235.

12 The monastery was burnt to the ground during the Napoleonic Peninsular War and was ruined until 1949, when it was restored. It is now inhabited by monks of the Pauline Order.

13 Smith, op. cit., p.234.

14 William Robertson, *History of Charles V* (Paris: Baudry, 1828), p.580.

15 Edward Armstrong, *The Emperor Charles V*, 2nd edn, 2 vols. (London: Macmillan, 1910), vol. 2, p.367.

16 Smith, op cit., p.234. Charles was interred in the monastery church but his remains were later reburied at San Lorenzo del Escorial.

17 *Report on MSS of Earl of Ancaster* (London: HMC, 1907), pp.454, 456.

18 TNA, SP 10/6/11.

19 TNA, SP 10/6/9.

20 *CSP Spain*, vol. 9, p.88.

21 Loach, op. cit., p.91.

22 John Gough Nichols (ed.), *Literary Remains of King Edward VI*, vol. 1 (London: Roxburghe Club, 1857), p.clvii.

23 Eric Ives, *Lady Jane Grey, A Tudor Mystery* (Chichester: Wiley-Blackwell, 2009), pp.11, 94.

24 For a discussion of Wriothesley's disgrace, see Slavin, 'The Fall of Chancellor Wriothesley...'.

25 TNA, SP 46/1/154, SP 46/2/78-81.

26 *APC*, vol. 2, p.400.

27 Muller, *Stephen Gardiner and the Tudor Reaction*, p.181.

28 Holinshed, *Chronicles*, vol. 4, p.2.

29 David Loades, *John Dudley, Duke of Northumberland* (Oxford: Clarendon Press, 1996), p.268.

30 A drawing of Anne of Cleves' funeral procession survives. BL, Add. MS, 35,324, f.1.

31 *CSP Venice*, vol. 5, p.200.

32 A delicate fabric made in the Iranian city of Ormuz.

33 *CSP Venice*, vol. 5, pp.191–203.

34 VSA, Consiglio di dieci, X, Criminale v, vii, p.3.

35 VSA Consiglio di dieci, X, Lettere Secrete, *buste* 4.

36 VSA, Avogaria di Comun, Filza Necrologia Nobili Veneti, *buste* 1.

37 TNA, E/23/4, f.5.

38 TNA, E/23/4, ff.7–8.

39 Higgins, 'On the Work of Florentine Sculptors...', p.143.

40 Margaret Mitchell, 'Works of Art from Rome for Henry VIII...', *Jnl. Warburg & Courtauld Institutes*, vol. 34 (1971), pp.189–90.

41 John Speed, *Historie of Great Britaine*, 2nd edn (London: George Humble, 1623), pp.796–7. See also 'Vertue's Note Book (BL, Add. MS. 21,111)', *Walpole Soc.*, vol. 18 (1929), pp.40–1.

42 My grateful thanks to Tim Tatton-Brown, for sharing his research with me and for helpful discussion about Henry's monument.

43 Hope, *Windsor Castle*, vol. 2, pp.482–6.

44 Ibid., p.483.

45 TNA, E 336/27/1.

46 Dr Roger Bowers, 'Henry VIII and St George's Chapel: his Chantry, Tomb & Testamentary Bequests 1547–65' (Maurice & Shelagh Bond Memorial Lecture, Friends of St George's, October 2002).

47 BL, Lansdowne MS 6, no.31; 116, no.13.

48 *Jnl. of the House of Commons*, vol. 4, p.502, 7 April 1646.

49 Higgins, op. cit., pp.177–80. The original casting of the candlesticks was poorly done. Several patches were inserted to cover defects. See ibid., fn. p.180. There is a cast of one candlestick in the Victoria & Albert Museum, London.

50 This miscreant was Richard Fishbourne, 'a gentleman of Windsor' who was a relation, by marriage of Sir Christopher Wren. See *King Charles I: His Burial and Relics at St George's Chapel, Windsor Castle* (Stroud: St George's Chapel, 2014), p.8.

51 On p.362 of the hand-foliated and heavily annotated copy of Pote's *History and Antiquities of Windsor Castle*, given to St George's Chapter in 1814 and now in the chapter archives.

52 Halford, *An Account of What Appeared . . .*, p.10.

53 Notes bound in the copy of Halford, *An Account of What Appeared . . .*, in the chapter archives at St George's.

54 *Annual Report of Friends of St George's*, 1933–50, p.10.

55 St George's Chapter, Acts VI B:9, p.109.

56 Tim Tatton-Brown, 'The Building of the New Chapel', in Nigel Saul & Tim Tatton-Brown, *St George's Chapel, Windsor: History & Heritage* (Wimborne: Dovecote Press, 2010), pp.77–8.

Bibliography

Primary sources – manuscript

BODLEIAN LIBRARY, OXFORD

Add. MS 43 – Costs of the wars and fortifications of Henry VIII and Edward VI, 30 September 1538–31 July 1552.

Ashmole MS 1729, ff.3–4r – Henry to his ambassador in France demanding extradition of 'Blanche Rose'; The Moor, Hertfordshire, 18 October 1540.

BRITISH LIBRARY, LONDON
Additional MSS

5,733, f.31 – Indenture dated 13 August 1544, for Robert Baker, to transport iron shot to siege of Boulogne.

6,716, f.98v – Fifteenth- and sixteenth-century medical recipes for curing Sweating Sickness.

8,716, f.67r – Letters of Cardinal Alessandro Farnese; Francis I's opinion of Henry VIII.

25,114, f.262 – Henry to Bishop Gardiner and Sir Francis Bryan; Greenwich, 25 April 1537.

30,536, f.194v – Obsequies at the French court for Henry VIII, 1547.

32,621, f.93 – Charles Brandon, duke of Suffolk, and Cuthbert Tunstall, bishop of Durham, to Privy Council, reporting torture; Darlington, 14 July [1543].

35,324, f.1 – Drawing of funeral procession of Anne of Cleves, 1557.

Arundel MSS

97 – Payments by the Treasurer of the King's Household, 1537–42; **f.186** – Payments for Margaret Pole, countess of Salisbury, in the Tower, April 1541.

Cotton MSS

Augustus I. i, f.49 – Map of the French town of Landrecy, *c.*1543.

Augustus I. ii, f.53 – Map of Boulogne's defences and new French fortifications drawn by John Rogers, 1546.

Caligula B, vii, f.289 – 'Transactions in Scotland' about the time of death of King Malcolm III.

———, **f.322** – Copies of two deeds proving the title of King Edward I of England to sovereignty over Scotland, deposited at Durham priory, 30 May 1291.

Caligula E, i, ff.63–66 – Sixteenth-century sketch of Boulogne and its surrounding forts.

Cleopatra E, v, ff.313–27v – Draft of Statute of Six Articles, corrected by Henry VIII.

Galba B, x, ff.21–25r – Stephen Vaughan to Thomas Cromwell, about allegations of supporting the Lutheran faith, December 1531.

———, **f.336** – Receipt for 152,000 Flemish pounds repaid to Anthony Fugger by Henry VIII; 24 September 1546.

Nero C, x, f.3 – Letter, signed by five doctors, to Cromwell describing the queen's [Jane Seymour's] worsening condition; Hampton Court, 17 October 1537.

———, **f.6** – Letter from Queen Katherine Parr to Prince Edward; Westminster; after 10 January 1547.

Otho C, x, f.232 – Order establishing commission to hear evidence and give sentence on the marriage of Henry and Anne of Cleves, 1540.

———, **ff.242–5** – Thomas Cromwell to Henry on his disgrace and being in the Tower of London, 1540.

———, **f.250** – Privy Council to Willian Paget, ambassador in Paris, concerning the offences of Queen Katherine Howard; Westminster, November 1541.

Titus B, i, f.94–96b – Norfolk to the Privy Council, vindicating himself of treason; Tower of London, December 1546.

———, **103ff.** – Declaration written by Richard Morison (with Cromwell's corrections), that Parliament should support the king because of military expenditure in 1539.

———, **f.365** – Augustine (as Wolsey's physician) to Thomas Cromwell, requiring medical assistance for the Cardinal; Esher, Surrey, 19 January 1530.

———, **ff.409–11** – 'Questions to be asked of the Lord Cromwell' about the Anne of Cleves marriage, 1540.

———, **f.551** – Proclamation declaring Henry VIII to be King of Ireland; 23 January 1542.

Titus B, ii, f.51 – Letter from Henry Radcliff, earl of Sussex, to his wife, announcing the death of Henry VIII and the regency of Edward VI. Ely Place, London, 31 January 1547.

———, **f.58** – Surrey to Sir William Paget, about his servants' offices at Boulogne, 14 July 1546.

Vespasian F, xiii, f.157 – Letter from Elizabeth Cromwell to Henry, appealing for pity for herself and her husband Gregory; after July 1540.

Appendix 28, f.69 – Accounts for work in the King's armoury at Greenwich, 1544.

Egerton MS

990, ff.414–6 – Secret annex to the Treaty of Crépy, 1544.

Harley MSS

78, f.5 – Sir Thomas Wyatt to the Privy Council about his ambassadorship at the court of Charles V; March 1541.

———, **f.24** – Surrey to the Privy Council promising to curb his 'heady will'; Fleet Prison; 15 July 1542.

295, f.146 – Thomas Perry's narration of his cruel usage by the Inquisition after saying that Henry VIII was a good Christian; 1539.

297, f.256 – Norfolk's confession, Tower of London; 12 January 1547.

304, f.136r – Exemption of a number of Knights of the Garter from attending the Order's feast at Windsor Castle on 6 May 1543.

353, f.1 – Proclamation of the death of Henry VIII and proclaiming his son Edward VI as King of England; London, 1 February 1547.

442, f.197 – Proclamation ordering destruction of books containing 'unauthorised news' about Hertford's invasion of Scotland; 1544.

3,362, f.17 – Thomas Cromwell's last words on the scaffold; 28 July 1540.

5,087, no 35 – Edward VI to Dowager Queen Katherine Parr; Tower of London, 8 February 1547.

6,074, f.57r – Creation of Thomas Cromwell as earl of Essex; Palace of Whitehall, 18 April 1540.

6,989, f.45 – Privy Council to Norfolk; Hampton Court, 23 February 1540.

———, f.121 – Privy Council to Norfolk, ordering the siege of Montreuil; 20 June 1544.

———, f.127 – Letter from the Privy Council to Norfolk, about secret plans to besiege Boulogne; London, 7 July 1544.

Lansdowne MSS

6, no.31 – Letter from Sir William Paulet, first marquess of Winchester, Lord High Treasurer, to Sir William Cecil about Henry VIII's tomb; 12 September 1563.

116, no.13 – Certificate on the state of the tombs of Henry VII at Westminster and Henry VIII at Windsor, with a view to their repair.

874, f.49 – Drawings of eight banners used in Henry VIII's funeral, hanging in St George's Chapel, Windsor, in early seventeenth century.

1,236, f.9 – Letter from Queen Katherine Parr to Henry in France, 'full of duty and respect and requesting to hear from him'; Greenwich, [July 1544].

Royal MSS

2A.XVI – *The Psalter of Henry VIII*, written and probably illuminated by John Mallard with Henry VIII depicted as the Biblical king David, 176ff; *c*.1540–1.

18B.VI, ff.153v–154 – Earl of Arran to Pope Paul III seeking papal protection for Scotland; Hamilton Castle, 14 May 1543, and a similar letter to the Cardinal of Carpi.

7C.XVI, f.60 – Wardrobe stuff at the Palace of Whitehall remaining in the hands of Anthony Denny.

7D.X – Collection of prayers and meditations translated into Latin, French and Italian by twelve-year-old Princess Elizabeth, with a Latin dedication to Henry VIII (ff.1r–5r) dated 30 December 1545.

Sloane MSS

1 – Guido de Cauliaco's fifteenth-century *Chirugia*, owned by John Ayliff, surgeon to Henry VIII.

1,017 – Collection of medical recipes, with, at **f.30v**, Henry's 'plaster' for Anne of Cleves.

1,047 – Collection of recipes for ointments and nostrums devised by Henry VIII and four of his doctors.

2,442, f.43 – Henry VIII's instructions to Dr Nicholas Wotton, his new ambassador to Charles V; 1543.

3,837 – Henry VIII's grant of privileges to Queen Katherine Howard; 1541.

Stowe MSS

396, ff.8–9 – Trial of Surrey; 1546.

559, ff.55–69r – Inventory of 'Certain Jewels . . . given by the King's Majesty unto Quene Katherine [Howard] his most dearest wife at the time of the solemnisation of their graces' marriage' and at New Year, 1541.

MSS OF MARQUESS OF SALISBURY
HATFIELD HOUSE, HERTFORDSHIRE

CP 1/22 – Deposition of Sir William Butts to the commission investigating the validity of the marriage to Anne of Cleves; 1540.

CP 1/23 – Henry VIII's deposition to the commission inquiring into the validity of his marriage to Anne of Cleves; 1540.

CP 1/27 – Letter from Thomas Cromwell to Henry VIII; Tower of London, 30 June 1540.

CP 1/28 – Letter to Henry VIII from Anne of Cleves agreeing to the terms of the annulment of her marriage; Richmond Palace, Surrey, 16 July 1540.

CP 1/29 – Letter from Anne of Cleves to her brother, signifying her 'willing consent' to the annulment of her marriage; Richmond Palace, Surrey, [21 July] 1540.

CP 36/21 – Note of £180,000 costs for victuals for Boulogne and Calais for December–May 1544/5.

CP 231/2 – Hertford to Privy Council, complaining about insufficient money to pay 'officers and mariners of the fleet'; 23 April 1544.

CP 231/15 – Sir Thomas Wriothesley to Hertford; Westminster, 25 November 1542.

CP 231/53 – Privy Council to Hertford, sending extra funds for the Scottish expedition; Westminster, 26 April 1544.

CP 231/98 – Privy Council to Hertford, expressing the king's approval of his military operations in Scotland; Westminster, 15 May 1544.

CP 231/108 – Privy Council instructions to Hertford for the invasion of Scotland; 1544.

CP 231/110 – Privy Council to Hertford on the Scots being 'most worthily and justly plagued' for their 'open untruth and disloyal behaviour'; Westminster, 20 May, 1544.

CP 232/17 – Henry VIII's ratification of peace treaty of Ardres, dated 17 July 1546.

CP 232/97 – Treaty of Ardres between Henry VIII and Francis I of France, dated 7 June 1546.

CP 232/103 – Draft abridgement of the articles of the peace treaty between England and Scotland, relating to the marriage of Mary, Queen of Scotland with Prince Edward, dated 1 July 1543.

LAMBETH PALACE LIBRARY
LONDON

Carew MSS 621, f.14 – Statement of the king's title to Ireland, listed as 1541 but probably written earlier.

MS 306, f.56r – 'A Memorial of the King's Charges at Boulogne'; 27 September–9 October 1545.

THE NATIONAL ARCHIVES
KEW, SURREY
Chancery Enrolment Office: Parliament Rolls

C 65/147/22 – Attainder of Margaret Pole, countess of Salisbury.

Court of Chancery, Six Clerks Office

C 1/1106/665-8 – Elizabeth, daughter and heir of Thomas Briggs of London, pressed into service with the King's Guard at Boulogne, *v* Kenelm Hydley, over half a messuage and land in Cradley, Worcestershire.

C 1/1244/32 – Petition by David Lewes, tailor, for a licence to beg by the friends and kin of William Dowding, killed at Boulogne.

C 1/1246/24 – Hugh Mathos and Joan and Alice his granddaughters and wards, daughters of Richard Smythe, killed at Boulogne, *v* Roger Edwards and Edward Cowper, entrusted with deeds of a leasehold property in Bodenham, Herefordshire.

Court of Requests

REQ 2/6/181 – Anne Whitney *v* John Sims and Joan Whitehead; plaintiff's claim to the goods of her late husband, victualler to Yeomen of the Guard at Boulogne; 22 April 1545–21 April 1546.

Exchequer
Treasury of the Receipt

E 23/4/1 – Henry VIII's will, dated 30 December 1546.

Treasury of the Receipt – Diplomatic Documents

E 30/1031 – Treaty of friendship and alliance between Charles V and Henry VIII; London, 11 February 1543.

E 30/1032 – Powers granted by Charles V to Don Fernando de Gonzaga and Eustace Chapuys, Imperial ambassador, to arrange with Henry VIII for an invasion of France; Brussels, 7 December 1543.

E 30/1041 – Oath of Francis I, king of France, to observe the Treaty of Ardres-Guînes; dated [1 August] 1546.

E 30/1315 – Powers granted by Francis I, king of France, to Claud d'Annebaut, Admiral of France, to conclude a treaty of perpetual peace with Henry VIII; Ferrières, 21 April 1546.

E 30/1318 – Treaty of peace between France and England concluded at Campagne, near Ardres; 7 June 1546.

E 30/1470 – Judgement of the United Convocations of Canterbury and York declaring the nullity of Henry's marriage with Anne of Cleves; Westminster, 9 July 1540.

E 30/1472/4 – Attestation before Suffolk and others of Anne of Cleves' consent to divorce from Henry; Richmond Palace, 11 July 1540.

E 30/1472/5 – Attestation of the marriage between Henry VIII and Katherine Parr.

E 30/1472/6 – Cranmer's licence for marriage of Henry VIII and Katherine Latimer, née Parr; Lambeth, 29 July 1543.

E 30/1480 – Safe-conduct granted by Henry VIII for two gentlemen sent by the Captain of Boulogne to negotiate cessation of hostilities; 'The camp before Boulogne', 12 September 1544.

E 30/1481 – Indenture between Suffolk and James de Courcy, Captain of Boulogne, for its surrender; 'The camp before Boulogne', 23 September 1544.

Lord Treasurer's Remembrancer, Accounts Various

E 101/60/22 – Accounts of Sir Walter Stonor, Lieutenant of the Tower of London, for expenses of prisoners held there, including Surrey and Norfolk.

E 101/422/15 – Expenses of Anne of Cleves as queen, 22 April 1539–21 April 1540.

E 101/423/12 – Expenses of the Queen's household, 22 April 1546–21 April 1548.

E 101/601/14 – Bond for repayment of loan to Thomas Cavalcanti and others of Florence; 1544–5.

E 101/601/16 – Bond for repayment of loan to Anthony Fugger and others; 1546.

E 370/2/23 – Enrolled account for 1545 Benevolence.

Court of Augmentations, Receipts and Payments Books

E 314/22 – Miscellaneous expenses of Queen Katherine Parr's household; 22 April 1545–28 January 1547.

E 315/160 – Household book of Sir Anthony Denny, Keeper of the Palace of Whitehall; 34 Henry VIII–2 Edward VI.

E 315/254 – Payments, 22 April 1544–21 April 1545 including wages of 'captains [of] Italians appointed to the Northern parts.

Pipe Office

E 351/43 – Accounts of Sir Thomas Chaloner, clerk to the Privy Council, for maintenance of Italians, Spaniards, Albanois, Clevois and Almains at their discharge from the late wars and conduct money for the wars in Scotland; 17 May 1545–28 February 1551.

Court of Augmentations/Office of Auditors, Land Revenue

LR 2/115 – Inventory of the goods of duke of Norfolk, at Kenninghall, Norfolk (ff.1–64) and at Castle Rising, Norfolk (ff.67–70) and of Henry Howard, earl of Surrey, at St Leonard's by Norwich (ff.71–4); of the duke's horses in Norfolk, Suffolk (ff.77–81); sheep (ff.84–5) and grain (f.86); December 1546.

Records of the Lord Chamberlain and Officers of the Royal Household

LC 2/2 – Wardrobe accounts for the funeral of Henry VIII, 1547.

Records of the Office of First Fruits and Tenths

E 336/27/1 – Accounts rendered by John Rok, deputy of John Gostwick, late Treasurer of Court of First Fruits and Tenths; payments to Giovanni Portinari, for work on Henry VIII's tomb; December 1543.

Probate Records, Prerogative Court of Canterbury

PROB/11/24/153 – Will of Dame Maud Parr, widow of Blackfriars, London.

PROB/11/30/180 – Will of William Bateman, 'petty captain' of Herefordshire, apparently killed during the siege of Boulogne.

PROB/11/37/171 – Will of Thomas Howard, third duke of Norfolk.

State Papers Domestic

SP 1/116/92 – Henry VIII to Norfolk; 22 February 1537.

SP 1/133/51-53 – Sermon of Thomas Cowley, alias Rochester, vicar of Ticehurst; 1538.

SP 1/158 f.124 – Henry Dawe's report on sermons by Barnes, Jerome and Garrett.

SP 1/161/61ff – File of indictments in London, each marked '*bills vera*'; 17 July 1540.

SP 1/163/46r – Declaration by John Lassells; September 1541.

SP 1/166/183 – Sir William Fitzwilliam, earl of Southampton and John, Lord Russell, to Henry VIII; Calais, 6 May 1541.

SP 1/167/14 – Queen Katherine to Thomas Culpeper; July 1541.

SP 1/167/100 – Confession of Mary Hall, 'taken by me William, earl of Southampton'; 5 November 1541.

SP 1/167/117-20 – Examination of Henry Monox by Cranmer and Sir Thomas Wriothesley; Lambeth, 5 November 1541.

SP 1/167/121 – Cranmer's interview with Queen Katherine Howard; November 1541.

SP 1/167/123 – Privy Council to Cranmer and others reporting that the Queen is to be removed to Syon House; Westminster, 11 November 1541 'at night'.

SP 1/167/127 – Sir Ralph Sadler to Cranmer and others urging that the Queen should be re-examined about Thomas Culpeper; 'The Court', 'Saturday 11pm'.

SP 1/167/131-4 – Examination of Katherine Tylney; Westminster, 13 November 1541.

SP 1/167/133-4 – Examination of Margaret Morton by Sir Anthony Browne; November 1541.

SP1/167/159 – Confession of Thomas Culpeper; Tower of London, November 1541.

SP 1/167/160 – Questions to be put to Agnes, dowager duchess of Norfolk; December 1541.

SP 1/167/161 – Confession of Francis Dereham; Tower of London, November 1541.

SP 1/176/137 – Privy Council to Suffolk, indicating the king's approval of the use of torture; 14 March 1543.

SP 1/182/40 – Sir John Wallop to Paget; Camp before Landrecy, 26 October 1543.

SP 1/184/24 – Rates of pay for German mercenaries.

SP 1/184/228ff – Detailed plans for Henry's invasion of France; 1544.

SP 1/190/23-5 – Sir William Paget to Suffolk, about the sieges of Boulogne and Montreuil; Gravesend, Kent, 12 July 1544.

SP 1/190/76 – Suffolk to Henry VIII; 'Camp besides Marquison', 18 July 1544.

SP 1/190/78-79v – Paget to Suffolk; Calais, 18 July 1544.

SP 1/190/85-85v – Suffolk and Sir Anthony Browne to Paget; Camp before Marquison, 19 July 1544.

SP 1/190/91-91v – Gardiner and Paget to Suffolk; Calais, 20 July 1544.

SP 1/190/96-96v – Lisle to Paget; from siege of Boulogne, 20 July 1544 'in the morning'.

SP 1/190/103 –Francis I to Henry VIII; St Mor de Fossez, 20 July 1544.

SP 1/190/112 – Norfolk and others to Henry VIII; Camp before Montreuil, 21 July 1544.

SP 1/190/126 – Russell to Henry VIII; Camp at siege of Montreuil, 22 July 1544.

SP 1/190/128 – Russell to Sir William Paget; Montreuil, 22 July 1544.

SP 1/190/155 – Queen Katherine Parr to Henry VIII; Hampton Court, 25 July 1544.

SP 1/190/165 – Henry VIII to Mary of Hungary, regent of Flanders; Boulogne, 27 July 1544.

SP 1/190/167 – Russell to Henry VIII; Montreuil, 28 July 1544.

SP 1/190/220 – Queen Katherine Parr to Henry VIII; Hampton Court, 31 July 1544.

SP 1/190/240 – Henry VIII's *pro forma* letter seeking loans for the French war; [July] 1544.

SP 1/193/92 – Norfolk and others to the Council; Calais, 9 October 1544.

SP 1/193/154 – Henry to Norfolk and Suffolk, following unsuccessful French attempt to recapture Boulogne; Westminster, 14 October 1544.

SP 1/202/15-18 – Mercenary agreement signed by Friedrich von Riffenberg; June 1545.

SP 1/202/66 – Philip of Hesse to Henry; 14 June 1545.

SP 1/209/209-12 – Fane to the Privy Council; 1 November 1545.

SP 1/209/215 – Paget to Riffenberg; Windsor, 2 November 1545.

SP 1/210/30 – Thomas Hussey, Treasurer to third duke of Norfolk, to earl of Surrey, about his debts; London, 6 November 1545.

SP 1/210/67-70 – Fane to Privy Council; Givey, 10 November 1545.

SP 1/213/47 – Council of Boulogne to Henry about skirmish at St Etienne; Boulogne, 8 January 1546.

SP 1/219/51 – Copy of articles demanded by the Dutch procurer général; 23 May 1546.

SP 1/220/60-9 – Confession of Robert Barker, servant to earl of Surrey.

SP 1/227/76 – Earl of Surrey, to the Privy Council; Tower of London, ?13 December 1546.

SP 1/227/84 – John Gates and others to Henry VIII about their 'dawn raid' at Kenninghall, Norfolk; Kenninghall, 14 December 1546.

SP 1/227/f.97 – Deposition of Sir Edmund Knyvett.

SP 1/227/103 – Deposition of Edward Rogers.

SP 1/227/ff.104-5 – Deposition of Sir Gawain Carew.

SP 1/227/106 – Deposition of John Torre.

SP 1/227/109 – Deposition of Hugh Ellis, secretary to the earl of Surrey.

SP 1/227/114 – Wriothesley's questions to be put to the earl of Surrey; December 1546.

SP 1/228/4 – William Grene's bill for 'making a close stool for the use of the king's majesty' delivered to Sir Anthony Denny; December 1547.

SP 2B/232 – Ordinances of Eltham, 1526; rules governing the conduct of the King's Barber.

SP 4/1 – List of documents issued under Henry VIII's 'dry-stamp', September 1545–January 1547.

SP 10/1/1 – Hertford to Sir William Paget; Enfield 'between 3 and 4am', 29 January 1547.

SP 10/1/2 – Hertford to Privy Council; Enfield, 1 dm, 30 January 1547.

SP 10/1/5 – Gardiner to Paget; Southwark, 5 February 1547.

SP 10/1/12 – Preamble of a grant by Edward VI to the duke of Somerset of certain properties; 15 February 1547.

SP 10/10/14 – Style and titles of the duke of Somerset; 15 February 1547.

SP 10/1/17 – Order of ceremonies at the funeral of Henry VIII.

SP 10/3/7 – Account of gold, rings and gems removed from secret jewel house at Whitehall for decorating various *objets d'art* and for Edward VI's crown; 20 January, 8 and 12 February 1547.

SP 10/3/9 – Discussions on order of service for coronation of Edward VI.

SP 10/6/9 – Deposition of Sir Richard Cotton.

SP 10/6/11 – Deposition of Lord Clinton.

SP 11/3/61 – Lord Chancellor Gardiner to Sir William Petre; Southwark, 11 February 1554.

SP 46/1/154 – Warrant to Sir Ralph Sadler, Master of the Great Wardrobe, to deliver clothing and bedding to the Tower for Thomas Howard, duke of Norfolk, and Edward Courtenay; Westminster, 3 March 1548.

SP 46/2/78-81 – Warrant to the Treasurer of the Exchequer to pay Sir John Markham, Lieutenant of the Tower, an annual sum for the apparel of Norfolk; 1548.

ST GEORGE'S CHAPEL, WINDSOR
Chapter Archives

Chapter Acts VI, B:9, p.109.

SGC. G.1 – *Liber Niger*, or 'Black Book of the Order of the Garter'

ARCHIVIO DI STATO DI VENEZIA (VSA)
CAMPO DEI FRARI, VENICE
Consiglio di dieci, X

VSA Criminale v, vii, p.36 – Council of Ten order for handcuffing Ludovico da l'Armi and the testing of his food for poison; 29 April 1547. His condemnation and orders for his execution; 11 May 1547.

VSA Lettere Secrete, *buste* 4 – Permission for the rector of St Luke's Church to hear da l'Armi's confession, 12 May 1547.

Avogaria di Comun

Filza Necrologia, Nobili Veneti, *buste* 1 – Record of da l'Armi's beheading, 12 May 1547.

Primary sources – printed

'APC' – *Acts of the Privy Council*, ns, vol. 1 (1542–7), vol. 2 (1547–50), ed. John Roche Dasent, London: HMSO, 1890.

'Bath MSS' – *Calendar of the Manuscripts of the Marquis of Bath Preserved at Longleat*, ed. S.C. Lomas and others, 5 vols., London: HMC, 1904–80.

Brigden, Susan (ed.), *Letters of Richard Scudamore to Sir Philip Hoby*, London: Camden Society, vol. 39 (1990), 67–148.

Caius, John, *A boke or counseill against the disease commonly called the sweate or sweatyng sicknesse*, London: Richard Grafton, 1552.

'Calais Chronicle' – *Chronicle of Calais in the Reigns of Henry VII and Henry VIII to the year 1540*, ed. John Gough Nichols, London: Camden Society, 1846.

CSP Spain – *Calendar of Despatches and State Papers, Spain.*

    vol. 4, pt. ii (1531–33), ed. Pascual de Gayangos, London: HMSO, 1882.

    vol. 5, pt. ii (January 1536–June 1538), ed. Pascual de Gayangos, London: HMSO, 1888.

    vol. 6, pt. i (July 1538–April 1542), ed. Pascual de Gayangos, London: HMSO, 1890.

    vol. 6, pt. ii (May 1542–December 1543), ed. Pascual de Gayangos, London: HMSO, 1895.

    vol. 7 (1544), ed. Pascual de Gayangos & Martin A.S. Hume, London: HMSO, 1899.

    vol. 8 (1545–46), ed. Martin A.S. Hume, London: HMSO, 1904.

    vol. 9 (1547–9), ed. Martin A.S. Hume & Royall Tyler, London: HMSO, 1912.

CSP Venice – *Calendar of State Papers, Venice*

    vol. 4, 1527–33, ed. Rawdon Brown, London: HMSO, 1871.

    vol. 5, 1534–54, ed. Rawdon Brown, London HMSO, 1873.

Eccles. Mems. – *Ecclesiastical Memorials relating chiefly to Religion and the Reformation of it,* by John Strype, 3 vols., Oxford: Clarendon Press, 1820–40.

Ellis, Sir Henry (ed.), *Original Letters Illustrative of English History*, 3 s., 11 vols, London: Harding, Triphook & Lepard, 1824–6.

Foxe, John, *Acts & Monuments*, G. Townsend & S.R. Cattley (eds.), 8 vols., London: R. B. Seeley & W. Burnside, 1837–41.

Giustinian, Sebastian, *Four Years at the Court of Henry VIII: Selection of*

Despatches written by the Venetian Ambassador Sebastian Giustinian, trans. Rawdon Brown, 2 vols., London: Smith, Elder & Co., 1854.

'Greyfriars Chronicle' – *Chronicle of the Greyfriars of London,* ed. John Gough Nichols, London: Camden Society, 1852.

Hall, Edward, *Chronicle containing the History of England,* London: J. Johnson et al., 1809.

'Hamilton Papers' – *Letters and Papers Illustrating the Political Relations of England and Scotland in the Sixteenth century, formerly in the possession of the dukes of Hamilton,* ed. Joseph Bain, 2 vols., Edinburgh: HM General Register House, 1890–2.

'Haynes' State Papers' – *A Collection of State Papers relating to Affairs in the Reigns of King Henry VIII, Edward VI, Queen Mary and Queen Elizabeth, 1542–70,* ed. Samuel Haynes, London: William Bowyer, 1790.

Hayward, Maria (ed.), *The 1542 Inventory of Whitehall: The Palace and its Keeper,* 2 vols., London: Society of Antiquaries of London, 2004.

Holinshed, Raphael, *Chronicles of England, Scotland and Ireland,* 6 vols., London: J. Johnson et al., 1808.

Howell, T.B. & T.J., *Complete Collection of State Trials,* 5th edn, 34 vols., London: Longman, Hurst, Rees, Orm & Brown, 1816–28.

Jenkyns, Revd. Henry, *The Remains of Thomas Cranmer DD, Archbishop of Canterbury,* 4 vols., Oxford: Oxford University Press, 1833.

Kaulek, J.B.L. (ed.), *Correspondence politique de mm. de Castillon et de Marillac, ambassadeurs de France en Angleterre 1537–42,* Paris: Commission des Archives diplomatique, 1885.

'LP' – *Letters & Papers, Foreign & Domestic, Henry VIII*

> vol. 8, pt. i (January–July 1535), ed. James Gairdner, London: HMSO, 1885.

> vol. 10, pt. ii (January–June 1536), ed. James Gairdner, London: HMSO, 1887.

> vol. 11 (July–December 1536), ed. James Gairdner, London: HMSO, 1888.

> vol. 12, pt. i (January–May 1537), ed. James Gairdner, London: HMSO, 1890.

> vol. 12, pt. ii (June–December 1537), ed. James Gairdner, London: HMSO, 1891.

> vol. 13, pt. i (January–July 1538), ed. James Gairdner, London: HMSO, 1892.

> vol. 14, pt. i (January–June 1539), ed. James Gairdner & R.H. Brodie, London: HMSO, 1894.

vol. 14, pt. ii (August–December 1539), ed. James Gairdner & R.H. Brodie, London: HMSO, 1895.

vol. 15 (January–August 1540), ed. James Gairdner & R.H. Brodie, London: HMSO, 1896.

vol. 16 (1540–1), ed. James Gairdner & R.H. Brodie, London: HMSO, 1898.

vol. 17 (1542), ed. James Gairdner, London: HMSO, 1900.

vol 18, pt. i (January–July 1543), ed. James Gairdner & R.H. Brodie, London: HMSO, 1901.

vol. 18, pt. ii (August–December 1543), ed. James Gairdner & R.H. Brodie, London: HMSO, 1902.

vol. 19, pt. i (January–July 1544), ed. James Gairdner & R.H. Brodie, London: HMSO, 1903.

vol. 19, pt. ii (August–December 1544), ed. James Gairdner & R.H. Brodie, London: HMSO, 1905.

vol. 20, pt. i (January–July 1545), ed. James Gairdner & R.H. Brodie, London: HMSO, 1905.

vol. 20, pt. ii (August–December 1545), ed. James Gairdner & R.H. Brodie, London: HMSO, 1907.

vol. 21, pt. i (January–August 1546), ed. James Gairdner & R.H. Brodie, London: HMSO, 1908.

vol. 21, pt. ii (September 1546–January 1547), ed. James Gairdner & R.H. Brodie, London: HMSO, 1910.

Addenda, vol. 1, pt. ii, (1538–47), ed. J.S. Brewer, London: HMSO, 1932.

'Lisle Letters' – *The Lisle Letters*, ed. Muriel St Clare Byrne, 6 vols., Chicago & London: University of Chicago Press, 1981.

Merriman, Roger, *Life and Letters of Thomas Cromwell*, 2 vols., Oxford: Clarendon Press, 1902.

Morison, Richard, *An Exhortation to styre all Englishe men to the defence of their countreye*, London: Thomas Berthelet, 1539.

Mueller, Janel (ed.), *Katherine Parr: Complete Works and Correspondence*, Chicago & London: University of Chicago Press, 2011.

Muller, James, *Letters of Stephen Gardiner*, Cambridge: Cambridge University Press, 1933.

Nicholas, Sir Harris (ed.), *Proceedings and Ordinances of the Privy Council of England*, vol. 7 (1540–2), London: Commissioners of the Public Records, 1837.

Nichols, John Gough (ed.), *Narratives of the Days of the Reformation*, London: Camden Society, 1859.

Parliamentary Rolls of Medieval England, ed. Chris Given-Wilson et al., 16 vols., Woodbridge: Boydell, 2005.

Ponet, John, *A Short Treatise on Political Power and of the True Obedience which Subjects owe to Kings and other Civil Governors*, first publ. 1556; in facsimile. Menston: Scholar Press, 1970.

Robinson, Revd. Hastings (ed.), *Original Letters Relating to the English Reformation*, 2nd edn, Cambridge: Cambridge University Press for Parker Society, 1847.

Sadler, 'State Papers' – *State Papers of Sir Ralph Sadler, knight-banneret*, ed. Arthur Clifford, 3 vols., Edinburgh: Archibald Constable, 1809.

SAL Proclamations – Bound folio of printed proclamations and broadsheets; vol.1: Henry VIII–Elizabeth I, Society of Antiquaries of London.

Spanish Chronicle – A Chronicle of King Henry VIII of England... written in Spanish by an unknown hand, trans. & ed. Martin Hume, London: George Bell & Sons, 1889.

'St. P' – *State Papers Henry VIII*, 11 vols., London: HMSO, 1830–52.

Starkey, David (ed.), *The Inventory of King Henry VIII: The Transcript*, London: Harvey Miller Publishers for the Society of Antiquaries of London, 1998.

Statutes of the Realm, ed. Alexander Luders et al., 11 vols., London: Dawsons of Pall Mall, 1810–28.

Stow, John, *Annals of England faithfully collected out of the most autuenicall authors, records and other monuments of antique, lately collected from the first habitation until this present*, London: George Bishop & Thomas Andrewes, 1605.

Tanner, J.R., *Tudor Constitutional Documents 1485–1603 with an Historical Commentary*, Cambridge: Cambridge University Press, 1951.

Wilkins, David, *Concilia Magnæ Britammiæ et Hiberniæ*, 3 vols., London: R. Gosling et al., 1737.

Wriothesley, Charles, *Chronicle of England during the Reigns of the Tudors 1485–1559*, ed. William Douglas Hamilton, 2 vols., London: Camden Society, 1875–7.

Secondary sources

Modern monetary values are derived from calculations, based on a number of economic factors, available on http://measuringworth.com/ukcompare/

Anglo, Sydney, *Spectacle, Pageantry and Early Tudor Policy*, Oxford: Clarendon Press, 1969.

Armstrong, C.D., 'English Catholicism Rethought?' *Jnl. Eccl. Hist.*, vol. 54 (2003), 714–28.

Ashrafian, Hutan, 'Henry VIII's Obesity Following Traumatic Brain Injury', *Endocrine, Int. Jnl. of Basic & Clinical Endocrinology*, vol. 42 (2012), 218–19.

Ayris, Paul, 'Preaching the Last Crusade: Thomas Cranmer the "Devotion" Money of 1543', *Jnl. Eccl. Hist.*, vol. 48 (1998), 683–701.

Bark, N., 'Did Schizophrenia Change the Course of English History? The Medical Illnesses of Henry VIII', *Med. Hypothesis*, vol. 59 (2002), 416–21.

Barrett, N.R. – 'King Henry the Eighth', *Annals Royal College of Surgeons of England*, vol. 52 (1973), 216–33.

Bayles, Howard, 'Notes on Accounts Paid to the Royal Apothecaries in 1546 and 1547', *Chemist & Druggist*, vol. 114 (1931), 794–7.

Bell, Doyne, *Notices of the Historic Persons Buried in the Chapel of St Peter ad Vincula in the Tower of London*, London: John Murray, 1877.

Bellamy, John, *The Tudor Law of Treason: An Introduction*, Abingdon: Routledge, Kegan Paul, 1979.

Bernard, G.W., 'The Making of Religious Policy 1533–46: Henry VIII and the Search for the Middle Way', *HJ*, vol. 41 (1998), 321–49.

Bindoff, S.T., *The House of Commons 1508–58*, 3 vols., London: Secker & Warburg, 1982.

Bishop, Jennifer, 'Currency, Conversation and Control: Political Discourse and the Coinage in mid-Tudor England', *EHR*, vol. 131 (2016), 763–92.

Blair, Claude, 'A Royal Swordsmith and Damascener: Diego de Çaias', [New York] *Met. Mus. Jnl.*, vol. 3 (1970), 149–98.

——— & Pyhrr, Stuart, 'The Wilton "Montmorency" Armor: An Italian Armor for Henry VIII', [New York] *Met. Mus. Jnl.*, vol. 38 (2003), 95–144.

Bloom, James & James, Robert, *Medical Practitioners in the Diocese of London Licensed under the Act of 3 Henry VIII, An Annotated List 1529–1725*, Cambridge: Cambridge University Press, 1935.

Bolland, Charlotte & Cooper, Tarnya, *The Real Tudors: Kings and Queens Rediscovered*, London: National Portrait Gallery, 2014.

Bonner, Elizabeth, 'The Genesis of Henry VIII's "Rough Wooing" of the Scots, *Northern Hist.*, vol. 33 (1997), 36–53.

Borman, Tracy, *Thomas Cromwell: The Untold Story of Henry VIII's Most Faithful Servant*, London: Hodder & Stoughton, 2014.

Brewer, Clifford, *The Death of Kings*, London: Abson Books, 2000.

Brewer, J.S., *The Reign of Henry VIII from his Accession to the Death of Wolsey*, ed. James Gairdner, 4 vols., London: John Murray, 1884.

Brigden, Susan, 'Henry Howard, earl of Surrey and the Conjured League', *HJ*, vol. 37 (1994), 507–37.

Brinch, Ove, 'The Medical Problems of Henry VIII', *Centaurus*, vol. 5 (1958), 339–69.

Brooks, Richard, *Cassell's Battlefields of Britain and Ireland*, London: Weidenfeld & Nicolson, 2005.

Burnet, Gilbert, *History of the Reformation*, 2 vols., London: W. Smith, 1841.

Carlton, Charles, 'Thomas Cromwell: A Study in Interrogation', *Albion*, vol. 5 (1973), 116–27.

Challis, C.E., 'The Debasement of the Coinage 1542–51', *Econ. Hist. Rev.* vol. 20 (1967), 441–66.

——— & Harrison, C.J., 'A Contemporary Estimate of the Production of Gold and Silver Coinage 1542–56', *EHR*, vol. 88 (1973), 821–35.

Chalmers, C.R. & Chaloner, E.J., '500 Years Later: Henry VIII, leg ulcers and the course of history', *Jnl. Royal Soc. Med.*, vol. 102 (2009), 513–17.

Chamberlin, Frederick, '*The Private Character of Henry VIII*', New York: Washburn, 1931.

Childs, Jessie, *Henry VIII's Last Victim: The Life and Times of Henry Howard, Earl of Surrey*, London: Jonathan Cape, 2006.

Clarke, Peter, 'Canterbury as the New Rome: Dispensations and Henry VIII's Reformation', *Jnl. Eccl. Hist.*, vol. 64 (2013), 20–44.

Colvin, Sir Howard et al., *History of the King's Works 1485–1660*, vol. 4, pts. 1 & 2 London: HMSO, 1982.

Copeman, William, *Doctors and Diseases in Tudor Times*, London: Dawson, 1960.

Crosby, Andrew W., 'The Early History of Syphilis: A Reappraisal', *American Anthropologist*, vol. 71 (1969), 218–27.

Currie, A.S., 'Notes on the Obstetric Histories of Catherine of Arragon [*sic*] and Anne Boleyn, *Edinburgh Med. Jnl.*, vol. 34 (1888), 294–8.

Davies, M.B., 'Surrey at Boulogne', *HLQ*, vol. 23 (1959–60), 343–5.

Dawson, Thomas, *Memoirs of St George the English Patron and the Most Noble Order of the Garter*, London: Henry Clements, 1714.

Devonald, G., 'Henry VIII', *Res Medica*, vol. 3 (1963), 18–23.

Dewhurst, J., 'The Alleged Miscarriages of Catherine of Aragon and Anne Boleyn', *Med. Hist.*, vol. 28 (1984), 49–56.

Dickens, A.G., 'Yorkshire Submissions to Henry VIII, 1541', *EHR*, vol. 53 (1938), 267–75.

Dietz, F.C., *English Public Finance 1485–1558*, Urbana, IL: University of Illinois Press, 1921.

Dillon, Viscount, 'The Rack', *Arch. Jnl.*, vol. 62 (1905), 48–66.

———, 'The Tudor Battle Flag of England', *Arch. Jnl.*, vol. 65 (1908), 282–6.

Donaldson, Gordon, *James VI – James VII* (Edinburgh History of Scotland, vol. 3), London: Oliver & Boyd, 1965.

Doran, Susan (ed.), *King Henry VIII: Man & Monarch*, London: British Library, 2009.

Dyer, Alan D., 'Influence of Bubonic Plague in England 1500–1667', *Med. Hist.*, vol. 22 (1978), 308–26.

Eaves, Richard Glen, *Henry VIII's Scottish Diplomacy 1513–24: England's Relations with the Regency Government of James V*, New York: Exposition, 1971.

Elton, G.R., *Policy and Police: The Enforcement of the Reformation in the Age of Thomas Cromwell*, Cambridge: Cambridge University Press, 1972.

———, *Reform & Reformation: England 1509–58*, London: Edward Arnold, 1977.

Evans, John, 'On a Counterfeit Groat of Henry VIII', *Jnl. Numismatic Soc.*, vol. 4 (1864), 248–51.

Fletcher, P.E., 'The Life of Andrew Boorde c.1490–1549', *Adverse Drug Reaction Toxicology Rev.*, vol. 21 (2002), 243–52.

Flugel, J.C., *Men and their Motives: Psycho-Analytical Studies*, London: Kegan Paul, Trench, Trubner, 1934.

———, 'On the Character and Married Life of Henry VIII' in *Psychoanalysis and History*, ed. Bruce Mazlish, rev. edn, New York: Grosset & Dunlap, 1971.

Frith, John, 'Syphilis: Its Early History and Treatment until Penicillin and the Debate on its Origins', *Jnl. of Military & Veterans' Health* (Australian Military Med. Ass.), vol. 20 (2002), 49–58.

Fuller, Thomas, *History of the Worthies of England*, 3 vols., London: Thomas Tegg, 1840.

Furdell, Elizabeth Lane, *The Royal Doctors 1485–1714: Medical Personnel at the Tudor and Stuart Courts*, Rochester, NY: University of Rochester Press, 2001.

———, 'Andrew Boorde (c.1490–1549), *ODNB*, vol. 6 (2004), 591–2.

Galassi, Francesco, Habicht, Michael & Růhli, Frank, 'Henry VIII's Head Trauma', *The Lancet Neurology*, vol. 15 (2016), 552.

Halford, Sir Henry, *An Account of What Appeared on Opening the Coffin of King Charles the First in the Vault of King Henry VIII*, London: Nichols & Son, 1813.

Hammond, E.A., 'Dr Augustine, Physician to Cardinal Wolsey and King Henry VIII', *Med. Hist.*, vol. 19 (1975), 215–49.

Harper, Kristin, et al., 'The Origin and Antiquity of Syphilis Revisited: An Appraisal of Old World Pre-Columbian Evidence for Treponemal Infection', *Yearbook of Physical Anthropology*, vol. 54 (2011), 99–132.

Harris, Frank, 'Law & Economics of High Treason in England from its Feudal Origins to the Early Seventeenth-Century', *Valparaiso University Law Review*, vol. 22 (1987), 81–108.

Harrison, Eric, 'Henry VIII's Gangster: the Affair of Ludovico da l'Armi', *Jnl. Modern Hist.*, vol. 15 (1943), 265–74.

Haugaard, William P., 'Katherine Parr: The Religious Convictions of a Renaissance Queen', *Renaissance Quarterly*, vol. 22 (1969), 346–59.

Head, David, 'Henry VIII's Scottish Policy: A Reassessment', *Scottish Hist. Rev.*, vol. 61 (1982), 1–24.

———, *The Ebbs and Flows of Fortune: The life of Thomas Howard, third duke of Norfolk*, Athens, GA: University of Georgia Press, 1995.

Herbert of Cherbury, Lord Edward, *The Life and Raigne of King Henry the Eight*, London: Thomas Whitaker, 1649.

Hetherington, Robert J., 'Health of King Henry VIII', *BMJ*, vol. 2 (6142) (1978), 956.

Higgins, Alfred, 'On the Work of Florentine Sculptors in England in the Early Part of the Sixteenth century, with Special Reference to the Tombs of Cardinal Wolsey and King Henry VIII', *Arch. Jnl.*, vol. 51 (1894), 129–220.

Hope, Sir William St John, *Windsor Castle, an Architectural History*, 2 vols., London: Country Life, 1913.

Hoskins, W.S., 'Harvest Fluctuations and English Economic History 1480–1619', *Agricultural Hist. Rev.*, vol. 12 (1964), 28–46.

Hoyle, Richard & Ramsdale, John, 'The Royal Progress of 1541, the North of England and Anglo-Scottish Relations 1534–42', *Northern Hist.*, vol. 41 (2004), 239–65.

Hutchinson, Robert, *The Last Days of Henry VIII*, London: Weidenfeld & Nicolson, 2005.

———, *Thomas Cromwell: The Rise and Fall of Henry VIII's most Notorious Minister*, London: Weidenfeld & Nicolson, 2007.

———, *House of Treason. The Rise and Fall of a Tudor Dynasty*, London: Weidenfeld & Nicolson, 2009.

———, *Young Henry. The Rise of Henry VIII*, London: Weidenfeld & Nicolson, 2011.

Ikram, Muhammad Q., Sajjad, Fazle H. & Salardini, Arash, 'The Head that Wears the Crown: Henry VIII and Traumatic Brain Injury', *Jnl. Clinical Neuroscience*, vol. 16 (2016), 16–19.

Ives, E.W., 'Henry VIII', *ODNB*, vol. 26 (2004), 522–51.

James, Susan E., 'The Devotional Writings of Queen Katherine Parr', *Trans. Cumberland & Westmorland Arch. Soc.*, vol. 82 (1982), 135–40.

———, *Kateryn Parr: The Making of a Queen*, Farnham: Ashgate Publishing, 1999.

———, 'Katherine Parr (1512–48)', *ODNB*, vol. 30 (2004), 901–6.

———, *Catherine Parr: Henry VIII's Last Love*, Stroud: Tempus, 2008.

Keynes, Milo, 'The Personality and Health of King Henry VIII' (1491–1547), *Jnl. Med Biog.*, vol. 15 (2005), 174–83.

Kybett, Susan Maclean, 'Henry VIII – A Malnourished King?', *History Today*, vol. 39 (1989), 19–25.

Lehmberg, Stanford E., 'Parliamentary Attainder in the Reign of Henry VIII', *HJ*, vol. 18 (1975), 703–24.

Lipscomb, Suzannah, *The King is Dead: The Last Will and Testament of Henry VIII*, New York: Pegasus Books, 2016.

Loach, Jennifer, 'The Function of Ceremonial in the Reign of Henry VIII', *Past & Present*, no. 142 (1994), 43–68.

———, *Edward VI*, New Haven & London: Yale University Press, 1999.

MacCulloch, Diarmid, *Thomas Cranmer, A Life*, New Haven & London: Yale University Press, 1996.

Mackie, J.D., 'Henry VIII and Scotland', *Trans. Royal Hist. Soc.*, vol. 29 (1947), 93–114.

MacLaurin, C., *Mere Mortals: Medico-Historical Essays*, London: Jonathan Cape, 1925.

MacLennan, Sir Hector, 'A Gynaecologist Looks at the Tudors', *Med. Hist.*, vol. 11 (1967), 66–74.

MacNalty, Sir Arthur, *Henry VIII: A Difficult Patient*, London: Christopher Johnson, 1952.

McLaren, Anne, 'Queenship in Early Modern England & Scotland', *HJ*, vol. 49 (2008), 935–52.

Marshall, Peter, 'Mumpsimus and Sumpsimus: The Intellectual Origins of a Henrician *Bon Mot*', *Jnl. Eccl. Hist.*, vol. 52 (2001), 512–20.

———, *Heretics & Believers; A History of the English Reformation*, New Haven & London: Yale University Press, 2017.

Martienssen, Anthony, *Queen Katherine Parr*, London: Secker & Warburg, 1973.

Matthews, Leslie G., 'Royal Apothecaries of the Tudor Period', *Med. Hist.*, vol. 8 (1964), 170–80.

———, *The Royal Apothecaries*, London: Wellcome Historical Medical Library, 1967.

Mayer, Thomas F., *Reginald Pole, Prince & Prophet*, Cambridge: Cambridge University Press, 2000.

Moore, Peter, 'The Heraldic Charge against the Earl of Surrey 1546–7', *EHR*, vol. 116 (2001), 252–68.

Moriarty, E.J., 'Henry VIII Medically Speaking', *Hist. Bull. of Calgary Associate Clinic*, vol. 20 (1955), 11–15.

Muir, Kenneth, *Life and Letters of Sir Thomas Wyatt*, Liverpool: University of Liverpool Press, 1963.

Muller, James, *Stephen Gardiner and the Tudor Reaction*, London: SPCK, 1926.

Murphy, Neil, 'Violence, Colonization and Henry VIII's Conquest of France 1544–1546', *Past & Present*, no. 233 (2016), 13–51.

Nott, George F., (ed.), *Works of Henry Howard, Earl of Surrey and of Sir Thomas Wyatt the Elder*, 2 vols., London: T. Beasley, 1815–16.

'ODNB' – *Oxford Dictionary of National Biography*, ed. Colin Matthew and Brian Harrison, Oxford: Oxford University Press, 2004, 60 vols.

O'Neil, B.H., 'Stefan von Haschenperg, an engineer to King Henry VIII and his work', *Archaeologia*, vol. 91 (1945), 137–55.

Outhwaite, R.B., 'The Trials of Foreign Borrowing: the English Crown and the Antwerp Money Market in the mid-Sixteenth Century', *Econ. Hist. Rev.*, vol. 19 (1966), 289–305.

Park, Bert E., *Ailing, Aging, Addicted: Studies of Compromised Leadership*, Lexington, KY: University of Kentucky Press, 1993.

Perkins, Peter, 'Henry VIII's leg ulcers', *Jnl. Royal Soc. Med.*, vol. 103 (2010), 81.

Pierce, Hazel, *Margaret Pole 1473–1541: Loyalty, Lineage and Leadership*, Cardiff: University of Wales Press, 2003.

Porter, Linda, *Katherine the Queen, The Remarkable Life of Katherine Parr*, London: Macmillan, 2010.

[Pote, Joseph], *History and Antiquities of Windsor Castle*, Eton: Joseph Pote, bookseller, 1749.

Potter, David, 'The International Mercenary Market in the Sixteenth Century: Anglo-French Competition in Germany 1543–50', *EHR*, vol. 111 (1998), 24–58.

———, *Henry VIII and Francis I: The Final Conflict 1540–7*, Leiden: Brill Academic, 2011.

Power, D'Arcy, 'Some Notes on Edmund Harman, King's Barber ?1509–76', *Proc. Royal Soc. Med.*, vol. 9 (1916), 67–88.

Pulvertaft, David, 'The Figurehead/Badge of the *Mary Rose* 1510–45', *Mariner's Mirror*, vol. 102 (2016), 331–5.

Redworth, Glyn, *In Defence of the Church Catholic: The Life of Stephen Gairdner*, Oxford: Blackwell, 1990.

Rex, Richard, 'The Religion of Henry VIII', *HJ*, vol. 57 (2014), 1–32.

Richardson, W.C., 'Some Financial Expedients of Henry VIII', *Econ. Hist. Rev.*, vol. 7 (1954), 33–48.

Rimer, Graeme, Richardson, Thom, & Cooper, J.P.D. (eds.), *Henry VIII: Arms and the Man 1509–2009*, Leeds: Royal Armouries, 2009.

Riordan, Michael & Ryrie, Alec, 'Stephen Gardiner and the Making of a Protestant Villain', *Sixteenth Century Jnl.*, vol. 34 (2003), 1039–63.

Rodger, N.A.M., *The Safeguard of the Sea: A Naval History of Britain*, vol. 1, 660–1649, London: HarperCollins/National Maritime Museum, 1997.

Russell, Gareth, *Young and Damned and Fair: The Life and Tragedy of Catherine Howard*, London: William Collins, 2017.

Ryrie, Alec, 'Divine Kingship and Royal Theology in Henry VIII's Reformation', *Reformation*, vol. 7 (2002), 49–77.

———, *The Gospel of Henry VIII: Evangelists in the Early English Reformation*, Cambridge: Cambridge University Press, 2003.

———, 'England's Last Medieval Heresy Hunt: Gloucestershire 1540', *Midland Hist.*, vol. 30 (2005), 37–52.

Samuels, Alec, 'What was the Medical Cause of Death of Henry VIII?' *Medico-Legal Jnl.*, vol. 65 (1995), 139–41.

Sansom, Christopher J., 'The Wakefield Conspiracy of 1541 and Henry VIII's Progress to the North Reconsidered', *Northern Hist.*, vol. 45, (2008), 217–38.

Scarisbrick, J.J., *Henry VIII*, New Haven & London: Yale University Press, 1997.

Sharpe, Kevin, *Selling the Tudor Monarchy. Authority and Image in Sixteenth-Century England*, New Haven and London: Yale University Press, 2009.

Shrewsbury, J.F.D., 'Henry VIII: A Medical Study', *Jnl. of History of Med. & Allied Sciences*, vol. 7 (1952), 141–85.

Skidmore, Chris, *Edward VI: The Lost King of England*, London: Weidenfeld & Nicolson, 2008.

Skoblo, Max & Leslau, Jack, 'Health of King Henry VIII', *BMJ*, vol. 2:6138 (1978), 700–1.

———, 'Health of King Henry VIII', ibid., vol. 2:6144 (1978), 1087–8.

Slavin, Arthur J., 'The Fall of Chancellor Wriothesley: A Study in the Politics of Conspiracy', *Albion*, vol. 7 (1975), 265–86.

Smith, Lesley, 'Henry VIII's Other Great Matter', *Jnl. of Family Planning & Reproductive Health Care*, vol. 38 (2012), 200–1.

Smith, Lacey Baldwin, *A Tudor Tragedy: the Life and Times of Catherine Howard*, London: Jonathan Cape, 1961.

———, *Henry VIII: The Mask of Royalty*, London: Jonathan Cape, 1971.

———, *Treason in Tudor England: Politics and Paranoia*, London: Pimlico, 2006.

Southworth, John, *Fools and Jesters at the English Court*, Stroud: Sutton Publishing, 1998.

Sowerby, Tracey A., *Renaissance and Reformation in Tudor England: the Careers of Sir Richard Morison, c.1513–56*, Oxford: Oxford University Press, 2010.

———, 'Richard Pate, the Royal Supremacy and Reformation Diplomacy', *HJ*, vol. 54 (2011), 265–85.

Starkey, David, *Henry: Virtuous Prince*, London: Harper Press, 2008.

Strickland, Agnes, *Lives of the Queens of England from the Norman Conquest*, 6 vols., London: Bell & Daldy, 1866.

Stride, P. & Lopes, Floro, K., 'Henry VIII, McLeod's Syndrome and Jacquetta's Curse', *Jnl. Royal Coll. Physicians of Edinburgh*, vol. 43 (2013), 353–60.

Strype, John, *Life of the Learned John Cheke, Knight*, Oxford: Oxford University Press, 1820.

Stubbs, S.G. Blaxland, 'Henry VIII and Pharmacy: Royal Recipes for Plasters, Ointments and Other Medicaments', *Chemist & Druggist*, vol. 114 (1931), 792–6.

Taviner, Mark, Thwaites, Guy & Gant, Vanya, 'The English Sweating Sickness 1485–1551: A Viral Pulmonary Disease?', *Med. Hist.*, vol. 42 (1998), 96–8.

Thomas, Duncan, 'Thomas Vicary and the Anatomie of Man's Body', *Med. Hist.*, vol. 50 (2006), 236–46.

———, 'Thomas Vicary, Barber Surgeon', *Jnl. Med. Biog.*, vol. 14 (2006), 84–9.

Thornley, I.D., 'The Treason Legislation of Henry VIII, 1531–4', *TRHS*, vol. 1, 3rd s. (1917), 87–123.

Thornton, Tim, 'Henry VIII's Progress through Yorkshire in 1541 and its Implications for Northern Identities', *Northern Hist.*, vol. 46 (2009), 231–44.

Thurley, Simon, *Hampton Court, A Social and Architectural History*, New Haven & London: Paul Mellon Centre for Studies in British Art/Yale Univerity Press, 2003.

Tighe, Robert & Davis, James, *Annals of Windsor and a History of the Castle and Town*, London: Longman, Brown, Green, Lowden & Roberts, 1858.

Von Arni, Eric Gruber, 'The Treatment of Injury and Disease' in Rimer, Richardson & Cooper (eds.) *Henry VIII: Arms and the Man*, 58–69.

Warnicke, Retha M., 'Katherine Howard (1518x1524–42)', *ODNB*, vol. 30 (2004), 906–10.

White, Micheline, 'The Psalms, War and Royal Iconography: Katherine Parr's Psalms or Prayers (1544) and Henry VIII's David', *Renaissance Studies*, vol. 29 (2015), 554–75.

Whitley, Catrina Banks & Kramer, Kyra, 'A New Explanation of the Reproductive Woes and Midlife Decline of Henry VIII', *HJ*, vol. 53 (2010), 827–48.

Williams, Neville, *Henry VIII and his Court*, London: Cardinal Books, 1973.

Worsley, Richard, *History of the Isle of Wight*, London: A. Hamilton, 1781.

Unpublished Theses

Clark, Nicola, *Dynastic Politics in Five Women of the Howard Family during the Reign of Henry VIII 1509–47*, Royal Holloway College, University of London, DPhil, 2013.

Hewerdine, Anita, *The Yeomen of the King's Guard 1485–1547*, London School of Economics, University of London, DPhil, 1998.

Index